TELECOMMUNICATIONS DEMAND IN THEORY AND PRACTICE

TELECOMMUNICATIONS DEMAND IN THEORY AND PRACTICE

by

LESTER D. TAYLOR

Department of Economics, University of Arizona, Tucson, Ariz., U.S.A.

KLUWER ACADEMIC PUBLISHERS

DORDRECHT / BOSTON / LONDON

Library of Congress Cataloging-in-Publication Data

```
Taylor, Lester D.
   Telecommunications demand in theory and practice / by Lester D.
 Taylor. -- [Rev. ed.]
     p.   cm.
   Rev. ed. of: Telecommunications demand. c1980.
   "March 1993."
   Includes bibliographical references and index.
   ISBN 0-7923-2389-0 (alk. paper)
   1. Telephone--United States.   2. Telephone--Mathematical models.
 I. Taylor, Lester D.  Telecommunications demand.   II. Title.
 HE8815.T395  1994
 384.6'0973--dc20                                         93-14522
```

ISBN 0-7923-2389-0

Published by Kluwer Academic Publishers,
P.O. Box 17, 3300 AA Dordrecht, The Netherlands.

Kluwer Academic Publishers incorporates
the publishing programmes of
D. Reidel, Martinus Nijhoff, Dr W. Junk and MTP Press.

Sold and distributed in the U.S.A. and Canada
by Kluwer Academic Publishers,
101 Philip Drive, Norwell, MA 02061, U.S.A.

In all other countries, sold and distributed
by Kluwer Academic Publishers Group,
P.O. Box 322, 3300 AH Dordrecht, The Netherlands.

Printed on acid-free paper

Printed in the Netherlands

To EDL and PBL,
whose efforts and support made
the 1980 book possible

TABLE OF CONTENTS

LIST OF FIGURES

LIST OF TABLES

PREFACE

Readers familiar with my 1980 book, *Telecommunications Demand: A Survey And Critique*, will find this edition almost entirely new. The only chapters from the 1980 book that are retained are the chapter on the theory of telephone demand (which is extended and now appears as two chapters) and the two chapters summarizing the empirical literature as it existed in the late 1970s. Those two chapters are now reproduced, with minor editing, in Appendices 1 and 2. The 1980 book consisted of five chapters and a Postscript; this edition consists of 11 chapters and three appendices, plus a greatly expanded bibliography. The 1980 book attempted to provide an exhaustive review of the empirical literature; this book is necessarily selective in its empirical review, as the post–1980 literature is simply too massive for an exhaustive review to be feasible.

Work on this edition was started in 1986, and has obviously taken much longer than I had planned. Much of the empirical work that is discussed reflects studies and research that I was involved with throughout the 1980s on a consulting basis at Southwestern Bell and Bell Canada and in very recent years in conjunction with the National Telecommunications Demand Study. Unlike the 1980 book, however, which was underwritten by AT&T, this edition has benefited from no corporate funding.

Although the changes that have transformed the structure of telecommunications in the U.S. are echoed in many other countries, the focus in this edition continues to be on North America. I regret not including studies on telecommunications demand from Europe and other parts of the world in the discussion, but to do so has simply not been feasible. I have, however, included several recent European and Australian studies in the bibliography.

As with the 1980 book, many people have given generously of their time and energy in chasing down studies and references, making unpublished studies available, offering advise, comments, and counsel, and providing ego-boosting encouragment that a new book was indeed worthwhile. The list includes to begin with: D. Kridel, A. Larson, J. Chen, J. Watters and D. Weisman of Southwestern Bell and T. Appelbe, J. Bodnar, P. Dillworth, S. Iacono, M. Manton, F.D. Orr, D.L. Solvason and S. Subisatti of Bell

Canada. Also: J. Alleman of the University of Colorado, A. Belinfante of the FCC, W. Boal of Pacific Telephone, J. Colias of Bell South, R. Dansby of BELLCORE, M. Ben-Akiva of M.I.T., G. Duncan of GTE Laboratories, B. Egan of Columbia University, D. Elixmann of the Wissenschaftliches Institut für Kommunikationsdienste GmbH, J. Gatto and P. Robinson of AT&T, J. Griffin of Texas A. & M. University, J. Hausman of M.I.T., R. Jacob of United Telecom, J. Kling of Michigan Bell, J. Langin-Hooper of Langin-Hooper Associates, S. Levin of the University of Southern Illinois at Edwardsville, A. Margeson of Andy Margeson Associates, J. Mayo of the University of Tennessee, P. Pacey of Pacey-Johnson Associates, T. Perez-Amaral of the University of Madrid, D. Perry and Dennis Trimble of GTE, L. Perl, T. Tardiff, W. Taylor and D. Zona of National Economic Research Associates, W. Pollard of the National Regulatory Research Institute, F. Sabetan of Pacific Bell, K. Train of the University of California at Berkeley, G. Wall of the Canadian Cable Television Association, and P. Zweifel of the University of Zürich.

I am particularly indebted to Judi Bodnar, Bruce Egan, Dieter Elixmann, Sandy Levin, Teodosio Perez, Tim Tardiff, and Peter Zweifel for careful reading and critique of the manuscript and to my colleague Leslie Stratton for her assistance in deriving some of the formulae in Section IV of Chapter 7. Special thanks are also due to Rick Emmerson, Don Michels and Paul Rappoport, my colleagues in the National Telecommunications Demand Study, for their contributions and support, as well as to my longtime collaborator, Don Kridel. I am especially indebted to R. Bruce Williamson of Southwestern Bell for making available his extensive bibliography on the regulated industries, much of which is reproduced in the bibliography at the end of the book.

Finally, I am grateful to Patricia Lenoir and Mary Flannery for expert word processing and preparation of the manuscript and to Alison Habel for preparation of the graphs and charts.

Lester D. Taylor   Heck of a Hill
March 1993   Wilson, WY.

CHAPTER 1

INTRODUCTION AND OVERVIEW

In the thirteen years since publication of *Telecommunications Demand: A Survey and Critique*,[1] much has occurred in the telecommunications industry. Most of what has happened is the result of the divestiture of AT&T and competition in markets that had historically been the preserve of natural monopoly.[2] In transforming the legal and organizational structure of the industry, the divestiture created a number of new players and redefined the lines along which competition was expected to ensure. Fueled by technological innovation in conjunction with the price distortions between the toll and access markets induced by many years of regulation, competition burgeoned not only in the equipment and toll markets as intended, but in the local market as well through "bypass", shared-tenancy, and mobile cellular services. All of this has created new challenges for demand analysis.

I. BACKGROUND

At the time of the 1980 book, telecommunications demand analysis had been concerned almost exclusively with the derivation of price elasticities that could be used in forecasting the impact on revenues of changes in the level and structure of rates. Price elasticities were acknowledged to be non-zero for most services, and it was recognized that not to take them into account could lead to serious errors in forecasts of revenues. Econometric demand models did not come into widespread use in the telephone industry until the mid-1970s. In the 1960s and early 1970s, the primary tool for assessing price effects, at least in the Bell System, was the LDI model, which was a large mathematical simulation model that had been developed in the Long Lines Department of AT&T.[3] The LDI model was designed for analyzing the revenue effects arising from changes in the interstate toll schedule, and was

---

[1] Hereafter referred to as the *Survey*.

[2] The events leading to the breakup of the Bell System are well-chronicled in a number of books. My personal favorites are Faulhaber (1986) and Temin (1987). See also Coll (1986).

[3] The LDI model is described in Appendix 1.

not intended for use in state jurisdictions. As it was essentially the "only game in town", however, it was often used in state proceedings as well.

Work on econometric models of toll demand began in earnest in the Bell Operating Companies (BOC's) in the mid-1970s. Demand analysis groups were formed in force at the BOCs, AT&T, and GTE during this time.[4] By 1978, the LDI model had been replaced at AT&T by the FIRM and RES econometric models, and econometric demand models for intrastate toll had been used in rate hearings in at least 34 states.[5] Until about 1980, the focus was almost exclusively on toll. Toll data were readily available and toll was where the money was to be made in the calculation of repression effects.[6]

By 1980, competition in the toll market was making it clear that the historical toll-to-local subsidy in the telephone industry was no longer viable and telcos were going to have to collect greater amounts of revenue from local markets, either through increased access charges or by instituting local measured-service. The prospect of this raised fears that higher local rates would cause many households to give up having a telephone or would make it impossible for many new households to have a telephone in the first place. Allaying these fears required knowledge of the price elasticities for local service (i.e., access to the network) and local use and whether these elasticities vary with income and across socio-demographic groups. There was also a great deal of interest in the so-called network externality.[7] The response was a sharp shift in focus to the local market and the econometric estimation of models for access and local use.

The focus of econometric research shifted again with divestiture:

1. Implementation of "access" charges by the FCC to alleviate problems of "bypass" of the local network by large toll users heightened concern about dropoff of low-income households from the network and a threat to Universal Service.[8]

---

[4] Econometric demand analysis was also active at Bell Canada, where econometric models had been used in calculating settlements with other telephone companies since the early 1970s.

[5] These models are discussed in Appendix 1.

[6] In the late 1970s, the head of a demand analysis district at a BOC made his budget case in terms of the potential repression revenues from intrastate toll at risk in the rate cases during the year ahead. He got his budget!

[7] The network externality is associated with the fact that the addition of a new subscriber to a telephone network means that there is now one more telephone that existing subscribers can reach. This presumably confers a benefit on existing subscribers and makes a large network more desirable to belong to than a small one. Externalities will be discussed in Chapters 2 and 9.

[8] Historically, the toll-to-local subsidy operated through an allocation of a part of the costs of local plant and equipment to the toll markets which was then recovered from toll revenues through the separations process. With divestiture, the interstate portions of these non-traffic

2. At least two new "markets" were created by divestiture. One related to the demand for "access" to the local network by intercity toll carriers acting on behalf of their toll customers, while the second related to the demand for "bypass" on the part of large toll users.

3. An unfortunate side effect of the divestiture for applied demand analysis was that much of the demand data that had previously been available to the public became proprietary. The result, accordingly, is that, in terms of data availability, it was easier for non-telco researchers to estimate econometric models of telephone demand 10 years ago than it is today.

II. RECENT METHODOLOGICAL DEVELOPMENTS

In 1980, as has been noted, the focus in telecommunications demand modeling was still largely on toll demand. Access and local use (especially as it related to measured local service) was beginning to attract attention, but toll demand still commanded the action. The standard Bell System model was to relate a physical measure of toll activity (calls, minutes, or price-deflated revenues) to income, price, market size, and "habit" (usually measured by the lagged value of the dependent variable). Linear regression was used, and estimation was by ordinary least squares or generalized least squares or maximum likelihood if autocorrelation in the error term was a problem.

As attention turned to access demand, for which decisions are the yes/no variety, quantal-choice models of the probit/logit type came into widespread use. Prior to 1980, I know of only one study, Perl (1978), that used a probit/logit framework. After 1980, many studies used this framework. Perl (1983) updated his 1978 study with data from the 1980 Census. Taylor and Kridel, in a study completed in 1985 but not published until 1990, estimated a model similar to Perl's for the five states in Southwestern Bell's service area, but with data at the Census tract level rather than for individual households. Canadian access demand in the Perl framework has been analyzed by Bodnar *et al.* (1988). Quantal-choice models have also been used to analyze the choice of class-of-service, notably by Train, McFadden and Ben-Akiva (1987) and Train, Ben-Akiva and Atherton (1989) for residential demand and by Ben-

sensitive costs were to be recovered partly through traffic-sensitive, per-minute charges at both local ends of a toll call and partly through a carrier-access line charge which was not traffic sensitive. Large toll users could avoid traffic-sensitive charges by bypassing the local exchange company, connecting directly with their toll carriers at their points of presence. To forestall this bypass, the FCC proposed imposing 'access' charges of several dollars per month on end users that would replace the traffic-sensitive charges. For quantitative assessments of the bypass problem, see Brock (1984) and Bell Communications Research (1984).

Akiva and Gershenfeld (1989) for business demand. All of these studies will
be discussed in subsequent chapters.

The theoretical basis for most of the access demand studies is the
consumer-surplus framework developed in the mid-1970s by Artle and Averous (1973), Rohlfs (1974), Von Rabenau and Stahl (1974), and Littlechild
(1975) in which the demand for access to a telephone network is related to
the net benefits from usage of the network as measured by consumer surplus.
This framework lends easily to the formulation of a quantal-choice model
by viewing consumer surplus as a random variable whose mean is related to
prices, income, and other relevant variables. A normal distribution leads to
the probit model, while logistic or Weibull distributions lead to the logit model. Probit and logit models can be alternatively be derived in a random utility
framework, as is the case for the models of Train, McFadden and Ben-Akiva
and Ben-Akiva and Gershenfeld.

As will be seen in chapters to follow, the consumer-surplus framework
provides an extremely versatile structure that allows for the modeling of a
wide variety of demands ranging from measured local service to the demands
for new products. Kling and Van der Ploeg, in a study completed in 1986
but also not published until 1990, analyze the demand for optional measured service using a sample of Michigan households. An earlier analysis of
the demand for optional local measured service was provided by Hausman,
Tardiff and Baughcum (1983). Kridel (1988) develops a model, based in
part on answers to "what if" questions obtained from potential customers,
for predicting the take-rate and traffic stimulation of newly offered Extended
Area Service to residents of a Dallas suburb.[9] Essentially the same methodology is used by Watters and Chen (1989a, 1989b) to predict the demands for
proposed new offerings of intraLATA 800 and private line services in some
of the Southwestern Bell's states.

In the modeling of toll demand, three important innovations occurred in the
1980s: refinement of the concept of market size, specification of models on a
point-to-point (or route-specific) basis, and estimation of random-coefficients
models. Market size, as noted earlier, has been a standard predictor in toll
demand models since the mid-1970s. The rationale is at base a simple one,
namely, that for a given level of income more calls will be made in a large
system than in a small system. The conventional measure of market size in
the toll models of the 1970s was simply a count of main stations and their
business equivalents.[10] In the early 1980s, demand analysts at Bell Canada
began measuring market size in terms of potential toll connections, defined

[9] The Kling-Van der Ploeg and Kridel studies are described in Chapter 7.
[10] See Table 5 in Appendix 1.

as the product of the number of telephones in sending areas with the number of telephones in receiving areas.[11]

Controversy concerning the specification of the market-size variable in the Bell Canada models erupted in hearings in 1984 before the Canadian Radio-television and Telecommunications Commission (CRTC) concerning the petition by CNCP to be allowed to compete with Bell Canada and B.C. Telephone as an interexchange toll carrier. CNCP argued that Bell Canada's specification, which yielded long-run price elasticities for toll traffic within Ontario and Quebec of the order of −0.4, implied implausibly large network externalities. In CNCP's view, network externalities should be zero in a mature network, and constraining them to be so yields a toll price elasticity that is of the order of −1.3, a value which is obviously much more supportive of competition![12]

A model of intra-state toll demand on a point-to-point basis was developed by Larson, Lehman, and Weisman (published in 1990, but completed in 1985) using data for 14 city-pairs in Southwestern Bell's service territory.[13] The model is specified as a 2-equation simultaneous system in which toll traffic between a city-pair in one direction is used as predictor for traffic in the other direction. Point-to-point models have also been developed at Telecom Canada (which is the Canadian inter-province long-distance consortium) for inter-provincial and Canada-U.S. toll traffic (Appelbe *et al.* 1988). Modeling toll demand on a point-to-point basis offers a number of attractive features, including allowing for interdependencies and the estimation of both uni-directional and bi-directional price elasticities, which are especially relevant in situations in which directional traffic is carried by different telcos. Reverse-traffic (or callback) effects are found to be quantitatively important in both the Southwestern Bell and Telecom Canada studies – indeed the results suggest that a call in one direction stimulates from half to two-thirds of a call in the

---

[11] See Bell Canada (1984).

[12] Of 30 days of hearings on the CNCP petition, fully five days of record were devoted to questions of the appropriate specification of market size and the size of the toll price elasticity. See Bell Canada (1984), Taylor (1984), and Breslaw (1985). The Bell Canada models will be discussed in Chapter 6. A critique of Breslaw's critique of Bell's models is presented in Appendix 3. Although the CNCP petition was denied by the CRTC, the issues continued through a generic price elasticity hearing before the CRTC. See Bell Canada (1989), Breslaw (1989), Globerman (1988), and CRTC (1990). Interestingly, however, the size of the toll price elasticity was not an issue in the Second Competition Hearing before the CRTC in 1990 and 1991 in which Unitel (the successor to CNCP) successfully petitioned to be allowed to enter the MTS market in competition with Bell Canada and B.C. Telephone.

[13] Point-to-point modeling of toll demand was pioneered by Larsen and McCleary (1970), Deschamps (1974), and Pacey (1983). The Larsen-McCleary and Deschamps studies are described in Appendix 2.

reverse direction. This means, among other things, that a price decrease in Telecom Canada's rates to the U.S., for example, can stimulate calls from the U.S. to Canada even though there is no change in the rates from the U.S. to Canada.[14]

Specification and estimation of random coefficients model for toll demand has been undertaken by Gatto, Kelejian, and Stephan (1988), and is the latest in a distinguished line of interstate toll models that have been developed at AT&T. Interstate toll demand is approached in a multi-equation framework in which toll demand is disaggregated by mileage bands, time-of-day, and non-operator/operator handled. The model is estimated in a random-coefficients variance-components format using a pooled time-series/cross-section data set consisting of quarterly observations for the 48 contiguous states plus the District of Columbia.[15]

The study breaks important new ground methodologically through the use of two novel concepts: stochastic symmetry and stochastic weak separability.Stochastic symmetry in the model means that the Slutsky symmetry conditions across commodities in a cross-section are only satisfied stochastically, while stochastic weak separability means that the price elasticities in a cross-section are stochastically proportional to the income elasticity.

III. CONFERENCES AND SPECIAL VOLUMES

A number of conferences were organized in the 1980s oriented to the presentation of new results and modeling methodologies. The first of these was held in Montreal in the fall of 1980 and focused on production and costs as well as demand. A substantial number of papers from this conference was published in a volume edited by Courville, Dobell, and de Fontenay (1983). In October 1985, Bell Communications Research (BELLCORE) organized a notable demand analysis conference in New Orleans and in recent years has collaborated with Bell Canada in sponsoring conferences in Key Biscayne (January 1988) and Hilton Head (April 1990). A selection of papers from the BELLCORE New Orleans conference, including several reviewed here, were published in a volume edited by de Fontenay, Shugard, and Sibley (1990). Five papers from the BELLCORE/Bell Canada Key Biscayne conference appeared in a special symposium issue of *Information Economics and Policy* (1988, Vol. 3, No. 4).[16]

[14] The Larsen-Lehman-Weisman and Appelbe *et al.* studies are discussed in Chapter 7.
[15] Although the model was estimated in early 1988, the data set ends with the fourth quarter of 1983 – an interesting data implication of competition and divestiture!
[16] Mention must also be made of a recent book on telecommunications demand modeling and forecasting (in French) by Curien and Gensellon (1989).

IV. PLAN OF THE BOOK

In the *Survey*, an effort was made to provide an exhaustive review of the econometric literature on telecommunications demand. This was feasible for two reasons: (1) the literature at the time was manageably small and (2) although much of it was unpublished, it was concentrated in the Bell System and was conveniently organized and made available to me by AT&T.[17] To do the same for the literature since 1980 has not been possible, and again for two reasons: (1) the literature has become too large and (2) because of competition and the divestiture, much of what is probably the best research on telecommunications demand is now proprietary. By necessity, therefore, the present book is selective in the material that is reviewed and discussed. This is made up, in part, by the inclusion at the end of the book of an extensive bibliography.

The book consists of 11 chapters and three appendices. Two of the appendices (1 and 2) reproduce, with minor editing, Chapters 3 and 4, from the *Survey*. Of the 11 chapters, five are theoretical and five (including the concluding chapter) are empirical. The basic theoretical structure for analyzing telecommunications demand is presented in Chapters 2–4. Chapters 2 and 3 are devoted primarily to household demand, while Chapter 4 focuses on business demand. Chapters 5–8 are empirical and contain discussions of a number of post-1980 empirical demand studies. Chapters 5 and 7 relate to access and local calling, while Chapter 6 is devoted to toll. Chapter 8 focuses on the demand for business telephone systems, fixed-bill effects, and socio-demographical effects (some discussion of which is reproduced from Chapter 1 of the *Survey*). Chapter 9 (together with Appendix 3) is devoted to a theoretical analysis of consumption externalities.

As the motivation for much of the econometric modeling of telecommunications demand continues to be the estimation of price elasticities for use in regulatory proceedings, I thought it would be useful to include a discussion on the use of econometrics in the hearing room. This is done in Chapter 10. There is a small but excellent literature on the role of econometrics in litigation, and my purpose in Chapter 10 is to introduce telecommunications demand analysts to this literature, as well as to provide my own thoughts as to how econometric demand models should be presented and defended in regulatory proceedings. The book concludes with an evaluation and conclusions in Chapter 11.

---

[17] Specifically by Edward D. Lowry and his staff of AT&T State Regulatory.

CHAPTER 2

THE THEORY OF TELEPHONE DEMAND

I: Basic Results

Meaningful empirical analysis of telephone demand must be accompanied by theory. At the time of the 1980 book, most existing studies of telephone demand were guided by the general canons of neoclassical demand theory, but the standard statement that demand depends upon price and income is of limited usefulness. The telephone and the network to which it belongs possess a number of singular features that must be taken into account in modeling its demand. By 1980, these features had been examined at a theoretical level in several places, but the discussions were highly abstract and had little impact empirically.

This is no longer the case. While there have been no major theoretical innovations since 1980, the key feature in question – notably the distinction between access and use and the network and call externalities – have received a great deal of empirical attention. The 1980s have also seen a marked shift in focus, from toll to local and from usage to access. This shift in focus reflected the concern (hastened by the breakup of AT&T on January 1, 1984) by state regulators and consumer groups that universal service was at risk from the higher local-service charges that were emanating from competition in the intercity toll market.

The purpose of this chapter and the next is to introduce essential concepts and to integrate them into a basic theoretical structure that can provide a framework for assessing the existing empirical record and for helping to organize an agenda for future research. The focus in these two chapters is almost entirely on households. Business demand will be discussed in Chapter 4.

I. SOME BASIC CONSIDERATIONS

The thing that most distinguishes telecommunications demand from the demand for most goods and services is the fact that telecommunications services are not consumed in isolation. A network is involved. This gives rise not only to certain interdependencies and externalities which affect how one models consumption but also a clear-cut distinction between access and usage. There must be access to the network before the network can be used.

A completed telephone call requires the participation of a second party, and the utility of this party is thereby affected. The second party is presumably also benefitted, but whether or not this is actually the case is beside the point. The point is that a completed call necessarily impinges upon a second party, and an externality is created. This is the first of two demand externalities associated with the telephone, and is usually referred to as the *call* (or *use*) externality.

A second type of externality arises when a new subscriber connects to the system. Connection of a new subscriber confers a benefit on existing subscribers because the number of telephones that can be reached is increased. This externality, which is usually referred to as the *network* (or *access* or *subscriber*) externality, gives the telephone system the dimension of a public good, since the benefit that a new subscriber confers on existing subscribers is shared in common. The call externality also has a public-good dimension, but this aspect of the externality has never received much attention because, in contrast with the network externality, only one party is involved.[1]

A further complication in modeling the telephone demand arises from the fact that benefits arise not only from completed calls, but also from calls that may not be made. Subscribing to the telephone network can be viewed as the purchase of options to make and receive calls. Some of these options will be exercised with certainty, while others will not be exercised at all. This is because many calls will only be made contingent upon particular states of nature whose realization is random and thus not known at the time that access is purchased. Emergency calls, such as for fire, police, or ambulance, are obvious cases in point, but compelling urgency is not the only determinant. Many calls arise from no more than mood or whimsy. *Option demand* is thus an important characteristic of telephone demand.[2]

Before turning to the formal aspects of the theory of telephone demand, it will be useful to list the points that must be kept in mind developing a meaningful theoretical superstructure:

1. The point of departure in modeling telephone demand should be the dis-

---

[1] These externalities will be discussed in detail in Chapter 9.

[2] The concept of option demand is well-known in the literature on conservation and exhaustible natural resources (see Kahn 1966, Weisbrod 1964), but apart from brief mention in Squire (1973), it is absent from the pre-1980 literature on telephone demand. In recent years, its relevance has come to the fore in analyzing the pricing of default capacity in the context of carrier-of-last resort obligations and in the demand for optional extended-area service. See Weisman (1988) and Kridel, Lehman and Weisman (1991).

tinction between demand for *access* to the telephone system and demand for *use* of the system once access is obtained.

2. Both the demand for access and the demand for use are complicated by the access and use externalities. The presence of these externalities means that, contrary to what is ordinarily assumed, *preferences are interdependent across subscribers.*

3. Option demand is an important component of telephone demand, for subscribers are generally willing to pay something for the option to make or receive calls even though the calls may never take place.

4. Finally, telephone calls come in a variety of shapes and forms – type (station, person, collect, etc.), time-of-day, day-of-week, distance, and duration – and it is often important that these be taken into account.

II. RECENT CONTRIBUTIONS TO THE THEORY OF TELEPHONE DEMAND

The problems associated with modeling telephone demand were clarified materially in the mid-1970s in a series of papers in the *Bell Journal of Economics* by Artle and Averous (1973), Von Rabenau and Stahl (1974), Squire (1973), Rohlfs (1974), and Littlechild (1975). The contributions of these authors, beginning with Artle and Averous, will be discussed in this section.

Artle and Averous consider a population consisting of N individuals that are a group in the sense that, over a period of time, each individual converses once with every other individual either by telephone or face-to-face. In addition, it is assumed that if an individual is not connected to the telephone system as a subscriber, there is no access at all (i.e., there are no pay phones and there is no use of another's phone). This, accordingly, defines two mutually exclusive and exhaustive subsets of individuals, say G_0 and G_1, where G_0 denotes the subset without access to the telephone system and G_1 denotes the subset with access.

The utility function for the ith individual is assumed to be given by

$$U^i = u^1(x^i, q^i), \tag{1}$$

$$q^i = \begin{cases} q & \text{for all } i \text{ in } G_1 \\ 0 & \text{for all } i \text{ in } G_0. \end{cases} \tag{2}$$

In (1), q^i stands for access by the ith individual to the telephone system, denoted by q,[3] while x^i denotes the ith individual's consumption of other goods. It is assumed that the goods included in x are all private.

---

[3] The units in which q is measured will be defined below.

Since the property of access or no access is dichotomous, it can also be represented by a dummy variable δ^i, where $\delta^i = 1$ if the ith individual has access to the telephone system and $\delta^i = 0$ if the individual does not have access. Consequently, an equivalent formulation of the utility function in (1) is

$$U^i = U^i(x^i, \delta^i, q^i), \tag{3}$$

where $q^i = q$ for all i and

$$q^i = \begin{cases} 1 & \text{for } i \text{ in } G_1 \\ 0 & \text{for } i \text{ in } G_0. \end{cases} \tag{4}$$

Artle and Averous next assume that all individuals connected by telephone (i.e., the members of G_1) consume the bundle of private goods, x^1. Similarly, it is assumed that the individuals not connected to the telephone system (i.e., the members of G_0) are also alike in that they, too, consume a common bundle of private goods, x^0. With these assumptions, the utility functions for individuals with and without a telephone can be written as[4]

$$U^1 = U^1(x^1, q), \quad \delta = 1 \tag{5}$$

$$U^0 = U^0(x^0, 0), \quad \delta = 0. \tag{6}$$

At this point, Artle and Averous postulate the presence of an omniscient planner who is equipped with a social-welfare function that embraces the well-being of all N individuals in the population. This omniscient planner is also provided with a social-production-possibility function that reflects the technological constraints imposed on the behavior of the N individuals. Finally, it is assumed that q (whose units have not previously been defined) is measured by the number of telephones, which implies, then, that q of the N individuals in the population are connected by telephone, while $N - q$ individuals are outside of the telephone system.[5] Question: What is the optimal value of q?

Let W denote the social-welfare function and F the social-production-possibility function. Artle and Averous assume that W has the form,

$$W = W\left[qU^1, (N - q)U^0\right]. \tag{7}$$

The question posed can be answered by maximizing the function,

$$\Psi(x^1, x^0, q) = W\left[qU^1, (N - q)U^0\right] - \lambda F(x^1, q) \tag{8}$$

---

[4] Artle and Averous actually assume that U^1 and U^0 have the same functional form.
[5] In the analysis that follows, q will be treated as though it varies continuously.

with respect to x^1, x^0, and q, where λ is the LaGrangian multiplier associated with the social-production-possibility function,

$$F(x, q) = 0 \tag{9}$$

and where

$$x = qx^1 + (N - q)x^0. \tag{10}$$

Assuming that an interior solution exists $(1 < q < N)$, the necessary conditions for an optimum will be given by:[6]

$$\frac{\partial \Psi}{\partial x^1} = W_1 q U_x^1 - \lambda F_x q = 0 \tag{11}$$

$$\frac{\partial \Psi}{\partial x^0} = W_0(N - q)U_x^0 - \lambda F_x(N - q) = 0 \tag{12}$$

$$\frac{\partial \Psi}{\partial q} = W_1\left(U^1 + qU_q^1\right) - W_0 U^0 - \lambda F_q = 0 \tag{13}$$

$$\frac{\partial \Psi}{\partial \lambda} = F(x, q) = 0. \tag{14}$$

From (11) and (12), we obtain the following optimality condition:

$$W_1 U_x^1 = W_0 U_x^0, \tag{15}$$

which simply states that the last unit of private consumer goods yields the same welfare, as measured by the social-welfare index, independent of the individual to which it is allocated. From (11), (12), and (13) we can derive

$$\left(\frac{U^1}{U_x^1} - \frac{U^0}{U_x^0}\right) + q\frac{U_q^1}{U_x^1} = ((x^1 - x^0) + \frac{F_q}{F_x}. \tag{16}$$

The interpretation of the condition in (16) is as follows. To begin with, the second term on the right-hand side is the usual marginal rate of transformation in production, which, in this case, represents the marginal amount of x that must be given up in order to produce (and service) one more telephone. The second term on the left-hand side gives the marginal rate of substitution in consumption between telephone and other goods. It is seen that the marginal rate of substitution is multiplied by q, the number of individuals with access

---

[6] In equations (11)–(13), W_1 denotes $\partial W/\partial(qU_1)$, W_0 denotes $\partial W/\partial(N - q)U^0$, F_q denotes $\partial F/\partial q$, and U_x^i denotes $\partial U^i/\partial x$.

to the telephone system. This result shows that access to the telephone system is indeed a public good.

As regards the two terms in parentheses, the term on the right-hand side measures the change in other goods that occurs when an individual enters the telephone system on the margin. Prior to entering the system, x^0 of other goods was consumed; after entry, x^1 of other goods is consumed. The difference, if negative, reduces the marginal rate of transformation of telephones for other goods. If the difference is positive, the difference must be produced, which will increase the marginal rate of transformation. The term in parentheses on the left-hand side shows the net difference in total welfare by having the marginal individual switch from the market basket $(x^0, 0)$ to (x^1, q). Since the terms in expression (16) are defined in units of x, both U^1 and U^0 are measured in the respective marginal utilities of x.

The Artle-Averous analysis makes two important contributions: (1) the public-good aspect of the telephone system is demonstrated with clarity and (2) the dichotomous access/no access decision is formulated in a way that allows conventional calculus methods to be used in deriving the optimal size of the telephone system. However, as a basis for a theory of telephone demand, the Artle-Averous analysis is incomplete. Prices and income are subsumed in the social-production-possibility function, and telephone use, as opposed to access, is assumed away by the assumption that each individual communicates with everyone else over some period of time, either by telephone or face-to-face. A further limitation with the Artle-Averous analysis is that the focus is on the optimal size of the system, rather than on individual demand.

Rohlfs (1974) extends the Artle-Averous analysis in several important respects, and in doing so overcomes some of the limitations just noted. Like Artle-Averous, Rohlfs, too, is concerned with the equilibrium number of telephones in a population, but he gives much greater attention to the demand component of the market. The public-good aspect of the telephone continues to be the central, but the focus is on individual demand, and an omniscient planner is not employed. The market demand function for telephones is obtained by summing over individual demand functions, which are derived from utility maximization.

The key construct for Rohlfs is the concept of an *equilibrium user set*, which is defined as a set of telephone users that is consistent with all individuals (users and non-users alike) maximizing their respective utility functions. A basic finding of Rohlfs is that, for any given price, there are typically multiple equilibria:

For example, a very small equilibrium may be consistent with utility maximization, since the smallness of the user set in itself make the service relatively unattractive to potential users. However, a much larger user set may also be possible for the same population at the same price. In this case the largeness of the user set would make the services attractive, and allow a high level of demand to be sustained. (Rohlfs 1974, p. 18.)

Rohlfs begins his analysis by defining (per Artle-Averous) a set of binary variables:

$$q_i = \begin{cases} 1 & \text{if individual } i \text{ has a telephone} \\ 0 & \text{if not} \end{cases} \tag{17}$$

for $i = 1, \ldots, N$. It is assumed that there is other goods in the economy (all of the private). Next, it is postulated that each individual possesses a *pair* of utility functions:

$$U_i^0 = U_i^0(x_{i1}, \ldots, x_{is}) \tag{18}$$

$$U_i^1 = U_i^1(q_1, \ldots, q_{i-1}, \ldots, q_N, x_{i1}, \ldots, x_{is}), \tag{19}$$

where:

U_i^0 = utility of individual i if the individual does not subscribe to the telephone system

U_i^1 = utility of individual i if the individual does subscribe

x_{ij} = consumption of (non-telephone) good j by individual i.

The utility function in (19) assumes that the utility of a telephone subscriber depends upon the other individuals who belong to the system. This interdependence of preferences reflects the consumption externalities of the telephone discussed earlier.

Per usual, Rohlfs assumes that, for $k = 0, 1$,

$$\frac{\partial U_i^k}{\partial x_{ij}} \geq 0 \quad \text{for all } j \tag{20}$$

and

$$\frac{\partial U_i^k}{\partial x_{ij}} > 0 \quad \text{for at least one } j. \tag{21}$$

Moreover, it is assumed that

$$U_i^0 \leq U_i^1 \tag{22}$$

for all i and for all values of the x_{ij}'s. Finally, it is assumed that

$$\frac{\Delta U_i^1}{\Delta q_w} \geq 0 \tag{23}$$

for all $i \neq w$ and for all $q_1, \ldots, q_{i-1}, q_{i+1}, \ldots, q_N, x_{i1}, \ldots, x_{is}$. This last assumption asserts that the addition of another subscriber to the system will never cause an existing subscriber to leave.

In deriving the demand function for access, Rohlfs postulates a two-step maximization procedure. First, the maxima of U_i^0 and U_i^1 are evaluated with respect to $q_1, \ldots, q_{i-1}, q_{i+1}, \ldots, q_N, x_1^i, \ldots, x_{is}$ subject to individual i's budget constraint. Denote these maxima by $\hat{U}_i^1$ and $\hat{U}_i^1$. The demand variable for individual i, q_i^d, is therefore defined as

$$q_i^d = \begin{cases} 1 \text{ if } \hat{U}_i^1 \geq \hat{U}_i^0 \\ 0 \text{ if } \hat{U}_i^1 < \hat{U}_i^0. \end{cases} \tag{24}$$

In order to concentrate on the interdependency in the telephone market, Rohlfs assumes income and the prices of all other goods to be constant, which allows i's *demand function* for access to the telephone system to be expressed as

$$q_i^d = q_i^d(r, q_1, \ldots, q_{i-1}, q_{i+1}, \ldots, q_N). \tag{25}$$

where r denotes the price of access. From earlier assumptions, it follows that q_i^d is nonincreasing in r – i.e., that an increase in r will never change q_i^d from 0 to 1 while a decrease in r will never change q_i^s from 1 to 0.

Finally, it follows from the assumption embodied in expression (23) that all q_i^d are nondecreasing with respect to all q_w ($w \neq i$).

Rohlfs defines an *equilibrium user set* as a set of telephone subscribers for which

$$q_i = q_i^d(r, q_1, \ldots, q_{i-1}, q_{i+1}, \ldots, q_N), \tag{26}$$

for all i. Thus, in equilibrium, all users demand access to the system, while nonusers do not. For fixed r, the equations in (26) comprise a system of N equations in N binary variables. However, Rohlfs shows that such a system does not in general have a unique solution. Indeed, in none of the simple models that Rohlfs investigates is the solution unique, except in the trivial cases where the price of access is so high that there is no demand at all or the price is zero. The reason for the nonuniqueness is the consumption externality. For, as noted earlier, an equilibrium user set can be very small because the smallness of the system makes the price unattractive to potential subscribers. On the other hand, a much larger equilibrium is possible because the largeness of the system makes the service more valuable.[7]

An important implication of multiple equilibrium user sets is the possibility that a telephone system can grow over time even though external factors (income, price, and population) do not change. If disturbed from an equilibrium with a small user set, the system might move to a new equilibrium with a much larger user set. Whether this would occur depends, as Rohlfs shows, on the direction of the disturbance and the nature of the disequilibrium adjustment process. However, the really important point is the role played by the consumption externality. For, as also stressed by Artle and Averous, endogenous growth can occur because of it.

Rohlfs' analysis makes the following contributions to the development of a framework for analyzing telephone demand:

1. Through the notion of an equilibrium user set, Rohlfs avoids the use of a social-welfare function to determine the equilibrium number of telephones in a population.
2. The demand function for access to the telephone network is approached in two steps: utility is evaluated with and without access, and whether access is demanded is then determined by comparing the resulting levels of utility. Not only does this seem descriptive of actual behavior, but it also provides a way (as we shall see) of integrating the best existing work on access demand, which is based on a consumer's-surplus analysis, into a utility framework.
3. Telephone price is an explicit argument in the analysis.

As with Artle and Averous, Rohlfs' analysis has some limitations. In particular, Rohlfs does not distinguish between access and use. Rohlfs employs just one price, which refers to access, as opposed to use. In this case, the customer would pay a flat charge per time period and make as many calls as desired. However, this ignores toll calls and those local calls for which there is an additional charge. Consequently, a meaningful theoretical framework for analyzing telephone demand must include a price for use (when use is priced), as well as a price for access.

To this end, we shall now turn our attention to an analysis first introduced by Squire (1973) that relates the demand for access to the demand for use in

---

[7] It should be noted that equation (26) defines equilibrium only with respect to the demand side of the market. It describes subscriber sets that are consistent with utility maximization at a given price of access, but these constitute only necessary, not sufficient conditions for an overall market equilibrium. The latter requires, in addition, that the subscriber set and the price of access be consistent with some specified model of supply behavior. (See Rohlfs 1974, p. 21.)

a consumer's-surplus framework. Let q be a dichotomous variable that takes the value of 1 if the consumer desires to subscribe to the telephone system and which takes the value of 0 if the consumer wishes not to subscribe. Let π denote the price of a call, r the subscription price of access to the telephone system, and μ the level of income of the consumer. Next, let Z denote the number of calls that the consumer would make if he were connected to the telephone system and let

$$\pi = g(Z, \mu) \tag{27}$$

denote the inverse demand function for calls.[8] Finally, let B_z denote the amount that the consumer would be willing to pay in order to make the Z calls.

Under Marshallian conditions, B_z will be given by[9]

$$B_z = \int_0^Z g(z, \mu)\, dz. \tag{28}$$

The consumer's surplus (S_z) associated with the Z calls will then be equal to

$$S_z = B_z - Z\pi. \tag{29}$$

Finally, it follows that the binary variable q will be determined according to

$$q = \begin{cases} 1 \text{ if } S_z \geq r \\ 0 \text{ if } S_z < r. \end{cases} \tag{30}$$

In words, expression (30) states that a consumer will demand access to the telephone system if the benefits from belonging to the system (measured by the consumer's surplus associated with the calls that would be made) are at least as great as the cost of subscribing to the system (measured by r).[10] From expressions (27) to (30), it follows, then, that (ignoring externalities) the demand for access is a function of income, the price of calls, and the price of access:

$$q = q(\mu, r, \pi). \tag{31}$$

---

[8] For now, the prices of other goods are absorbed into the shape of g. Note, too, that the customer index i is suppressed.

[9] For convenience, we shall treat the number of calls Z as though this were a continuous variable.

[10] It should be noted that a consumer may desire access to the system even though no calls are made. In this case, $g(0, \mu)$ would measure the benefits of receiving calls. If these benefits are greater than r, the consumer will demand access just to receive incoming calls. The benefits generated by incoming calls are clearly related to call externality referred to earlier, and will be discussed below and also in Chapter 9.

Thus, we see that the demand for access to the telephone system depends in a fundamental way on the demand for use of the system. In making this connection precise and rigorous – and especially in showing that the relationship flows from use to access, rather than from access to use – Squire makes a fundamental contribution to the theoretical analysis of telephone demand.

In arriving at expressions (30) and (31), access and call externalities (except as noted in footnote 10) have been ignored. We shall now indicate how these externalities can be integrated into the analysis. The discussion that follows is once again based upon Squire. To begin with, let us distinguish between a *conceptual* market demand curve for calls and an *observed* demand curve. The conceptual demand curve refers to the relationship between the total number of calls that a group of subscribers would make and the price of a call on the assumption that the number of subscribers is constant. However, because of consumption externalities, there is an entire family of conceptual demand curves. Moreover, only a single point on each member of this family can be observed. For if we were to increase the price of a call to all subscribers, there would be a reduction in both the number of calls and the number of subscribers.

The number of subscribers would be reduced because the increase in the price of a call will decrease the net benefits of being connected to the telephone system, and this will cause subscribers that were previously on the margin to disconnect. Moreover, because of the externality associated with the number of subscribers, the decreased system size will lead to a still further attrition of subscribers. The reduction in the number of subscribers therefore means that, for any given size of the system, the conceptual demand curve will be less elastic than the observed demand curve.

The foregoing is illustrated in Figure 1. The total number of calls in the system is measured along the horizontal axis, while the price of a call is measured on the vertical axis. Three members of the family of conceptual demand curves are drawn. These are labeled $\bar{N}_1$, $\bar{N}_2$ and $\bar{N}_3$, and correspond to a system consisting of N_1, N_2, and N_3 subscribers, respectively, where $N_1 < N_2 < N_3$.[11] That the curve corresponding to N_3 lies to the right of the curve for N_2, which is to the right of the curve for N_1, reflects the positive externalities generated by the telephone system.

The conceptual demand curves, as mentioned, cannot be observed. What can be observed is the one point on each curve that corresponds to the equilibrium number of calls for that number of subscribers. (These points

---

[11] The bars over the Ns are to remind us that the conceptual demand curve is derived with the number of subscribers held constant.

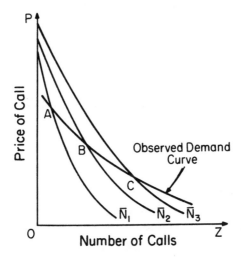

Fig. 1.   Relationship between the Conceptual and Observed Market Demand Curve for Calls.
Source: Squire (1973), p. 571).

correspond to the equilibrium user sets discussed by Rohlfs.) The focus of
these points yields the observed demand curve as drawn in the figure. As
noted earlier, the elasticity of the observed demand function is greater than
the elasticity of the conceptual demand function.

With a slight modification to our earlier notation, the benefit derived by
the nth subscriber from outgoing calls can be written as

$$B_n(\bar{N}) = \int_0^{Z_n} g_n(z, \bar{N}) \, dz, \tag{32}$$

where Z_n is the number of calls made by the nth subscriber and g_n is this
subscriber's conceptual inverse demand function.[12] The total benefit from
outgoing calls is obtained by summing over the N subscribers,

$$\sum_{n=1}^{N} B_n(\bar{N}) = \sum_{n=1}^{N} \int_0^{Z_n} g_n(z, \bar{N}) \, dz. \tag{33}$$

If we define

$$G(Z, \bar{N}) = \sum_{n=1}^{N} g_n(Z_n, \bar{N})$$

---

[12] Income has been absorbed into the shape of g_n.

as the market conceptual inverse demand function,[13] expression (33) can be written as

$$\sum_{n=1}^{N} B_n(\bar{N}) = \int_0^z G(z, \bar{N}) \, dz. \tag{34}$$

Finally, Squire defines the benefit from outgoing calls for the *marginal* (i.e., the Nth) subscriber as

$$B_N(\bar{N}) = \sum_{n=1}^{N} B_n(\bar{N}) - \sum_{n=1}^{N-1} B_n(\bar{N}). \tag{35}$$

The foregoing describes the benefits associated with outgoing calls, but what about incoming calls? Squire states (p. 518): "When one's telephone rings, one has no idea of the possible benefit of the incoming call." Presumably, the expected benefit is positive, but there is no guarantee that this will be the case, for the call may be a nuisance call or the caller may be someone with whom the callee would prefer not to speak. However, as Squire notes, the benefit of an incoming call can, in principle, be measured by asking how much a person would be willing to pay in order to be allowed to answer the call. This reduces the problem to asking for the certainty-equivalent value of an uncertain return.

Specifically, let us assume, following Squire, that the possible benefit (i.e., return) from an incoming call can be represented by a probability distribution, where the expected return is measured by the mean of the distribution (θ) and the risk associated with the return by its variance (σ^2). Assume that a subscriber is willing to accept greater risk (i.e., is willing to accept a greater uncertainty of the possible benefit of an incoming call) only in return for a larger expected benefit. We can then define a curve, as in Figure 2, that shows the nth subscriber's tradeoff between risk (i.e., higher variance) and expected benefit.[14] The point b_n on the μ-axis measures the certainty equivalent of the uncertain benefit of the incoming call. Hence, in this case, the subscriber is willing to pay up to b_n to answer the phone. We can therefore interpret b_n as the benefit from an incoming call.[15]

Squires observes:

----

[13] The three conditional demand curves in Figure 1 correspond to $G(Z, \bar{N})$ for $\bar{N} = \bar{N}_1, \bar{N}_2, \bar{N}_3$.

[14] The curve in Figure 2 is drawn on the assumption that the subscriber is risk averse. The conventional procedure is to represent risk by the standard deviation. I have followed Squire in using the variance. The conclusion is obviously not affected.

[15] In commenting on this section in the 1980 book, the late Arthur Okun remarked that this analysis focuses on the benefit or nuisance of an incoming call in isolation, rather than on how the information conveyed by the call interacts with other uncertainties about the world.

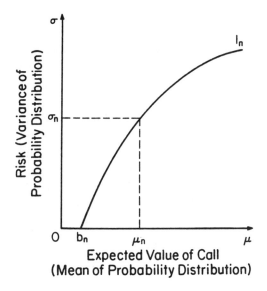

Fig. 2.   Certainty-Equivalent of an Incoming Call for a Risk-Averse Subscriber. Source: Squire (1973), p. 519.

We can deduce something about the probable value of b_n from observed behavior. In the first place, most subscribers do answer their phones, which operation presumably involves some private cost in terms of effort expended. (This private cost must be quite high in the case of the subscriber who gets out of his shower to answer his phone!) In some cases, the private cost may be negligible, but in general we can assume that it is not negative (i.e., subscribers do not derive utility from lifting the receiver), from which observation we can deduce that $b_n \geq 0$. This is not to say that b_n will never be negative. The subscriber who receives a *prolonged* series of nuisance calls learns not to answer his phone, and in extreme instances may even have his phone disconnected. Such behavior indicates that $b_n < 0$ for this subscriber. Alternatively, the subscriber may request an unlisted number which may be interpreted as an attempt to insure that b_n is positive, because the unlisted number will only be given to people from whom the subscriber wishes to receive calls. (Squire 1973, p. 518, italics

To the extent that the information conveyed by an incoming call helps to reduce overall risk, then answering the phone is beneficial. Okun noted that it was always bad for his wife when he is going to be home late for dinner, but the bad news was less costly if she learned of it in advance by a call. The bad outcome is made less bad by answering the phone than by not answering it, so that total risk is reduced. Thus it follows that the certainty-equivalent value of an incoming call can exceed the expected value of the call.

in original.)

As Squire goes on to note, there is not much more that can be deduced about the value of b_n. At present, I know of only three market mechanisms whereby subscribers can express their preference concerning incoming calls. First, and most obvious, is the acceptance of collect calls. The second is the firm that offers a toll-free number, while the third is call forwarding, in which the subscriber can have calls to his/her regular number automatically forwarded to another number. In each case, the value on incoming calls must be at least as much as the price the subscriber has to pay for the service.[16]

In the end, Squire assumes that $b_n = b$ for all subscribers. With this assumption, the total benefits derived from making and receiving calls in the telephone system will be given by

$$TB = \sum_{n=1}^{N} B_n(\bar{N}) + bY = \int_0^Z G(z, \bar{N}) \, \mathrm{d}z + bY, \tag{36}$$

where Y denotes the total number of incoming calls. For a closed system Y will actually equal Z, since an incoming call is also an outgoing call for someone.

The size of the telephone system is determined in Squire's analysis from the condition that the marginal subscriber will equate the private benefit and cost of belonging to the telephone system. Specifically, for the marginal subscriber, the benefit from making calls $[B_n(N)]$ plus the anticipated benefit from receiving calls (bY_N) will just be equal the cost of making calls (πZ_N) plus the cost of access to the system (r), that is,

$$B_N(\bar{N}) + bY_N = \pi Z_N + r, \tag{37}$$

where Y_N denotes the number of incoming calls anticipated by the marginal subscriber and Z_N denotes the number of calls made by this subscriber.

I have described the analysis of Squire in detail because of the insights that it provides into the nature of access and call externalities and also because of its identification of the dependence of the demand for access on the benefits conferred by use of the telephone system. These are important contributions, and clearly complement the contributions of Artle and Averous and Rohlfs.[17]

---

[16] The use of answering service and recording devices are consistent with a positive b_n, but since these services also enable calls to be screened, it would be incorrect to identify the expenditure for them solely with b_n. As with an unlisted number and services which display the number from which a call is placed, their purchase can be viewed as helping to insure that b_n is positive.

[17] Before leaving this discussion, I would like to comment briefly on Squire's use of the

III. Consumption Externalities and Communities of Interest

Thus far consumption externalities have been discussed with reference to the total number of telephones. While this makes sense in the context of option demand, for most subscribers the absolute size of the system is probably secondary to the subscriber's individual community of interest. What matters to most people is whether the circle to which they "belong" is on the telephone system. If so, then belonging to the system will probably be quite independent of how many other telephones can be reached. Consequently, to identify the network externality solely with system size is probably to abuse the concept.

De Fontenay and Lee (1983) and Breslaw (1985) have sought to clarify the meaning of the network externality by distinguishing between the two forms that an expansion in the number of telephones in a system can take. The first is through an increase in the penetration rate (i.e., an increase in the proportion of a population that has a telephone), population remaining constant, while the second is through an increase in population, the penetration rate remaining constant. These are referred to by de Fontenay and Lee as *Type 1* and *Type 2* expansions, respectively. The question we wish to focus on for a few moments is the implications of these two types of expansions for the network externality, specifically on that aspect of the externality associated with communities of interest.

In a mature system, such as in the U.S. and Canada, which have effectively had universal service for years, it has been argued by de Fontenay and Lee (1983), and especially ardently by Breslaw (1985), that it is doubtful that consumption externalities are any longer a factor with either type of expansion. The argument is essentially that in a mature system, communities of interest are also mature. Existing communities of interest are unlikely to enlarge in direct response to an increase in the number of telephones, and new ones that form are likely the result of increases and movements in population.

conceptual demand function in measuring the benefits from outgoing calls. One way to interpret the conceptual experiment that gives rise to the conceptual demand function for an individual consumer is to assume that income is varied across the other subscribers in such a way as to keep the number of subscribers constant. In this case, the conceptual demand function is an income-compensated demand function, and is accordingly an interesting and useful construct. In particular, it can be used, as Squire suggests (p. 517), to assess a consumer's willingness-to-pay. However, I question that aggregate willingness-to-pay can be defined, as in expression (33), by summing over individual willingnesses-to-pay. For individual willingnesses-to-pay cannot be meaningfully summed, as in expression (33), because the individual demand functions are not independent. A particular subscriber's conceptual demand function is derived on the assumption that his income is held constant, while other incomes are varied so as to keep the number of subscribers constant. To sum across individual willingnesses-to-pay thus involves an inconsistency. Partial-equilibrium analysis is being used in a situation that requires a general-equilibrium framework.

The network externality is undoubtedly a factor in the penetration rate being higher in a mature system than what it would be in its absence – 95% instead of (say) 90% – but it is no longer a factor making for endogenous growth. Put another way, existing subscribers, because of the externality, may be willing to pay more to remain subscribers than what they would in its absence, but the addition of a new subscriber (for whatever reason) does not make the system more valuable to nonsubscribers and cause some of them to subscribe who otherwise would not. Put still a third way, a mature system is basically in equilibrium and in particular is in equilibrium with respect to the network externality.

Usually, the focus of the network externality is on access rather than on usage. However, Breslaw (1985) poses the externality in terms of usage, specifically whether one should expect usage per telephone to be greater, everything else being constant, in a large system as opposed to a small system. Breslaw's view is that, again in a mature system, this should not be the case. Breslaw's argument for this will be examined in detail in Appendix 3. Here, I wish only to note that, while the question is legitimate and interesting, to pose it as a reflection of the network externality is incorrect. The problem is with option demand. The larger number of telephones that can be reached in a larger system, as opposed to a smaller one, can induce a greater willingness-to-pay to belong to a larger system without there necessarily being any increase in planned usage per telephone. In short, a network externality can exist which affects access but not usage.

When all is said and done regarding communities of interest, the problem is not the conceptual basis for their importance, but difficulties of measurement. Essentially for lack of anything better, the usual practice has been to identify community-of-interest with the number of telephones that can be reached, but this (as we have seen) is unsatisfactory, especially when the focus is on a single-individual or household. What is to be done? The fact is that economists probably need help from the disciplines that study networking and how personal networks form. The telephone is clearly an important factor in increasing the efficiency with which personal networks can function, but it is an enabling device rather than a *causa causen*.

IV. A Framework for Analyzing Telephone Demand

In this section we shall attempt to mold the ideas and concepts just discussed into a cohesive theoretical structure. Our focus will be strictly on demand, and the question of pricing will be of interest only to the extent that particular pricing schemes have important theoretical and econometric implications.

Problems caused by two-and multi-part tariffs are particular cases in point. Similarly, the question of the size of the telephone system will enter into the analysis only to the extent that telephone demand can grow endogenously because of the consumption externalities.

In the discussion that follows, our concern will be with a consumer whose *potential* market basket consists of two goods, telephone calls (q) and a composite good (x) that represents all other goods and services.[18] Let N denote the number of subscribers to the telephone system, and following Artle and Averous and Rohlfs, define a dichotomous variable δ such that

$$\delta = \begin{cases} 1 & \text{if the consumer is connected to the telephone system} \\ 0 & \text{otherwise.} \end{cases} \tag{38}$$

We assume that the consumer has a utility function U with q, x, and N as arguments:[19]

$$U = U(q, x, N). \tag{39}$$

Finally, let the consumer's budget constraint be given by

$$(r + \pi q) + px = \mu, \tag{40}$$

where:

$r =$ price of access to the telephone system

$\pi =$ price of a call

$p =$ price of the composite good x

$\mu =$ income of the consumer.

The utility function in (39) differs from the utility function postulated by Artle and Averous in that the number of calls and the number of subscribers appear as arguments, rather than just the number of calls. The number of calls represents the purely private benefits of using the telephone system, while the

---

[18] The representation of the other goods in the consumers' market basket by a composite good is strictly an assumption of convenience.

[19] We make the standard neoclassical assumptions concerning the properties of U with respect to q and x. In addition, we also assume $\partial U/\partial N > 0$. Also, in reviewing this chapter in the first edition, Merton Peck suggested that the system externality might be measured better by the proportion of the population having a telephone rather than just the number of subscribers, which is to say that we assume that the system externality is always positive. However, the popularity of unlisted and unpublished numbers in large systems suggests that this may not always be the case. For reasons discussed in the preceding section, the effect of the externality is almost certainly nonlinear.

number of subscribers represents the external benefits of system size. Unlike Artle and Averous, we do not assume that each individual communicates with everyone else in the population, and unlike Rohlfs, we do not allow for interdependence among subscribers by including as arguments the calls made by every other subscriber to the telephone system.

Rohlfs' procedure is, in principle, superior to the one that is being followed here because it allows for the call externality as well as the access externality. Also, it can be seen as an effort to define the community of interest. But the present procedure is clearly more tractable empirically. Also, as noted, by Littlechild (1975), when the consumption of a large group of subscribers is considered – as is the case for most empirical studies of telephone demand – the *individual* effects of call externalities will tend to balance out. For when people have repetitive contacts, each person can return the benefit of receiving a call.[20] However, since the call externalities are not, in general, reflected in either the price of access or the price of use, there will be an unallocated benefit for the *system* as a whole. On the other hand, the size of this benefit, which represents the collective benefits from incoming calls, should be closely related to the size of the system, and (for a large group of subscribers) will thus also tend to be reflected in the number of subscribers.

Let me now turn to the derivation of demand functions for use and access. These will be obtained by postulating, following Rohlfs, a two-step maximization procedure. In the first step, the net benefits from use of the telephone system by an individual are calculated conditional on access, while in the second step, the net benefits are compared with the cost of access in order to determine whether access will in fact be purchased.

In step 1, therefore, we assume that $\delta = 1$ and then maximize the LaGrangian function,

$$L = U(q, x, N) - \lambda(\pi q + px - \mu + r) \tag{41}$$

with respect to q and x, where λ is the LaGrangian multiplier associated with the (conditional) budget constraint,

$$\pi q + px = \mu - r. \tag{42}$$

The first-order conditions are accordingly [in addition to (42)]:

$$\frac{\partial L}{\partial q} = U_q - \lambda \pi = 0 \tag{43}$$

$$\frac{\partial L}{\partial x} = U_x - \lambda p = 0. \tag{44}$$

---

[20] We shall return to this point in Chapter 3 and also in Chapter 9.

From these three equations, we can in principle derive the demand functions for calls and all other goods:

$$q = q(\pi, p, N, \mu - r) \tag{45}$$

$$x = x(\pi, p, N, \mu - r). \tag{46}$$

These functions differ from conventional demand functions in two respects: (1) the budget constraint is $\mu - r$, rather than μ, which reflects the conditionality of use on having purchased access to the telephone system, and (2) the demand functions depend upon the number of subscribers, which reflects the access and call externalities. Determination of the net benefits for the consumer from use of the telephone system proceeds by evaluating the consumer's surplus generated by use of the telephone system. Accordingly, let

$$\pi = g(q, p, N, \mu - r) \tag{47}$$

be the inverse demand function for calls [obtained by solving equation (45) for π]. The consumer's surplus (S) from making q calls will consequently be given by

$$S = \int_0^q g(z, p, N, \mu - r) \, dz - \pi q. \tag{48}$$

In step 2, the consumer's net benefits from using the telephone system are compared with the cost of access to the system. If S is at least as great as r, the benefits from belonging to the telephone system outweigh the cost of access, and the consumer will subscribe to the system. Thus,

$$\delta = \begin{cases} 1 & \text{if } S \geq r \\ 0 & \text{if } S < r. \end{cases} \tag{49}$$

If it is found in step 2 that the consumer does subscribe to the system, the conditional analysis in step 1 becomes unconditional – that is, the demand functions for calls on other goods and services given in expressions (45) and (46) are the actual demand functions. However, if step 2 shows that the consumer will not subscribe, then equations (45) and (46) do not apply, for $\lambda = 0$ also implies that $q = 0$. The utility function in (39) will therefore be given by

$$U = U(x) \tag{50}$$

and the budget constraint will be reduced to

$$px = \mu. \tag{51}$$

The demand function for x will consequently be given by

$$x = \mu/p. \tag{52}$$

The two-step maximization process for determining the demand for use and access combines the procedures of Rohlfs and Squire. Rohlfs, it will be recalled, also employs a two-step maximization framework, but uses the utility function directly to calculate benefits, rather than calculating consumer's surplus as does Squire. In principle, using the utility function to calculate benefits is preferable because it is exact, whereas consumer's surplus provides only an approximation to the benefits. However, as Willig (1976) has shown, the error involved in using a consumer-surplus framework is seldom serious.[21]

The next task is to extend the analysis to an entire population. In the discussion that follows, the demand for use will continue to be identified with the number of calls, while the demand for access will be identified with the proportion of the population that subscribes to the telephone system. Let Q denote the total number of calls that are made by system subscribers.[22] We assume Q to be a function of the price of a call (π), the price of other goods and services (p), the cost of access (r), the number of subscribers (N), and aggregate income (Y):

$$Q = Q(\pi, p, r, N, Y). \tag{53}$$

In arguments, the only difference between the aggregate (or market) demand function and the demand function for an individual subscriber in (45) is that the cost of access (r) is included separately, rather than as a subtraction from income. However, we could just as plausibly postulate the budget constraint to be $Y - rN$.[23]

Turning now to the aggregate demand for access, let M denote the size of the population and, as before, let N denote the number of subscribers. In line with (49), define

$$\delta_n = \begin{cases} 1 & \text{if individual } n \text{ subscribes to the telephone system} \\ 0 & \text{otherwise.} \end{cases} \tag{54}$$

Then,

$$N = \sum_{n=1}^{N} \delta_n. \tag{55}$$

---

[21] See also Hausman (1981).

[22] At this point, all calls are treated as toll calls with π as the price of a call.

[23] Problems of aggregation are being glossed over at this point.

The quantity that we wish to explain is the proportion of the population having access to the telephone system, N/M.

Next, define S_n [as in expression (48)] to represent the consumer's surplus of individual n associated with his or her use of the telephone system, that is

$$S_n = \int_0^{q_n} g_n(q, p, N, \mu_n - r) \, dq - q\pi. \tag{56}$$

From (49),

$$\delta_n = \begin{cases} 1 & \text{if } S_n \geq r \\ 0 & \text{if } S_n < r. \end{cases} \tag{57}$$

Hence, it follows that δ_n is a function of π, p, N, r, and μ_n. Since π, p, N, and r are independent of n, δ_n will vary across individual consumers in the population either because of differences in preferences or because of differences in income. For now, however, we shall assume that everyone has the same preferences.

Since $N = \Sigma \delta_n$ and since δ_n depends on the value of $S_n - r$, N will depend on the distribution of $S_n - r$. However, since preferences are assumed not to vary, it follows that the distribution of $S_n - r$ will depend on the distribution of income. Hence, N, too, will depend on the distribution of income.[24] In particular, for given M, and with S_n treated as a random variable, N will be determined by the probability that S_n is greater than r, namely:

$$P(S_n > r) = 1 - F(r) = 1 - \int_0^r f(S_n) \, dS_n, \tag{58}$$

where $f(S_n)$ and $F(S_n)$ are the density and distribution functions of S_n. Under our assumptions, the distribution of S_n will be related to the distribution of income via the "change-of-variable" from μ_n to S_n as defined in expression (56).

More precisely, let $h(\mu_n)$ represent the density function of μ. Then, employing the formula for a change in variable, $f(S_n)$ will be related to $h(\mu_n)$ according to

$$f(S_n) = h\left[\mu_n(S_n)\right], \tag{59}$$

where $\mu_n(S_n)$ describes μ_n as a function of S_n, obtained from equation (56) by solving it for μ_n. The other arguments in (56), namely, q_n, p, N, and r, are

[24] If everyone were also to have the same income, there would be only two equilibrium values that N could take, O or M. Either no one would belong to the telephone system, or else everyone would.

subsumed into the shape of $\mu_n(S_n)$.[25] Let H denote the distribution function of μ_n. We can now reformulate expression (58) as

$$P(S_n > r) = P\left[\mu_n > \mu^*(r)\right] = 1 - H\left[\mu^*(r)\right]$$

$$= 1 - \int_0^{\mu^*(r)} h(\mu_n)\, d\mu_n. \tag{60}$$

Equivalently, $\mu^*(r)$ can be determined by solving the equation

$$H(\mu^*) = F(r) \tag{61}$$

for μ^* in terms of r. To summarize: given M and the assumption that tastes do not vary, the proportion of the population that subscribes to the telephone system will be given by:

$$\frac{N}{M} = P(S_n > r) = P\left[\mu_n > \mu^*(r)\right] = 1 - \int_0^{\mu^*(r)} h(\mu_n)\, d\mu_n, \tag{62}$$

or

$$\frac{N}{M} = \int_{\mu^*(r)}^{\infty} h(\mu_n)\, d\mu_n. \tag{63}$$

Readers will recognize the expression described by equation (63) as a discrete-choice model, which is a type of model that has been used extensively in analyzing model choice in transportation demand[26] and fuel and appliance choice in energy demand.[27] It has also found extensive use since 1980 in telecommunications demand. In discrete-choice terminology, $\mu^*(r)$ can be interpreted as the "threshold" value of income. If the threshold is exceeded, the consumer subscribes to the telephone system; if the threshold is not reached, the consumer does not subscribe. In the present context, however, we are able to specify how the threshold arises, for it is determined by the consumer's surplus generated by the use of the telephone system compared with the cost of access. Under our assumptions, variation in consumer's surplus across consumers is caused by variation in income. Hence, in this case,

---

[25] Since it is assumed that the marginal utility of a call is always positive, S_n in equation (56) is a positive function of μ_n, so that equation (56) is in fact invertible.

[26] See McFadden (1974), Domencich and McFadden (1975), and Hausman and Wise (1978). For surveys of discrete-choice models, see Amemiya (1981) and McFadden (1976). For textbook treatments, see Ben-Akiva and Lerman (1985), Maddala (1983), and Train (1986).

[27] See Baughman and Joskow (1975), and Lin, Hirst, and Cohn (1976).

the proportion of the population demanding access to the telephone system will be determined by the distribution of income, according to equations (62) or (63).[28]

In view of equations (56), (58), and (59), we can rewrite expression (63) as

$$\frac{N}{M} = \Phi(\pi, p, r, N, Y), \tag{64}$$

where Φ is a highly complicated composite function embodying S_n in expression (56), the change-of-variable in equation (59), and the integral in equation (63).[29] The distribution of income is represented in (64) by the variable Y, which (for expositional convenience) we shall identify with the aggregate level of income. In view of the complexity of equation (63), empirical application will require specification of the demand function (or functions) for use and a more detailed representation of the income distribution.

Equations (53) and (64) comprise, in general form, a bare-bones model of telephone demand for a population of residential consumers. Equation (53) describes the total number of calls that are logged by subscribers to the telephone network, while equation (64) describes the proportion of the population that demands access to the network. Equation (53) thus represents the aggregate demand for use of the telephone system, and equation (64) represents the aggregate demand for access to the system. In later sections, we shall extend this model to take into account flat-rate pricing for local calls and toll prices that vary by mileage, duration, time of day, and type of call.

V. RELATIONSHIPS BETWEEN PRICE AND INCOME ELASTICITIES FOR ACCESS AND USAGE

We have seen how the demand for access to a telephone network depends upon the consumer surplus from usage. In view of this, it is not correct, as it

---

[28] If tastes also vary, then the proportion of the population demanding access will depend upon the joint distribution of tastes and income. Allowing tastes to vary is mandatory if one is going to deal realistically with situations where consumers can choose among several types of basic service-one-party flat-rate, two-party flat-rate, one-party measured, and so on. This will be discussed in Chapters 5 and 7.

[29] The argument leading up to expression (63) contains a problem similar to the one discussed in connection with Squire's derivation of the aggregate willingness-to-pay function: the number of subscribers, N, is assumed to be fixed in deriving the individual S_n; however, at the aggregate level, N is variable. As expression (64) stands, it is an implicit function in N, and accordingly can in principle be solved for N. A more practical solution is suggested in Section 3.4 below.

is often attempting to do, to treat access and usage as independent markets, and in particular to treat the price elasticity for access as independent of the price elasticity for usage. For, as we will now show, there is a relationship which connects the price and income elasticities for access with the price and income elasticities for usage.

For notation, let S (as before) denote the consumer surplus from usage and r the price of access. From the discussion leading to equation (58) in the preceding section, we can conclude that, for a household picked at random, the probability that the household will subscribe to the telephone network will be given by

$$P(\text{access}) = P(S > r) = 1 - F(r), \tag{65}$$

where F denotes the distribution function of S.

We want now to calculate the partial derivatives of expression (65) with respect to π and r at the margin of subscription, which is at the point where $S = r$. Denote this value of S by S^*. Accordingly:

$$\frac{\partial P}{\partial \pi} = -f(r)\left(-\frac{\partial S^*}{\partial \pi}\right), \tag{66}$$

$$\frac{\partial P}{\partial r} = -f(r)\left(1 - \frac{\partial S^*}{\partial r}\right), \tag{67}$$

where f denotes the density function of S. Since $\partial S/\partial \pi = -q$, we can rewrite (66) as

$$\frac{\partial P}{\partial \pi} = -f(r)q^*, \tag{68}$$

where q^* represents the value of q associated with $S^* = r$.

For $\partial S^*/\partial r$, we will have as a first approximation:[30]

$$\frac{\partial S^*}{\partial r} = \left[q^{*2} + \left(\frac{q^*}{\frac{\partial q}{\partial \pi}}\right)^2\right]^{1/2}\frac{\partial q}{\partial r}$$

$$= q^*\left(1 + \phi^2\right)^{1/2}\frac{\partial q}{\partial r} = -q^*\left(1 + \phi^2\right)^{1/2}\frac{\partial q}{\partial \mu}, \tag{69}$$

since $\partial q/\partial r = -\partial q/\partial \mu$ and where ϕ represents the price flexibility of q [defined as $1/(\partial q/\delta \pi]$. Thus for $\partial P/\partial r$ we will have

$$\frac{\partial P}{\partial r} = -f(r)\left[1 + q^*\left(1 + \phi^2\right)^{1/2}\frac{\partial q}{\partial \mu}\right]. \tag{70}$$

[30] This approximation involves linearizing the demand function for usage and then using the Pythagorean Theorem.

Dividing (68) by (70) then yields:

$$\frac{\frac{\partial P}{\partial \pi}}{\frac{\partial P}{\partial r}} = \frac{q^*}{1 + q^* \left(1 + \phi^2\right)^{1/2} \left(\partial q / \partial \mu\right)} \tag{71}$$

or in terms of elasticities:

$$\frac{\eta_{m\pi}}{\eta_{mr}} = \frac{\pi q^*}{r} \cdot \frac{1}{1 + \left(\frac{q^{*2}}{\mu}\right)\left(1 + \phi^2\right)^{1/2} \eta_{q\mu}}, \tag{72}$$

where $\eta_{m\pi}$ denotes the elasticity of the probability of access with respect to the price of usage, etc. Since q^{*2}/μ (which represents the square of usage divided by income at the margin of subscription) will in general be a small number of the order of 0.1, the second factor on the right-hand side of (72) can be ignored, in which case we will have

$$\frac{\eta_{m\pi}}{\eta_{mr}} \cong \frac{\pi q^*}{r}. \tag{73}$$

In words, expression (73) states that the ratio of the elasticities of access demand with respect to the prices of usage and access, respectively, is approximately equal to the ratio of their respective expenditures. This result, which is given in more exact form in expressions (71) and (72), expresses the fundamental connection between the price slopes and elasticities of the demand functions for usage and access. In view of the fact that econometric efforts to estimate $\eta_{m\pi}$ have been generally unsuccessful, the empirical usefulness of expression (73) is evident.

VI. Option Demand

It was noted earlier that subscription to the telephone system is closely related to option demand. Option demand was first discussed by Kahn in a provocative article in *Kyklos* in 1963 and also by Weisbrod in the *Quarterly Journal of Economics* in 1964, and has since figured prominently in the economics of natural resources, particularly in the preservation of irreplaceable places of natural beauty. As described by Krutilla (1967),

> [option] demand is characterized as a willingness to pay for retaining an option to use an area or facility that would be difficult or impossible to replace and for which no close substitute is available. Moreover, such a demand may exist even though there is no current intention to use the area or facility in question and the option may never be exercised. (Krutilla 1967, p. 780.)

In the present context, option demand refers to where the making of a call is contingent upon a state of nature whose realization is uncertain. In this situation, the consumer is willing to pay something for the option to make the call even though the option may not be exercised. Let us assume that, during a given period of time (say a month), a consumer is willing to buy options to make R calls, but that, on the average, only a proportion θ of these calls will actually be made.[31] Assume that both θ and R are known to the consumer. Assume, further, that the expected value of the number of options that will be exercised, θR, is included in q (defined in previous sections), so that the net benefits from these calls are already reflected in the consumer's surplus measure defined in expression (56).

However, the benefits from the $(1 - \theta)R$ options that are not exercised are not reflected in S_n, which means that S_n *understates* the amount that the consumer is willing to pay in order to have access to the telephone system. Let w denote the benefit conferred by an option that is not exercised.[32] The benefits associated with the $(1 - \theta)R$ unexercised options will then be equal to $w(1 - \theta)R$. This, then, is the amount by which S_n will understate the consumer's willingness-to-pay for access to the system.

With option demand in the picture, expression (57) for δ_n becomes

$$\delta_n = \begin{cases} 1 & \text{if } S_n + w(1 - \theta)R \geq r \\ 0 & \text{if } S_n + w(1 - \theta)R < r \end{cases} \tag{74}$$

Expression (45) remains valid as the demand function for use; similarly, equation (53) continues to describe the demand for the total number of calls in the system. However, in deriving the function describing the aggregate demand for access, the threshold value for income in expression (60) must be replaced by $\mu^*(r) - w(1 - \theta)R$, which means that expression (62) becomes

$$\frac{N}{M} = \int_{\mu^{**}}^{\infty} h(\mu_n)\, d\mu_n, \tag{75}$$

where

$$\mu^{**} = \mu^*(r) - w(1 - \theta)R. \tag{76}$$

Hence, expression (64) must be revised to[33]

$$\frac{N}{M} = \Phi(\pi, p, r, N, Y, R). \tag{77}$$

---

[31] These R calls are in addition to those the consumer knows will be made with certainty. R may be very large, but for most consumers θ will be very small.

[32] Since the value of the benefit associated with an option will almost certainly vary with the call involved, w should be viewed as an expected value.

[33] The value of w is assumed to be absorbed into the shape of Φ.

Although the foregoing is straightforward in principle, the important question is whether option demand can be dealt with empirically. Since it is unlikely that information on θ and R can be found, their presence will have to be inferred indirectly. To this end, let us consider two types of option calls: (1) calls of an emergency nature (police, fire, medical, etc.) and (2) calls of a non-emergency nature relative to pleasure or business.

Generally speaking, calls of an emergency nature should be reasonably independent of the size of the local network (or exchange), since small communities, as well as large communities, require doctors and police and fire protection. However, this type of option demand is probably relatively more important in small as opposed to large exchanges and in rural as opposed to urban areas. In a rural area, having access to a telephone is probably more urgent than in an urban area because of the absence of immediate neighbors and because distances are likely to be longer. In a large exchange, on the other hand, option demand of this form is likely to be of lesser relative importance because the option demand of the second type is likely to be of greater absolute importance.

Option calls of the second type will be primarily related to a subscriber's income and community of interest, both of which are likely to be larger with a larger exchange. Income is higher in a large exchange, because large exchanges are in urban areas and urban incomes are higher than rural incomes. Consequently, since R would seem almost certainly to be heavily weighted with option calls of the second type, network size (as noted in Section IV), in addition to everything else that it might measure, ought also to stand as an indicator of option demand. On the other hand, since option calls of the first type are probably of greater relative importance in communities with low population density, a measure of urbanization should probably be included as a predictor in the equations describing the demand access.[34]

---

[34] The discussion in this section has only scratched the surface of option demand and its relation to the demand for access. At the time of the *Survey*, there was no knowledge of either the quantitative importance of option demand or how it may vary across customer classes or sizes of exchange. Option demand was thought to be a factor in subscribers' apparent preference for flat-rate pricing for local service, even though measured service may result in a smaller expected overall bill, but there again there was no quantitative information. At the 1990 Hilton Head conference sponsored by Bell Canada and BELLCORE, three papers were devoted to option demand in the context of class-of-service choice. D. Kridel, D. Lehman and D. Weisman analyzed extended area service, while in two separate papers, K. Train and T. Tardiff analyzed the premium associated with flat-rate service when local measured service is available as an option.

CHAPTER 3

THE THEORY OF TELEPHONE DEMAND

II: Extensions of Basic Results

This chapter continues the discussion of the basic theory of telephone demand and adds a number of extensions to the model derived in Chapter 2.

I. THE DURATION AND DISTANCE DIMENSIONS OF TELEPHONE DEMAND

For a given customer class, a telephone call possesses four dimensions: type of call, time, distance, and duration. Since the cost of "supplying" a call varies in each of these dimensions, telephone companies have priced calls accordingly. In some cases, the pricing schemes used have been in some accordance with the principles of marginal-cost pricing (day/night and weekday/weekend differentials, a lower charge for direct dialing, etc.), while in other cases, the motivation has been primarily to subsidize the access and local-service markets by the long-distance market. In the present context, however, the issue is not *why* a telephone call is priced in multi-dimensions, but rather *that* it is so priced. Our task in this section and the next will be to illustrate how this fact can be integrated into the theoretical structure.

The first thing that we shall focus on is the complications caused by multi-part tariffs. Most telephone services are priced on some form of multi-part tariff, and care must be taken in the way that price is introduced to the analysis. A toll call, for example, is supplied on a two-part tariff, the initial period carries one charge, and subsequent periods (or parts thereof) carry a lower charge. As a consequence, the average price per call-period is no longer the same as the marginal price.

To see what is involved with a multi-part tariff, let us assume that q is supplied according to the following rate schedule:[1]

---

[1] For the next several paragraphs, q should be viewed as an abstract good that is sold on a multi-part tariff. The point of these paragraphs is to describe the problems caused by multi-part tariffs under highly simplified assumptions. However, if readers prefer at this point to identify q with telephone calls, then q should be viewed as a single call measured in call-minutes (or call-seconds).

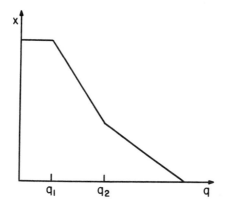

Fig. 1.   Budget constraint with decreasing block pricing.

1st q_1 units of q or less: r\$'s

q_1 to q_2 units of q: π_0/unit of q

more than q_2 units of q: π_1/unit of q,

where it is assumed that $\pi_0 > \pi_1$. Assume that a second good x can be purchased in unlimited quantities at price p per unit. As usual, we shall assume that the consumer possesses a utility function $U(q, x)$ that is maximized subject to the level of income.[2]

With the multi-part tariff for q, the budget constraint becomes nonlinear. Its general appearance is as given in Figure 1, while algebraically it is given by[3]

$$r + \Psi_0(\pi_0, q, q_1, q_2) + \Psi_1(\pi_1, q, q_2) + px = \mu, \tag{1}$$

where

$$\Psi_0(\pi_0, q, q_1, q_2) = \begin{cases} 0 & \text{if } q \leq q_1 \\ \pi_0(q - q_1) & \text{if } q_1 < q \leq q_2 \\ \pi_0(q_2 - q_1) & \text{if } q > q_2 \end{cases} \tag{2}$$

---

[2] The following discussion is taken from Taylor (1975, pp. 76–79). There is now a large literature on the economics and econometrics of non-linear and piece-wise linear budget constraints. Blattenberger (1977) provides the most extensive theoretical treatment. See also Dubin (1985), Moffitt (1986, 1990), and Pudney (1989).

[3] It is assumed that the amount r is spend independently of whether any q is actually consumed.

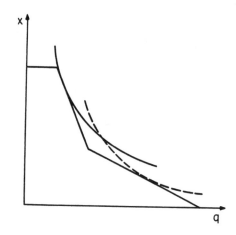

Fig. 2.   Consumer equilibria with decreasing block pricing.

$$\Psi_1(\pi_1, q, q_2) = \begin{cases} 0 & \text{if } q \leq q_2 \\ \pi_1(q - q_2) & \text{if } q > q_2 \end{cases} \tag{3}$$

The horizontal segment of the budget constraint in Figure 1 corresponds to the "fixed charge" of r for consumption of the first q_1 units of q. The linear segment between q_1 and q_2 has slope equal to $-\pi_0/p$, and corresponds to the π_0 block of the tariff schedule. Finally, the segment from q_2 on, with slope equal to $-\pi_1/p$, corresponds to the π_1 part of the schedule.

The nonlinear, nonconvex budget constraint in (2) and (3) has a number of consequences for the demand functions and Engel curves, and we shall now analyze these with the aid of Figures 2 through 7. Figure 2 shows the point of equilibrium for two different indifference maps. The indifference map corresponding to the solid curve gives an equilibrium on the facet of the budget constraint having slope equal to $-\pi_0/p$, while the one corresponding to the dashed curve gives an equilibrium on the facet with slope equal to $-\pi_1/p$.

Figure 3 describes an increase in π_0, but keeps π_1 constant, while Figure 4 depicts an increase in π_1 as well. In Figures 3 and 4, equilibrium following a price increase remains on the same facet of the budget constraint, but it is clear from Figure 5 that this need not always be the case, since the price increase in this figure leads the consumer to drop back to a higher rate class. Switching into a different marginal rate class can also come about by a change in income, as is evident in Figure 6. Finally, Figure 7 shows a case in which the budget constraint is tangent to the same indifference curve at two different points, thereby resulting in multiple equilibria.

Figures 2 through 7 thus support the following conclusions:

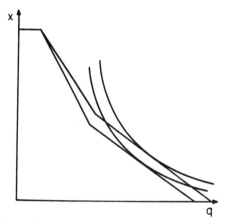

Fig. 3.   Effect of a change in intramarginal price.

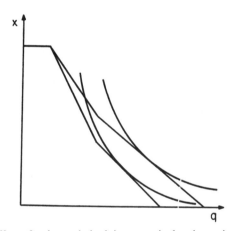

Fig. 4.   Effect of a change in both intramarginal and marginal price.

1. Because of the piece-wise linearity of the budget constraint, the equilibrium of the consumer cannot be derived, as is conventionally the case,
   using the differential calculus. Mathematical programming must be used
   instead. Demand functions and Engel curves still exist, but they cannot
   be obtained as closed-form expressions from solution of the first-order
   conditions for utility maximization.
2. From Figure 5, it is evident that the demand functions are discontinuous,
   with jumps at the points where equilibrium switches from one facet of
   the budget constraint to another.
3. From Figure 6, the same is seen to be true of the Engel curve.
4. From Figure 7, it is evident that for normally shaped indifference curves,

40   *Chapter 3*

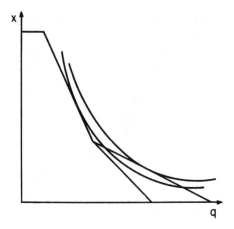

Fig. 5.   Price change that leads to switching of blocks.

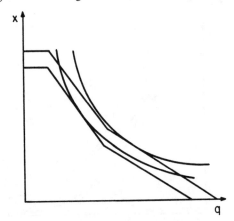

Fig. 6.   Effect of an income change.

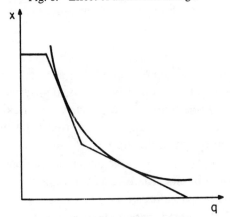

Fig. 7.   Multiple equilibria.

there will be a particular configuration of price for which the demand functions are not singled-valued. This is, of course, a consequence of the non-convexity of the budget constraint. In particular, the demand functions will be multi-valued whenever there is a configuration of prices that yield multiple tangencies of the budget constraint to the same indifference curve.

Putting aside the nonanalyticalness of the demand functions, how is a multi-part tariff to be represented in an empirical demand function? Suppose that the consumer is in equilibrium in the π_1 block, and consider the following cases:

1. An increase in the "fixed charge" r, π_0 and π_1, remaining the same;
2. An increase in π_0, r and π_1 remaining the same;
3. An increase in π_1, r and π_0 remaining the same.

In Figure 8, the increase in r is seen to shift the budget constraint downward, and leads to a reduction in the amount of q consumed. In Figures 3 and 9, it is seen that q is decreased for Cases 2 and 3 as well. It will be noted, however, that the reductions in q in Cases 1 and 2 *arise strictly from an income effect.* That is, an increase in the "fixed charge" or an increase in an intra-marginal price are equivalent in the sense that they give rise to income effects, but not to substitution effects.[4] An increase in π_1 (the marginal price) yields in traditional fashion, however, both an income effect and a substitution effect.

From this simple exercise, it is evident that all parts of a multi-part tariff up to and including the price in the marginal block belong in the empirical demand function. Changes in intramarginal prices (so long as they do not cause the consumer to shift blocks) give rise to income effects only, while a change in the price in the marginal block gives rise to both an income effect and a substitution effect.

Let us now interpret the foregoing as a highly simplified model of telephone demand. One can define r (as before) as the price of access to the telephone system, π_0 as the charge for the initial period of a call, and π_1 as the charge for each overtime period (or part thereof). In this case, then, q will represent the duration of a call. The value of q will depend on all three telephone prices (as well as on income and the price of other goods), but the price effect, as we ordinarily think of it, will only be reflected in the charge for an overtime period. Provided that the call lasts into at least one overtime

---

[4] The only qualification to this statement arises in the situation where the increase in π_0 or r is sufficiently large that equilibrium switches from the π_1 block to the π_0 block. In this case, there would be a substitution effect as well as an income effect.

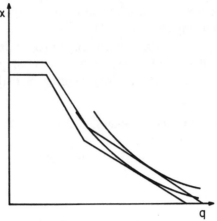

Fig. 8.   Change in fixed charge.

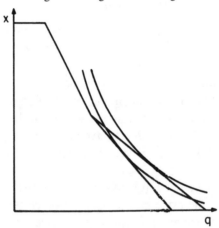

Fig. 9.   Change in marginal price.

period, the price of access and the initial-period charge will affect duration only through an income effect.[5]

The fact that the demand functions (with a multi-part tariff) are multi-valued and discontinuous for certain configurations of prices means that the demand functions for individual subscribers cannot be represented by analytic functions. However, conventional econometric estimation of price and income elasticities requires the use of an analytic function, which means

---

[5] Also, this conclusion ignores the possibility that a person who speaks frequently with another may substitute a large number of short calls for a small number of long calls if the charge for overtime periods becomes large relative to the charge for the initial period. In this case, the initial period charge would also affect duration directly.

that use of micro data necessarily involves an error. At present, the evidence is limited as to how serious this error may be.[6] Fortunately, though, the problem tends to disappear with aggregation, for as one aggregates over a population of consumers, the average demand functions for the population become continuous as the size of the population becomes large. A sufficient condition for this to occur is that income or tastes vary across consumers.[7] Since most empirical analyses of telephone demand are based on aggregate data, the problems caused by multi-valuedness and discontinuities can thus safely be ignored.

We now turn to the main purpose of this section, which is to incorporate the duration and distance dimensions of a telephone call into the theory of telephone demand. The discussion that follows will be facilitated by assuming a specific functional form for the demand function in equations (53) and (77) of Chapter 2. For ease in exposition, we shall postulate these functions to be linear. Hence, for the demand function for use [equation (53) of Chapter 2], we assume:

$$Q = \alpha_0 + \alpha_1 \pi + \alpha_2 p + \alpha_3 r + \alpha_4 N + \beta_5 Y, \tag{4}$$

while for the demand function for access [equation (77) of Chapter 2], we assume:[8]

$$m = \beta_0 + \beta_1 \pi + \beta_2 p + \beta_3 r + \beta_4 N + \beta_5 Y, \tag{5}$$

where

$$m = \frac{N}{M}. \tag{6}$$

We shall consider, first, the case where a telephone call is timed and charged according to duration. However, we shall continue to assume that the cost of the call does not vary by type, time-of-day, or length-of-haul. The only modification in equation (4) that is required is that Q is now more properly interpreted as referring to the number of call-minutes, rather than to just the number of calls. The price variable, π, in both equations (4) and (5) will, of course, refer to the charge measured in some unit of connect time

---

[6] See Wade (1980). Wade's results, in the context of residential electricity demand, suggest that the problem may not be as severe as I had once thought.

[7] The theorem involved was proven by Gail R. Blattenberger in her Ph.D. dissertation at the University of Michigan (Blattenberger 1977). The theorem is also discussed in Taylor and Blattenberger (1986). See also Chipman (1982).

[8] For convenience, it is assumed that θ and R, the parameters describing option demand, are reflected in N. Also, we ignore until Section IV the fact that N appears on both sides of the equation.

(most likely a minute or fraction thereof). With the redefinition of π, equation (4) does not require further modification.

We shall now complicate the situation (but also make it more realistic) by assuming that a call is priced on a two-part tariff. In particular, assume that the first minute of a call costs π_0, while each subsequent minute, or part thereof, costs π_1, where $\pi_0 > \pi_1$. As we have just seen, a two-part tariff introduces a complication in that the average price per call-minute of a call is no longer the same as the marginal price. There are accordingly three ways that we can proceed. The first, which follows from the preceding discussion, is to include both π_0 and π_1 in the demand functions as predictors, that is,

$$Q = \alpha_0 + \alpha_1 \pi_0 + \alpha_1' \pi_1 + \alpha_2 p + \alpha_3 r + \alpha_4 N + \alpha_5 Y \tag{7}$$

$$m = \beta_0 + \beta_1 \pi_0 + \beta_1' \pi_1 + \beta_2 p + \beta_3 r + \beta_4 N + \beta_5 Y. \tag{8}$$

In this case, α_1' (assuming that not all calls terminate within the initial period) will measure the traditional price effect (since π_1 is the price on the margin), while α_1 will measure an income effect. Naturally, we expect both α_1 and α_1' to be negative.

Alternatively, equation (4) can be replaced by two equations. The first equation will explain the *number* of calls that are made, while the second equation will explain the *mean duration* of a call. Let Z denote the former, and t the latter. Then,

$$Q = Zt. \tag{9}$$

The relationship between Z and t can be approached in the same framework as the demand for access and the demand for use. Making a call corresponds to the decision to purchase access, while the duration of the call corresponds to use.[9] The first part of the two-part tariff, π_0, represents the "buy in" price for the call, while π_1 represents the "running cost". Thus, π_1 will be most relevant in explaining t, but both π_0 and π_1 should figure in the equation for Z. The inclusion of π_1 in the equation for Z reflects the fact that, in line with the link between access and use expressed in equation (57) of Chapter 2, the amount that a subscriber is willing to pay to make a call will depend on the net benefits that the call confers, and this will clearly depend on π_1.

For the equation explaining the number of calls, we therefore postulate:

$$Z = \gamma_0 + \gamma_1 \pi_0 + \gamma_2 \pi_1 + \gamma_3 p + \gamma_4 r + \gamma_5 N + \gamma_6 Y, \tag{10}$$

while for the equation explaining mean duration, we assume:

$$t = \eta_0 + \eta_1 \pi_0 + \eta_2 \pi_1 + \eta_3 p + \eta_4 N + \eta_5 Y. \tag{11}$$

---

[9] Cf. Khadem (1976).

Strictly speaking, r should also be an argument in equation (11) since the duration of a call is clearly conditional on access. However, the contribution of this variable will operate only through an income effect, and its net influence on it will almost certainly be small.[10] On the other hand, one might question whether system size belongs in equation (11), for, once a call is made, the number of subscribers might seem irrelevant to how long the call lasts.[11]

The third way of dealing with a multipart tariff is through a two-level budgeting framework that is based upon the Almost Ideal Demand System of Deaton and Muellbauer (1980). The two levels in this approach correspond to an initial decision on the part of consumers of how much of their total income to allocate to telecommunications services in general and then an allocation of this expenditure amongst the various services. This approach is especially useful in situations in which several services are being analyzed jointly, such as measured local calling, intraLATA toll, and interLATA toll. All of the prices that are involved (including all up-front charges) are included in a price index that is used in the initial- (or first) level allocation, while the relative prices of the individual services are used in determining the shares of the first-level expenditures amongst these services. Two-level budgeting was initially applied in the analysis of energy demand by Hausman, Kinnucan and McFadden (1979) and also by Hausman and Trimble (1984). In telecommunications demand, it has been employed by Zona and Jacob (1990) in testing for "total bill" effects and by Hausman (1991) and Trimble (1992) in analyzing intraLATA toll demand in rate hearings in California and Florida. The Zona-Jacob study will be discussed in Chapter 8.

Continuing down the list of complications, we shall now assume that the price of a call varies with distance (i.e., length-of-haul). We shall retain the

[10] The initial-period charge (π_0) will also affect Z through an income effect. However, in commenting on the 1980 book, William Shew (then of NERA, now of Putnam, Hayes and Bartlett) suggested that there may be a substitution effect as well, because there may be situations where the number of calls and duration can be substitutes. For example, suppose that a person is weighing making three-minute calls to a relative in the middle and at the end of the month or six-minute call at the end of the month. If π_0 is greater than π_1, then the former would be more expensive, but could be of greater value because the information conveyed is more current. The choice in this situation will therefore depend in part on the incentive created by the tariff to substitute call frequency for call duration. With present day tariffs, in which the difference between π_0 and π_1 is small for customer-dialed calls, there is probably little incentive to do so.

[11] William Shew has also questioned this conclusion. Shew points out that if a portion of A's calls to B consist of information that B is to convey to C, who does not have a telephone, then C's getting a telephone would shorten A's conversations with B, since A could now talk to C directly. Shew also noted that if all eight of A's closest friends have telephones, A's average length of conversation is likely to be shorter than if only four of the eight have telephones. Thus, it seems that whether system size affects duration has to be left as an empirical question.

assumption that a call is charged by the call-minute, but (for now) we shall drop the assumption that this is on a two-part tariff. Further, we shall assume that there are D cities that a subscriber can call. Let these be indexed by j, and assume that they are ordered by the distance that they are from the subscriber. Let π_j denote the price per call-minute of a call to city j and assume that $\pi_j < \pi_k$. The question that we wish now to ask is: What will determine the subscriber's demand for call-minutes to city j?

In approaching this question, it will once again be useful to decompose call-minutes into the product of the number of calls and the mean duration of a call. Hence, parallel to equation (9), we have for calls to city j,[12]

$$q_j = z_j t_j. \tag{12}$$

We shall focus first on the determinants of z_j.

As before, it is clear that z_j will depend on prices, income and some measure of system size. Concerning prices and income, no new questions of principle arise, and these variables can be represented as previously. However, how to represent system size is another matter, for in this case, system size is ambiguous. To this point, it has more or less been implicit that the subscriber's community of interest is geographically local. However, the community of interest has now been extended to another telephone system, and the size of that system will be the relevant measure of size, rather than the size of the local system. Everything else being constant, the larger is city j, the more people in that city the subscriber is likely to know, and, therefore, the more calls that are likely to be made. But distance will also be a factor. In particular, the more distant is city j, the fewer people in city j the subscriber is likely to be acquainted with, and hence the fewer calls that are likely to be made.

For the demand function for z_j, we therefore postulate[13]

$$z_j = \gamma_0 + \gamma_1 \pi_j + \gamma_2 p + \gamma_3 r + \gamma_4 \mu + \gamma_5 N_j + \gamma_6 d_j, \tag{13}$$

where μ denotes income, N_j denotes the number of telephones that can be reached in city j, and d_j denotes the distance of city j from the subscriber. As noted, we expect γ_5 to be positive and γ_6 to be negative. For the equation for mean duration, t_j, we assume

$$t_j + \eta_0 + \eta_1 \pi_j + \eta_2 p + \eta_3 \mu + \eta_4 N_j + \eta_5 d_j. \tag{14}$$

---

[12] The focus in the next several paragraphs will be on an individual subscriber. This is indicated by the use of lower-case letters, q and z, in place of Q and Z.

[13] The cities other than j that the consumer might call are ignored at this stage. It is not clear *a priori* how much interdependence there is (if any) among calls to different cities; besides, it is best not to try to cover everything in the present discussion.

As in equation (11), the price of access, r, is excluded from this equation, although in principle it does belong. Note, too, that, also as in equation (11), the number of subscribers in city j is included as an argument. In this case, though, it is clear that the impact of a larger system size on duration (assuming that system size is important at all) will be positive. For (as noted earlier), the larger is city j, the more people in that city the subscriber is likely to know, so that a call to city j may be longer as a result of more messages being conveyed to acquaintances in city j through the person who is called (and also more information being acquired through the callee by the caller). Finally, since a positive relationship between the duration of a call and distance is a well-established empirical regularity, we expect η_5 to be positive.

Let us now turn to the total volume of one-way traffic between the subscribers in one system and the subscribers in another system. Let i and j denote the two systems involved, and let Q_{ij} denote the one-way toll volume, measured in call-minutes, from system i to system j. Let Z_{ij} denote the number of calls from i to j, and let t_{ij} denote the mean duration of a call. Then,

$$Q_{ij} = Z_{ij} t_{ij}. \tag{15}$$

For the model explaining Z_{ij}, we propose:

$$Z_{ij} = \lambda_0 + \lambda_1 \pi_{ij} + \lambda_2 p + \lambda_3 r_i + \lambda_4 N_i + \lambda_5 N_j + \lambda_6 Y_i + \lambda_7 d_{ij}, \tag{16}$$

where

$$\pi_{ij} = \text{price/call-minute of a call from system } i \text{ to system } j$$

$$p = \text{price of other goods and services}$$

$$N_i = \text{number of telephone subscribers in system } i$$

$$N_j = \text{number of telephone subscribers in system } j$$

$$Y_i = \text{income in system } i$$

$$d_{ij} = \text{distance between systems } i \text{ and } j.$$

The variables in equation (16) require little comment. We should, of course, expect λ_1 and λ_3 to be negative and λ_2 and λ_6 to be positive. Since the volume of traffic should vary directly with the sizes of the systems involved, we should also expect λ_4 and λ_5 to be positive. Finally, as in equation (13), we should expect λ_7 to be negative.[14] For the equation explaining the mean duration of a call, we postulate [in line with equation (16)]

$$t_{ij} = \xi_0 + \xi_1 \pi_{ij} + \xi_2 p + \xi_3 N_j + \xi_4 Y_i + \xi_5 d_{ij}. \tag{17}$$

[14] A model will be analyzed in Chapter 6 in which calling from city i to city j depends upon the reverse traffic from city j to city i.

As in equation (14), the coefficient on N_j may be positive, as should be also the coefficient on d_{ij}.

No new questions of principle arise when (as is in fact the case) a toll call is supplied on a two-part tariff. With slight modification to our previous notation, let π^0 denote the first part of the tariff, and let π^1 denote the second part. In line with equations (10) and (11), equations (13) and (14) for the number of calls and mean duration of a call by a single subscriber to city j become

$$z_j = \gamma_0 + \gamma_1 \pi_j^0 + \gamma_2 \pi_j^1 + \gamma_3 p + \gamma_4 r + \gamma_5 \mu + \gamma_6 N_j + \gamma_7 d_j. \tag{18}$$

and

$$t_j = \eta_0 + \eta_1 \pi_j^0 + \eta_2 \pi_j^1 + \eta_3 p + \eta_4 N_j + \eta_5 \mu + \eta_6 d_j. \tag{19}$$

Similarly, equations (15) and (16) describing the total volume of traffic from system i to system j become

$$Z_{ij} = \lambda_0 + \lambda_1 \pi_{ij}^0 + \lambda_2 \pi_{ij}^1 + \lambda_3 p + \lambda_4 r_i + \lambda_5 N_i$$
$$+ \lambda_6 N_j + \lambda_7 Y_i + \lambda_8 d_{ij} \tag{20}$$

$$t_{ij} = \xi_0 + \xi_1 \pi_{ij}^0 + \xi_2 \pi_{ij}^1 + \xi_3 p + \xi_4 N_j + \xi_5 Y_i + \xi_6 d_{ij}. \tag{21}$$

II. TIME-OF-DAY PRICING

In an effort to smooth out peak-load traffic, telephone companies have for years priced toll calls differently depending on the time of the day or day of the week that a call is placed. We shall now consider the implications of this type of pricing, under the assumption that there are two pricing periods, day and night. Let the price of a call be π^d during the day and π^n at night, and let q^d and q^n denote the number of day and night calls respectively. The utility function in expression (39) of Chapter 2 will therefore become

$$U = U(q^d, q^n, x, N), \tag{22}$$

and the budget constraint becomes

$$(\pi^d q^d + \pi^n q^n + r) + px = \mu. \tag{23}$$

The demand functions for q^d and q^n *conditional* on access [cf. expression (45), Chapter 2] will be given by

$$q^d = q^d(\pi^d, \pi^n, p, N, \mu - r) \tag{24}$$

$$q^n = q^n(\pi^d, \pi^n, p, N, \mu - r). \tag{25}$$

Whether or not access is purchased will be determined by the consumer's surplus generated by *both* day calls and night calls in comparison with the cost of access, r. That is, access will be purchased (i.e., δ will be equal to 1) if

$$S_d + S_n \geq r, \tag{26}$$

where

$$S_d = \int_0^{q_d} g^d(z, \pi^n, p, N, \mu - r)\, \mathrm{d}z - \pi^d q^d \tag{27}$$

$$S_n = \int_0^{q_n} g^n(z, \pi^d, p, N, \mu - r)\, \mathrm{d}z - \pi^n q^n \tag{28}$$

and where $g^d(\cdot)$ and $g^n(\cdot)$ are the inverse demand functions from (24) and (25).

From the foregoing, it should be clear that the introduction of a day/night price differential does not raise any new questions of principle. There will be a demand function for day calls and a demand function for night calls, and π^d and π^n will be arguments in both functions. In general, we should expect day and night calls to be substitutes, which is to say that $\partial q^d / \partial \pi^n$ and $\partial q^n / \partial \pi^d$ should both be expected to be positive.

We shall illustrate the modifications required by time-of-day tariffs using the equations describing the volume of one-way traffic between two systems discussed at the end of the preceding section. That is, we shall assume that a call is charged according to time (day/night), distance, and duration and, further, that duration is charged on a two-part tariff. For the equations explaining the total number of calls, we will have [cf. equation (20)]

$$
\begin{aligned}
Z_{ij}^d = {}& \lambda_0 + \lambda_1 \pi_{ij}^{0d} + \lambda_2 \pi_{ij}^{1d} + \lambda^3 \pi_{ij}^{0n} + \lambda_4 \pi_{ij}^{1n} + \lambda_5 r_i \\
& + \lambda_6 p + \lambda_7 N_i + \lambda_8 N_j + \lambda_9 Y_i + \lambda_{10} d_{ij},
\end{aligned} \tag{29}
$$

$$
\begin{aligned}
Z_{ij}^n = {}& \lambda_0' + \lambda_1' \pi_{ij}^{0d} + \lambda_2' \pi_{ij}^{1d} + \lambda_3' \pi_{ij}^{0n} + \lambda_4' \pi_{ij}^{1n} + \lambda_5' r_i \\
& + \lambda_6' p + \lambda_7' N_i + \lambda_8' N_j + \lambda_9' Y_i + \lambda_{10}' d_{ij},
\end{aligned} \tag{30}
$$

while for the equations explaining the mean duration of a call, we will have [cf. equation (23)]:

$$
\begin{aligned}
t_{ij}^d = {}& \xi_0 + \xi_1 \pi_{ij}^{0d} + \xi_2 \pi_{ij}^{1d} + \xi_3 \pi_{ij}^{0n} + \xi_4 \pi_{ij}^{1n} \\
& + \xi_5 p + \xi_6 N_j + \xi_7 Y_i + \xi_8 d_{ij}
\end{aligned} \tag{31}
$$

$$t_{ij}^n = \xi_0' + \xi_1'\pi_{ij}^{1d} + \xi_2'\pi_{ij}^{1d} + \xi_3'\pi_{ij}^{0n} + \xi_4'\pi_{ij}^{1n}$$

$$+ \xi_5'p + \xi_6'N_j + \xi_6'N_j + \xi_7'Y_i + \xi_8'd_{ij}. \tag{32}$$

III. Operator-Handled Versus Direct-Dialed Calls

When a subscriber wishes to make a toll call, there is a choice of dialing the call directly or using an operator. Since an operator-handled call necessarily involves the time of an operator, telephone companies charge more for this type of call, but an operator-handled call also provides more service in that the call can be sent person-to-person, collect, or billed to a third party. This section provides a brief discussion of the factors that enter into the choice of operator-handled versus nonoperator-handled calls. Most of the focus will be on station-to-station versus person-to-person calls. Let π^p denote the price of a person-to-person call, and let π^s denote the price of a station-to-station call.[15] Let η denote the probability that the person the subscriber wishes to talk with can in fact be reached.[16] Then, given a choice between a person-to-person or a station-to-station call, the subscriber will choose the station call if

$$\pi^s \leq \eta\pi^p, \tag{33}$$

that is, if the price of the station-to-station call is no greater than the probability that the person that it is desired to reach is in fact reachable times the price of the person-to-person call. To illustrate, if the probability of reaching the desired party is 0.5, then the caller will be better off making the call station-to-station if the price of the station-to-station is no greater than one-half of the price of the person-to-person call.[17]

---

[15] If a call is charged on a two-part tariff, π^p and π^s are assumed to refer to the first part of the tariff. Current rate schedules typically distinguish between person-to-person and station-to-station calls only in the charge for the initial period. Overtime periods are charged the same.

[16] The probability η is defined on the assumption that the call is completed. If there is no answer or the line is busy, the caller does not pay. The analysis that follows assumes that the call is completed.

[17] The decision rule expressed in expression (33) can be complicated for a business call by the likelihood that the caller will attempt to shift part of the cost of the call onto the callee when the latter cannot be reached by asking that the call be returned. In this case, a caller may choose a station-to station call even when the probability of reaching the person desired is zero. Also, it should be noted that this analysis ignores the fact that the charge for a person-to-person call does not begin until the desired party is actually on the line. In some cases, therefore, a person-to-person call may be cheaper than a station-to-station call.

Turning now to the toll calls of a system of subscribers, let r denote the proportion of the toll calls from the system that are station-to-station calls. We assume that, in the aggregate, this proportion will depend on the *ratio* of π^s to π^p. In particular, we shall postulate

$$\tau = w_0 \left(\frac{\pi^s}{\pi^p} \right)^{w_1}. \tag{34}$$

In this expression, the effect on τ of the probability of callers reaching desired callees is represented in the parameters w_0 and w_1.[18]

The other two types of operator-handled calls, collect calls and third-party billings, should be closely related to travel. This should especially be the case for third-party billings. Collect calls, on the other hand, should be particularly sensitive (among other things) to college enrollments and military maneuvers, but are probably less sensitive than third-party billings to changes in income and price. The income elasticity for credit-card calls, in particular, is probably substantial.

IV. SOME FURTHER DYNAMICS

The purpose of this section is to introduce some dynamical elements into the theory, in addition to those inherent in the access/use distinction, by allowing for inertia (or habit formation) in both the access and use equations. In order to keep the analysis simple, we shall revert to our very first price assumption, namely, that there is just one price π that applies to all calls. Our focus in the discussion that follows will be on equations (45) and (49) in Chapter 2 for an individual subscriber and equations (53) and (77) in Chapter 2 for a full system of subscribers.

We shall begin with an individual subscriber's demand for telephone calls. Let us assume that when there is a change in price or income, a subscriber does not adjust immediately to a new equilibrium number of calls, but that adjustment occurs over a period of time. Let q_t^* denote the desired (i.e. equilibrium) number of calls during period t for given prices, income, and the number of subscribers. In particular, assume

$$q_t^* = \alpha_0 + \alpha_1 \pi_t + \alpha_2 p_t + \alpha_3 N_t + \alpha_4 (\mu_t - r_t). \tag{35}$$

Next, let q_t denote the actual number of calls that the subscriber makes during the period. Finally, we postulate that whenever q and q^* diverge, a proportion

---

[18] The probability of the desired party being reached will almost certainly vary from call to call, which means that, for the system as a whole, τ in expression (34) will be described by a probability distribution. Provided that this distribution is independent of π^s/π^p (which should be the case), its parameters can be represented in the parameters w_0 and w_1.

θ of the discrepancy is eliminated within any one period. That is, we assume
that

$$q_t - q_{t-1} = \theta(q_t^* - q_{t-1}), \tag{36}$$

where $0 < \theta \le 1$. Substituting expression (35) into (36) for q_t^* we obtain
(after some rearrangement)

$$q_t = \alpha_0\theta + (1 - \theta)q_{t-1} + \alpha_1\theta\pi_t + \alpha_2\theta p_t + \alpha_3\theta N_t + \alpha_4\theta(\mu_t - r_t). \tag{37}$$

Readers will recognize this expression as the estimating equation for the
Koyck geometric distributed-lag model, although in this case it has been
derived from a Stone-Rowe-Nerlove partial-adjustment mechanism.

The dynamics that are implicit in expression (37) are simple and easy to
derive. Assuming that θ is less than 1, the underlying dynamical process is
stable, and long-run equilibrium will be achieved when $q_t = q_{t-1}$, or when
$q_t = q^*$. Hence, when there is a change in price (say), the long-run impact of
this change on q will be given by α_1 [cf. expression (35)]. However, this will
be achieved only after an infinity of periods have passed. In the short run,
the impact on q will be tempered by the parameter θ. One way that we can
define the short run is as the elapse of one period following a change in price
(or income). From equation (37) we see that the one-period effect on q of a
one unit change in price will be equal to $\alpha_1\theta$. Thus the short- and long-run
derivatives of q with respect to price are equal to $\alpha_1\theta$ and α_1, respectively.
Similarly, the short- and long-run derivatives of q with respect to income are
$\alpha_4\theta$ and α_4, and so on for the derivatives with respect to the other predictors.

As before, the demand function in (37) has to be interpreted as conditional
on access to the telephone network. However, since the demand for access
depends on the consumer's surplus generated by use, it is clear that, unless
we assume otherwise, the demand for access will be affected by the inertia in
use. At one extreme, we could assume that the consumer's surplus from use
(S) is calculated using the demand function in (37). In this case, the access/no
access decision would be reopened each period within the adjustment interval.
The other extreme would be to assume that S is calculated using the long-run
equilibrium value of q, q^*, in which case the demand for access would be
insulated completely from the inertia in use.

The problem with the first assumption is that, for a marginal subscriber,
$S(q_t)$ [i.e., the consumer's surplus calculated on the basis of q_t in expression
(37)] could be seen less than r_t for some t within the adjustment interval even
though $S(q^*)$ is greater than r_t. If the subscriber were already connected to
the system he or she would not subscribe during the time that $S(q_t)$ were
less than r_t, but would subscribe as q_t approaches q^7. Such stop-go behavior

seems highly implausible empirically, and we shall therefore assume that S is calculated using q^*.[19]

Let us now turn to the full system of subscribers. For the aggregate demand for calls, we shall postulate a partial-adjustment mechanism parallel to the one in (36):

$$Q_t - Q_{t-1} = \Psi \left(Q_t^* - Q_{t-1} \right). \tag{38}$$

Similarly, we shall assume for Q_t^*:

$$Q_t^* = \alpha_0 + \alpha_1 \pi_t + \alpha_2 p_t + \alpha_3 r_t + \alpha_4 N_t + \alpha_5 Y_t. \tag{39}$$

Consequently,

$$Q_t = \alpha_0 \Psi + (1 - \Psi) Q_{t-1} + \alpha_1 \Psi \pi_t \alpha_2 p_t + \alpha_3 \Psi r_t$$
$$+ \alpha_4 \Psi N_t + \alpha_5 \Psi Y_t. \tag{40}$$

Equation (40) has the same form as equation (37) and therefore has the same dynamical properties.

To be consistent with the behavior postulated for an individual subscriber, the inertia assumed in the aggregate call-market cannot affect the aggregate demand for access. However, this does not mean that the aggregate market for access cannot be assumed to be dynamical in its own right. Such an assumption is plausible *per se* and also provides a solution to the problem that was noted earlier in deriving the aggregate demand for access. This problem, it will be recalled, involved the proportion of a population subscribing to the telephone system itself being a function of the number of subscribers.[20]

Let m^* denote the equilibrium proportion of a population that purchases access to the telephone system for given values of the population, prices, and the distribution of income. In view of expression (64) in Chapter 2, we will have

$$m^* = (\pi, p, r, N^*, Y), \tag{41}$$

where N^* denotes the equilibrium number of subscribers corresponding to m^*.[21] Let $m_t = N_t/M$ denote the observed value of m during period t. We now assume that m_t is determined according to

$$m_t = \beta_0 + \beta_1 + \beta_2 p_t + \beta_3 r_t + \beta_4 N^* + \beta_5 Y_t. \tag{42}$$

[19] Insulating the demand for access from short-run inertia in use is consistent with the view that the demand for access involves primarily long-run considerations, while the demand for calls is much more sensitive to short-run phenomena. Also, service-connection charges, which have been ignored throughout this chapter, are an important factor in diminishing stop-go connection/disconnection behavior.

[20] See footnote 29 of Chapter 2.

[21] N^* corresponds to an equilibrium user set in the sense of Rohlfs (1974).

However, stability requires that β_4 be smaller than $1/M$. If this condition holds, long-run equilibrium will be achieved when $N_t = N_{t-1} = N^*$. Hence, we will have

$$m^* = \beta_0 + \beta_1 + \beta_2 p + \beta_3 r + \beta_4 N^* + \beta_5 Y. \tag{43}$$

The equilibrium number of subscribers can then be obtained by solving this expression for N^*.

V. THE USE OF PRICE DEFLATED REVENUES

A question that often comes up is how price elasticities that are estimated in models in which the dependent variable is price deflated revenues are related to elasticities that are estimated in models in which the dependent variable is messages or minutes. This section examines this question.

For notation, let:

$R = $ revenues

$p^* = $ an appropriate price index for telephone services

$M = $ number of messages

$\bar{d} = $ average duration of a message

$m = $ total minutes of calls

$\quad = m\bar{d}$

$\bar{r} = $ average revenue per minute.

Then:

$$R = m\bar{r} = M\bar{d}r. \tag{44}$$

Thus, for price-deflated revenues (PDR):

$$\text{PDR} = \frac{R}{p^*} = \frac{m\bar{r}}{p^*} = \frac{M\bar{d}r}{p^*}, \tag{45}$$

so that

$$\ln \text{PDR} = \ln m + \ln(\bar{r}/p^*) = \ln M + \ln \bar{d} + \ln(\bar{r}/p^*). \tag{46}$$

For elasticities, therefore:

$$\frac{\partial \ln \text{PDR}}{\partial \ln p^*} = \frac{\partial \ln m}{\partial \ln p^*} + \frac{\partial \ln \bar{r}}{\partial \ln p^*} - 1 = \frac{\partial \ln M}{\partial \ln p^*} + \frac{\partial \ln d}{\partial 1np^*} + \frac{\partial \ln \bar{r}}{\partial \ln p^*} - 1. \tag{47}$$

From the first line of expression (47), we see that the elasticity for PDR differs from the elasticity for minutes to the extent that $\partial \ln \bar{r}/\partial \ln p^*$ differs from 1. For $\partial \ln \bar{r}/\partial \ln p^*$ to be equal to 1 would require p^* to be a perfect continuously chained index. Since this will almost certainly not be the case in practice, $\partial \ln \bar{r}/\partial \ln p^*$ will be different from 1 depending upon:

1. How elasticities differ across mileage bands;
2. How frequent are the chain points in p^*.[22]

The econometric implications of $\partial \ln \bar{r}/\partial \ln p^*$ being different from 0 will be illustrated using the following model of toll demand:

$$\ln \text{ PDR } = \alpha + \beta \ln p^* + \gamma \ln y + \lambda \ln T + u, \tag{48}$$

where y denotes income, T is a measure of "market size", and u is a random error term.[23]   Since PDR $= m\bar{r}/p^*$ as defined above, we can rewrite this model as:

$$\ln(m\bar{r}/p^* = \alpha + \beta \ln p^* + \gamma \ln y + \lambda \ln T + u, \tag{49}$$

or alternatively as:

$$\ln m = \alpha + \beta \ln p^* + \gamma \ln y + \lambda \ln T + v, \tag{50}$$

where $v = u - \ln(\bar{r}/p^*)$.

Equation (48) represents a model with the logarithm of price-deflated revenues as the dependent variable, while equation (50), represents a model with the logarithm of the number of minutes as the dependent variable. Note that the error term in equation (50) contains $\ln(\bar{r}/p^*)$ as an omitted variable. In view of this, the estimate of β in equation (48) will be biased by an amount that depends upon the covariance between $\ln p^*$ and $\ln(\bar{r}/p^*)$. Specifically, from the theorem on the impact of an omitted variable:[24]

$$E[\beta \mid (50)] = E[\beta \mid (48)] - b[\ln p^*, \ln(\bar{r}/p^*)],$$

where $\beta \mid (50)$ denotes the estimate of β from equation (50) while $\beta \mid (48)$ denotes the estimate of β from equation (48), and where $b[\ln \bar{p}, \ln(\bar{r}/p^*)]$ denotes the regression coefficient for $\ln p^*$ in the regression of $\ln (\bar{r}/p^*)$ on

---

[22] From the second line in expression (47), we see that the elasticity for minutes is equal to the elasticity for messages plus the elasticity for average duration. As there is no reason *a priori* to expect the elasticity for duration to be 0, the elasticity for messages will accordingly be smaller than the elasticity for minutes.

[23] This model will be discussed in Chapter 6 in connection with Bell Canada's modeling of toll demand.

[24] See Theil (1959, pp. 328–329).

a constant, $\ln \bar{p}$, $\ln y$, and $\ln T$. From this, we see that the coefficient in the minutes model will tend to be smaller (in absolute value) if the covariance between $\ln p^*$ and $\ln (\bar{r}/p^*)$ is negative.

A priori one should probably expect this covariance in fact to be negative. This is because price elasticities tend to be larger in longer-haul mileage bands, so that across-the-board changes in rates will affect average revenue per minute more than they will affect the price index p^* (unless p^* is continuously chained). A rate increase will increase p^* more than $\bar{r}$. The result will be a negative covariance between $\ln p^*$ and $\ln(r/p^*)$.

VI. FIRM *VS* MARKET ELASTICITIES

One of the central tenets of economics is that the demand function faced by a firm selling in an industry in which there are several suppliers will be more elastic than the demand function faced by a monopoly supplier. With monopoly, the firm and industry demand functions are one and the same, whereas with competition customers can migrate between firms in response to price differentials. Because of entry of MCI and the other OCCs into the interexchange toll market, it is clear that the price elasticity faced by AT&T is now almost certainly larger than the price elasticity for the industry overall. The purpose of this section is to illustrate, using a simple analytical framework, how firm and industry elasticities are related. For simplicity, it will be assumed that there are just two firms.

Let the demand functions for the two firms be given by:

$$q_1 = a_0 - a_1 p_1 - a_2(p_1 - p_2) \tag{51}$$

$$q_2 = b_0 - b_1 p_2 - b_2(p_2 - p_1), \tag{52}$$

where q_1, q_2, p_1, p_2 denote the two firm's outputs and prices, respectively. The industry demand function will obviously be given by

$$q = q_1 + q_2 = a_0 + b_0 - (a_1 + a_2 - b_2)p_1 - (b_1 + b_2 - a_2)p_2. \tag{53}$$

The price slopes faced by the two firms will be given by

$$\frac{\partial q_1}{\partial p_1} = -a_1 - a_2 + a_2\frac{\partial p_2}{\partial p_1} \tag{54}$$

$$\frac{\partial q_2}{\partial p_2} = -b_1 - b_2 + b_2\frac{\partial p_1}{\partial p_2}, \tag{55}$$

where $\partial p_2/\partial p_1$ represents the competitive (price) response by firm 2 to a change in p_1 by firm 1, and similarly for $\partial p_1/\partial p_2$. For the industry demand function, the price slopes will be given by

$$\frac{\partial q}{\partial p_1} = -a_1 - a_2 + b_2 - (b_1 + b_2 - a_2)\frac{\partial p_2}{\partial p_1} \tag{56}$$

$$\frac{\partial q}{\partial p_2} = -b_1 - b_2 + a_2 - (a_1 + a_2 - b_2)\frac{\partial p_1}{\partial p_2}. \tag{57}$$

A variety of competitive price responses are obviously possible, the two extremes being where the firms ignore each other's price changes – $\partial p_i/\partial p_j = 0$ – and where responses are dollar-for-dollar – $\partial p_i/\partial p_j = 1$. Firm elasticities for the former will be given by

$$\eta_{p1} = -(a_1 + a_2)\frac{p_1}{q_1} \tag{58}$$

$$\eta_{p2} = -(b_1 + b_2)\frac{p_2}{q_2}, \tag{59}$$

while for the latter they will be given by

$$\eta_{p1} = -a_1\frac{p_1}{q_1} \tag{60}$$

$$\eta_{p2} = -b_1\frac{p_2}{q_2}. \tag{61}$$

Since a_2 and b_2 are both positive, the elasticities in (58) and (59) are clearly larger than in (60) and (61).

In order to attract customers, a new firm entering a previously single-supplier market clearly has to price at a discount in relation to the incumbent. This will have two effects: some customers of the incumbent will migrate and some of those who migrate will increase their usage because of the lower price. Two questions come up: (1) who is likely to migrate and (2) is the price elasticity of those who migrate likely to be different from the price elasticity of those who remain with the incumbent?

In analyzing these questions, it will be useful to assume a convenient functional form for individual demand functions, namely,

$$q = Ay^\alpha e^{-\beta p}, \tag{62}$$

where q, y, and p denote toll usage, income, and price, respectively. For a customer of the incumbent to migrate to the new firm, the benefits must outweigh the costs. As before, benefits will be measured by the consumer surplus from usage, which for the demand function in (62) is given by

$$CS = \frac{Ay^\alpha e^{-\beta p}}{\beta}. \tag{63}$$

For reasons that will become clear shortly, the costs of migration will be approached in terms of a threshold of benefits, which we will denote by B^*. A customer will accordingly migrate if

$$CS > B^*. \tag{64}$$

Figures 10 and 11 show the demand function in expression (62) for two values of β and two levels of income. β varies in Figure 10, while income varies in Figure 11. The curve labeled β_1 in Figure 11 has the larger value of β, while the curve labeled y_2 in Figure 11 has the larger income. The price charged by the incumbent is denoted by p_1 in the figures, while p_2 represents the discounted price charged by the entrant. The benefits from migration are given by the shaded areas. The gains for the demand function labeled β_2 are obviously larger than for the demand function labeled β_1, and similarly for the gains for y_2 in relation to y_1. From these figures, we can conclude that, *ceteris paribus*, a customer will be more likely to migrate:

1. The smaller is the customer's price elasticity of demand, and
2. The larger is the customer's income.

The first result may seem counter-intuitive, for price elasticity is associated with responsiveness to price and sensitivity to alternatives. In the case described in Figures 10 and 11, however, intuition is misleading, for the real drive of migration is the level of usage. Customers with large usage will gain more in consumer surplus from a discounted price than customers with a small usage and, as under the assumption made in Figures 10 and 11, a customer with a small price elasticity will have a higher usage, *ceteris paribus*, than a customer with a large price elasticity. Large users with small price elasticities are thus strong candidates for migration.[25]

Let us now turn to the costs of migration, which will include not only the objective transactions costs of switching, but also more subjective factors

---

[25] *Ceteris paribus* in Figure 10 assumes that customers have the same values for A, y, and α, so that they would have the same usage at price equal to zero. If, in contrast, usage were held constant (i.e., both customers had the same usage at p), then obviously the customer with the larger price elasticity would gain the most from a discounted price and would be the one more likely to migrate. The essential point, however, is that usage will be the main driver for migration, and in many cases high-usage will be associated with a lower-than-average price elasticity. I am grateful to Teodosio Perez Amaral and Stanford Levin for discussions on this point.

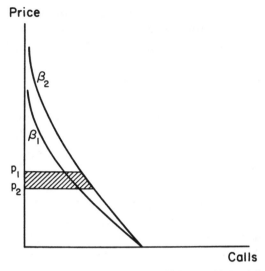

Fig. 10. Benefits of migration for different values of β.

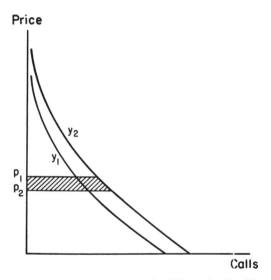

Fig. 11. Benefits from migration for different levels of income.

such as brand-name attachment to the incumbent together with inertia and ignorance. All of these factors are represented in B^* in expression (64). The subjective factors can be overcome, at least to some degree, through advertising and other marketing efforts. From the preceding discussion, it is clear that important targets of such marketing efforts will be large users with small price elasticities.

We can conclude from the foregoing that customers who migrate to an entrant will be larger users who have smaller price elasticities than the smaller customers who remain with the incumbent. This, too, might seem counter-intuitive, but it is a clear implication of the demand curves in Figure 10. This provides some theoretical basis for a narrowing of discounts as market shares stabilize in the years following entry. Once there is a cadre of satisfied customers, the entrant can allow the discount to fall without much fear of ill effects on revenue. This is because the discount effectively segments the market, so that the discount (so long as it is positive) can narrow without inviting reverse migration.[26]

Earlier, we defined price elasticities that refer to individual firms. We now consider some expressions for the price elasticity for the industry as a whole. For this, we will return to the demand functions in expressions (51) and (52). It will be assumed that firm 1 is the dominant firm and that firm 2 prices at a discount $1 - \lambda$ relative to p_1 $(0 < \lambda < 1)$. Assume that firm 1 is the price leader and let $p = p_1$ and $p_2 = \lambda p_1 = \lambda p$. From expression (53), we will then have

$$\frac{\partial q}{\partial p} = -a_1 - a_2 + b_2 - (b_1 + b_2 - a_2)\lambda. \tag{65}$$

The industry price elasticity will accordingly be given by

$$\eta_p = [(a_1 + a_2 - b_2) + (b_1 + b_2 - a_2)\lambda]\frac{p}{q}. \tag{66}$$

An industry price elasticity such as this is probably of limited interest. It will be of some relevance to analysts interested in the industry as a whole, but because of the rigid relationship assumed between p_1 and p_2 it does not provide insight into how industry output will respond to non-proportional changes in p_1 and p_2. In analyzing this question, we return to expressions (56) and (57) and define two "partial" industry price elasticities as follows:[27]

$$\eta_{p_1}^q \equiv \frac{\partial q}{\partial p_1} \cdot \frac{p_1}{q} = -\left[a_1 + a_2 - b_2 + (b_1 + b_2 - a_2)\frac{\partial p_2}{\partial p_1}\right] \cdot \frac{p_1}{q} \tag{67}$$

$$\eta_{p_2}^q \equiv \frac{\partial q}{\partial p_2} \cdot \frac{p_2}{q} = -\left[b_1 + b_2 - a_2 + (a_1 + a_2 - b_2)\frac{\partial p_1}{\partial p_2}\right] \cdot \frac{p_2}{q} \tag{68}$$

[26] All of this assumes that the service of the entrant is identical with that of the incumbent. If the entrant provides a lower quality service, then the necessary condition is not just a positive discount, but positive beyond some threshold. On the other hand, if the entrant offers a superior service (as might be the case for intraLATA toll), the entrant might be able to price at a premium to the incumbent.

[27] Note that, in contrast to the firms' elasticities defined in expressions (58)–(61), industry output q is used as the divisor rather than the firm outputs q_1 and q_2.

Unfortunately, too many parameters are involved to draw a definitive conclusion regarding the relative sizes of these two elasticities. As before, their absolute sizes depend crucially on the two firms' competitive responses to one another's price changes. In view of the discussion just concluded concerning migration, we should probably expect (once market shares have stabilized) firm 1 to be more responsive to price changes by firm 2 than vice versa, but this will probably depend upon whether firm 2 is raising its price or lowering it. Firm 1 will probably respond more strongly to a price decrease by firm 2 than to a price increase. From this, it follows that the sizes of the two price elasticities will probably depend upon whether firm 2's discount is widening or narrowing.

From the earlier discussion, we can expect $a_1 > b_1$ and possibly $a_2 > b_2$. Finally, $p_2 < p_1$ by hypothesis. Despite these relationships, it is impossible to conclude that either of η_{p1}^q or η_{p2}^q will be larger than the other, and neither can we conclude that either or both will be larger than η_p in expression (66). Perhaps the most striking conclusion that can be drawn is the *possibility* that η_{p2}^q will be smaller than η_{p1}^q.

VII. LOGISTIC APPROACHES TO FORECASTING

Before leaving this chapter, it will be useful to devote a few paragraphs to the logistic model, which found frequent use in forecasting telephone development in the 1960s and early 1970s.[28] Although the logistic framework has fallen by the wayside in modeling access demand in the U.S. and Canada (which is the focus of most of this book), its parsimonious data demands commends its use in countries which are just beginning to modernize and develop their telecommunications systems. The purpose of this section is to provide a brief description of the logistic model and to show how it can be related to the models discussed in earlier sections.

For notation, let:

z = the number of households having a telephone

M = the "saturation" level of households having a telephone.

The point of departure for the logistic model is the differential equation,

$$\frac{\dot{z}(t)}{z(t)} = \varphi[M - z(t)], \tag{69}$$

---

[28] See Chaddha and Chitgopekar (1971) and the references cited therein. Also in the opening presentation of the Hilton Head conference sponsored by Bell Canada and BELLCORE in April 1990, Jerry Hausman described a study for cellular radio which combined quantal choice methods with logistic diffusion curves.

where $\dot{z} = dz/dt$ and φ (> 0) is a parameter. The solution of this equation is

$$z(t) = \frac{M}{1 + \frac{M-z_0}{z_0}e^{-M\varphi t}}, \quad -\infty < t < \infty, \tag{70}$$

where z_0 denotes the number of households with telephones at $t = 0$. The standard procedure is to rewrite expression (70) in simplified form as

$$z(t) = \frac{M}{1 + \exp(\alpha + \beta t)}, \tag{71}$$

where $\alpha = \ln[(M - z_0)/z_0]$ and $\beta = -M\varphi$.[29]

Under the assumption that y is positive, expression (71) describes a familiar S-shaped penetration curve that is asymptotic to the horizontal axis as $t \rightarrow \infty$ and asymptotic to the saturation level M as $t \rightarrow \infty$. If data on $z(t)$ are available at equally spaced intervals $(t_1, t_2, \ldots, t_k)$, the parameters α and β can be estimated by applying nonlinear least squares to the model [obtained from expression (71)],

$$\ln\left(\frac{z_t - M}{z_t}\right) = \alpha + \beta t + u_t. \tag{72}$$

The logistic model has an obvious appeal in forecasting telephone penetration because of its minimal data requirements. All that is needed is a time series on the number of telephones. The downside is the assumption of a constant saturation rate. This is a plausible assumption over short intervals of time, but not over longer intervals of time. For as Chaddha and Chitopekar note, the saturation level is clearly related to population, prices, and income.

To bring these factors into the analysis, let us return to the differential equation in expression (69), but rewrite it as

$$d\ln z(t) = \varphi[M(t) - z(t)]\, dt. \tag{73}$$

Note that the saturation level M is now written as a function of time. Specifically, let

$$M(t) = \gamma_0 + \gamma_1 y(t) + \gamma_2 p(t) + \gamma_3 \pi(t), \tag{74}$$

where y denotes the aggregate income and p and π denote the prices of usage and access, respectively. The terms in y and p in this expression can

---

[29] The parameters α and β can be interpreted as a scale effect and growth rate, respectively. See Chaddha and Chitgopekar (1971, p. 544) for diagrams which depict different values for α and β.

be interpreted as representing the aggregate consumer surplus from usage. Substitution of (74) for M_t in expression (73) then yields

$$d \ln z(t) = \varphi[\gamma_0 + \gamma_1 y(t) + \gamma_2 p(t) + \gamma_3 \pi(t) - z(t)] \, dt. \tag{75}$$

An estimating equation can be obtained from expression (75) using the finite-approximation procedures employed by Houthakker and Taylor (1970),[30] namely:

$$Z_t = A_0 + A_1 Z_{t-1} + A_2(y_t + y_{t-1})$$
$$+ A_3(p_t + p_{t-1}) + A_4(\pi_t + \pi_{t-1}) + v_1, \tag{76}$$

where:

$$Z_t = \ln z_t - \ln z_{t-1} A_1 z_{t-1}$$

$$A_0 = \psi \gamma_0$$

$$A_1 = -\frac{\varphi}{2}$$

$$A_2 = \frac{\varphi \gamma_1}{2}$$

$$A_3 = \frac{\varphi \gamma_2}{2}$$

$$A_4 = \frac{\varphi \gamma_3}{2}.$$

Note that, since the dependent variable Z_t is a function of A_1, nonlinear least squares will have to be used in estimation.

Equation (76) clearly bears an affinity to equation (40) in Section III above. In essence, what the exercise in the last several paragraphs has shown is that, in an access/usage framework, the logistic model really entails a specification of disequilibrium dynamics.

VIII. CONCLUDING COMMENTS

The primary purpose of Chapters 2 and 3 has been to lay out the key characteristics of a theoretical framework for analyzing the residential demand for telephone service. To this end, a collection of demand models has been analyzed that reflects the peculiar features of the telephone. The discussion has focused on the distinction between access and use, the call and access

[30] Cf. also Bergstrom and Chambers (1989) and Taylor and Houthakker (1991).

externalities, and option demand. The problems caused by pricing telephone services on multi-part tariffs have also been emphasized. However, the discussion in this chapter, provides little more than a point of departure. While each of the models discussed in Sections V and VI, in Chapter 2 and Sections I and IV in this chapter have been specified with empirical application in mind, the primary motivation has been the illustration of ideas and concepts, and, as a consequence, the models are, for the most part, *ad hoc* and highly simplified. Linearity, for example, has been assumed in most cases, but this has been strictly an assumption of convenience. Nonlinear functional forms are perfectly feasible, and in most situations yield superior empirical results.

Finally, readers must be warned not to take the models that have been presented too literally. Telephone demand is a complex subject, and there is much that is not known. Business demand which is discussed in the next chapter, stands out in this regard, and an entire monograph could easily be devoted to its study. I have emphasized repeatedly the importance of the call and access externalities, option demand, and communities of interest, but how are these concepts to be measured? I have tended to roll both the externalities and option demand into the size of the system (as measured by the number of subscribers), but this can hardly be considered a satisfactory solution, since it leaves the individual contributions underidentified. We will return to these matters in Chapter 9. Also, much remains to be done in incorporating the joint distribution of tastes and income into the aggregate demand for access. Some progress in this direction is reported in Chapter 5. Finally, mention has been made only in passing to the demand for custom-calling features such as call-waiting and call forwarding. This topic will be taken up in Chapter 7.

CHAPTER 4

BUSINESS TELECOMMUNICATIONS DEMAND

Business telecommunications demand was singled out in the 1980 book as one of the areas most in need of attention. This is still the case. While information has accumulated on business usage demand, especially MTS, cross-elasticities between MTS, WATS, and private line remain elusive and knowledge of business access demand remains close to being a void. The biggest problem in modeling business demand is heterogeneity. Compared with households, businesses are an amorphous mass with respect to telecommunications use and attempts to model business telecommunications demand in terms of the generic needs of a generic firm are simply not very useful.

The standard approach to modeling business demand is in a production function framework in which telecommunications are treated as an input alongside capital and labor. Demand functions are derived in the usual manner from cost minimization conditions. The trouble with this approach is that, at least in its usual application, it is too aggregative and is therefore too narrow and inflexible. Telecommunications serve a variety of needs in a business, some complementary to other inputs, others substitutes, some related to production, others related to marketing, some internal to the business, others external. To treat telecommunications as a single input is to gloss over this variety of uses and probably to fail to capture the real structure of business telecommunications demand.

My purpose in this chapter is to approach business telecommunications demand in a framework which recognizes the immense diversity amongst business customers in the uses to which telecommunications are put. The discussion will be informal and nonrigorous, but with a practical goal, namely, the development of a framework that will prove useful for organizing the empirical analysis of business demand. In doing this, I will be guided in considerable part by my own (often frustrating) recent experience in analyzing business demand with Bell Canada and Southwestern Bell.

I. SOME BASIC CONSIDERATIONS

To begin with, it will be useful to discuss what seems to me to be the stylized facts which, at least in broad measure, characterize business telecommunications demand.

1. Business Access

Fact one would seem to be that no business in this day and age can be without telephone service. Accordingly, to approach business demand in an access/no access framework as with residential demand is simply not relevant.[1] What is relevant is the type of access that a business demands and the number of lines. To attempt to explain the number of business customers is really to explain the number of businesses, and it stretches credulity to imagine that this number depends in any fundamental way on the monthly charge for single-line business access.

2. Internal vs External Communication Needs

Unlike a household, much of business telecommunications demand is driven by internal needs. These needs vary depending upon the size and type of business, and increase rapidly with the number of locations. For large national and multinational corporations, the demand for internal communications probably outweighs the external demand. Large private networks are a reflection of this. The presence of multiple locations, perhaps more than any other factor, is what makes modeling business demand so difficult, for one must focus on communications between and among locations as well as between the firm and the outside world.

   In one sense, the distinction between internal and external communication is an artificial one because they reflect different aspects of a firm's overall community of interest. For small firms, even those with several locations, the internal community of interest will be served through the public network because that is the cheapest way of doing so. The larger the firm, the more sharply defined will be the internal segment of its community of interest and a point will be reached where the possibility of its being served by a separate private network can be considered. A firm may continue to use the public network to serve its internal communication needs, but the decision to do so will be continuously monitored in light of the costs of alternatives, both public and internal.

---

[1] This is not to argue that all businesses necessarily have telephones, but just as there are high-income households without telephones, there are undoubtedly successful businesses for which the same is true. Numbers cannot be large, however, and the reasons are almost certainly noneconomic.

3. Marketing vs Production

Another factor which complicates analyzing business demand in the standard neoclassical framework is the heavy use of telecommunications in marketing. For many businesses, the telephone is a primary instrument of selling, whether it be in terms of direct communication with customers or maintaining contact with a sales force in the field. Obviously, the importance of telecommunications in marketing will depend upon a number of factors, including the type of product or service involved, the type of output market, whether the market is local, regional, national or international, the organizational structure of the firm, etc.

4. Customer-Premise Equipment

During pre-competition days in the telephone industry, modeling the demand for customer-premise equipment was no big deal. Equipment was basic, it had to be rented, and its price was for the most part bundled into the monthly service charge. Access and equipment were essentially one and the same, and to explain the demand for one was essentially to explain the other. Technological change and competition changed this. Access and equipment were unbundled, and customers were allowed to purchase or rent their equipment from whomever they wanted. As a consequence of this change, customer-premise equipment has become one of the most problem-plagued areas to model. Equipment is no longer slave to the choice of access, but is a decision variable of stature commensurate with access and usage.

At one level, the emergence of customer-premise equipment as a decision to be modeled is too recent for any stylized facts to be apparent. Technological change has been so rapid that stable structures have had little opportunity to emerge, and even if one were to have emerged, data series are in most cases too scant to enable its parameters to be identified and estimated.[2] On a broad scale, the experience at Bell Canada provides a good illustration. Customer-premise equipment in Ontario and Quebec was opened to competition in late 1980. Businesses could continue to rent their equipment from Bell Canada or alternatively could buy it from Bell or buy or rent from any number of vendors. Prices were unbundled, and the demand for PBX trunks soared as digital technology combined with deregulation greatly lowered the cost of customer-premise switching. To model the shift from single lines to trunks requires, among other things, a price index that captures this lowering of cost,

---

[2] A review of recent telecommunications trade press made this clear as professional telecommunications managers of large firms find the best mix of equipment and service a complex and moving target, with no clear long-run solution.

but constructing such an index is impossible in the circumstances because prior to competition the price of equipment was bundled into the monthly service charge.

5. The Opportunity Cost of Time

One of the obvious consequences of economic growth is that time becomes more valuable. Businesses (as well as individuals acting simply in their capacities as consumers) seek ways to make more efficient use of time and often turn to increased use of telecommunications. While this may seem paradoxical since time spent on the telephone is real time generally unavailable for any other use,[3] the point is obvious when one considers the savings that can arise from replacing salespeople in the field with advertising and 800 service. The widespread use of fax provides another example.

In my view, the use of telecommunications to make labor and capital more efficient has been, and will continue to be the major force driving business telecommunications demand. As real wages increase, the time to be saved by increased use of telecommunications also increases in value. If this value is greater than the cost of achieving it, telecommunications demand will in fact increase. The modeling problem lies in identifying and measuring the appropriate opportunity cost, for in most situations the cost of increased telecommunications usage is not the out-of-pocket cost of the increased usage, but the cost of the labor and other resources that are replaced. Measuring these costs can be a devilish problem. The first step to their measurement, however, is recognition that they exist. Once this happens, I am confident that ways can be found to take them into account.

II. A GENERAL MODEL OF BUSINESS DEMAND

The biggest challenge facing the modeling of business telecommunications demand is to find a way of making heterogeneity and diversity manageable. Of the factors that have been discussed to this point, the one that is probably most instrumental in creating heterogeneity is the need for internal communications, for which there is no counterpart in a household. As the size of a business increases, especially as it expands to multiple locations, its internal communications needs increase sharply, indeed far more sharply than any simple proportionality with size would suggest. It is this fact more than any

---

[3] A secretary I once observed who could simultaneously talk on the telephone and type a hundred words a minute would seem an exception.

other which makes modeling business demand so perplexing. One generally does not have to deal with multiple locations with residential demand.

Our basic approach will be to develop stylized models for four generic businesses, beginning with a business that operates from a single address. Each generic type will be referred to as a stage. Stage 1 defines a business with just one location. Stage 2 defines a business with multiple locations in the same locality. The internal communications requirements increase rapidly at this stage, at least for most businesses, because of the need to communicate among locations. Stage 3 defines a firm with multiple locations in multiple localities. The complication at this stage, which can include firms that are regional to national, is that intrafirm communication will require toll as well as local-exchange services, and alternatives to the public switched network become an important factor to consider. Finally stage 4 defines a firm that is multinational, with locations that cross country boundaries. All considered, there is probably less of a difference between the telecommunications needs of firms in stages 3 and 4 than in firms in stages 2 and 3.

Let us now turn attention to Table 1, which is intended to describe the telecommunications needs in terms of usage, type of access, and customer premise equipment for businesses in each of the four stages. This is a detailed table, and it is important that the information it is attempting to convey be understood. The first line for each stage refers to the "smallest" firm for that stage. Thus, in stage 1, a firm is assumed to be "born" with single-line business service that is used to communicate solely with the outside world (customers, suppliers, etc.) with the only customer-premise equipment being a main station and possibly some extensions. Within a stage, several generic sizes of firms are considered with their attendant usage, access, and equipment requirements. As mentioned earlier, the volume and configuration of usage is assumed to drive the type (or types) of access, while usage and access together drive the amount and type of customer-premise equipment. The table is not intended to be exhaustive, especially with regard to the "communities of interest" listed under usage or with regard to customer-premise equipment.

1. Stage 1 Firms

As mentioned, businesses in stage 1 are assumed to be born with single-line telephone service. A firm's initial telecommunications needs are simple. Usage arises from communications with the external world, and customer-premise equipment may consist of nothing more than a main telephone and extensions. The volume of usage will be determined primarily by the number of employees and the type of business that the firm is engaged in. Increased usage will be accommodated for some time by simply adding additional lines.

TABLE 1
Business telecommunications needs

Stage	Usage Drivers	Types of Access	Customer Premise Equipment
Stage 1 (Single Location)			
Birth	Customers, Suppliers, Employees	Single Line	Main, Extensions
a	Customers, Suppliers, Employees Sales Force	Multi-Single Lines	Smart Phone, Extensions, Modems, Fax, PC(data)
b	" "	PBX Trunks	PBX, Extensions, Modems Fax, PC(data)
b'	" "	PBX Trunks, WATS,	" "
c	" "	800, Centrex	Extensions, Modems, Fax PC(data)
c'	" "	Centrex, WATS, 800	" "
Stage 2 (Multi-Locations Same Locality)			
a	Customers, Suppliers, Sales Force, Inter-Office	Multi-Single Lines	Mains, Smart Phone Extensions, Modems, Fax
b	" "	PBX Trunks	PBX, Extensions, Modems, Fax, PC(data)
c	" "	PBX Trunks, Private Line	" "
d	" "	PBX Trunks, PL, WATS, 800	" "
e	" "	Centrex	Extensions, Modems, Fax, PC(data)
f	" "	Centrex, WATS, 800	" "
Stage 3 (Multi-Locations, Multi-Localities)			
a	Customers, Suppliers, Employees Sales Force, Inter-Office Extensions, Fax, PC(data)	Multi-Single Lines	Mains, Smart Phones, Modem
b	" "	Multi-Single Lines, Private Line	" "
c	" "	PBX Trunks, Private Line	PBX, Extensions, Modems Fax, PC (data)
d	" "	PBX Trunks, PL, WATS, 800	PBX, Extensions, Smart Switch Modems, Fax, PC(data)
e	" "	Centrex, PL, WATS, 800	Smart Switch, Extensions Modems, Fax, PC(data)
f	" "	PBX Trunks/Centrex, PL, WATS, 800	PBX, Smart Switch, Extensions, Modems, Fax PC(data)
Stage 4 (Multi-National)			
	Customers, Suppliers, Employees Sales Force, Inter-Office	PBX Trunks/Centrex, PL, WATS, 800	PBX, Smart Switch Extensions, Modems, Fax, PC(data)

A key system or new smart phones may be acquired to serve as an internal system until the number of lines becomes large enough that the firm can consider the purchase (or rental) of a small PBX, at which point individual line access to the local telephone exchange would be replaced by one or more PBX trunks. Expansion would now occur through adding more PBX trunks and increasing the capacity of the PBX. Eventually, usage volume might reach a point where centrex were economic, in which case the firm might switch to centrex.[4] Technologically, centrex and PBX trunks are essentially equivalent forms of access, and which is done, and when, will depend upon relative costs and the particular needs of the firm.

The foregoing would seem to provide a plausible growth scenario for a single location business even in the absence of toll usage. When a business is small, its toll needs will probably be met in the conventional way – i.e., by accessing its toll carrier through the local telephone company using its regular mode of access. In most circumstances, regular MTS service will be all that is needed. The primary determinants of toll usage by stage 1 businesses will be the number of employees and the nature of the business, particularly as it relates to the markets in which the firm buys and sells (i.e., whether local, regional, or national) and the nature of its marketing efforts (i.e., whether marketing is by telephone or salespeople visits, etc.). As toll volume increases, points can be reached where WATS and 800 service (again according to the nature of its business and markets) will be considered as well as direct links to its toll provider (i.e., bypass of the local exchange company).

2. Stage 2 Firms

Stage 2 businesses are those with multiple locations in the same locality. The new element, obviously, is the need to communicate between locations, and telecommunications acquires new importance because of the greatly increased cost of face-to-face contact. Everything else being constant, a given number of employees will have higher telephone usage if they are dispersed across several locations than if they are all at the same place. More lines will be needed for the firm overall, but it is not clear *a priori* whether the introduction of PBX's or centrex service will be retarded or hastened in comparison with a comparably sized single-location firm. What really matters is the size of the individual locations. Large locations may have PBX or centrex service, while smaller locations function equally well with multiple lines and key systems.

In the choice between PBX and centrex service, it is again not clear *a priori* as to whether large multi-location firms might lean to one as opposed

---

[4] In many areas, centrex is now available as a service option for anyone requiring two or more lines.

to the other. Centrex service would provide centralized switching, but so too would a central PBX connected by private-line trunks. The decision in the end will be determined by the overall telecommunications needs of the firm (the nature of its business, the types of markets bought and sold in, the volume of toll usage, etc.) in relation to relative costs of the two types of access.

With regard to toll usage, the needs of multi-location businesses are probably not much different in form from those of single-location businesses. Volume will tend to be large because the firms are on average larger. There will consequently be a higher incidence of WATS and 800 service and direct linkages to toll carriers.

3. Stage 3 Firms

The "new kid on the block" in stage 3 is that communication between locations in different cities requires the use of toll services (which since the AT&T divestiture are available in a host of alternatives). Telecommunications needs will be enhanced in this stage both because firms tend to be much larger than in stage 2 and because face-to-face contact on a casual basis between intercity offices becomes prohibitively expensive. Powerful incentives are accordingly created for firms to buy toll services in bulk (via WATS and 800 service) or to avoid the public switched network altogether through the setting up of private networks.

A point that is probably underappreciated is that the use of private lines and private-line networks is primarily for internal needs. Private lines, to be cost-effective, require heavy volumes between fixed points. Multiple offices in different cities provide the fixed points, while largeness provides the volume. A large stage 3 business will essentially have every type of toll service and form of access (with possible exceptions of single-line business numbers) that telecommunications companies have to offer (and will probably use multiple carriers).

Access to, or interconnection with, the public switched network will still be required for external needs, while internal needs will be catered to largely by private lines and private-line networks. Most switching will be on premise, with trunks to the central office of the local exchange company and to the firm's toll carrier (or carriers). In some cases, non-internal calls will be routed over the private network and then into the appropriate local network through a PBX in the area. So-called "smart" switches can be used to select the least-cost mode for a call, whether internal or external, to be sent.

4. Stage 4 Firms

The only essential difference between stage 4 and stage 3 businesses is that the internal communications needs of stage 4 businesses extend across national boundaries. The only obvious implication of this is that it will expand the firm's demand for international services for both internal and external reasons. Multi-national firms tend to be large, so like a large stage 3 firm, internal communications needs will be large as well. In some cases, depending primarily on proximities and the nature of the business and markets engaged in, international interoffice communication may be handled by extensions of domestic private-line networks. In most circumstances, however, volumes will be too small for this to be economic and public carriers will be used instead.

III. SOME SPECIFIC MODELS OF BUSINESS DEMAND

Let us now turn our attention to Table 2, which describes a set of models for analyzing business telecommunications demand. As the table is intended to be self-contained, only a few expository comments will be given in the text.

1. Models are specified for each of the four stages described in the proceeding section.
2. For each stage, demand is modeled along three dimensions: usage, type of access, and customer-premise equipment.
3. Usage drives type of access, and type of access and usage together drive customer-premise equipment.
4. Except for stage 1 businesses (for which usage is assumed to be primarily external), usage is decomposed into usage related to communication with the external world and usage related to communications within the firm.
5. Usage is modeled in a standard regression format in which the volume of usage is related to vectors of determining variables depicting internal and external communications needs.
6. Access, in contrast, is modeled in a quantal-choice framework in which the demands for different types of access are described in terms of the probabilities of their selection.
7. The probability models describing access choice are assumed to be conditional on usage, both in terms of total volume of usage and its split between internal and external.
8. Customer-premise equipment can be modeled in either a quantal-choice or a regression format, depending upon the data that are available and the detail desired.

TABLE 2.

Suggested models for business usage, access, and customer premise equipment

Stage	Form of Model	Predictors			
		Firm	Market	Price	Comments
STAGE 1					
Usage	Regression	# of employees	Type of markets sold in,	Price of local usage (if LMS),	Most important factors will be number of employees (especially non-production) and the types of markets bought and sold in. Once the number of employees is taken into account, output may not be of much importance.
		# of non-production employees	Types of markets purchased in,	All relevant toll prices,	
		Type of firms – manufacturing, processor, etc.	Local, regional, national,	Opportunity cost of time to firm including prices of substitutes/complements	
		Type of product – finance real estate, etc.	Type of marketing effort,		
			Sales people in field		
		Single or multiple products,			
		Level of output,			
		Type of corporate structure			

Table 2 (continued)

Stage	Form of Model	Predictors			Comments
		Firm	Market	Price	
STAGE 1 (continued)					
Access	Quantal choice/ regression		All firms and market variables listed for usage.	Price of single-line business access, access,	Main issue on access is point at which firm begins replacing single lines with PBX trunks and onsite switching. Firm may bypass LEC if toll usage is sufficiently high. Models for explaining choice of type of access should be quantal-choice. Models for explaining number of lines or number of PBX trunks can be regression.
				Price of PBX trunks,	
				Price of onsite switching,	
				Price of contrex lines,	
				Price of bypass facilities	
Customer Premise Equipment	Quantal choice/ regression	Volume and structure of usage		All relevant prices of customer premise equipment.	Models can be quantal choice regression depending upon how or variable is defined.

Table 2 (continued)

Stage	Form of Model	Predictors			Comments
		Firm	Market	Price	
STAGE 2					
Usage	Regression	All Stage 1 predictors plus number of locations.		Price of local usage (if LMS), All relevant toll prices, All relevant private line prices, Price of centrex lines, Price of bypass of LEC Opportunity cost of time to firm including prices of substitutes/complements	Internal communication needs take a big jump. Main factors will be number of locations and the number of employees per location.
Access	Quantal choice/ regression	All firm and market variables listed for usage.		Price of single-line business usage	Key question on Stage 2 access is whether firm is large enough to set up a local private network. If firm's usage is primarily local and firm large, centrex may be preferred mode.
Customer Premise Equipment	Quantal choice/ regression	Volume and structure of usage.		All relevant prices of customer premise equipment	Models can be quantal choice or regression depending upon how dependent variable

Table 2. (continued)

Stage	Form of Model	Predictors			Comments
		Firm Market	Price		
STAGE 3					
Usage	Regression	Same as for Stage 2.			Internal communications needs take another big jump because of need to connect locations in different localities. Key question is whether firm is large enough to justify formation of private network.
Customer Premise Equipment	Quantal choice/ regression	Volume and structure of usage.	All relevant prices of customer premise equipment		Key questions are whether firm leases or purchases CPE and whether private network is leased or owned.

STAGE 4

Stage 4 firms will in general be driven by the same factors as stage 3 firms. The only notable difference is the need to take into account the number of countries in which there are locations and the cost of connecting them through the public network as opposed to a private network. Differential prices between and among countries will affect where facilities will be located.

9. The vantage point for the models is the firm. Some comments on specifying models from the vantage point of the serving telephone company
   will be given in the next section.
10. Regarding estimation, the intent is that the models for each stage be
    estimated (once they are given parametric forms) from cross-sectional
    data consisting of observations on individual firms at a particular point
    in time. If multiple observations are available, pooled time-series/cross-
    sectional estimation can be used.
11. The models are specified on the assumption that structures differ across
    stages. This does not preclude pooling over stages if some structures are
    found to have parts in common.

A central theme of this chapter has been the complications that are associated with multiple locations. Not the least of these complications are problems
of measurement. Telecommunications usage almost certainly increases more
than proportionately with size, and especially so as locations multiply. But
how is this greater-than-proportional dependence to be measured? Grouping
businesses into the four stages that has been proposed in this chapter allows
for the obvious discontinuities in internal telecommunications needs as a
business moves from one to two-or-more locations, to two-or-more localities,
and to two-or-more countries, but there remains the question of how size is
to be measured within a stage.

For a network with N nodes, the number of connecting paths is $N(N-1)$.
If every node in the network communicates with every other nodes, say for
one minute a day, then total "usage" of the network would be $N(N-1)$
and would increase with the number of nodes as N^2. This is the basis for
the statement that the communication needs of a firm increase more than
proportionately with size.[5]

Taken at face value, the foregoing suggests (as a first cut, anyway) that
size be measured for the four stages as follows.

Stage 1
A single variable $N(N-1)$, where N denotes the number of employees.

Stage 2
Two variables:

1. $\sum_{i=1}^{L} N_i(N_i-1)$, where N_i denotes the number of employees in location
   i and L denotes the number of locations.
2. $L(L-1)$.

---

[5] Of course, the probability of use of any path will in fact decline as N increases.

Stage 3
Three variables:

1. $\sum_{j=1}^{H} \sum_{i=1}^{L_j} N_{ij}(N_{ij} - 1)$, where N_{ij} denotes the number of employees in locations i in locality j, L_j denotes the number of locations in locality j, and H denotes the number of localities.
2. $\sum_{j=1}^{L} L_j(L_j - 1)$.
3. $H(H - 1)$.

Stage 4
Four variables:

1. $\sum_{k=1}^{M} \sum_{j=1}^{H_k} \sum_{i=1}^{L_{ij}} N_{ijk}(N_{ijk} - 1)$, where N_{ijk} denotes the number of employees in location i in locality j in country k, L_{jk} denotes the number of locations in locality j in country k, H_k denotes the number of localities in country k, and M denotes the number of countries.
2. $\sum_{k=1}^{M} \sum_{j=1}^{H_k} \sum_{i=1}^{L_{ij}} L_{jk}(L_{jk} - 1)$.
3. $\sum_{k=1}^{M} H_k(H_k - 1)$.
4. $M(M - 1)$.

Let N denote the total number of employees that a firm has.[6] The assumption that underlies the variables in this list is that, for firms with multiple locations, the internal communication network does not consist of the $N(N - 1)$ paths that would connect every employee, but is hierarchical: employees communicate with employees within a location, but locations communicate with locations within a locality, localities communicate with localities within a country, and countries communicate with countries. Obviously, this is overdrawn, but it allows in a straightforward way for internal communications needs to vary between locations, localities, and countries. Addition of 100 employees to an existing location should be expected to affect a firm's communications needs differently than the opening of a new 100-employee location in an existing locality or expansion to a new locality or country.

As mentioned earlier, size in my view is best measured by the number of employees (or more particularly by the number of non-production employees), rather than by sales or the level of output.[7] It is people that make calls (computers talking with computers notwithstanding), not output and sales.

---

[6] For stage 4 firms, $N = \Sigma\Sigma\Sigma N_{ijk}$.
[7] The reference here is to internal communication. Sales and output are clearly relevant to communication with the external world.

IV. Business Demand From the Point of View of the Local Exchange Company

The standard practice in the telecommunications demand literature is to estimate models that are derived with reference to the household or the firm with data that are collected by telephone companies. In pre-divestiture, pre-competition days, this was essentially the equivalent of using market data to estimate individual demand functions under the usual representative consumer or representative firm assumptions. These may or may not be good assumptions in general, but their use in the monopoly days in telephone industry did not *per se* raise new questions of principle.

The situation is different now. Firms do not deal with a single telecommunications company but with several, so that the data for any one telephone company will represent only a part of the total telecommunications-related expenditures by the firms in the area it serves. Among other things, this means that when the focus is on demand as seen by a serving telephone company, the models to be estimated must be formulated with care. Often it is assumed that they have the same form as for the firms that they serve, but this is incorrect.[8] The demand functions faced by the telco are aggregations of its customers' demand functions. This means, then, that a primary determinant of a telco's load and service-mix will be the size-distribution of its customer base. A local exchange, for example, whose business customer base is heavily skewed to stage 1 firms will face a much different PBX trunk demand than a company with a strong representation of Fortune 500 companies.

In the remainder of this section, some of the principles to be taken into account will be illustrated by focusing on the demands for two of the major business services provided by local exchange companies, single-line access and PBX trunks. As our presumption is that businesses are born with telephone service, changes in the total number of business single-line access lines can arise only because of births of new firms, death of old firms, or changes in the number of lines that existing firms have. The ebb and flow of firms in a telco's service area will depend upon the general business climate and is clearly beyond the control of the telco.

As has been noted, a new firm's needs for additional access will take the form of adding single lines until it becomes economic to replace the single lines with centrex or trunks and on-site switching.[9] The primary determinants of the number of single-line business access lines will accordingly be:

---

[8]   I specifically have in mind here the estimation of models derived as input demand functions with data from telephone companies serving these demands.

[9]   In the discussion that follows, the focus will be on the switchover from single lines to trunks.

1. The number of businesses in the area served (which, as noted, will be determined by factors beyond the telco's control), and
2. The number of employees per firm.

Employees per firm should be expected to have a nonlinear effect because of the threshold whereby it becomes economic to replace multiple single lines with trunks. Below the threshold, single lines will be a positive function of the number of employees per firm; beyond the threshold, the relationship will be negative because of the substitution of trunks. In view of this nonlinearity, simply to include the number of employees or the number of employees per firm would be inappropriate. If the threshold were known, the nonlinearity could be dealt with (assuming data are available) by inclusion of two employee variables, E_1 and E_2, say, where:

$E_1 =$ the number of employees at firms below the threshold,

$E_2 =$ the number of employees at firms above the threshold.

The coefficient for E_1 would be expected to be positive, while the coefficient for E_2 would be expected to be negative.[10]

Refinements and additional factors to be kept in mind are as follows:

1. In discussion to this point, the reference has been to businesses in stage 1. In stage 2, the nonlinearity identified above continues to apply, but at the level of the location rather than the firms as a whole. E_1 and E_2 for stage 2 firms should accordingly be measured in terms of mean values per location.
2. The nonlinearity also applies to stage 3 and 4 businesses, but only with reference to the locations that are served by the telco in question. If for example, the telco in question is Bell Canada and the purpose is to explain single-line business access in the Bell-served areas of Ontario and Quebec, E_1 and E_2 should be defined only with respect to locations within the Bell-served areas.

Let us now turn to PBX trunks. As with single-line business access, the primary determinants of the number of lines will be the number of businesses in the area served and the number of employees that these businesses have per (local) location. With PBX trunks these two factors continue to be important, but with an obvious difference. In view of the definitions of E_1 and E_2, E_1

---

[10] This is obviously a simplification of a complicated telecommunications network engineering structure problem, which will involve, among other things, the number of nodes, node availability and configuration, and spatial distribution of employees. The discussion in the text is intended simply as a point of departure.

will be irrelevant to explaining PBX trunks while the effect of E_2 will be positive, rather than negative.

The number of PBX trunks will also be related to:

1. The number of locations for businesses in stages 2–4;
2. The number of localities for businesses in stages 2 and 3;
3. The number of countries with locations for businesses in stage 4.

Thus far, nothing has been said about prices. The prices that are relevant are the price of single-line business access, the price of PBX trunks, and the cost of on-site switching and central office based services like centrex and bypass. For businesses below the PBX threshold (which is in itself a function of all three prices), the price of single-line business access can only affect the number of additional lines. Apart from helping to determine the PBX threshold, the prices of PBX trunks and on-site switching are irrelevant for these businesses. For businesses above the PBX threshold, the price of PBX trunks will be the primary driver, as it will have a direct effect on the number of PBX trunks as well as an indirect effect via the threshold. The prices of single-line business access and on-site switching will affect PBX trunk demand only through the value of the PBX threshold.

Two specific models emerge from the discussion of this section. For notation, let:

$L\ =\ $ the number of single-line business access lines in the area served

$T\ =\ $ the number of PBX trunks

$B\ =\ $ the number of businesses in the area served

$E_1\ =\ $ the mean number of employees per (local) location for businesses smaller than the PBX threshold

$E_2\ =\ $ the mean number of employees per (local) location for businesses larger than the PBX threshold

$P_L\ =\ $ the price of single-line business access

$P_T\ =\ $ the price of PBX trunks

$P_S\ =\ $ the price of on-site switching

$G\ =\ $ the number of local locations in the area served

$H\ =\ $ the mean number of localities in which firms in the area served are located

$M\ =\ $ the mean number of countries in which firms in the area served are located

u = random error term.

The models for single-line business access lines and PBX trunks, in logarithmic form, are as follows:

$$\ln \left(\frac{L}{B}\right) = \alpha_0 + \alpha_1 \ln E_1 + \alpha_2 \ln E_2 + \alpha_3 \ln P_L + \alpha_4 \ln \left(\frac{P_T P_S}{P_L}\right) + u \quad (1)$$

$$\ln \left(\frac{T}{B}\right) = \beta_0 + \beta_1 \ln E_2 + \beta_2 \ln P_T + \beta_3 \ln \left(\frac{P_T P_S}{P_L}\right)$$
$$+ \beta_4 \ln G + \beta_5 \ln H + \beta_6 \ln M + u. \quad (2)$$

In the model for single-line business access lines [equation (1)], E_1 and E_2 measure the nonlinearity of the effect of the number of employees in relation to the PBX threshold discussed above, P_L measures the direct effect of the price of single-line business access, while the last term measures the relative price of on-site switching via PBX. In the model for PBX trunks [equation (2)], E_1 is excluded (since PBX customers necessarily exceed the PBX threshold) and G, H, and M are included as measures of the community of interest. As the PBX threshold is in general not observable, it becomes an additional parameter to be estimated.

V. WRAP-UP AND SUMMARY

This chapter has emphasized five basic themes:

1. As always, usage drives access, and type of access and usage drives customer-premise equipment.
2. Multiple locations and their spatial distribution are the biggest complicating factors in modeling business telecommunications demand.
3. As a business expands and branches into multiple locations, internal communications needs increase in relation to external needs. Growth in internal communications needs is what drives the construction of private networks.
4. The primary determinant of usage (for a given technology and service configuration) is the number of people employed by a business. The effect on usage of additional employees depends upon whether the employees are added at existing locations, through the opening of new locations in existing localities, or through expansion into new localities.

5. The telecommunications services purchased by firms in a telco's serving area are not synonymous with the services sold by that telco. Telco sales must be explained in the framework of models that reflect the distributional characteristics of the telco's customers.

Since business telecommunications demand is clearly a derived demand, fans of Shepherd's Lemma may be shocked that it has not been mentioned once in this chapter. This has been deliberate. In my view, what is in shortest supply in modeling business is not rigor, but simply greater understanding of how a firm's telecommunications needs, especially those internal to the firm, evolve as the firm grows and branches into multiple locations. Classifying firms as to whether they are single or multiple locations, located in single or multiple localities, national or multinational is a step in this direction. Hopefully, one of the things that might emerge from the suggestions that have been made here is the establishment of a coherent set of stylized facts that theory can seek to connect and explain. At that point, Shepherd's Lemma can assume its rightful place in the analysis.

CHAPTER 5

RECENT STUDIES OF RESIDENTIAL ACCESS DEMAND

In this chapter, we shall take a detailed look at four recent studies of the demand for access to the telephone network by households. The four studies are Perl (1983), Taylor and Kridel (1990), Bell Canada (Bodnar *et al.* 1988), and Train, McFadden, and Ben-Akiva (1987). The early 1980s saw a shift in focus from toll demand to access demand, particularly residential access demand. Competition in the toll market was shrinking the pool of revenue that for many years had been subsidizing residential local rates. The consequent upward pressure on local rates was causing concern that a large number of households would be forced to give up telephone service. There was especially concern that certain socio-demographic groups – low income, the elderly, black, hispanic – would be burdened disproportionately. Tiny access elasticities for the population at large might mask much larger values for specific groups.

It was with this in mind that in early 1983 the about-to-be-divested Bell Operating Companies approached Lewis Perl of National Economic Research Associates through the then Central Services Organization of Bell Communications Research to update and expand Perl's 1978 study. The study was completed in late 1983 to the accompaniment of immediate, widespread attention. Perl subsequently extended the analysis to GTE, United Telecommunications, and Continental, but only the Bell results will be discussed here.

The second study to be discussed was initiated in early 1984 at Southwestern Bell under the direction of myself and Donald Kridel. The Southwestern Bell study was prompted by two concerns with the Perl study. The first was that the socio-demographic detail of the Perl model was not sufficiently specific to Southwestern's subscribers, while the second concern related to the matching of rates with households in rural areas. Census rules preclude identifying the location of individual households in areas of less than 100,000 populations, which means that all that can be known of some rural households is that they live in some 20-county area in west or north Texas. Matching households to the rates they faced in these circumstances is problematic at best.

The third study to be discussed was undertaken by Bell Canada to analyze the likely effects of rate "rebalancing" in the jurisdictions served by Bell Canada in Ontario and Quebec. Although telecommunications in Canada is characterized by different market and regulatory structures than in the U.S., rate structures are essentially the same in that residential access is heavily subsidized by toll users. In recognition of the distortions that such a pricing structure entails, Bell Canada has proposed to its regulator, the Canadian Radio-television and Telecommunications Commission (CRTC) that it be allowed to "rebalance" rates. Toll rates would be reduced toward cost. A residential access-demand model along the lines of Perl's was developed to assist in assessing the effects of such a rebalancing.

The fourth, and final, model to be discussed was developed by Cambridge Systematics Incorporated of Berkeley, California for an eastern Bell Operating Company. The study was authored by Kenneth Train, Daniel McFadden, and Moshe Ben-Akiva. The TMB study differs from the other three studies in that the focus is not on access *per se*, but on the *type* of access – i.e., flat-rate, measured, or flat-rate/measured – given that access is demanded. A conditional nested logit model is specified in which a household is assumed to select a local-calling portfolio in which a portfolio is defined in terms of type of access and the number, duration, and length-of-haul calls.

I. THE 1983 PERL STUDY[1]

In his 1978 study, discussed in Appendix 1, Perl used data for individual households from the Public Use Sample of the 1970 U.S. Census to analyze residential access to the telephone network. The decision to have or not to have access was analyzed in a discrete choice framework in which the presence or absence of telephone service was related to the cost of the monthly service, income, and a host of socio-demographic factors. The 1983 study extends the analysis to data from the 1980 Public Use Sample.

Beside being based on more recent data, the 1983 study offers several important innovations over the 1978 study, including an improved treatment of the price of access and greater socio-demographic detail. The price of access in the 1978 study was defined in terms of average rates for 100 Bell System Revenue Accounting Offices (RAOs). Each household in the sample was assigned the rate for the RAO in whose geographic area the household was located. The 1983 study attempts to match households with exchanges.

---

[1] The discussion in this section is based upon Perl (1983), which was completed in December 1983. The model was subsequently re-estimated, with similar results, using a revised data set. The re-estimated model is given in Perl (1984).

The matching is good in dense urban areas, but less so in rural areas because of the need to protect against disclosure.

The 1980 Public Use Sample contains information on 80,428 households (a 1-in-1000 sample of all U.S. households) assigned to one of 1154 geographic areas. The geographic areas are either cities, counties, or country groups selected so that each area contains at least 100,000 households. Unlike in the 1970 census in which households were asked whether they simply had access to a telephone (irrespective of whether they were subscribers), the 1980 census targeted actual subscription. The analysis proceeds in a logit framework in which the logarithm of the odds of having a telephone is related to a long list of price variables, household characteristics, and area characteristics. Many of the variables are dummy (i.e., 0–1 indicator) variables. Estimation is by maximum likelihood. The independent variables with their estimated coefficients and asymptotic standard errors are given in Table 1.

Access in 1980 was offered in a variety of forms. Traditional flat-rate service was available to nearly all households in the sample. Many households had a choice between flat-rate and measured service, while most had an option of single-or multi-party service. In view of this, the price of access is measured by four different variables:

1. The flat-rate price in flat-rate only areas.
2. The flat-rate price in areas with a measured option.
3. The measured-rate access price.
4. The measured-rate calling price.

The installation charge is also included as a predictor, as is a variable which measures the availability of measured service. The model thus allows for price to operate in three dimensions, through an access charge (whether service is flat-rate or measured), through a usage charge (when measured service is an option), and the installation charge. That measured service when it is available as an option may not be available to all of the households in a geographic area to which a household is assigned is taken into account by the variable which measures the proportion of households (in the geographic area) for which measured service is an option. Finally, the model allows for the effect of the access charge to be different depending upon whether or not measured service is available as an option.[2]

The variables relating to household characteristics include income, age of head of household, education, race, sex of head, and employment status, size and age distribution of household, language spoken other than English, and

---

[2] The price variables are constructed from rates that were in effect at the time that the 1980 Census was taken. 7260 Bell Operating Company exchanges are represented in the prices in contrast with the 1978 study which used average revenue data for 100 RAOs.

TABLE 1

1983 Nera telephone access demand equation: Parameters and mean values of variables.

	Units	1980 Mean Values[1]	Coefficient[2]	t-Statistic[3]
	(1)	(2)	(3)	(4)
Intercept			-1.8125	9.54
Price Variables				
Flat Rate Price (Flat Rate Area only)	Dollars	9.051	-0.0492	4.46
Flat Rate Price (Measured Rate Area)	Dollars	9.679	-0.0175	2.50
Measured Rate Access Price	Dollars	5.695	-0.0414	2.13
Measured Rate Calling Price	Dollars	0.096	-1.7179	1.92
Installation Price	Dollars	28.304	-0.0034	1.25
Proportion with Measured Rate Service	Decimal	0.543	0.1526	0.82
Household Characteristics				
Household Income	$1,000	20.026	0.1296	20.83
Household Income Squared	$1,000,000	621.158	-0.0011	13.67
Age of Householder	Years	47.156	0.0446	26.31
Income* Age	$1,000– Years	917.958	-0.0003	2.55
Education of Householder	Years	12.125	0.1489	26.52
Race of Householder	Indicator[4]	0.102	-0.5133	11.24
Employment Status	Indicator[5]	0.697	0.3874	9.29
Persons in Household	Number	2.764	-0.0503	3.26
Proportion Less Than 6	Decimal	0.070	-0.7417	6.29
Proportion 6–12	Decimal	0.061	0.4242	2.86
Proportion 65+	Decimal	0.042	1.3412	6.61
Language Other Than English Spoken	Indicator	0.103	-0.3920	7.07
English Spoken Poorly Or Not At All	Indicator	0.018	-0.1477	1.50
Family Household, No Wife Present	Indicator	0.025	-0.8722	10.18
Family Household, No Husband Present	Indicator	0.102	0.1162	2.06
Nonfamily Household, Male Householder	Indicator	0.107	-1.2436	22.36
Nonfamily Household, Female Householder	Indicator	0.152	0.1453	2.20
Area Characteristics				
Nonfarm Area	Indicator	0.827	0.1096	2.51
South	Indicator	0.328	-0.3588	8.20
Phone Density 1 (1–100)	Indicator[6]	0.336	-0.247	3.43
Phone Density 4 (1,000–2,500)	Indicator[6]	0.120	0.2516	3.40
Phone Density 5 (2,501–5,000)	Indicator[6]	0.083	-0.2189	2.61
Phone Density 6 (5,001+)	Indicator[6]	0.034	-0.3344	3.67
Number of Subscribers in Local Calling Area (in Natural Logs)	1n-1,000	4.693	0.0990	4.91
Number of Observations		71,979	71,979	
R^2			0.099	

Notes to Table 1:

[1] The mean values are the means for the sample used to estimate this equation, *i.e.*, for the 71,979 households for which rate data were available.

[2] Coefficients measure the change in the natural log of the odds of a household having a telephone for a 1 unit change in the variable.

[3] The *t*-statistic is the ratio of the coefficient to its standard error. Since parameter estimates are normally distributed, these *t*-statistics can be used to test hypotheses about the true value of each coefficient.

[4] Rate = 1 if the householder is black, and 0 otherwise.

[5] Employment = 0 if the householder is unemployed or not in the labor force and 1 otherwise.

[6] The ranges for the phone density indicators are in numbers of mains per square mile. The range 101–1000 phones per square mile is the reference group.

Source: Perl (1983, Figure 1)

whether the household is family or nonfamily. Both the level and square of income is included to allow for the effect of income to be nonlinear. Income is also interacted with the age of the head of household. With regard to area characteristics, account is taken of whether a household is rural or urban and resides in the South. Four density variables (defined in terms of the number of main-stations per square mile) and the number of subscribers in the local-calling area complete the list of predictors. These last five variables are intended to capture the network (or subscriber) externality.

Perl summarizes the results of his 1983 study as follows:

First, the new study suggests that there has been a substantial increase in demand for telephone service between 1970 and 1980. As a result, increasing access prices will have a *smaller* effect on access demand than indicated by [the] earlier study. Price elasticity as estimated from the 1983 model is about 60 percent of that derived from the 1978 model.

Second, the 1983 model confirms the assumption which was implicit in the 1978 model that access demand is primarily a function of minimum rather than average access charges. This result suggests that the provision of measured-rate service, with relatively low access but high usage charges or the provision of low-priced two-party service can be expected to maintain relatively high levels of access demand even in the face of substantial increases in the prices of flat-rate service.

But, *third*, demand also depends on local-calling prices and even at very low access prices *some* households will not subscribe to telephone service unless they can make a large number of local calls at a low price. Thus, any increases in local-service charges, whether for access or local usage

TABLE 2

1978 Nera telephone access demand equation: Parameters and mean values of variables.

	Units	1980 Mean Values[1]	Coefficient[2]	t-Statistic[3]
	(1)	(2)	(3)	(4)
Intercept			-1.8125	9.54
Price Variables				
Flat Rate Price (Flat Rate Area only)	Dollars			
Flat Rate Price (Measured Rate Area)	Dollars	11.907[4]	-0.0624	5.37
Measured Rate Access Price	Dollars			
Measured Rate Calling Price	Dollars	–	–	–
Installation Price	Dollars	15.566	-0.0105	2.21
Proportion with Measured Rate Service	Decimal	0.348	0.2425	5.25
Household Characteristics				
Household Income	$1,000	18.781	0.0778	12.31
Household Income Squared	$1,000,000	582.997	–	–
Age of Householder	Years	48.203	0.0350	19.14
Income* Age	$1,000– Years	872.925	-0.0003	2.36
Education of Householder	Years	11.960	0.1164	22.10
Race of Householder	Indicator[5]	0.097	-0.5953	13.23
Employment Status	Indicator[6]	0.736	0.2337	5.07
Persons in Household	Number	3.110	-0.0486	4.12
Proportion Less Than 6	Decimal	NA	–	–
Proportion 6–12	Decimal	NA	–	–
Proportion 65+	Decimal	NA	–	–
Language Other Than English Spoken	Indicator	NA	–	–
English Spoken Poorly Or Not At All	Indicator	NA	–	–
Family Household, No Wife Present	Indicator	0.025	-0.6235	6.32
Family Household, No Husband Present	Indicator	0.088	–	–
Nonfamily Household, Male Householder	Indicator	0.073	-1.2900	22.09
Nonfamily Household, Female Householder	Indicator	0.124	-0.1900	3.10
Area Characteristics				
Nonfarm Area	Indicator	0.805	0.3551	7.64
South	Indicator[7]	0.303	-0.3480	7.62
Phone Density 1 (1–100)	Indicator[7]	NA	–	–
Phone Density 4 (1,000–2,500)	Indicator[7]	NA	–	–
Phone Density 5 (2,501–5,000)	Indicator[7]	NA	–	–
Phone Density 6 (5,001+)	Indicator[7]	NA	–	–
Number of Subscribers in Local Calling Area (in Natural Logs)	1n-1,000	NA	–	–
Number of Observations		63,444	36,703	
R^2			0.146	

Notes to Table 2:

[1] The mean demographic values are the means for the entire sample, including households for which rate data were not available, whereas the model was estimated using only those households for which data were available.

[2] Coefficients measure the change in the natural log of the odds of a household having a telephone for a 1 unit change in the variable. The coefficients of price and income variables have been adjusted for inflation to make them comparable with the new model.

[3] The *t*-statistic is the ratio of the coefficient to its standard error. Since parameter estimates are normally distributed, these *t*-statistics can be used to test hypotheses about the true value of each coefficient.

[4] In the 1978 model, the access price was an estimate of the lowest available rate prevailing in each of the areas sampled. Where measured rate service was available, these estimates were based on the rate data which included some people subscribing to measured rate services.

[5] Rate = 1 if the householder is black, and 0 otherwise.

[6] Employment = 0 if the householder is unemployed or not in the labor force and 1 otherwise.

[7] The ranges for the phone density indicators are in numbers of mains per square mile. The range:

101–1000 phones per square mile is the reference group.

NA = Not Available.

Source: Perl (1983, Figure 2)

will cause some decreases in the percentage of households with phones (telephone penetration). This result suggests that decreases in telephone penetration do not necessarily reflect decreases in the *affordability of access* to telephone service.

Fourth, there has been a marked narrowing in income-related differences in telephone penetration from 1970 to 1980. Nevertheless, there is still a significant disparity in penetration between the lowest and highest income households and this disparity will widen if prices increase markedly. This widening can be avoided by providing a low-cost "life-line" service to low-income households. Revision of life-line service is also a relatively effective way to assure high telephone penetration and still charge *most* subscribers cost based prices.

Fifth, the market for telephone service is characterized by an externality. The value of telephone service to each subscriber increases as the number of subscribers on the network increases. This suggests that the price of telephone access *should* be set somewhat below the cost of access to promote the optimal-sized network. *But*, the welfare gains from subsidizing access are quite small and may not justify the efficiency losses that would result from any practical subsidy program. (Perl 1983, pp. 2–3), italics in original.)

From Table 1, we see that the price of access has an expected negative effect on the probability of having a telephone, while income, age, education, and size of household have positive effects. Income becomes less important as the level of income increases and also as a household ages. Households with female heads are more likely to have a telephone than households with husband present or a male head. Unemployment or absence from labor force depresses the probability of having a telephone, as does also being black, having English as the non-primary language, or having pre-school children. With regard to the area characteristics, urban households are more likely than rural households to have a telephone, while households in the South are less likely to have one than households elsewhere in the country. Density (as measured by the number of telephones per square mile) is seen to have a mixed effect, while the number of main stations in the local-calling area has a positive effect. Finally, a glance at the column of t-ratios shows that household characteristics are the strongest predictors by a wide margin.

Besides being based on 1980 data, the 1983 study differs from the 1978 study in the use (as noted) of more precise price data and in the inclusion of prices for both flat-rate and measured service. The 1983 model also takes into account the size of the local-calling area, which the 1978 model did not. Finally, the 1983 includes some household characteristics not examined in the 1978 study. The parameters of the 1978 model are presented in Table 2 for reference.

Since the model is logit, elasticities vary both with the level of penetration and with the level of the predictor. Some representative access price elasticities are given in Table 3 for penetration rates of 88, 93, and 97% and for flat-rate/measured-rate access charges of \$10/\$6, \$20/\$16, and \$30/\$26. Elasticities are shown for the 1978 model as well as for the 1983 model.[3] Although small in absolute value, the elasticities are seen to increase sharply with the level of access prices and to decrease sharply with the level of penetration. The elasticities in the 1983 are smaller than in the 1978 model.

Because telephone penetration is lower at low-income levels, low-income households are also more sensitive to price changes. This is illustrated in Table 4, which uses the 1983 model to predict telephone penetration at different income levels at different levels of flat-and measured-rate access prices. Dropoff is seen to be much larger at low income than at high income.

---

[3] The price elasticity in this context is defined as the elasticity of the probability of having a telephone with respect to the price of access. In calculating the elasticities, it is assumed that flat-rate and measured-rate access prices change in the same proportion. Also, it is assumed in the 1983 model that 54% of the population have measured service available as an option.

TABLE 3

Price elasticity at alternative prices and telephone penetration rates; Perl study

Telephone Penetration	Access Price[1]	Price Elasticity	
		1983 Model	1978 Model
(1)	(2)	(3)	(4)
88.0%	$ 10/6	-0.0654	-0.0749
	20/16	-0.1307	-0.1498
	30/26	-0.1961	-0.2246
93.0	10/6	-0.0381	-0.0437
	20/16	-0.0763	-0.0874
	30/26	-0.1144	-0.1310
97.0	10.6	-0.0163	-0.0187
	20/16	-0.0327	-0.0374
	30/26	-0.0490	-0.0562

[1] The access price shown in column (2) are flat rate/measured rates. The computed elasticities assume the same percentage increase in all access prices. In computing these effects using the 1983 model, 54 percent of the population was assumed to have access to measured rate service.

Source: Perl (1983, Figure 5)

The elasticities in Table 3 are calculated on the assumption that flat-and measured-rate access charges vary in the same proportion. Table 3 shows what could be expected to happen to penetration rates if the flat-rate price were increased at different levels of the measured-rate access charge and at different prices per call. In making the calculations, it is assumed that measured service is universally available. The results indicate that about half of the dropoff that would be expected by a doubling or tripling of the flat-rate charge from $10 per month could be avoided by keeping the measured-rate access charge at $5 per month but increasing the calling price to 20 cents per call. This is the basis for Perl's conclusion that the level of penetration depends more on the minimum price of access than on the average price. The policy implications of this will be discussed below.

One of Perl's most interesting findings is that the value of having a telephone appears to have increased between 1970 and 1980. Holding all other

TABLE 4

Telephone penetration rates at alternative flat and measured rate prices; Perl study

| Measured Rate | | Flat Rate Access Price | | |
Access Price	Calling Price	$10	$20	$30
(1)	(2)	(3)	(4)	(5)
$ 5	$ 0.05	93.99%	93.05%	92.01%
	0.10	93.54	92.55	91.45
	0.20	92.57	91.47	90.23
10	0.05	92.87	91.80	90.60
	0.10	92.36	92.13	89.97
	0.20	91.25	89.99	88.60
15	0.05	91.59	90.37	89.02
	0.10	91.01	89.72	88.30
	0.20	89.75	88.33	86.77

Assumes 100 percent measured rate availability.

Source: Perl (1983, Figure 8)

factors constant, households appeared willing to pay more to have a telephone in 1980 than in 1970. This is shown in Figure 1, which describes the relationship between the price of access and the percentage of households that would have access at that price. The curve for 1980 is seen to lie everywhere above the curve for 1970. In 1970, for example, 73% of households were willing to pay $30 or more to have a telephone, whereas in 1980 84% were willing to pay $30 or more.

Perl notes that this increase in demand for access is primarily attributable to changes in the economic and demographic variables included in the model:

> ... decreases in access price, increases in income, and changes in other household characteristics occurring over the decade of the 1970s would account for about a 2.0 percentage point increase in telephone demand. But over this period the percentage of households with phones increased by 7.0 percentage points. Thus, taste changes and other variables excluded from the model account for a 5.0 percentage point increase. (Perl 1983, p. 13.)

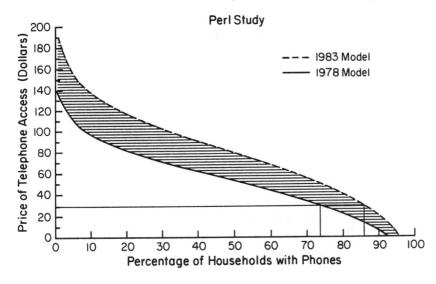

Fig. 1.   Access price and demand for telephone service 1983 and 1978 models; Perl study. Source: Perl (1983, Figure 4).

Perl mentions several factors that could have led to the increased value of telephone service: increased prices for other forms of communication, reduced long-distance toll rates, increases in the number of services available by phone, and an increased need for the phone as a source of security. Reduced toll prices led to increased toll calling and thus to increased consumer surplus from usage, while increased prices of alternative forms of communication – especially the cost of face-to-face contact which was increased sharply by the 1973 and 1979 energy crises – shifted calling demands to the right.[4] The last two factors – shopping by phone and security concerns – are perhaps most usefully seen as operating on option demand.

The increase in the willingness-to-pay to have a telephone in 1980 over 1970 is presented in a different light in Table 5, which shows penetration rates by income group for the 1983 and 1978 models. As in Table 4, income is measured in terms of multiples of the poverty level. The 1983 model predicts higher penetration at every income level, but the differences are seen to be greatest at the low-income levels. At the poverty level or below, the 1983 model predicts a penetration rate nearly nine percentage points higher than the 1978 model, 80.2% versus 71.5%. At the highest levels of income, the

---

[4] The substitution of telephone for face-to-face contact may be even more pronounced for local calling as a result of urban congestion. Congestion not only accompanies economic growth and development but also increases the cost of coping with it.

TABLE 5

Telephone penetration by income group 1983 and 1978 models; Perl study

| Income Group | Telephone Penetration | |
	1983	1978
	(1)	(2)
Below Poverty	80.22%	71.45%
1–2 Times Poverty	89.79%	81.34%
2–3 Times Poverty	93.90%	86.89%
3–4 Times Poverty	96.26%	90.79%
4–5 Times Poverty	97.38%	93.01%
5–6 Times Poverty	96.15%	94.74%
Above 6 Times Poverty	98.95%	97.59%
All	93.39%	87.54%

Source: Perl (1983, Figure 1)

difference is only 1.4 percentage points.

The size and density variables are included in the model for the purpose of controlling for a network externality. Returning to Table 1 for a moment, density is seen to have a positive effect for densities up to 2,000 telephones per square mile, but a negative effect for densities greater than 2,000 telephones per square mile. The size of the local-calling area (as measured by the number of subscribers) is seen to have a positive effect. The implications of these results will be discussed in Chapter 9.

II. SOUTHWESTERN BELL'S RESIDENTIAL ACCESS DEMAND MODEL: TAYLOR AND KRIDEL (1990)

In the discussion of Perl's model we noted that there is a problem with Census data in matching up individual households and rates. To forestall the identifying any individual household, the Census Bureau discloses place of residence only for areas of at least 100,000 population. This creates major problems in matching rates with households, as in virtually all cases areas of 100,000 or more contain several wire centers. Since rate data refer to wire centers, this means that it is impossible with the Public Use Sample to get an accurate matching of households and rates. The consequences of this may be

unimportant when the focus is national, but problems clearly emerge when
attention shifts to specific socio-demographic groups and areas.

An alternative to Perl's procedure is to use data aggregated to the level
of a census tract. The census tract is the smallest geographical area that
can be analyzed with census data, and provides a better match between rates
and place of residence than is possible using data for individual households.
Although aggregation leads to loss of information, census tracts are sufficiently diverse in income levels and socio-demographic characteristics that
the parameters of most interest can continue to be isolated.

The present section, accordingly, reports on a model of residential access
demand that uses census tracts as the unit of observation. The model was
developed at Southwestern Bell for use in estimating the impacts of higher
local-service rates on its residential customers. The model that is estimated
is a model similar to Perl's, but with an extension that takes into account
differences in the distribution of income across census tracts. The model is
estimated from a data set consisting of 8423 census tracts in the five states
(Arkansas, Kansas, Missouri, Oklahoma, and Texas) served by Southwestern
Bell. The results corroborate existing views concerning the price elasticity
for residential access demand. Perl's finding with regard to the importance of
socio-demographic factors are also confirmed, but the present model provides
a better vehicle for quantifying specific effects.

Following Perl (1983), we assume that the demand for use is given by

$$q = Ae^{-\alpha p}y^\beta e^u, \tag{1}$$

where q denotes use of the telephone network, p denotes the price of use, y
denotes income, and u denotes a random error term.[5] We ignore at this point
complications of network and call externalities, and we also ignore for now
socio-demographic factors.

The consumer's surplus from q units of use will be given by

$$CS = \int_0^p Ae^{-\alpha z}y^\beta e^u \, dz = \frac{Ae^{-\alpha p}y^\beta e^u}{\alpha} \tag{2}$$

or in logarithms,

$$\ln CS = a - \alpha p + \beta \ln y + u, \tag{3}$$

where $a = \ln A/\alpha$. Let π denote the price of access. In line with earlier
discussion, access will be demanded whenever

$$\ln CS > \ln \pi, \tag{4}$$

[5] Use for present purposes refers to local calling. The demand function in (1) accordingly
allows for both flat-rate ($p = 0$) and measured ($p > 0$) service.

i.e., when

$$a - \alpha p + \beta \ln y + u > \ln \pi, \tag{5}$$

or alternatively when

$$u > \ln \pi - a + \alpha p - \beta \ln y. \tag{6}$$

If u is $N(0, \sigma^2)$, the probability of access will accordingly be given by

$$P(\text{access}) = 1 - \Phi(\ln \pi - a + \alpha p - \beta \ln y), \tag{7}$$

where Φ denotes the distribution function for the normal distribution. In probit form, this is essentially the model applied by Perl to individual households.

With census tracts as the unit of observation, equation (6) must be aggregated over the households in a tract. Our procedure will be to aggregate equation (6) over the joint distribution of u and y, where assume that y is lognormally distributed, independent of u, with mean μ_y and variance σ_y^2. Let

$$v = u + \beta \ln y. \tag{8}$$

Under our assumption, it follows that v will be $N(\mu_y, \sigma^2 + \beta^2 \sigma_y^2)$. Let P_j denote the proportion of households in census tract j that have a telephone. This proportion will be given by

$$P_j = P(v_j > \ln \pi_j - a + \alpha p_j), \tag{9}$$

or equivalently,

$$P_j = P(w_j > w_j^*) = 1 - \Phi(w_j^*), \tag{10}$$

where

$$w_j = \frac{v - \beta \mu_{yj}}{[\sigma^2 + \beta^2 \sigma_{yj}^2]^{1/2}} \tag{11}$$

$$w_j^* = \frac{\ln \pi_j - a + \alpha p_j - \beta \mu_{yj}}{[\sigma^2 + \beta^2 \sigma_{yj}^2]^{1/2}}. \tag{12}$$

Let F_j denote the probit for census tract j calculated from equation (10), and write:

$$F_j = \frac{\ln \pi_j - a + \alpha p_i - \beta \mu_{yj}}{[\sigma^2 + \beta^2 \sigma_{yj}^2]^{1/2}}. \tag{13}$$

Clearing the fraction, we have

$$F_j \left(\sigma^2 + \beta^2 \sigma^2_{Yj} \right)^{1/2} = \ln \pi_j - a + \alpha p_j - \beta \mu_{Yj} + \varepsilon^*_j, \tag{14}$$

where

$$\varepsilon^*_j = \left(\sigma^2 + \beta^2 \sigma^2_{Yj} \right)^{1/2} \varepsilon_j. \tag{15}$$

Equation (14) offers a number of challenges for estimation, but before discussing these the fact that customers in some areas can choose between either flat-rate or measured service must be taken into account. Three possibilities must be considered:

1. Only flat-rate service is available;
2. Only measured service is available;
3. Both flat-rate and measured service are available.

In flat-rate only areas, access will be demanded if [from equation (6), since $p = 0$]

$$u > \ln \pi_f - a - \beta \ln y, \tag{16}$$

while in measured-rate only areas, access will be demanded if

$$u > \ln \pi_m - a + \alpha p - \beta \ln y, \tag{17}$$

where π_f and π_m denote the monthly fixed charges for flat-rate and measured services, respectively. In areas where both flat-rate and measured service are options, access will be demanded if *either* (16) *or* (17) hold. From these two inequalities, it follows that access will be demanded if

$$u > \min(\ln \pi_f, \ln \pi_m + \alpha p - a - \beta \ln y). \tag{18}$$

Finally, given that access is demanded, flat-rate service will be selected if

$$\ln \pi_f < \ln \pi_m + \alpha p, \tag{19}$$

while measured service will be chosen if[6]

$$\ln \pi_m + \alpha p < \ln \pi_f. \tag{20}$$

---

[6] While choice is deterministic (given α), bill minimization is *not* assumed. Flat-rate expenditures may exceed measured-rate expenditures, but equation (17) could still hold. Rearranging the inequality in (19), flat-rate will be chosen over measured service if $\ln \pi_f - \ln \pi_m < \alpha p$, i.e., if the difference in the logarithms of the monthly fixed charges is less than the price elasticity of usage (under measured service) with respect to the price of usage.

To incorporate these choices into the analysis, we define:

$$\delta_1 = \begin{cases} 1 & \text{if only flat-rate service is available} \\ 0 & \text{otherwise} \end{cases}$$

$$\delta_2 = \begin{cases} 1 & \text{if only measured service is available} \\ 0 & \text{otherwise} \end{cases}$$

$$\delta_3 = \begin{cases} 1 & \text{if both flat-rate and measured service are available} \\ 0 & \text{otherwise} \end{cases}$$

With these dummy variables, we can rewrite equation (14) as

$$F_j \left(\sigma^2 + \beta^2 \sigma_{Yj}^2 \right)^{1/2} = \delta_1 \ln \pi_{fj} + \delta_2 (\ln \pi_{mj} + \alpha p_j) \tag{21}$$
$$+ \delta_3 \min(\ln \pi_{fj}, \ln \pi_{mj} + \alpha p) - a - \beta \mu_j + \varepsilon_j^*.$$

This (with the addition of socio-demographic variables) is the equation to be estimated.

Several things are to be noted regarding the estimation of equation (21):

a)   The equation is nonlinear in β.
b) σ^2, the variance of u is a parameter to be estimated.
c) $\text{Min}(\ln \pi_{fj}, \ln \pi_{mj} + \alpha p_j)$ must be calculated for the areas in which both flat-rate and measured service are available. But to do this requires knowledge of α.

We begin by rewriting the model as follows:

$$z_j = -a - \beta \mu_{yj} - \sum_i \gamma_i X_{ij} + \varepsilon_j^*, \tag{22}$$

where:

$$z_j = F_j \left(\sigma^2 + \beta^2 \sigma_{Yj}^2 \right)^{1/2} - \delta_1 \ln \pi_{fj} - \delta_3 \min(\ln \pi_{fj}, \ln \pi_{mj} + \alpha p_j), \tag{23}$$

and where X_{ij} denotes the socio-demographic factors thought to be relevant. As none of Southwestern Bell's service territory has mandatory measured service, δ_2 is dropped from equation (23).

If σ^2, β and α were known, z_j could be calculated (using observed values for F_j, σ_{yj}^2, π_{fj}, π_{mj}, and p_j) and equation (22) could be estimated as a linear regression. However, these parameters are not known, so estimation proceeds by an iterative search procedure as follows:

1. The initial search is over values of σ^2 for fixed values of β and α. The value of σ^2 which is finally selected is the one which maximizes the correlation between the actual and predicted values of F_j.

2. The second step is to fix σ^2 at the value obtained in step (i), keep β fixed as in step 1, and search over α. Again, the value of α selected is the one which maximizes the correlation between the actual and predicted values of F_j.
3. The third and final step involves iteration of β. An iteration consists of the estimation of equation (20), with z_j [from equation (23)] calculated using the values of σ^2 and α obtained from steps 1 and 2 and β from the immediately preceding iteration. Iterations proceed until the estimate of β stabilizes.[7]

The model represented by equation (22) and (23) has been estimated from a data set consisting of 8423 census tracts from the 1980 Census in the five states served by Southwestern Bell, Arkansas, Kansas, Missouri, Oklahoma, and Texas. Written in full, the model estimated is as follows:

$$F_j \left(\sigma^2 + \beta^2 \sigma_{yj}^2 \right)^{1/2} - \delta_1 \ln \pi_{fj} - \delta_3 \min \left(\ln \pi_{fj}, \ln \pi_{mj} + \alpha p_j \right)$$
$$= -a - \beta \mu_{yj} - \gamma_1 \text{RENTER}_j - \gamma_2 \text{RURAL}_j - \gamma_3 \text{BLACK}_j$$
$$- \gamma_4 \text{SPANISH}_j - \gamma_5 \text{AMINDIAN}_j - \gamma_6 \text{IMMOB}_j$$
$$- \gamma_7 \text{AVGAGE}_j - \gamma_8 \text{MILAGE}_j - \gamma_9 \text{EMP}_j - \gamma_{10} \text{LINES}_j$$
$$- \gamma_{11} \text{AVESZHH}_j + v_j, \tag{24}$$

where:

F = probits corresponding to the proportion of households in a census tract that have a telephone

σ^2 = variance of error term for individual households (a nuisance parameter that must be estimated)

β = coefficient for income

σ_y^2 = within-tract variance of the logarithm income (calculated for each tract from Census data)

δ_1, δ_3 = dummy variables as defined above

$\ln \pi_f$ = logarithm of flat-rate monthly service charge

---

[7] The estimation procedure was evaluated before applying it to the Southwestern Bell data set by a Monte Carlo study. The Monte Carlo results show that the estimators have a moderate bias which appears to diminish with sample size. The results also show that the variance of the error term u has little effect on the accuracy of the coefficients. For details, see Taylor and Kridel (1990) or Kridel (1987).

$$\ln \pi_m \ = \ \text{logarithm of measured-rate monthly service charge}$$

$$\alpha \ = \ \text{coefficient for price of a local call}$$

$$p \ = \ \text{price/minute for a local call}$$

$$a \ = \ \text{a constant}$$

$$\mu_y \ = \ \text{geometric mean of income within a census tract}$$

$$\text{RENTER} \ = \ \text{\% of census tract that rents home}$$

$$\text{RURAL} \ = \ \text{\% of census tract that is rural}$$

$$\text{BLACK} \ = \ \text{\% of census tract that is black}$$

$$\text{SPANISH} \ = \ \text{\% of census tract of hispanic origin}$$

$$\text{AMINDIAN} \ = \ \text{\% of census tract that is American Indian}$$

$$\text{IMMOB} \ = \ \text{\% of census tract that has not moved since 1975}$$

$$\text{AVGAGE} \ = \ \text{average age of population of census tract}$$

$$\text{MILAGE} \ = \ \text{\% of census tract that pays a local-loop mileage charge}$$

$$\text{EMP} \ = \ \text{\% of census tract that suffered no unemployment in 1979}$$

$$\text{LINES} \ = \ \text{number of lines that can be reached in "local-calling area"}$$

$$\text{AVESZHH} \ = \ \text{average number of people per household in census tract}$$

$$v \ = \ \text{error term.}$$

At the start of the empirical analysis, the three standard discrete choice models – linear probability, probit, and logit – were estimated, but without taking into account differences in the variance of income across census tracts. The results were surprising, at least with regards to the price of access. The access price was significant in the linear probability model, but not in the probit or logit models. For reasons relating to the strength of a poverty variable (defined as the percentage of households in the census tract with income below the poverty level) in these models, the simplistic treatment of income was singled out as the cause of this disturbing result, and the present model was settled on in which the full distribution of income is taken into account.

The estimated coefficients for the model in expression (24) are given in Table 6. Except for the constant, the t-ratios are seen to be well in excess of two. Mileage has the smallest t-ratio (3.8), while the proportion of households that are black has the largest t-ratio (24.9). The t-ratio for income is 19. T-

TABLE 6

Coefficient estimates; Taylor-Kridel Study

Variable	Coefficient	t-Statistic
Constant	0.43	1.2
INCOME	0.98	19.0
PRICE OF LOCAL MINUTE	-6.87	–
PRICE OF ACCESS	-1.00	–
RENTER	-1.56	14.3
RURAL	-0.82	19.0
BLACK	-1.18	12.9
SPANISH	-2.78	24.9
AMINDIAN	-7.38	14.2
IMMOB	0.51	4.7
AVGAGE	0.05	9.9
MILAGE	-0.45	3.8
EMP	2.88	14.3
LINES	0.37	4.8
AVESZHH	0.55	10.3
Nuisance Variance (σ^2)	5.60	–
$R^2 = 0.420^*$		

* The R^2 is calculated as the square of the correlation
  between the actual and predicted values for F_j.

Source: Taylor and Kridel (1990, Table 1)

ratios for the price of a local call and the "nuisance" variable (σ^2) cannot be obtained directly because of the way they are estimated. Standard errors for these parameters could in principle be obtained by a jackknife technique, but efforts to do so got sidetracked.

As expected, the sign for income is positive, while the sign for price terms are negative. Mileage charges also have a negative effect. As regards the socio-demographic factors, penetration is lower for blacks, hispanics, or American Indians, lower for renters than for homeowners, and lower in rural areas than in urban. Unemployment also has a negative effect, while residence longevity (IMMOB) has a positive effect, as do average age and the number of lines in the local-calling area.

Care is required in interpreting the coefficients, however. The coefficient for income, 0.98, represents the elasticity for *usage* with respect to income. Likewise, 0.51 times the mean (0.52) of IMMOB is the usage elasticity with respect to mobility, and similarly for the other variables. The *access* elasticity, on the other hand, cannot be observed directly, but must be induced by changing a variable and then calculating the resulting change in penetration. For example, consider a 10% increase in income. This yields 0.42% increase in penetration, and hence an access elasticity of 0.042 with respect to income.[8]

Of special interest is the elasticity of access with respect to the number of lines in the local-calling area, for this is usually interpreted as a measure of the subscriber (or network) externality. While the elasticity is positive, any suggested externality is tiny at present levels of development, for an increase of 10% in the number of (local) lines implies an increase of only 0.027% in penetration. We will take up the implications of this result in Chapter 9.

The main purpose of the Southwestern Bell study was to quantify the impact on development in Southwestern's jurisdictions of higher access charges. To this end, Tables 7 to 9 show the predicted effects on development of some of the most widely discussed pricing scenarios. Table 7 shows that predicted effects of a doubling of flat-rate and measured-rate access charges in each of the five states served by Southwestern Bell. The predicted impacts across several socio-economic-demographic groups in Texas are shown in Table 8.[9] Finally, Table 9 shows predicted impacts on penetration of the FCC-mandated end-user subscriber-line charge (EUCL) of $1 that went into effect June 1, 1986.

Tables 7, 8 and 9 make several points. In the first place, it is clear that access repression, while small, is not zero. In Table 7, we see that the predicted effect across all five states of a doubling of access charges is to reduce development from 92.5 to 88.8. Arkansas, because of low income levels and socio-demographic factors, has the largest predicted repression, while Kansas has the least.

As noted earlier, tiny elasticities applied to huge bases give large numbers, and this is what alarms those concerned with universal service. In Texas, for example, the predicted decrease in development of 3.7 percentage points from a doubling of access charges translates into more than 200,000 households,

---

[8] Two points must be kept in mind in making this calculation. First, since the variance of income is also on argument in the model, only small changes in income should be considered. Second, the implied income elasticity may seem small at first glance. However, since 93% of households (on the average) already have access, an increase in income can have no effect on their access decision.

[9] Texas has been singled out because it had the highest measured-service availability of the five states. The effect of having a lower-priced alternative to flat-rate service can accordingly be more easily seen.

TABLE 7

Development and repression for 100% access price increases*; Taylor-Kridel study

	100% Increase Actual Development	with Lower Priced Alternative**	100% Increase All Prices***
AR	89.1	83.6	83.2
		(5.5)	(-5.9)
KS	95.3	–	93.0
			(-2.3)
MO	95.4	92.3	92.3
		(-3.1)	(-3.1)
OK	92.7	–	89.3
			(-3.4)
TX	91.4	89.3	87.7
		(-2.1)	(-3.7)
SWBT	92.5	89.6	88.8
		(-2.9)	(-3.7)

Numbers in parenthesis are repression estimates in basis points.

* No measured service was available in Kansas or Oklahoma.
   Measured availability for the other three states was as follows:
   AR: 10.48%; MO: 2.2% and TX: 58.4%.

** Measured service, where available, is the lower priced alternative
   and its price is unchanged.

*** Both flat rate and measured rate, where available are doubled.

Source: Taylor and Kridel (1990, Table 2)

which is a frighteningly large number. Numbers like this are grist to consumer groups, congressmen, state legislators, and regulators who are opposed to higher access charges, and attempts by telephone companies to increase local rates not surprisingly trigger choruses of emotional responses.

The 200,000-plus Texas households predicted to be affected by a doubling of access charges assumes a doubling of all local rates, measured as well as flat-rate. In Table 8, we see that the availability of a lower-price alternative substantially lessens the predicted impact of higher access charges. This is in keeping with the results that Perl obtained in his 1983 model. If only flat

TABLE 8

Development and repression for 100% access price increases for Texas; Taylor-Kridel study

	Actual Development	100% Increase for Lower Priced Altnerative	100% Increase All Prices*
Poor, Rural**	80.4	73.9	73.3
		(-6.5)	(-7.1)
		[-6,400]	[-6,900]
Poor, Urban	83.1	79.6	75.4
		(-3.5)	(-7.7)
		[-24,000]	[-53.300]
Poor, Nonwhite Rural	75.5	67.5	66.6
		(-8.0)	(-8.9)
		[-3,800]	[-4,200]
Not Poor, Not Nonwhite, Urban	94.6	93.7	92.0
		(-0.9)	(-2.6)
		[-20,300)	[-60,200]

Numbers in parenthesis are repression estimates in basis points. Numbers in brackets are estimates of number of households affected.

* Same definition as in Table 2.

** "Poor" refers to the poorest 25% of the tracts. "Not poor" refers to other 75%, while "rich" would refer to the richest 25% of the tracts and all rural tracts. The other groups are defined similarly.

Source: Taylor and Kridel (1990, Table 3)

rates are doubled, with no changes in measured rates, the predicted decrease in penetration, in the five Southwestern Bell states combined, is 2.9 percentage points rather than 3.7. In Texas, the predicted decline is even smaller – 2.1 percentage points vs. 3.7 – because of the greater availability of measured service.

The importance of a lower-priced alternative is even more sharply delineated in Table 8. Again, the reference is to Texas. While measured service was most widespread in Texas in 1980 for the five Southwestern Bell states, only 58% of households had access to it, and this mostly in urban areas.

TABLE 9

Impact of "current" FCC access charge plan Southwestern Bell; Taylor-Kridel study

	Actual Predicted	$1 EUCL	$1 EUCL Poor Exempted
Total # Subscribers	6,608,500	6,569,300	6,579,900
ALL			
development	92.5	92.0	92.1
(change)		(-0.5)	(-0.4)
POOR, RURAL			
development	83.7	82.6	82.9
(change)		(-1.1)	(-0.8)
POOR, URBAN			
development	85.0	84.0	84.3
(change)		(-1.0)	(-0.7)
POOR, NONWHITE, RURAL			
development	78.5	77.0	77.5
(change)		(-1.5)	(-1.0)
NOT POOR, NOT NONWHITE, URBAN			
development	95.3	95.0	95.1
(change)		(-0.3)	(-0.2)

Source: Taylor and Kridel (1990, Table 4)

Comparing column 3 with column 2 in Table 8 and urban with rural, the availability of measured service is seen to make a dramatic difference.

What this exercise emphasizes is that, with properly structured lower-priced alternatives, higher local-service charges need not be a threat to universal service. While the Southwestern Bell study confirms Perl's findings that development has racial and ethnic dimensions, it also confirms that income is the most important factor and that its scarcity can be overcome with low-priced measured offerings that target the poor.

III. BELL CANADA'S RESIDENTIAL ACCESS DEMAND MODEL

Telephone rates that are out of line with costs is not exclusive to the United States, but is a concern also in Canada. In early 1987, Bell Canada petitioned the Canadian Radio-television and Telecommunications Commission for permission to begin a "rebalancing" of rates. Toll rates would be reduced, while local rates would be increased. Fears in Canada are the same as in the United States, the higher local rates will cause a substantial number of households to give up telephone service. In anticipation of these concerns, Bell Canada (Bodnar *et al.* 1988) developed a model of residential access demand that could be used to predict the impact of the proposed rate rebalancing. As South of the Border, fears were that certain socio-demographic groups would bear the brunt of the impact.

The Bell Canada study is based upon household survey data for 1985 that were collected by Statistics Canada.[10] Information on 34,262 Canadian households is contained in the microdata files that were analyzed; 34,168 of these are in the sample used in estimation. A binary logit model along the line of the Perl model is specified in which the logarithmic odds in favor of a household having telephone service are related to a long list of economic, socio-demographic, and regional factors. The estimated coefficients for the variables in the model are given in Table 10. Definitions of the variables are given in Table 11.

The coefficients in Table 10 provide nothing by way of surprise. The probability of having a telephone varies negatively with price and positively with income, age and education. Single male-headed households are less likely to have a telephone than other types of households, those who rent are less likely to have a telephone than those who own their homes, and the self-employed, unless they fish or farm, are more likely to have a telephone than those who work for others. The recently-moved have a lower probability of having a telephone than those who have been at the same address for more than three years. The probability of having a telephone is higher in urban than in rural areas and increases monotonically with urban size. Finally, holding all else constant, the probability of having a telephone is higher in Ontario and Quebec and lower in Newfoundland and New Brunswick than elsewhere in Canada.

As in the Perl and Southwestern Bell models, the price elasticity varies with the point at which it is calculated and depends upon price and the predicted probability of subscription, which in turn depends upon all of the

[10] See Statistics Canada (1986). The HIFE data set was created by Statistics Canada by linking the contents of four surveys: Household Facilities and Equipment Survey (HFES), Labour Force Survey (LFS), Survey of Consumer Finances, and the Rent Survey. These surveys were conducted in April 1985 except for the HFES, which was conducted over the same sample as a supplement to the LFS in May 1985. Accordingly, the data refer to April or May 1985 except for household income and income-related measures, which refer to 1984 annual values.

TABLE 10

Estimation Results; Bell Canada Study

Variable	Coefficient	Asymptotic t-Statistic
CONSTANT	0.87	2.7
PRICE	-0.045	-2.4
INCOME	0.065	15.3
HHAGE	0.017	6.4
HHED1	0.34	3.4
HHED2	0.87	7.9
HHED3	1.44	9.9
HHED4	1.82	7.3
MALE	-1.33	-14.7
MOBILE	-0.55	-6.0
RENT	-0.78	-7.6
AREA1	1.96	13.7
AREA2	1.45	8.3
AREA3	1.24	9.3
AREA4	0.79	7.5
ROOMS	0.42	14.1
SELF-EMP	0.56	2.8
FARM/FISH	-0.32	-2.6
MIN INCOME	-0.10	-8.1
ONT + QUE	0.73	7.1
NFLD + NB	-0.37	-3.5

Adjusted likelihood ratio index $(\bar{p}^2)$ 0.272.

Likelihood ratio test statistic 2290.4.

Source: Bodnar *et al.* (1988, Table 2)

independent variables in the model.[11] A variety of results are presented in Tables 12 and 13. In Table 12, we see that the price elasticity for Canada as a

[11] Bell Canada encountered the same problem in constructing a price variable as did Perl. Because of possible problems with disclosure, domicile is only known by size of residence area, so that households could only be assigned a price that represented a weighted average price for the size of residence area in the province in which they reside. Price, accordingly, only varies across sizes of residence areas across provinces. This could lead to an errors-in-variables problem.

TABLE 11

Description of explanatory variables; Bell Canada study

Mnemonic	Description
PRICE	Weighted average price of residence single-party service including the rental charge for one basic set and any applicable provincial sales tax
INCOME	1984 after-tax household income (in thousands of dollars)
HHAGE	Age of household head (in years)
EDUCATION:	
HHED1	1 if the household head has 9–10 years of schooling; and 0 otherwise
HHED2	1 if the household head has 11–13 years of schooling; and 0 otherwise
HHED3	1 if the household head has some post-secondary education or has an associated certificate or diploma; and 0 otherwise
HHED4	1 if the household head has a university degree; and 0 otherwise
HOUSEHOLD COMPOSITION:	
MALE	1 if the household head is a single male unit (with or without children; and 0 otherwise
MOBILITY:	
MOBILE	1 if the household moved into its residence within 3 years of the survey; and 0 otherwise
TENURE:	
RENT	1 if the household rents its dwelling; and 0 otherwise
SIZE OF AREA:	
AREA1	1 if the household resides in a large urban centre with a population greater han 499,999; and 0 otherwise
AREA2	1 if the household resides in a large urban centre with a population between 100,000–499,999; and 0 otherwise
AREA3	1 if the household resides in a minor urban centre with a population between 30,000–99,999; and 0 otherwise
AREA4	1 if the household resides in a small urban centre with a population under 30,000; and 0 otherwise
ROOMS	the number of rooms in the household's dwelling
OCCUPATION:	
SELF-EMP	1 if the household's major source of income is net income from self-employment; and 0 otherwise
FARM/FISH	1 if the household head is employed in farming; horticultural and animal husbandry, fishing, hunting, trapping, forestry or logging; and 0 otherwise
MIN INCOME	the 1984 low income cut-off value for households of size k in area i; where k represents the number of persons in the household and i represents the size of area of residence (in thousands of dollars)
PROVINCE:	
ONT + QUE	1 if the household resides in Ontario or Quebec; and 0 otherwise
NFLD + NB	1 if the household resides in Newfoundland or New Brunswick; and 0 otherwise

Source: Bodnar *et al.* (1988, Table 3)

whole, calculated at 1985 predicted penetration rates and prices, is estimated to be -0.009, which might seem almost too small to be noticed. By province, the elasticity varies from -0.03 for New Brunswick to -0.005 for Ontario. In Table 13, we see that the size of the price elasticity decreases (in absolute value) with size of urban area, age, and income. For Canada as a whole, the elasticity for households residing in cities of 500,000 or more is only half the elasticity for households living in rural areas (-0.007 vs. -0.014). In the basis of these tables, it is clear that the Canadian households that would be most vulnerable to rate rebalancing would be young, low-income, rural households.

In comparing the Bell Canada model with the Perl and Southwestern Bell models, the most notable difference is the relative strengths of the price effects. However, it does not follow from this that price is more important in the U.S. than in Canada, for the difference simply reflects the fact that penetration rates are higher in Canada than in the U.S. For whatever reason, the overall penetration rate is about four percentage points higher in Canada than in the U.S. When calculated using the 1980 U.S. penetration rate of 93.4% (but 1985 Canadian values for all the other variables), the price elasticity in the Bell Canada model turns out to be -0.034. This compares with -0.032 in the Perl model.

IV. TRAIN, MCFADDEN, AND BEN-AKIVA (1987)

The final study to be discussed in this chapter is a study of the demand for local service (Train, McFadden, and Ben-Akiva 1987) undertaken for a large east coast local exchange company by Cambridge Systematics, Inc.[12] Unlike in the three preceding studies where the focus is on the choice of access/no access, the TMB study focuses on the choices of class of service given that access of some form is already demanded. What sets the TMB study apart is that the class of service is determined jointly with a portfolio of calls. Calls are distinguished according to number, duration, distance, and time-of-day, and a portfolio of calls accordingly consists of a particular number of calls of a particular duration to a set of specific locations at specific times of the day. Households in the data set analyzed faced a variety of service options ranging from budget-measured to metropolitan-wide flat-rate, so that the cost of a portfolio varies with the particular service option selected.

TMB proceed in a conditional (i.e., nested) logit framework in which the choice of service is assumed to be conditional on the portfolio of calls that

---

[12] See also Train, Ben-Akiva, and Atherton (1989) wherein the TMB model is applied to similar data for Delaware.

TABLE 12

Penetration elasticities by province*; Bell Canada study

Province	Elasticity
NFLD	-0.028
PEI	-0.021
NS	-0.021
NB	-0.030
QUE	-0.009
ONT	-0.005
MAN	-0.007
SASK	-0.010
ALTA	-0.010
BC	-0.012
CANADA	-0.009

* Calculated at 1985 predicted penetration rates and prices.
Source: Bodnar *et al.* (1988, Table 5)

is selected. With this structure, the probability of a household choosing a particular service option can be interpreted as depending upon the household's expected portfolio of calls (reflecting, for example, the tendency of households that place many calls to choose flat-rate service). Since usage is in turn conditional on access, however, the portfolio that a household will actually choose in a month will depend upon the service option that has been selected as this determines the cost per call.

Turning now to a description of the model, let the distinct times of the day that calls can be made be denoted by $t = 1, \ldots, T$ and let the geographic areas (or zones) to which calls can go be denoted by $z = 1, \ldots, Z$. Let N_{tz} represent the number of calls to zone z during time period t and let D_{tz} represent the average duration of these calls. A portfolio, accordingly, can be written as the vector with elements $(N_{11}, \ldots, N_{TZ}, D_{11}, \ldots, D_{TZ})$. Denote the set of all possible portfolios by A and a particular portfolio by $i \in A$. Finally, index the available service options by $s = 1, \ldots S$. In the data set analyzed, three service options are available to all households and two additional services are available to some households. The options are listed in Table 14. Portfolios are defined for the 21 time-zones listed in Table 15.

The probability of observing a particular (s, i) service-portfolio combina-

TABLE 13

Penetration price elasticities by size of area of residence, age and income*; Bell Canada study

Size of Area	Canada	Ont & Que
Urban		
> 499,999	-0.007	-0.006
100,000–499,999	-0.006	-0.006
30,000–99,999	-0.010	-0.006
< 30,000	-0.013	-0.009
Rural	-0.014	-0.009
Age (in years)	**Canada**	**Ont & Que**
< 26	-0.024	-0.016
26–44	-0.009	-0.006
45–64	-0.007	-0.005
> 64	-0.008	-0.006
Income**	**Canada**	**Ont & Que**
1st Quintile	-0.026	-0.019
2nd Quintile	-0.012	-0.008
3rd Quintile	-0.006	-0.004
4th Quintile	-0.002	-0.002
5th Quitnile	-0.0005	-0.0004
Low Income Cut-Off	**Canada**	**Ont & Que**
Below	-0.025	-0.019
At or Above	-0.005	-0.004

* Calculated at 1985 predicted penetration rates and prices.

** The 1984 after-tax household incomes that correspond to these quintiles for Canada and for Ontario and Quebec are as follows:

Quintile	Canada	Ont & Que
	($)	($)
First	< 12270	< 12580
Second	12270–20169	12580–20619
Third	20170–28339	20620–28169
Fourth	28340–38509	28620–38709
Fifth	> 38509	> 38709

Source: Bodnar *et al.* (1988, Tables 6–8)

TABLE 14

Service options in TMB study

Service	Availability	Charges for Calls to Nearest Zone	Charges for Calls to Other Zones
Budget Measured	Available to all customers.	Each call charged seven cents.	Each call charged at rate that varies with time, distance, and duration of call.
Standard Measured	Available to all customers.	$4.00 worth of calling is at no extra charge, then each call is charged as under budget measured service.	
Local Flat-Rate	Available to all customers.	No extra charge.	Each call charged at rate that varies with time, distance, and duration of call.
Extended Local	Available to customers in only some exchanges.	No extra charge.	No extra charge for calls to some exchanges; charged as under local flat-rate service for calls to other exchanges.
Metropolitan Area Flat-Rate	Available to nonrural customers.	No extra charge.	No extra charge.

Source: Train, McFadden, and Ben-Akiva (1987, Table 1)

tion, given available service and portfolio options, is assumed to be nested logit. In the nesting, alternatives [where an alternative is an (s, i) combination] are nested together with the same portfolio but different service options.[13] Let P_{is} denote the probability of observing the combination (i, s),

[13] TMB provide an excellent discussion of the considerations that determine an appropriate nesting. The key consideration is the pattern of correlations among the omitted factors. For local calling, most of the specific factors that determine portfolio choice – such as where the household's friends and relatives live, the time and location of activities that require use of the telephone, etc. – are not observed. These factors, however, are similar across all service offerings for any porfolio. This leads to nesting together alternatives with the same portfolio but different service options. On the other hand, the primary factor affecting the choice of service is price which is observable. (The price of a portfolio under a particular service option is simply the cost of the portfolio under the rate schedule associated with that option.) Since alternatives with the same service option but not the same portfolio of calls can be similar with respect to observed factors, but not (at least relatively) with respect to unobserved factors,

TABLE 15

Time & Zone Categories in TMB study

Zones		Times	
		Times of Week during which Different	Rates during
Number	Description	Rates Are Charged for Calls to that Zone	Time
1	Zone immediately surrounding the household's residence.	9 A.M.–9 P.M., Monday–Friday	Full tariffs
		7 A.M.–9 A.M., and 9 P.M.–Midnight, Monday–Sunday	50% off
		Midnight–7 A.M., Monday–Sunday	86% off
2–6	Geographic bands successively more distant from household's residence.	9 A.M.–9 P.M., Monday–Friday	Full tariffs
		All other times	50% off
7	Specific exchanges of zones 1–6, applicable only to households in certain exchanges within a metropolitan area.	9 A.M.–9 P.M., Monday–Friday	12% off, on average
		7 A.M.–9 A.M., 9 P.M.–Midnight, Monday–Sunday	48% off, on average
		Midnight–7 A.M., Monday–Sunday	60 off, on average
		9 A.M.–9 P.M., Saturday–Sunday	56% off, on average
8	Remainder of metropolitan areas in which household resides, applicable only to households in certain exchanges within a metropolitan area.	9 A.M.–9 P.M., Monday–Sunday	12% off, on average
		7 A.M.–9 A.M., 9 P.M.–Midnight, Monday–Sunday	48% off, on average
		Midnight–7 A.M., Monday–Sunday	60% off, on average
		9 A.M.-9 P.M., Saturday–Sunday	56% off, on average

Source: Train, McFadden, and Ben-Akiva (1987, Table 2)

let $P_{s|i}$ denote the conditional probability of choosing service option s given portfolio i, and let P_i denote the marginal probability of selecting portfolio i, so that (from the definition of conditional probability):

$$P_{is} = P_{s|i}P_i. \tag{25}$$

these are not nested.

In particular, it is assumed that

$$P_{is} = \frac{e^{y_{is}}}{\sum_j e^{y_{ij}}} \left(\frac{\sum_j e^{y_{ij}}}{\sum_k \sum_j e^{y_{kj}}} \right)^{\lambda}, \tag{26}$$

where:

$$P_{s|i} = \frac{e^{y_{is}}}{\sum_j e^{y_{ij}}} \tag{27}$$

$$P_i = \left(\frac{\sum_j e^{y_{ij}}}{\sum_k \sum_j e^{y_{kj}}} \right)^{\lambda}, \tag{28}$$

and where y_{is} is a parametric function of factors specific to service option s and portfolio i. Without loss of generality, y_{is} can be written as the sum of two terms.

$$y_{is} = w_{is} + v_i/\lambda, \tag{29}$$

where w varies with both i and s, but v varies only with i. Consequently, we will have for $e^{y_{is}}$,

$$e^{y_{is}} = e^{(w_{is}+v_i/\lambda)} = e^{v_i/\lambda} e^{w_{is}}. \tag{30}$$

Similarly, for $\sum_j e^{y_{ij}}$

$$\sum_j e^{y_{ij}} = \sum_j e^{(w_{ij}+v_i/\lambda)} = e^{v_i/\lambda} \sum_j e^{w_{ij}}, \tag{31}$$

so that

$$P_{s|i} = \frac{e^{w_{is}}}{\sum_j e^{w_{ij}}}. \tag{32}$$

Next, let

$$I_i = \ln \left(\sum_j e^{w_{ij}} \right). \tag{33}$$

$\sum_j e^{w_{ij}}$ can then be written as

$$\sum_j e^{w_{ij}} = e^{I_i}. \tag{34}$$

Consequently, for P_i:

$$P_i = \left(\frac{\sum_j e^{y_{ij}}}{\sum_k \sum_j e^{y_{kj}}} \right)^\lambda = \left(\frac{e^{v_i/\lambda} \sum_j e^{w_{ij}}}{\sum_k e^{v_k/\lambda} \sum_j e^{w_{kj}}} \right)^\lambda = \frac{e^{v_i + \lambda I_i}}{\sum_k e^{v_k + \lambda I_k}}. \quad (35)$$

The term I_i is interpreted as the "inclusive price" of portfolio i, and its coefficient λ measures the substitutability across portfolios. For $0 < \lambda < 1$, substitution is greater within nests than across nests, while for $\lambda > 1$, substitution is greater across nests than within nests. Given the nesting structure, the parameter will be less than one if households shift to different service options more readily than they shift to different portfolios. It will be greater than one if they shift to different portfolios more readily than if they shift to different service options.

TMB note that the specification contained in expressions (32), (33), and (35) have several advantages:

First, since P_i and $P_{s|i}$ are both logit, the model is relatively inexpensive to estimate and easy to interpret. Second, the cost of any portfolio under any service option is simply the bill that the household would receive if it made that portfolio of calls and chose that service option. [Since cost varies over i and s, it enters as an element of w_{is}. We estimate its impact on choice of portfolio and service option in $P_{s|i}$.] Threshold values for calling at no extra charge, which are based on either the number or the dollar value of calls, enter the calculation of the cost of a portfolio under a service option in the same way as in the telephone company's calculation of bills. Consequently, we can readily and consistently examine the impact of changes in tariffs and thresholds. Finally, this specification incorporates interrelations among calling patterns and service option choices. The probability of a household's choosing any particular portfolio changes as the tariffs or thresholds associated with any service option change and depends on the portfolio of calls that the household makes. (Train, McFadden, and Ben-Akiva 1987, p. 114.)

It remains to specify forms for v_i and w_{is}. As the only difference among service offerings is in the billing procedure, w_{is} is assumed to depend only on the cost to the customer of portfolio i under option s and option-specific constants. The specification of v_i is more complex. To begin with, it is assumed that a portfolio yields benefits through the information transmitted in calls and extracts opportunity costs through the time spent on the telephone. Suppressing for the moment variations in coefficients across time and zone categories and households, TMB specify v_i for a portfolio of N_i calls of average duration N_i (with the i deleted to simply notation) as:

$$v = \theta N \ln \phi D - \alpha N D = \theta N \ln D - \gamma N - \alpha N D, \tag{36}$$

where $\gamma = -\theta \ln \phi$.

The first term on the right-hand side in this expression measures the benefits of the portfolio. Each call provides a benefit, $\theta \ln \phi D$, which is assumed to increase at a decreasing rate with duration. The parameter ϕ can be interpreted as measuring the rate of information transfer. It is expected to be positive, but can be either greater or less than one. As θ can be interpreted as measuring the benefits from the information that can be transferred by a call, this is necessarily positive. Consequently, γ can be either negative or positive. The model assumes that the benefits from N calls is simply N times the benefits from a single call. The term $\alpha N D$ measures the opportunity cost of the portfolio. ND represents the total amount of time spent in calling, while α measures the opportunity cost per minute.

The parameters are allowed to vary in two ways. Benefits depend upon the destination of a call, while the opportunity cost depends upon the time of day. θ accordingly, is allowed to vary over distance zones and α over time periods. In addition, θ is assumed to vary with income and the number of telephone users in the household. Income is also assumed to affect α, the time opportunity cost of calling.

TMB note that estimation of the parameters entering P_i is complicated by the large number of possible portfolios. As enumeration of every possible portfolio is out of the question, estimation proceeds on the basis of a sample of portfolios for each household. The sample includes the portfolio chosen by the household plus a subset of portfolios that the household did not choose. Samples are constructed by drawing from the set of all possible portfolios and then adding each household's chosen alternative. Let B denote the sample of portfolios constructed for a particular household, and let $\pi(B|i)$ denote the conditional probability of constructing subset B given that the chosen alternative is i. [Since B necessarily includes the chosen portfolio, $\pi(B|j) = 0$ *for* $j \notin B$.]

The joint probability of drawing a chosen alternative i and a subset of alternatives B is

$$\pi(i|B) = \pi(B|i)P_i. \tag{37}$$

Consequently, from Bayes theorem, the conditional probability of i being chosen, given B, is

$$\pi(i|B) = \frac{\pi(B|i)P_i}{\sum_{j \in B} \pi(B|j)P_j}, \tag{38}$$

which exists if $\pi(B|j) > 0$ *for all* $j \notin B$. Rewritten in logit form, with P_i given by equation (35), (38) becomes

$$\pi(i|B) = \frac{e^{[v_i + \lambda I_i + \ln \pi(B|i)]}}{\sum_{j \in B} e^{[v_j + \lambda I_j + \ln \pi(B|i)]}}. \tag{39}$$

McFadden (1978) has shown that under usual regularity conditions maximizing the conditional logarithmic likelihood function,

$$L = \sum_{h=1}^{H} \ln \pi_n(i|B), \tag{40}$$

(where h denotes particular households in a sample of H households) yields consistent estimators of the unknown parameters.

It will be noted that the logit model in (39) is the same as in equation (35) except that the summation is over the set of constructed portfolios B, rather than over the set of all possible portfolios A. Also, the exponential terms contain an additive alternative-specific factor which corrects for the bias introduced by the sampling of alternatives.[14] The coefficient on this factor is constrained to be one. Estimation is based on a constructed subset of alternatives for each household that consists of ten portfolios, the one actually chosen by the household plus nine other sampled portfolios.

Empirical results for the TMB study are given in Tables 16, 17 and 18. The data set used in the analysis consists of observations on individual households in the service area of a large east coast local telephone company. The service options available to households in the sample together with the number in the sample choosing each option are given at the top of Table 16. The bottom of Table 16 gives the estimated parameters service-option choice conditional on portfolio for each of three specifications of the cost function that enters $P_{s|i}$. In each specification, cost has an expected negative effect, with the best fit being obtained with $\ln C_{is}$, which has a coefficient of about -2. This implies that the ratio of probabilities for any two service options is essentially inversely proportional to the square of the ratio of their costs:

$$\frac{P_{s|i}}{P_{s'|i}} = k \left(\frac{C_{is'}}{C_{is}} \right)^{2.08},$$

which implies that the relative probabilities change at an accelerated rate as relative costs change. TMB note that this result is consistent with the popular view that households are relatively insensitive to small cost differences when they select service options but become increasingly sensitive as the differences become large.

---

[14] See McFadden (1978).

TABLE 16

Logit model of service choice for given portfolio; TMB study

Service Options	Number of Customers with Altneratives Available	Number of Customers Who Chose the Alternative
Budget Measured	2963	579
Standard Measured	2963	855
Local Flat-Rate	2963	1120
Extended Local Flat-Rate	84	20
Metropolitan Area Flat-Rate	1873	389

	Estimated Parameters (t-statistics in parentheses)		
	Model 1: $\ln C$	Model 2: C_{is}	Model 3: C_{is} Divided by Income of Household in Thousands of Dollars
C_{is}: cost of portfolio under designated service option (includes monthly fixed fee and charges for calls, in 1984 dollars; specified differently in each model).	-2.081 (23.87)	-0.0111 (17.42)	-0.4538 (14.51)
Option-Specific Constants:			
Standard Measured	1.228 (17.83)	0.6135 (11.04)	0.5079 (9.282)
Local Flat-Rate	2.635 (24.74)	1.5 (20.94)	1.081 (18.07)
Extended Local Flat-Rate	2.254 (7.880)	1.123 (3.922)	0.8614 (3.279)
Metropolitan Area Flat-Rate	3.757 (21.82)	3.474 (17.23)	1.317 (13.60)
Number of Households	2963	2963	2963
Initial Log Likelihood	-3812.4	-3812.4	-3812.4
Log Likelihood at Convergence	-3356.0	-3487.8	-3562.3

Source: Train, McFadden, and Ben-Akiva (1987, Table 3)

Mechanically, the option-specific constants are those that result in the average probability (i.e., the predicted share) for each option being equal to the observed share in the sample. As can be seen, these constants, which capture the average option-specific effect of all excluded variables, are highly significant. TMB suggest that the most important excluded factor may be the insurance quality of the option. Under flat-rate pricing, the customer, for a fixed fee, is provided an upper limit on charges for calling within a specified geographic area. The larger the area of calling at no extra charge, the more valuable is the insurance that the option provides. The estimated coefficients, measured as deviations from budget measured service, are consistent with this: all are positive, which is consistent with budget measured service having no insurance value (since all calls are charged), and except for extended local service whose coefficient is smaller than for regular local service,[15] the coefficients increase with the size of the free-calling area.

The estimated parameters for the model of portfolio choice are given in Table 17. All of the coefficients have the expected sign and are reasonable in magnitude. In assessing signs and sizes of coefficients in this model, it is important to keep in mind just what it is that is being predicted: namely, the probability of selection of the portfolio that the household in question actually selected. The logic of the model states that this probability ebbs and flows with the distance calls go, when they are made, how many in the household can make them, the income of the household, etc. The coefficients on the total duration of calling ($n \ln D$) accordingly indicate that the probability of selecting a selected portfolio increases with length-of-haul, as the more outlying the calling zone the larger its coefficient. A portfolio is selected with greater "tenacity" the more it is weighted to calls of longer distance.

The coefficient on the "inclusive value" of a portfolio is greater than one, which indicates that households respond to price changes more readily by adjusting their patterns of calling than by shifting to different service options. Also, it is seen that the probability of choosing portfolio i decreases with the number of calls. TMB comment on this as follows:

1. Recall that there are multiple time-of-day and destination zone categories. As the total number of calls increases, the number of portfolios that are possible with that number of calls increases. For example, there is only one portfolio of no calls, but there are 21 portfolios – when we ignore duration – associated with making a total of one call

---

[15] However, TMB note that the coefficients for local flat-rate and extended local flat-rate are not strictly comparable because the latter is not universally available and so the excluded factors are averaged over different populations.

TABLE 17

Logit model of service option choice conditional on portfolio; TMB study
Alternative Set: The household's chosen portfolio plus nine portfolios selected randomly
from the set of all available portfolios.

Explanatory Variable	Coefficient	t-Statistic
Benefits of Information (θ):		
$N \log D$ for calls to zone 1	0.0239	11.8
$N \log D$ for calls to zones 2–6	0.0410	13.10
$N \log D$ for calls to zones 7–8	0.0474	11.11
Σ_{zones} (pop of zone in millions) $N \log D$ for zone	0.00752	14.58
(Income of households in thousands of $)		
($N \log D$ for all zones)	0.213×10^{-3}	3.13
(Number of telephone users in household)		
($N \log D$ for all zones)	-0.755×10^{03}	4.035
Rate of Information Transfer ($-\gamma$):		
Total number of Calls (N to all zones)	-0.890	8.525
Opportunity Cost of Conversation Minutes ($-\alpha$):		
Total duration 9 A.M.–9 P.M. to zone 1	-0.00472	10.11
Total duration 7 A.M.–9 A.M. and		
9 P.M.–Midnight to zone 1	-0.00438	8.475
Total duration Midnight–7 A.M. to zone 1	-0.00141	1.866
Total duration for 9 P.M.–9 A.M. to zone 2–8	-0.0111	12.56
(Total income in households of $)		
(Total duration all zones and times)	-0.060×10^{-3}	3.22
Other Variables:		
Inclusive value of service option choice		
(using model 1 of Table 3)	4.178	13.68
Sampling correction factor (coefficient		
is constrained to 1.0)	1.0	–
Number of households	3038	
Log likelihood at zero	-7125.9	
Log likelihood at convergence	-6242.8	

Source: Train, McFadden, and Ben-Akiva (1987, Table 4)

– a portfolio for each time and zone category in which that one call could be made. Therefore, if the probability of making a certain total number of calls increases with the number of calls, but increases less rapidly than the number of portfolios that are possible with that number of calls, then the probability of each portfolio must decrease in the number of calls. This is what is occurring in the estimated model.

2. It is reasonable to expect that the probability of a household's making a particular number of calls reaches a maximum at some finite number of calls. The number of portfolios that are possible with a certain number of call increases with the number of calls, but does so at a continuously decreasing rate. Consequently, if V_i decreases linearly with the number of calls (as the estimates in Table 4 indicate), then the probability of making a certain number of calls first increases with the number of calls (with the expansion of the number of possible portfolios dominating the decrease in V_i minus the cost of each portfolio), but eventually decreases (when the decrease in V_i, which is linear in the number of calls, starts to dominate the diminishing expansion in the number of portfolios). (Train, McFadden, and Ben-Akiva 1987, p. 118.)

The estimated aggregate price elasticities for the TMB model are given in Table 18. Price elasticities in the model vary over customers and, for any customer, depend upon current prices and all other factors entering the model. Aggregate elasticities are accordingly specific to a particular population at a particular time. The numbers in the table refer to the sample used in estimation.

The own-price elasticities for the monthly fixed charge for each service are seen to be fairly large. Since all of the households in the sample had telephone service under one service option or another, these numbers do not represent access elasticities in the sense of service/no service, but rather substitution among service options. The relatively large own-price elasticities accordingly indicate a high degree of substitutability among services. The size of both the own-and cross-price elasticities depend upon market share. Consider local flat-rate service whose market share (74%) is large in relation to the other service options. Because of this, its own-price elasticity (at -0.46) is smallest of all the service options, yet the shift in demand that results from an increase in the local flat-rate access charge represents a relatively high percentage increase in the demand for other service options, as evidenced by the substantial cross elasticities for the other options with respect to the flat-rate price. In contrast, the extended flat-rate option has only 1% of the market, so that an increase in its fixed charge has a relatively small effect

TABLE 18

Estimated price elasticities; TMB study

Monthly Fixed Charges for Service
(initial shares in parentheses)

Number of Households Choosing:	Budget Measured (0.05)	Standard Measured (0.15)	Local Flat-Rate (0.74)	Extended Local Flat-Rate (0.01)	Metropolitan Area Flat-Rate (0.05)	Charge for Calls to Zone 1	Charge for 1st Min. for Calls to Zones 2–8	Charge for Addl. Mins. for Calls to Zones 2–8
Budget Measured	-1.06	0.16	1.52	0.02	0.11	-0.41	-0.04	-0.04
Standard Measured	0.05	-1.38	1.36	0.01	0.14	-0.26	-0.04	-0.03
Local Flat	0.07	0.25	0.46	0.01	0.11	0.08	-0.00	-0.01
Extended Local Flat	0.11	0.11	0.45	-0.91	0.34	0.08	0.06	0.06
Metro Flat	0.04	0.22	1.07	0.04	-2.19	0.07	0.21	0.21
Number of Calls	0.14	0.14	-0.29	-0.00	-0.06	-0.02	-0.00	-0.00
Average Duration	0.00	0.00	0.00	0.00	0.00	0.00	0.01	-0.01
Total Revenues	0.04	0.18	0.56	0.01	0.02	0.05	0.07	0.06

Source: Train, McFadden, and Ben-Akiva (1987, Table 5)

on the demand for the other options, and this is the case even though the own-price elasticity for extended flat-rate service is double the local flat-rate elasticity.

Other results of interest include:

1. Increasing the fixed charge for each service option affects the number of calls made by households in an expected way. Increase in the fixed charge for measured services shifts customers to flat-rate services, under which customers make more calls because of the marginal price of calling is zero. Conversely, increasing flat-rate charges decreases the amount of calling because it shifts customers to measured services which charges for calls.

2. Increasing the charges for marginal calls – particularly for zone 1 calls, which comprise about 80% of all local calls – shifts customers from measured to flat-rates services. The elasticities, however, are small.

3. Charges for marginal calls have a small effect on the total number of calls that households make. Largely, this is because in the great majority of cases customers are not charged for the marginal calls that they make. Zone 1 calls are free to 80% of customers (those choosing flat-rate services). All zone 8 calls are free to customers with metropolitan flat-rate service, and many of these calls are free under extended flat-rate service. Moreover, customers with standard measured service do not pay for marginal calls if they are below the threshold of calling at no extra charge.

V. EVALUATION

Of the four studies that have reviewed in this chapter, three – Perl, Taylor and Kridel, and Bell Canada – were motivated primarily by concerns with dropoff, that spiraling local rates would cause large numbers of households to give up telephone service. The three studies are similar in many respects, in the use of a binary choice logit or probit model that relates the probability of a household having a telephone to the price of access, income, and a wide range of socio-demographic variables related to particular social and ethnic groups. All three studies find that the probability of having a telephone is sensitive to price, but a sensitivity that in the aggregate is quantitatively small. All three studies also find that the households most vulnerable to dropoff from rising local rates would be young, low-income, poorly educated households living in rural areas. Actually, when all-is-said-and-done, the primary factor is really income, or rather its absence.

As noted at the beginning of this chapter, the problem with small (or even tiny) elasticities is that they can lead to large numbers when applied to a large base. In the U.S., the population of residential telephone subscribers is approaching 100 million; in Bell Canada's service territory, it is close to six million. Applied indiscriminately, an elasticity as small as -0.02 would imply a "dropoff" from a doubling of local rates of 120,000 households in Ontario and Quebec, and two million in the U.S. Absolutely, these are large numbers, and become staggeringly so if they are concentrated within disadvantaged, low-income groups.

It is important, however, that the elasticities that have been estimated in the Perl, Southwestern Bell, and Bell Canada's models not be used in this manner, especially the implication that a doubling of rates would lead to dropoffs of the magnitudes indicated. To begin with, it must be kept in mind that the question being asked is essentially temporal in nature, whereas the elasticities in question are based upon parameters that are estimated from cross-sectional data. Households do not react immediately to higher access charges, but adjust over a period of time, possibly as long as several years in the unlikely event of a sudden doubling of rates. During the period of adjustment, other factors – social, demographic, and economic – will be changing that could offset the impact of the rate increase. Once adjustment is complete, the number of telephone subscribers could very well be smaller than in the absence of the rate increase, but the "shortfall" would almost certainly be smaller than the dropoff indicated by a straight-forward application of the access price elasticity.

A second point to keep in mind relates to the fact that dropoff refers to a household giving up a service that it has had as opposed to refusing to take the service in the first place. The effect could be asymmetrical. The price increase needed to cause a dropoff might need to be much larger than the price decrease that could induce another household in otherwise similar circumstances but which has never had telephone service to subscribe. All three of the models in question assume that this is not the case, but because none of the samples contains information as to whether households may once have had telephone service that was subsequently renounced, this restriction is imposed *a priori* rather than through testing. Consequently, the ultimate effects on telephone subscription of sharply higher access rates may reflect failure to "drop in" as much or more as inducement to dropoff.

In view of all this, the Perl, Southwestern Bell, and Bell Canada models are of limited usefulness in my opinion in predicting the amount of dropoff that might ensue in the event of sharp increases in residential access charges. The models are most useful in establishing that the price of access has a negative effect, albeit small, on the probability of a household having a telephone, that income is the primary factor in determining subscription, and in identifying the socio-demographic and economic dimensions along which a targeted subsidy program, should (for whatever reason) it be decided that one is desired, could be designed. Indeed, all three models are unambiguous in identifying low-income households as the households most likely to be harmed by rising local-service rates.

The three models are also informative in identifying density and size of local-calling area as factors increasing the probability of having a telephone. That a larger system increases the value (i.e., willingness-to-pay) of belonging to the system, there is little doubt. Significant positive coefficients for size and density accord with common sense on this score. However, one must be careful in concluding from this the existence of a network externality that would support, on social-welfare grounds, an access price that is less than cost. As was noted in Chapter 2, whether a network externality supports a subsidized access price depends upon the willingness-to-pay of those not on the system in relation to the benefits that their presence would confer on the subscribers already on the system. At present sizes of systems, it is not clear that these benefits are all that large. We will examine this question in detail in Chapter 9.

In contrast with the Perl, Southwestern Bell, and Bell Canada studies, which focus on the access/no access decisions, the Train-McFadden-Ben-Akiva study focuses on the choice of class of service given that access is already demanded. The question that is investigated is how service choice is affected by different service options becoming available, as relative prices of the options change, and as calling patterns change. The TMB study is ambitious and highly innovative. It approaches a household's choice of service as a portfolio choice problem in which the household not only selects a service option but also a portfolio of calls. Portfolios are defined along each of the dimensions that calls are priced – time-of day, distance, and duration. The price of a portfolio under a particular service option is simply the bill that would be generated by that portfolio under the option.[16] The model is formulated as a nested logit model in which the nesting proceeds from choice of portfolio to the choice of service option conditional on the portfolio.

With regard to price effects, the conclusion which emerges from the four studies is that, in the aggregate and at present levels of development, the decision to access the telephone network is relatively insensitive to price, but not the form. For the TMB results indicate substantial substitution among service

---

[16] This way of defining price avoids the usual problems presented by a multi-part tariff. Simultaneity bias is avoided, also the need to reduce a complicated tariff to a few parameters. Responses to changes in access and usage changes, pricing periods, and the number of "free" calls are easily estimated by simulation.

options in response to changes in relative prices. This is an important result for policy purposes, for it provides strong support for the view, discussed at length by Perl, that the threat to universal service caused by elimination of the toll-to-local subsidy can be contained by a carefully designed budget measured-service.

CHAPTER 6

RECENT STUDIES OF TOLL DEMAND

As noted in Chapter 1, concerns with the effect on residential subscribers of rising local-service rates led to a sharp shift in emphasis in the early 1980s to research on access demand. The analysis of toll demand not only ceased being center stage in terms of resources devoted to it, but the nature of toll-demand research shifted as well. Prior to divestiture, the toll market in the U.S. was split, for regulatory reasons, between intrastate and interstate. Intrastate rates were regulated by state PUCs, while interstate rates were regulated by the FCC. With divestiture came the creation of LATAs (local access transport areas), which are within-state geographical areas consisting of a single population center and its environs. The terms of the divestiture stipulated that the only toll service that local exchange carriers can provide is in the LATAs within which they operate. The post-divestiture toll market thus came to entail three segments: intraLATA, interLATA-intrastate, and interLATA-interstate. Intrastate rates (both intraLATA and interLATA) continued to be regulated by the states, while interstate rates continued under FCC jurisdiction.

Even before the divestiture, emergent competition in the toll market was causing toll price elasticities for the long-distance carriers to become increasingly proprietary. As MCI, Sprint, and other IX carriers acquired market share, the price elasticities faced by AT&T ceased referring to the industry at large, but became AT&T specific. Not surprisingly, AT&T – as also the other carriers – viewed these elasticities as important company secrets, to be revealed only in regulatory proceedings on a proprietary basis. The result has been that research on toll demand at AT&T no longer finds its way into the open literature, and has not since 1980.[1]

A consequence of the divestiture for the analysis of toll demand was to create two wholly new markets, namely, the market for "access" to the interLATA toll network(s) and the market for "bypass" of the LECs on the part of toll users. In an important sense, both markets were creatures of the toll-to-local subsidy that had evolved historically through the separations

---

[1] Two exceptions to this are Gatto, Kelejian, and Stephan (1988) and Gatto et al. (1988). The former is described briefly in Chapter 11, while the latter is discussed later in this chapter. In keeping with the point just made, the price elasticities presented by Gatto, Kelejian, and Stephan are highly aggregated and camouflaged as to state.

process. At the time of divestiture, some \$16 billion of annual costs associated with local plant and equipment was allocated to the toll arena to be recovered through toll revenues. The \$16b involved was divided about equally between interstate and intrastate. At divestiture, much of the interstate portion was set up to be recovered through per-minute charges at both the originating and terminating ends of a toll call.

These "access" charges were set initially at about 6 cents per minute, but were to be recalculated annually on the basis of forecasts of interstate "access" minutes submitted by the LECs. Preparation of these forecasts was coordinated by the National Exchange Carriers Association (NECA) in annual hearings before the FCC. One of the studies to be discussed in this chapter (Gatto *et al.* 1988) arises out of this activity.

The fact that the "access" charges are usage-sensitive means that they can be avoided if toll users were to connect directly to their IX carrier at the latter's point-of-presence. Whether this is accomplished through the users' own facilities or through facilities leased from the LECs, the result is to bypass the switching facilities of the LECs and thereby avoid the per-minute "access" charges (at least at the originating end). This is the market for "bypass" referred to earlier.[2]

As a way of introducing readers to the substantive developments in the analysis of toll demand during the 1980s, I have singled out four particular studies for detailed discussion in the remainder of this chapter. Two of these, Bell Canada (1984) and Appelbe *et al.* (1988), were undertaken at Bell Canada, so that the focus is on Canada, rather than the U.S. The remaining two studies refer to the U.S.

I. TOLL DEMAND IN ONTARIO AND QUEBEC

I shall begin with Bell Canada's recent work in modeling the toll market in Ontario and Quebec (or what Bell Canada refers to as Bell-Intra). Bell's current models are of especial interest because of their extension of the concept of market size to areas.[3] The price elasticities from these models figured prominently in hearings regarding inter-exchange competition before the Canadian Radio-television and Telecommunications Commission (CRTC) in 1984. The treatment of market size in the models triggered a spirited but useful debate,

---

[2] For detailed analyses of the bypass problem, see Bell Communications Research (1984) and Brock (1984). For an exchange involving the concept of "uneconomic" bypass, see Wenders (1986) and Egan and Weisman (1986).

[3] My focus in this section will be on the model in Bell Canada (1984). An updating of the Bell-Intra results appears in Bell Canada (1989).

which (as will be seen in Chapter 9) has helped to clarify the effects associated with the network externality.

To facilitate the discussion, it will be helpful to present a simplified version of the model which underlies Bell Canada's analyses. Suppose that we have two exchanges, A and B, that are not part of the same local-calling area, so that calls between the exchanges are toll calls. Let the number of telephones in the two exchanges be T and R, respectively. The total possible connections between the two exchanges will therefore be $T \cdot R$. Let M denote the number of calls that are "sent paid" from A to B during some period of time (a quarter, say), and let θ denote the proportion of the potential connections ($T \cdot R$) that are realized, so that

$$M = \theta(T \cdot R). \tag{1}$$

Equation (1) might describe the relationship that would be observed in a stationary world – i.e., where income, price, and all other factors that affect toll calling are constant. However, these other factors do not remain constant, and we can allow for them through the value of θ. In particular, let us suppose that income (Y) and the price (P) of a toll call from A to B affect θ according to

$$\theta = aY^\beta P^\gamma, \tag{2}$$

where a, β, and γ are constants. The relationship in expression (1) accordingly becomes

$$M = aY^\beta P^\gamma(T \cdot R). \tag{3}$$

Finally, let us suppose that M is affected by a change in potential toll connections that may be either more or less than proportional, in which case the model becomes

$$M = aY^\beta P^\gamma(T \cdot R)^\lambda, \tag{4}$$

where λ is a constant, presumably of the order of 1.

Taking logarithms of both sides of equation (4), we obtain

$$\ln M = \alpha + \beta \ln Y + \gamma \ln P + \lambda \ln(T \cdot R), \tag{5}$$

where $\alpha = \ln a$. With the addition of a random error term, this equation represents the model that was used by Bell Canada in the Interexchange (IX) Hearings before the CRTC. The model was applied to four toll markets in Ontario and Quebec using quarterly data for the period 1974Q1–1983Q3. The four markets refer to peak/off-peak, short-haul/long-haul.[4]

---

[4] The peak period is defined as weekdays 8am–6pm, off-peak as all other hours. Short-haul is 0–100 miles, while long-haul is greater than 100 miles.

The results for the four models are presented in Table 1. The price elasticities are seen to lie in a range of -0.324 (sum of price 1 + price 2) for off-peak short-haul to -0.370 for peak long-haul, while the elasticities for market size vary 0.829 for peak long-haul to 1.158 for off-peak short-haul. Income elasticities vary between 0.469 for off-peak long-haul to 0.640 for short-haul peak.

In light of results presented in the 1980 book, these results seem reasonable. The price elasticities are somewhat smaller than counterparts in the U.S., but not unduly so. Also, not unreasonably the elasticities with respect to potential toll connections are generally of the order of 1. The equations were scarcely out of the computer, however, before controversy swirled. CNCP, the petitioner in the IX Hearing, challenged the validity of Bell's market size variable, arguing that coefficients of the order of 1 on (the logarithm of) potential toll connections imply implausibly large network externalities. Because of the debate that followed is a prime illustration of the pitfalls, trials, and tribulations of econometrics in the hearing room, detailed discussion of the controversy is put off until Chapter 9 and Appendix 3. For now, I will simply note that when the coefficient for market size is constrained to a value considered plausible by CNCP, the price elasticities increase substantially, to values in excess of 1 (in absolute value).

II. Point-to-point Toll Demand

Competition in the interLATA market has quite naturally stirred interest in disaggregation and the development of toll demand models that are route-specific. We now turn to two recent studies that are at the forefront of point-to-point modeling. The first was completed by Southwestern Bell in 1985, while the second is from an on-going study at Telcom Canada that was started in early 1987. The model of the preceding section provides a convenient vehicle for organizing the discussion.

As before, the concern is with two areas, A and B, that are not part of the same local-calling area. Let Q_{AB} denote calls from A to B, Y_A income in A, P_{AB} the price from A to B, T_A the telephones in A, and T_B the telephones in B. With this notation, the model of the preceding section becomes

$$\ln Q_{AB} = \alpha_0 + \alpha_1 \ln Y_A + \alpha_2 \ln P_{AB} + \alpha_3 (\ln T_A \cdot T_B). \tag{6}$$

We now make two modifications to this model. The first is to allow for telephones in the sending and receiving areas to have different elasticities, while the second modification is to allow for a "reverse-traffic" effect whereby calling from A to B is affected by the volume of traffic from B to A. Expression

TABLE 1

Bell Canada Bell-Intra models double logarithmic (t-ratios in parentheses)

Variable	Peak		Off-Peak	
	0–100 Miles	101+ Miles	0–100 Miles	101+ Miles
Constant	-29.525	-22.828	-33.291	-27.893
	(-19.29)	(-7.66)	(-14.36)	(-9.46)
Q1 Seasonal	0.031	0.033	0.020	0.047
	(3.69)	(4.33)	(1.77)	(2.09)
Q2 Seasonal	0.077	0.061	-0.002	-0.039
	(11.40)	(8.71)	(-0.26)	(-3.94)
Q3 Seasonal	0.092	0.072	-0.032	-0.064
	(12.70)	(7.77)	(-3.23)	(-4.91)
Price*	-0.282	-0.370	-0.265	-0.354
	(-4.96)	(-3.74)	(-3.40)	(-3.99)
Price 2**	–	–	-0.059	-0.036
			(-4.82)	(-2.35)
Income*	0.640	0.547	0.635	0.469
	(8.4)	(6.96)	(6.28)	(5.51)
Market Size	1.025	0.829	1.158	1.043
	(88.71)	(13.13)	(40.35)	(16.57)
Spike Dummy, 1980 Q1	0.024	0.040	–	–
	(2.30)	(3.13)		
Step Dummy, 1976 Q4	–	0.022	–	0.042
		(2.41)		(3.03)
$\bar{R}^2$	0.998	0.997	0.997	0.996

* Both price and income are represented as polynomial distributed lags.

** Two price variables are included in the off-peak models to take into account a change in the weekend discount structure which occurred in June 1977.

(6) accordingly becomes

$$\ln Q_{AB} = \alpha_0 + \alpha_1 \ln Y_A + \alpha_2 \ln P_{AB} + \alpha_3 \ln T_B$$
$$+ \alpha_4 \ln T_A + \alpha_5 \ln Q_{BA}. \tag{7}$$

As the reverse-traffic effect is reciprocal, there will also be an equation for the traffic from B to A:

$$\ln Q_{BA} = \beta_0 + \beta_1 \ln Y_B + \beta_2 \ln P_{BA} + \beta_3 \ln T_B$$
$$+ \beta_4 \ln T_A + \beta_5 \ln Q_{AB}. \tag{8}$$

These two equations form a simultaneous system and must be estimated jointly.

Larson, Lehman, and Weisman (1990), who were the first to formulate a model incorporating reverse calling, rationalize the phenomenon in terms of implicit contracts, that if I call you today, then tomorrow it is your turn to call me.[5] Among other things, the effect of this is to internalize over a period of time the benefits that a calling party confers on the party called. Larson, Lehman, and Weisman (LLW) estimated their model using city-pair data from Southwestern Bell's service area. The data are quarterly time-series for the period 1977Q1 through 1983Q3. Nine city pairs are analyzed. The city pairs were defined *a priori* and for the most part were selected on a natural community-of-interest based on nearness, with each pair being defined in terms of a larger city and a smaller city. The larger cities are designated as points A and the smaller cities as points B. The nine city pairs thus form 18 routes to be analyzed, 9 AB routes and 9 BA routes.

The two-equation model estimated by LLW is as follows:

$$\ln Q_{it} = \alpha_0 + \sum_{j=1}^{g} \alpha_i \delta_{ij} + \sum_{j=0}^{h} \beta_j \ln P_{it-j} + \sum_{j=0}^{1} \gamma_j \ln Y_{t-j}$$
$$+ \lambda \ln POP_t + \xi \ln Q_{it}^* + u_{it} \tag{9}$$

$$\ln Q_{it}^* = a_0 + \sum_{j=1}^{g} a_i \delta_{ij} + \sum_{j=0}^{m} b_j \ln P_{it-j} + \sum_{j=0}^{n} c_i \ln Y_{t-j}$$
$$+ d \ln POP_t + e \ln Q_{it} + v_{it}, \tag{10}$$

where:

Q_i = Total minutes of intraLATA long-distance traffic between the ith AB city pair. Traffic refers to DDD calls only, aggregated over a rate periods, that originate in city A and terminate in city B.

Q_i^* is defined similarly and represents the reverse traffic B to A.

---
[5] See also Larson and Lehman (1986).

P_i = Real price of an interLATA toll call on the ith route. Defined as a fixed-weight Laspeyres price index, expressed as average revenue per minute, and deflated by the appropriate state or SMSA CPI.

Y_i = Real per-capita personal income in the originating city. Derived from county-level wages and salaries disbursements data.

POP = Market size defined as the product of the population in city A and the population in city B.

δ_{ij} = 1 for $i = j$, 0 otherwise.

The models were estimated with pooled data for the nine city pairs by two-stage least-squares. The error terms u and v are assumed to be homoscedastic within a route, but heteroscedastic across routes. Contemporaneous covariance across routes is allowed for, as in first-order autocorrelation within routes. Finally, it is assumed that $E(u_{it}v_{jt'} = 0$ for all i, j, t, and t'. Estimation proceeded as follows:[6] To begin with, reduced-form equations were estimated using LSDV, corrected for autocorrelation and heteroscedasticity and tested for functional form (Box-Cox format). Fitted values from these equations were then used in direct 2SLS estimation of the structural equations. The 2SLS residuals were tested for autocorrelation and heteroscedasticity, and the structural equations were re-estimated with appropriate corrections for autocorrelation and heteroscedasticity and then tested for the correct functional form. Final estimation of the structural equations was performed by LSDV (using the initial fitted values for the endogenous variables) with an additional correction for contemporaneous covariances (across routes, but not across equations).

The empirical results are given in Tables 2 and 3. Table 2 contains the estimated coefficients and summary statistics for both AB and BA routes,[7] while Table 3 presents the long-run flow-through (i.e., reduced-form) price and income elasticities. These flow-through elasticities measure the full effects of price and income changes, including the feedbacks through reverse traffic. From Table 2, we see that reverse-traffic effects are strong, with elasticities of 0.75 and 0.67 and large t-ratios to match. From Table 3, we see that the flow-through elasticities are -0.75 for price and about 0.5 for income. Market size was excluded from the AB equation because of a low t-ratio.

---

[6] Full details of the estimation are given in Larson (1988).

[7] Although significant as groups in both equations, the route-specific intercepts are not tabulated. Also, only the sum of the distributed-lag coefficients for price and income are presented.

TABLE 2

Point-to-point model of Larson, Lehman, and Weisman (*t*-ratios in parentheses)

Variable	$\ln Q$ (AB routes)	$\ln Q^*$ (BA routes)
$\ln P$	-0.18	-0.26
	(-3.3)	(-3.5)
$\ln Y$	0.27	0.23
	(3.3)	(2.0)
lnPOP	–	0.30
		(2.4)
$\ln Q$	–	0.67
		(7.2)
$\ln Q^*$	0.75	–
	(15.6)	
$\bar{R}^2$	0.990	0.987

Note: The coefficients for $\ln P$ and $\ln Y$ represent
the sum of the distributed-lag coefficients.
Source: Larson, Lehman, and Weisman (1990,
Tables 3–4)

In view of the earlier discussion which identified market size with potential toll connections, this could reflect a problem with population as a proxy for lines.[8]

The LLW study is a pioneering effort, and is accordingly subject to the usual problems of something being cut from whole cloth with only a vague pattern for guidance. The use of per-capita income while the dependent variable is not per-capita is questionable, and almost certainly confuses the elasticities for market size and probably for income as well. There may also be a problem in constraining the elasticities for the sizes of the two calling areas to be equal. Such a constraint makes sense when calling between the two areas is aggregated, but probably not when the model is directional and feedback from reverse traffic are allowed for. In this case, separate elasticities for the two market sizes are in order. Traffic from the sending

[8] An alternative explanation, to be discussed below, is in the constraint that is implicitly imposed on the population in A by income, but not the dependent variable, being per-capita.

TABLE 3

Flow-through price & income elasticities;
Larson-Lehman-Weisman study

Elasticity	AB Routes	BA Routes
Price	-0.75	-0.76
Income	0.54	0.46

Source: Larson, Lehman, and Weisman
(1990, p. 312)

area will continue to depend upon the number of telephones in that area, but the reverse-traffic variable will probably swamp the effect of the number of telephones in the receiving area, if for no other reason than it is a better proxy for the community of interest.[9] As noted above, the use of population as a proxy for the number of telephones may be a problem as well.

The final question regarding the LLW study concerns the choice of routes for analysis. LLW chose the routes, in terms of a large-city/small-city pairing, on an *a priori* basis. This was reasonable in the circumstances, but the question emerges of whether the results might depend upon the particular routes selected. All routes should in principle be encompassed, but organizing the requisite data set was considered too costly to undertake. Consequently, whether an alternative grouping of city pairs might lead to different results, especially as regards the price and income elasticities, remains an open question.

These criticisms in no way undermine LLW's central result, namely, that calls tend to generate calls in return that are independent of price and income. This result is statistically strong, and I am confident it would be robust with respect to the respecifications that would be needed to take the criticisms into account. Clearly, the reverse-calling phenomenon is most relevant in situations in which the same telephone company does not serve both directions of a route. In this situation, a decrease in the price on the AB route will lead to a stimulation of the traffic on the BA route in the absence of a price change on that route. Failure to take this into account could lead to serious biases in estimates of price elasticities.

Let me now turn to the point-to-point models that have been developed by

---

[9]   We will return to this point in Chapter 9.

Telecom Canada (Appelbe *et al.* 1988).[10] Two models have been constructed, one analyzing interprovincial toll traffic and the other analyzing calling
between Canada and the U.S. The models have a common structure and take
their cue from the Larson-Lehman-Weisman model in that bi-directional traffic is modeled in a two-equation pooled time-series/cross-section format that
allows for the influence of reverse traffic.

The model used by Telecom Canada is as follows:

$$\ln Q_A = a_0 + a_1 \ln P_A + a_2 \ln I_A + a_3 \ln M_A + a_4 \ln X_A$$
$$+ a_5 \ln Q_B + u_A \tag{11}$$

$$\ln Q_B = b_0 + b_1 \ln P_B + b_2 \ln I_B + b_3 \ln M_B + b_4 \ln X_B$$
$$+ b_5 \ln Q_A + u_B, \tag{12}$$

where:

Q_A = demand from A to B

P_A = real price from A to B

I_A = real income (or level of economic activity in A)

X_A = other factors in A (postal strike, seasonals, etc.)

u_A = error term in A.

$Q_B, P_B, I_B, X_B,$ and u_B are similarly defined for B.

The model in equations (11) and (12) differs from the LLW model in two
important respects: (1) income (or the level of economic activity) appears as
total income rather than income per capita and (2) market size is represented
by the number of network access lines in the sending area only rather than by
potential toll connections. The analyses also differ in the levels of aggregation. In the LLW analysis, A and B are defined in terms of city-pairs, while
in the Telecom Canada analyses, they are defined in terms of provinces and
regions.

The interprovincial models are estimated by pooling data for specific pairs
of Telecom Canada member companies. The "points" used in the analysis
are

1. British Columbia Telephone Company (BCT)

[10] Telecom Canada is the consortium of Canadian telephone companies which (except for
calls between Ontario and Quebec) provides interprovincial toll calling.

2. Alberta Government Telephones[11] (AGT)
3. Saskatchewan Telecommunications (SASK)
4. Manitoba Telephone System (MTS)
5. Bell Canada (BELL)
6. Atlantic[12] (ATL)

Routes are defined in terms of calls between pairs of member companies, BCT-BELL and BELL-BCT defines two such routes. All pairs are modeled except for the BCT-AGT link as the data for traffic between these adjacent companies are not available to the Telecom Canada staff.

Models are estimated for three different groupings of routes depending upon length-of-haul and two tariff periods, full-rate and discount. Full-rate applies 8 a.m. to 6 p.m. Monday through Saturday, while the discount period applies 6 p.m. to 8 a.m. Monday through Saturday and all day Sunday. The first grouping of routes consists essentially of adjacent provinces from Manitoba west and has a majority of calls under 750 miles, with an average length-of-haul of about 450 miles. Group 2 has a majority of calls between 750 and 1600 miles, with an average length-of-haul of about 850 miles. Finally, the majority of the third grouping's calls are greater than 1600 miles in length-of-haul, with an average of about 2100 miles. Group 1 includes eight routes, while group 2 and 3 each contain ten.

The interprovincial models are estimated with quarterly data, 1977Q1–1986Q4, pooled across routes. Estimation is by essentially the same TSLS iterative maximum-likelihood procedure as used by LLW, except that contemporaneous covariances across equations are allowed for as well as across routes. The models allow for different elasticities on market size across routes; they also allow for route-specific patterns in a LSDV format. Unlike the LLW model, however, coefficients on like variables across equations are constrained to be equal – i.e., elasticities for B to A are assumed to be the same as for A to B.

The results for the interprovincial models are summarized in Table 4. Both uni-directional and bi-directional elasticities are presented, as is also the coefficient for reciprocal calling.[13] The uni-directional elasticities assume that price or income changes in the sending area only, while the bi-directional elasticities assume that price or income changes by the same proportion in the receiving area as well. The bi-directional elasticities accordingly correspond to the elasticities that are obtained in models in which the directional traffic

---

[11] Includes all calls originating and terminating in Edmonton Telephone Company.

[12] Atlantic comprises the New Brunswick Telephone Company; Maritime Telegraph and Telephone Company; the Island Telephone Company; Newfoundland Telephone Company.

[13] Since they vary across routes, the market size elasticities are omitted.

TABLE 4

Telecom Canada models price and income elasticities Canada–Canada (*t*-ratios in parentheses)

| | Price | | Income | | |
| | Uni- | Bi- | Uni- | Bi- | Reverse Traffic |
Model	Directional	Directional	Directional	Directional	Coefficient
Group 1	-0.21	-0.36	0.33	0.57	0.72
	(-2.49)	(-2.51)	(3.67)	(3.66)	(26.38)
Group 2	-0.35	-0.48	0.39	0.54	0.38
	(-5.38)	(-5.58)	(5.00)	(4.88)	(11.53)
Group 3	-0.48	-0.73	0.62	0.95	0.53
	(-5.27)	(-5.36)	(4.57)	(4.43)	(14.80)
Discount Rate:					
Group 1	-0.39	-0.59	0.23	0.35	0.50
	(-6.63)	(-6.56)	(3.83)	(3.66)	(13.61)
Group 2	-0.48	-0.70	0.54	0.79	0.46
	(-12.60)	(-13.04)	(11.41)	(10.63)	(15.98)
Group 3	-0.49	-0.75	0.29	0.44	0.53
	(-5.72)	(-5.76)	(4.30)	4.17)	(17.58)

Source: Appelbe *et al.* (1988, Tables 1–6)

on a route is aggregated.

In Table 4, we see that, as in the LLW model, reverse traffic is strong statistically, with elasticities that range from 0.38 to 0.72. Price elasticities, when reverse traffic is taken into account, range from -0.21 to about -0.49 for the uni-directional elasticities and from -0.36 to -0.75 for the bi-directional elasticities. As usual, the price elasticities increase (in absolute value) with average length-of-haul in both tariff periods, and the bi-directional elasticities are in general about a third larger than the uni-directional elasticities. The income elasticities are less than one in all of the models.

The Telecom Canada Canada-U.S. models have the same basic structure as the interprovincial models, but they differ in that estimation is restricted to the one-way traffic from Canada to the U.S. U.S.-to-Canada equations are specified, but figure only in estimation of the reduced forms for the Canada-U.S. equations. Canada-U.S. equations are not themselves estimated. Routes are defined in terms of traffic from six member companies of Telecom Canada (as defined in the interprovincial models) and four broad census regions in the U.S., West, North Central, North East, and South. Of the 24 routes that this defines, only 10 are modeled. These 10 routes represent about 87% of 1986 Telecom Canada's Canada-U.S. revenues.

As in the interprovincial analysis, routes are grouped according to average length-of-haul. Two groupings are defined. The first group consists of four routes, the majority of whose calls are less than 800 miles and an average length-of-haul of about 300 miles. The second group consists of six routes, the majority of whose calls are greater than 800 miles and an average length-of-haul of about 1150 miles. Both full-fare and discount period models are estimated. Two different measures of economic activity are used in the first grouping, employment for Manitoba and exports for the other member companies. Employment is used exclusively in the second grouping. Both economic activity and market size are allowed to have different coefficients across routes within a grouping. Finally, it will be noted that a travel variable which measures the number of Canadians traveling to the U.S. South in the winter months appears as a predictor in the discount equation for the second grouping.

The empirical results for the Canada-U.S. models are tabulated in Table 5.[14] Since only Canada-U.S. models are estimated, only uni-directional elasticities are calculated. The elasticities reflect changes in U.S. calling to Canada that are caused by changes in Canadian rates, but they are net of any changes in U.S. rates. The price elasticities follow the same general pattern as the Canada-Canada elasticities – slightly larger for discount-rate and for calls of longer haul. The elasticities for the level of economic activity display considerably more variation and clearly depend upon the measure of economic activity that is used, employment or exports. All are less than one.

The Canada-U.S. results once again confirm the existence of a strong reverse-traffic effect, suggesting that each 1% increase in U.S.-Canada calling (for whatever reason) leads to about a 0.4% stimulation to Canada-U.S. calling. The shorter haul discount-period routes are the only exception. The reverse-traffic effect is still strong statistically, but the elasticity is much smaller.

III. The Demand for Interstate Access Minutes

As noted earlier, in separating AT&T and the Bell operating companies the divestiture created a "market" for access to the toll network. I put market in quotation marks, because really what is represented is an interface between

---

[14] Income and market-size elasticities are omitted.

TABLE 5

Telecom Canada models Canada–U.S. (*t*-ratios in parentheses)

Model	Uni-Directional Price Elasticity	Reverse-Traffic Coefficient
Full-Rate:		
Group 1	-0.43	0.42
	(-8.77)	(4.91)
Group 2	-0.49	0.47
	(-4.58)	(7.17)
Discount-Rate:		
Group 1	-0.45	0.24
	(-5.62)	(4.86)
Group 2	-0.53	0.40
	(-7.93)	(11.12)

Source: Appelbe *et al.* (1988, Tables 7–10)

local networks (which the divestiture left as monopoly domains of the LECs) and a set of competing connecting toll routes (or trunks). Access in this context is usually taken to mean access to the toll network from the local network, but since every call has a receiving end as well as a sending end, access also means access to local networks from the toll network.

For a sender of a toll call, both forms of access are obviously necessary because a toll necessarily originates in one local network and terminates in another. There are accordingly two "gates" that have to be gone through, and under the original FCC rules,[15] passage through each gate was charged for on a real-time basis. Since most of these charges consisted of recovery of the joint and common costs of local plant and equipment that are allocated to toll usage, and since the amounts to be recovered are nontraffic-sensitive but are recovered on a traffic-sensitive basis, the per-minute charges have to be recalculated annually for use during the year ahead. These are determined in annual proceedings before the FCC.

The model to be described next (Gatto, Langin-Hooper, Robinson, and Tyon 1988) was developed at AT&T using data on Carrier Common Lines (CCL) demand that has been submitted to the FCC by the LECs as part of

---

[15] The reference here is to interstate calls.

the Annual Access Tariff Filings.[16] The model is a pooled time-series/cross-section model that relates the minutes-of-use (MOU) of interstate switched access to the price of a unit of MOU, the level of income, population, and the price of all other goods, as measured by the CPI. In addition to these factors, the model also includes variables or adjustments which capture the effects that regulatory and structural changes have had on CCL demand.[17]

The data set used in estimation consists of monthly observations for the 48 contiguous states plus the District of Columbia for the 36-month period July 1984 through June 1987. The dependent variable in the model is the logarithm of monthly CCL MOU for a state, adjusted for state-level resold WATS MOU. Independent variables include state-specific intercepts, the logarithm of a composite service-weighted AT&T, AT&T WATS, and OCC price index for a state deflated by a state-specific CPI, the logarithm of state-specific disposable personal income deflated by the state-specific CPI and total population, the logarithm of population, a dummy variable that captures the impact of the direct assignment of WATS to specific access starting in June 1986 (WATDA) and a variable that accounts for the transition from non-measured to measured local service starting in September 1985 (MDUM). Polynomical distributed lags are specified on price and income. Estimation is by LSDV, with corrections for within-state first-order autocorrelation and across-state heteroscedasticity. All coefficients are constrained to be equal across states, except for the WATS direct-assignment variable (WATDA).

The results are tabulated in Table 6. The long-run price and income elasticities are seen to be -0.723 and 0.827. Both estimates are highly significant statistically. All of the state-specific intercepts are highly significant, as are most of the state-specific coefficients on the WATS direct-assignment variable.

Although it might not be apparent at first glance, the model in Table 6 has essentially the same form as the Bell-Intra model discussed in Section II of this chapter. That this is the case can be seen by rewriting the model (ignoring the state-specific intercepts, MDUM, and WATDA and using an obvious notation) as:

$$\ln Q = \alpha + \beta \ln(Y/\text{POP}) + \gamma \ln P + \xi \ln \text{POP}$$

$$= \alpha + \beta \ln Y + \gamma \ln P + (\xi - \beta) \ln \text{POP}, \qquad (13)$$

which is the same as expression (5), except for $\ln \text{POP}$ in place of $\ln(T \cdot R)$. $T \cdot R$, it will be recalled, represents the number of potential toll connections,

---

[16] This model has been updated several times, most recently in 1990.

[17] One such adjustment takes into account the direct assignment, effective June 1, 1986, of the closed end of WATS calls, which caused a precipitous drop in recorded CCL demand. For other adjustments, see Gatto *et al.* (1988, pp. 340–341).

TABLE 6

All state pooled PDL model for interstate access minutes

	Long-Run Elasticity	t-Ratio		
Price	-0.723	-17.744		
Income	0.827	5.006		
POP	1.208	3.918		
MDUM	-0.002	-0.295		

State	Intercept	t-Ratio	WATDA	t-Ratio
AL	8.594	18.731	-0.086	-4.941
AR	8.703	24.824	-0.136	-7.805
AZ	9.086	21.276	-0.103	-3.784
CA	8.008	8.163	-0.154	-8.536
CO	9.163	20.690	-0.151	-5.605
CT	9.060	19.741	-0.185	-7.578
DC	10.321	22.212	-0.208	-4.738
DE	9.710	22.812	-0.128	2.798
FL	8.752	11.809	-0.089	-2.112
GA	8.831	15.632	-0.199	-12.542
IA	8.614	21.182	-0.056	-1.152
ID	9.318	28.637	-0.155	-2.852
IL	8.411	11.266	-0.166	-12.894
IN	8.551	15.685	-0.135	-7.930
KS	8.718	22.367	-0.115	-6.892
KY	8.412	18.981	-0.050	-2.385
LA	8.575	17.519	-0.060	-3.462
MA	8.814	15.316	-0.120	-6.734
MD	8.685	16.942	-0.037	-1.552
ME	8.899	27.655	-0.090	-1.782
MI	8.211	12.064	-0.101	-4.007
MN	8.492	17.304	-0.177	-3.899
MO	8.622	16.323	-0.199	-8.295
MS	8.827	24.899	-0.032	-1.569
MT	9.081	26.801	-0.202	-3.798
NC	8.511	14.861	-0.113	-4.791
ND	9.021	23.428	-0.064	-1.680
NE	8.983	26.258	-0.191	-4.879

Table 6 (continued)

State	Intercept	t-Ratio	WATDA	t-Ratio
NH	9.411	25.801	-0.075	-3.492
NJ	8.987	13.966	-0.133	-7.534
NM	9.144	29.264	-0.067	-1.341
NV	9.584	25.551	-0.122	-8.139
NY	8.503	9.801	-0.121	-8.835
OH	8.343	11.548	-0.165	-7.492
OK	8.751	20.147	-0.106	-5.281
OR	8.910	22.218	-0.135	-2.796
PA	8.431	11.229	-0.111	-5.710
RI	9.264	25.734	-0.036	-0.840
SC	8.644	20.720	-0.068	-3.159
SD	9.136	24.811	-0.161	-3.324
TN	8.797	17.500	-0.160	-7.342
TX	8.217	9.771	-0.080	-5.363
UT	9.164	29.085	-0.163	-2.873
VA	8.683	15.397	-0.083	-2.621
VT	9.411	22.096	-0.013	-0.407
WA	8.673	17.200	-0.119	-3.951
WI	8.359	16.236	-0.077	-3.529
WV	8.775	27.237	-0.029	-0.594
WY	9.547	21.068	-0.105	-2.933

Source: Gatto *et al.* (1988, Table 1)

which in a closed system is essentially $T \cdot T$, so that $\ln(T \cdot R) = 2 \ln T$. Since telephones and the population are highly correlated, $\xi - \beta$ in expression (13) will equal 2λ in expression (5). From the top of Table 6, we see that the estimate of $\xi - \beta$ is 2.035, which (given that λ should be of the order of 1) is within the range we should expect.

IV. THE DEMAND FOR BYPASS OF THE LEC

Earlier, it was noted that recovery of nontraffic-sensitive local plant and equipment costs that are allocated to the toll market through usage-sensitive access charges provides incentive for large toll users to connect directly with their IX carriers, and thereby avoid the per-minute access charges. We now turn to a study undertaken at Southwestern Bell (Watters and Grandstaff 1988) which provides some evidence on the elasticities involved. Watters and Grandstaff postulate a model in which the demand for access minutes is derived from end-users' demand for switched services sold by interexchange carriers.

The vantage point for the analysis is the IX carriers. Carriers are assumed to be cost minimizers and to have a demand for access minutes that depends upon their (exogenously given) outputs. The demand for switched access minutes is then derived, using Shepherd's lemma, from an IX carrier's cost function. A translog cost function is assumed. Access can be either switched, for which per-minute access charges are incurred, or special, for which per-minute access charges are avoided. Total access minutes consists of the sum of switched originating and terminating minutes plus the minutes (both originating and terminating) that funnel through special access.

The access-minutes demand functions, expressed as shares, estimated by Watters and Grandstaff are as follows:

$$\frac{P_0 Q_0}{C} = \alpha_0 + \alpha_1 \ln P_0 + \alpha_2 \ln P_T + \alpha_3 \ln P_d + \alpha_4 \ln \hat{Q} \qquad (14)$$

$$\frac{P_T Q_T}{C} = \beta_0 + \beta_1 \ln P_0 + \beta_2 \ln P_T + \beta_3 \ln P_d + \beta_4 \ln \hat{Q} \qquad (15)$$

$$\frac{P_d Q_d}{C} = \gamma_0 + \gamma_1 \ln P_0 + \gamma_2 \ln P_T + \gamma_3 \ln P_d + \gamma_4 \ln \hat{Q} \qquad (16)$$

where

$$C = \text{total cost of access}$$
$$= P_0 Q_0 + P_T Q_T + P_d Q_d$$

$P_0 = $ access price for originating switched minutes

$P_T = $ access price for terminating switched minutes

$P_d = $ prices for dedicated (i.e., special) access

$Q_0 = $ originating access minutes

$Q_T = $ terminating access minutes

$Q_d = $ special access channels and mileage

$\hat{Q} = $ estimated output of the IX carriers.

The model is estimated from a pooled time-series/cross-section data set consisting of monthly observations for Southwestern Bell's five states (ARK,

KN, MO, OK, TX) for the period March 1985 through September 1987. The usual homogeneity, adding-up, and symmetry restrictions are imposed in estimation, which is by least-square-dummy-variables.[18]

The estimated elasticities obtained by Watters and Grandstaff are tabulated in Table 7. Both partial and full elasticities are presented. Partial elasticities hold output of the IX carriers [$\hat{Q}$ in equations (14), (15), and (16)] constant, while full elasticities allow carriers' output to vary. Watters and Grandstaff use a value of -0.47 for the interstate toll elasticity.[19] Two comments are in order about the results: (1) the own-price elasticity for originating switched access minutes differs from the elasticity for terminating switched access minutes [0.08 vs. (an insignificant) 0.02] and (2) there are significant cross-price elasticities between switched and dedicated access. Note, too, that the full elasticity for originating access minutes is estimated to be about double its value for terminating access minutes. This is not surprising, because toll calling is clearly much more concentrated at the sending end of a call than at the receiving end, so that bypass is much more likely to occur at the sending end.

V. WRAP-UP

The important innovations in my view in the modeling of toll demand during the 1980s were a reinterpretation of the market-size variable that was a standard predictor in toll demand models in the 1970s in terms of potential toll connections and the estimation of bi-directional point-to-point models that allow for call-back (or reverse-traffic) effects. These innovations feature prominently in the Larson-Lehman-Weisman, Bell Canada, and Telecom Canada studies. The study of Gatto *et al.*, whose model is essentially the same as Bell Canada's Bell-Intra model, is of interest because, among other things, it is only one of two national-in-scope studies of U.S. toll demand [Gatto, Kelejian, and Stephan (1988) being the other] that reached the open literature. Since the data in this study refer to interstate MTS minutes, it is of considerable significance that the long-run price elasticity that is obtained is -0.72, which is in keeping with the *long-haul* values that were thought to hold at the time of the 1980 book.

The Watters-Grandstaff study is of interest because it is one of the few attempts to quantify the effects on switched access to the toll networks of the

---

[18] Estimation of the model requires estimates of the IX carriers' output, $\hat{Q}$. See Watters and Grandstaff (1988, pp. 6–7) for a description of how these were devised.

[19] See Watters and Grandstaff (1988, p. 11). It would have been preferable in my view, to have used a value closer to the estimate of -0.72 from the access-minute model of Gatto *et al.*

TABLE 7

Price elasticities for switched and dedicated access; Watters and Grand-staff study

| | Partial Elasticities | | |
	O	T	D
O	-0.7780*	0.0107	-0.0350
T	0.0829*	0.0222	0.1018*
D	-0.0223	-0.0679	-0.1459
	Full Elasticities**		
	O	T	D
O	-0.17	-0.09	-0.04
T	-0.004	-0.09	0.06
D	-0.09	-0.09	-0.04

* Share elasticity significantly differs from the value that would correspond to elasticy of 0 at mean share.

** Only the partial elasticities significantly different from 0 are used; otherwise a value of 0 is used for the partial elasticity.
Full elasticities assume a value of –0.47 for the price elasticity for IX carriers' output.

Source: Watters and Grandstaff (1988, Tables 2–3)

divestiture-induced usage-sensitive access charges. Their results show small, yet statistically significant, own- and cross-price elasticities for originating switched access and dedicated (or special) access. Since volume must be considerable for special access to pay, the price elasticities for high-volume toll users are obviously much larger than the values shown by Watters and Grandstaff.

In closing this chapter, it should be noted that the study of Train, McFadden, and Ben-Akiva (1987) discussed in the preceding chapter also provides important information concerning short-haul toll price elasticities. The toll price elasticity obtained (through simulation) by TMB is -0.47. As the data set from which this estimate is derived is post-divestiture, this estimate refers to an intraLATA elasticity.[20]

[20] See also Train, Ben-Akiva, and Atherton (1989).

CHAPTER 7

THE DEMAND FOR LOCAL CALLS AND RELATED LOCAL SERVICES

This chapter returns to the local market, but the focus will shift from access *per se* to some of the services that are supplied by local exchange companies. The services to be examined include local calling, Extended Area Service (EAS), and custom calling features such as call-forwarding and call-waiting. Four studies will be reviewed in detail, Kling and Van der Ploeg (1990), Kridel (1990), Park, Wetzel, and Mitchell (1983), and Kridel and Taylor (1993). Kling and Van der Ploeg focus on the residential demand for local calls in an environment in which customers can choose between flat- and measured-rate service. The model is estimated with data obtained in a Subscriber Line Utilization Study in an exchange served by Michigan Bell. Kridel, on the other hand, is concerned with estimating the proportion of residential customers that will subscribe to Extended Area Service in situations where EAS was not previously available. Park, Wetzell, and Mitchell utilize data from the well-known GTE measured-service experiment involving three exchanges in central Illinois. Finally, the Kridel-Taylor study provides a glimpse, based on the initial results of the National Telecommunications Demand Study,[1] at price elasticities for a variety of custom-calling options.

I. LOCAL CALLING AND THE CHOICE BETWEEN FLAT-RATE AND MEASURED SERVICE

By the mid-1970s, it was clear that incipient intercity toll competition posed a serious threat to the toll-to-local subsidy, and telephone companies began looking for ways to soften the inevitable upward pressure on local-service charges. One of the ways considered was measured local service, whereby

---

[1] The National Telecommunications Demand Study is an on-going study of the demand for the services provided by local telephone companies and is a joint undertaking of INDETEC, Inc. of Del Mar, CA. and PNR & Associates of Jenkintown, PA, and myself in collaboration with a consortium of telephone companies and others. The motivation and format of the study is described in Chapter 11.

149

local calls would be charged for, albeit at much lower rates, in the same manner as toll calls. However, as experience nationwide with measured local service was extremely limited, little information was available concerning the effects on call repression of a shift from flat-rate to measured service.

One of the first attempts to quantify these expressions effects was in the study of Carl Pavarini that is discussed in Appendix 1 (Pavarini 1978). Pavarini analyzed data that were collected in connection with the conversion to measured service of customers in several exchanges in metropolitan Denver that had been subscribers to an optional extended area service. One of the things to be contended with in modeling the demand for local calls under flat-rate local service is the fact that, despite the fact that local calls are "free", demand is always finite. Pavarini dealt with this by treating a household's volume of local calling as a random variable whose mean was changed (presumably reduced) by the introduction of a non-zero price for a local call. Subsequent work at Bell Laboratories by Mary Shugard, Mark Hoffberg, and others integrated Pavarini's notion of a satiation level of local calling into a utility framework by viewing the satiation level of calling as a parameter of the utility function.[2] In the study to be reviewed in this section, Kling and Van der Ploeg (1990) reformulate the Bell Laboratories approach in the access/usage consumer's-surplus framework that was discussed in Chapter 2.

The point of departure for Kling and Van der Ploeg – hereafter KP – is to assume a semi-logarithmic demand function for the demand for local calls:

$$q_i = \theta_i \exp(\beta p), \tag{1}$$

where:

q_i = local calls demanded by the ith household

θ_i = unrepressed (i.e., satiation) usage for the i household

β = price response

p = marginal price of a local call.

A semi-logarithmic function is postulated because, unlike for a double-logarithmic function, it is defined at $p = 0$ and therefore allows for a satiation level of usage under flat-rate service, namely, θ_i.[3]

With income and demographics taken into account, the demand function becomes:

$$q_i = \theta_i \exp(\alpha x + y^\gamma \beta p), \tag{2}$$

---

[2] See Shugard (1979), Infosino (1980), Hoffberg and Shugard (1981), and Shugard (1982).

[3] Cf. the demand function as described in Chapter 5, employed by Perl (1983) and Taylor and Kridel (1990).

where y denotes income and x denotes (possibly a vector of) demographic factors. By including income as a non-linear multiplicative term with the marginal price, it is assumed that income affects local calling only through the price response. The level of income does not affect the level of satiation usage, but it does affect the sharpness with which the household responds to a non-zero price for local calls.[4]

Let us now assume that households have a choice between flat-rate service at a fixed monthly fee of P_f or measured service at a fixed monthly fee of P_m and a price per unit of usage of p. The consumer surplus under flat-rate service will be[5]

$$S_i^f = \int_0^\infty \theta_i \exp(\beta p) \, dp - P_f = -\frac{\theta_i}{\beta} - P_f. \tag{3}$$

The consumer surplus under measured service will be

$$S_i^m = \int_{P_m}^\infty \theta_i \exp(\beta p) \, dp - P_m = -\frac{\theta_i}{\beta} \exp(\beta P_m) - P_m. \tag{4}$$

The difference in consumer surplus between measured and flat-rate service is accordingly:

$$S_i^m - S_i^f = \frac{1}{\beta}(\theta_i - q_{im}) + (P_f - P_m), \tag{5}$$

where $q_{im} = \theta_i \exp(\beta P_m)$ denotes the level of local usage under measured service. Expression (5) shows that the choice of service depends upon three factors:

1. the difference between usage levels under flat-rate and measured service,
2. the difference between fixed monthly fees of the two services, and
3. the price coefficient β.

KP next considers the implications for choice-of-service when (as is typically the case) the measured option includes a local call allowance. In Michigan during the time that the data analyzed by KP were collected, subscribers to measured service were allowed \$3.10 in local calls a month (50 calls), while calls beyond 50 were charged at a rate of \$0.052 per call. Measured service with a call allowance can thus be viewed as a mixture of pure measured service and flat-rate service.

---

[4] Specifically, KP shows that, assuming decreasing marginal utility of income, that the price response to measured service will be weaker for high-income households than for low-income households.

[5] We will now assume that αx is absorbed into θ_i.

The difference in consumer surplus between measured and flat-rate service when the measured option includes a call allowance is calculated as follows:

$$S_i^m - S_i^f = \frac{1}{\beta}(\theta_i - q_i) + (P_f - P_m) + p_i^* A, \tag{6}$$

where q_i denotes the local usage demanded under measured service, A represents the usage allowance, and p_i^* denotes the household's valuation of each unit of the allowance. p_i^* can be interpreted as the call price that would cause the customer to choose the call allowance volume of usage, and can be obtained from the demand equation as:

$$p_i^* = \ln(A/\theta_i)/\beta. \tag{7}$$

The first-term on the right-hand side of expression (6) represents the consumer surplus that is lost in the reduction of local usage from θ_i under flat-rate service to q_i under measured service. The second term represents the gain in consumer surplus that arises from the difference in the fixed monthly fees of the two services. Finally, the third term measures the value to the customer of the call allowance.

Expression (6) can generate three different cases. The first case arises when the call allowance A exceeds the consumer's unrepressed (or satiation) call volume – i.e., $A > \theta_i$ – as shown (for a linear demand function) in Figure 1. In this case, the difference in consumer surplus between the two services is simply the difference in the fixed monthly fees,

$$S_i^m - S_i^f = P_f - P_m. \tag{8}$$

Since usage with measured service equals the flat-rate usage (i.e., $q_i = \theta_i$), the difference in consumer surplus does not depend upon either the usage level or the value of the call allowance.

The second case arises when the repressed usage under measured service is greater than the call allowance (i.e., $\theta_i > q_i > A$). This case is illustrated in Figure 2. The difference in consumer surplus in this case will be given by:

$$S_i^m - S_i^f = \frac{1}{\beta}(\theta_i - q_i) + (P_f - P_m) + pA. \tag{9}$$

This expression is the same as the general expression in (6) except that the value of the call allowance is determined by the marginal call price.

In the third case, which is illustrated in Figure 3, the call allowance exceeds the repressed usage volume of measured service without a call allowance, but is less than the satiation usage under flat-rate service (i.e., $q_i < A < \theta_i$). In this case, the subjective value of a marginal call p_i^* is less than the market price

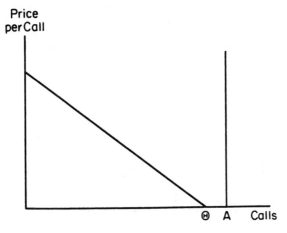

Fig. 1.

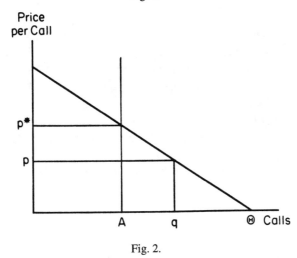

Fig. 2.

of the marginal call p. The contribution of the call allowance to consumer surplus is evaluated at the subjective value of a marginal call, not its market value. The expression for the difference in consumer surplus for this case is given by

$$S_i^m - S_i^f = \frac{1}{\beta}(\theta_i - A) + (P_f - P_m) + p_i^* A. \tag{10}$$

This expression differs from the previous case in the value of the call allowance (p_i^* instead of p) and in the usage-sensitive term (A instead of q_i). Unlike in the first case, the call allowance will necessarily be used up (since A is less than θ_i).

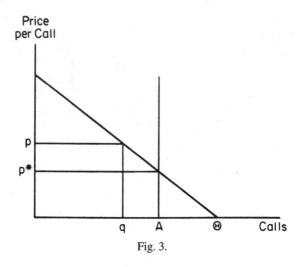

Fig. 3.

KP extended the analysis to include "zone" toll calls, whereby the call allowance under measured service can be extended on either local calls or long-distance calls to a designated zone. With zone calls eligible for the call allowance, the measured-service option becomes a mixture of pure measured service and EAS. With the assumption that the demand function for zone calls has the same semi-logarithmic form as the demand function for local calls, the difference in consumer surplus in this situation can be written as follows:[6]

$$ S^m - S^f \ = \ \frac{1}{\beta}(\theta - q) + \frac{1}{\gamma}(Z_f - Z_m) + (P_f - P_m) $$

$$ + \ \Phi(p_q^* q_A, p_z^* Z_A), \tag{11} $$

where:

$\theta \ = \ $ local usage with flat-rate service

$q \ = \ $ local usage with measured service

$Z_f \ = \ $ zone usage with flat-rate service

$Z_m \ = \ $ zone usage with measured service

$q_A \ = \ $ local usage that could be purchased with the call allowance

$\beta, \gamma \ = \ $ price response coefficients for local and zone usage

$Z_A \ = \ $ zone usage that could be purchased with the call allowance

$p_q^*, p_z^* \ = \ $ household's evaluations of each unit of call allowance

---
[6] The subscript i is suppressed for convenience.

Φ = value of call allowance to consumer.[7]

Expression (11) again allows for a number of cases. In the first case, the call allowance results in the satiation of both local and zone calls. Measured service, in this situation, gives flat-rate characteristics in both types of calls, in contrast to flat-rate service which results in satiation in local, but not zone calls. The difference in consumer surplus for this case would be

$$S^m - S^f = \frac{1}{\gamma}(Z_f - \theta_z) + (P_f - P_m), \tag{12}$$

where θ_z denotes the satiation level of zone usage at a zero price.

The second case is when the consumption of both local and zone calls exceeds the amounts that would be permitted by the call allowance. Zone usage in this case would be the same with measured service as with flat-rate service, so that the difference in consumer surplus will depend upon local usage, the monthly fixed fees, and the value of call allowance:

$$S^m - S^f = \frac{1}{\beta}(\theta - q) + (P_f - P_m) + p_q q_A. \tag{13}$$

Note that since $q > q_A$, the value of the call allowance will be the same for both types of usage and is simply equal to the cash value of the allowance. Consequently, the value of the allowance can be represented by either $p_q q_A$ or $p_z Z_A$.[8]

A third case arises when the amount of local usage permitted by the call allowance is greater than what would be consumed under measured service, but is less than the satiation level under flat-rate service – i.e., $q < q_A < \theta$. Two subcases need to be distinguished, depending upon whether Z_m is greater or less than Z_A. The situation for $Z_m > Z_A$ is illustrated in Figure 4. The key to calculating the value of the call allowance in this situation is to note that, with $Z_m > Z_A$, the fact that $q < q_A$ is irrelevant to the amount of zone usage that will be purchased. Consequently, we can rule out any allocation of the call allowance that involves a division of it between local and zone usage. The only way that the "unused" call allowance can lead to an increase in consumer surplus is for the consumer to increase local usage up to the

---

[7] The KP expression for the difference in consumer surplus writes Φ as $p_q^* q_A^* + p_z^* Z_A^*$, where q_A^* and Z_A^* denote the volumes of local and zone usage that would (as opposed to could) be purchased with measured service. The reason for the reformulation will become clear in the next footnote.

[8] To include both, as KP do would entail double-counting.

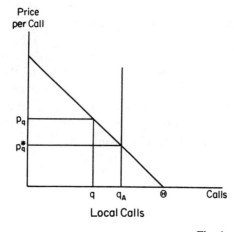

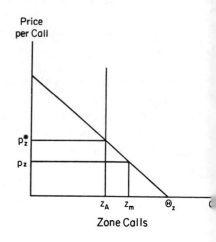

Fig. 4.

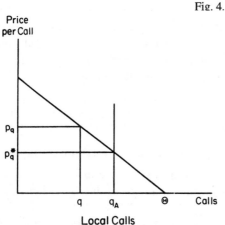

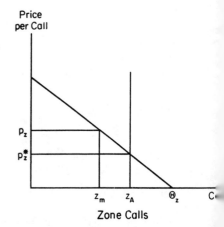

Fig. 5.

level permitted by the allowance. The difference in consumer surplus will accordingly be given by

$$S^m - S^f = \frac{1}{\beta}(\theta - q_A) + (P_f - P_m) + p_q^* q_A. \tag{14}$$

The second subcase, where $Z_m < Z_A < \theta_z$, is illustrated in Figure 5. The key to evaluating this situation is to note that, since $q_A < \theta$ and $Z_A < \theta_z$, the only way that the "unused" allowance can lead to increased consumer surplus is if the allowance is dedicated exclusively to one type of call. If the allowance is used only for local calls, its value will be equal to $p_q^* q_A$, while if it is used only for zone calls, its value will be equal to $p_z^* Z_A$. The difference in consumer surplus will therefore be given by

$$S^m - S^f = \max\{\phi_q, \phi_z\}, \tag{15}$$

where:

$$\theta_q = \frac{1}{\beta}(\theta - q_A) + (P_f - P_m) + p_q^* q_A, \tag{16}$$

$$\theta_z = \frac{1}{\beta}(\theta - q) + \frac{1}{\gamma}(Z_A - Z_m) + (P_f - P_m) + p_z^* A_A. \tag{17}$$

Stochastic elements enter the model in three ways: (1) as variation in the mean satiation level among households, (2) in the variation of calling over time by a household, and (3) in the probability that a household will choose measured service, given the systematic part of the difference between expected utility (as measured by the difference in consumer surplus) from the available service options. A household's mean level of satiation for local calling is assumed by KP to be a random variable with a gamma distribution. The number of calls per day is assumed to have a Poisson-geometric (or Polya-Aeppli) distribution, which is a distribution which has been used in epidemiology. Finally, the probability that a household selects measured service as the utility-maximizing choice is modeled with a single logistic function of the systematic part of the difference in expected consumer surplus between services. Each of these stochastic elements will now be examined in detail.

The SLUS data base analyzed in the Michigan Bell study consisted of eight months of daily call volume for a sample of 1456 households. The data reveal that the volume of calls per day is typically zero or a small number, but that the variation is large. There also appears to be a contagious element in the distribution. An appropriate distribution for these circumstances is the Polya-Aeppli distribution, which has the form:

$$f(x) = \left\{ \begin{array}{l} \Pr(x = 0) = \exp(-\lambda) \\ \Pr(x = k) = \exp(-\lambda)\Gamma^k \sum_{j=1}^{k} \left(\frac{k-1}{j-1}\right) \frac{1}{j!} \left\{\frac{\lambda(1-\Gamma)}{\Gamma}\right\} \\ k = 1, 2, \ldots \end{array} \right\} \tag{18}$$

The assumptions underlying this distribution are that the number of purposes for which telephone communications are used in a given day has a Poisson distribution with parameter λ, and that the number of calls required for any purpose has the geometric distribution,

$$h(x) = (1 - \Gamma)\Gamma^{x-1}, \quad x = 1, 2, \ldots, \quad 0 < \Gamma < 1, \tag{19}$$

with parameter Γ. The Polya-Aeppli distribution has mean $\lambda/(1 - \Gamma)$ and variance $\lambda(1 + \Gamma)/(1 - \Gamma)^2$. The sum of n independently and identically distributed Polya-Aeppli variables accordingly has mean $n\lambda/1 - \Gamma)$ and variance $n\lambda(1 + \Gamma)/(1 - \Gamma)^2$.[9]

Not surprisingly, the most prominent characteristic of the usage distribution across households is the great variation in average usage. It is assumed that λ has a gamma distribution across households and that Γ has a beta distribution. The average monthly unrepressed (i.e., satiation) usage, $E(\theta_i)$ will accordingly be equal to:

$$E(\theta_i) = n(\lambda_i)/(1 - \Gamma), \tag{20}$$

where n denotes the number of days in the month.

When satiation usage is modified by the influence of price or demographics, the parameter λ_i is likewise modified by the appropriate parameters of the demand function. For the semi-logarithmic demand function that is assumed for usage, the parameter with measured service is assumed to be given by

$$\lambda_i^* = \lambda_i \exp(\alpha p), \tag{21}$$

where p is the price per unit of local usage. If income and other demographics are taken into account, the modification becomes

$$\lambda_i = \lambda_i \exp(\alpha_i x_i + \ldots + \alpha_n x_n). \tag{22}$$

With stochastic factors present, the choice of service is assumed to depend upon the expected difference in consumer surplus between measured and flat-rate service. The semi-logarithmic demand function makes calculation of the expected difference in consumer surplus straightforward. In the case in which the call allowance is applicable only to local calls, the difference in expected consumer surplus for household i will be given by:[10]

$$\begin{aligned}
E_i &= E_i^m(S_i^m - S_i^f) \\
&= P_f - P_m + P(C_2)\left[\frac{1}{\beta}E(\theta_i|C_2)(1 - \exp(\beta p)) + pq_A\right] \\
&\quad + P(C_3)\frac{1}{\beta}\left[E(\theta_i|C_3) - q_A\left(1 - E(\ln(\theta_i/q_A)|C_3)\right)\right],
\end{aligned} \tag{23}$$

where C_2 refers to Case 2 ($q_A < q_i$) and C_3 refers to Case 3 ($q_i < q_A < \theta_i$). The evaluation of the difference in expected consumer surplus thus

---

[9] For a discussion of the Polya-Aeppli distribution, including a convenient recursive formula for calculating Polya-Aeppli probabilities, see D.A. Evans (1953).

[10] Income and demographics are suppressed for the moment.

requires calculation of the probabilities of Cases 2 and 3 and calculation of the conditional expectations of θ_i and $\ln \theta_i$. In general, these conditional expectations will depend upon income and demographical variables and will therefore vary across households.

Expression (23) represents the systematic component in the choice of service. However, as many unobservable individual characteristics are also present, the choice of service is inherently stochastic and can only be determined in terms of probabilities. KP assume a logit framework in which the difference between the expected consumer surplus is transformed into a probability of choice of service as follows:

$$P(M) = \pi \left[\frac{\exp(\xi E_i^*)}{1 + \exp(\xi E_i^*)} \right], \tag{24}$$

where:

$$E_i^* = \text{bias} + E_i + \sum_{k=1}^{m} \alpha_k x_{ik}$$

$$E_i = E(S_i^m - S_i^f)$$

bias = constant introduced to capture household preference for flat-rate service over measured service that is not related to usage or price

x_{ik} = the value of the kth socio-demographic variable

π = the probability that the household knows that the measured-rate choice exists.

Under the assumption that daily call volumes are independently and identically distributed, the observed distribution of daily calls for a particular household can be calculated using the Poly-Aeppli distribution. The calculations are conditional upon particular values of the unobservable gamma and beta variables λ and Γ. Unconditional probabilities are obtained by integration over λ and Γ to yield an expression for the probability of the joint occurrence actually observed of the choice of service and the distribution of calls. This probability represents the likelihood function (L) of the sample:

$$L = \int_\lambda g(\lambda | B_1, B_2) \int_\Gamma h(\Gamma | v_1, v_2)$$

---

[11] See Infosino (1980).

$$\times \left[\sum_{j=1}^{2} P\left(\text{COS}_j | \lambda_i^*\right) P\left(q_1^i, \ldots, q_n^i\right) | \left(\lambda_i^*(\text{COS}_j \delta_{ij})\right) \right] \, d\Gamma \, d\lambda_j, (25)$$

where:

$$\delta_{ij} = \begin{cases} 1 & \text{if household } i \text{ has class of service } j \\ 0 & \text{otherwise} \end{cases}$$

$$g(\lambda | B_1, B_2) = \text{gamma density function with parameters } B_1 \text{ and } B_2$$

$$h(\Gamma | v_1, v_2) = \text{beta density function with parameters } v_1 \text{ and } v_2$$

$$\text{COS}_j = \text{class of service } j$$

$$n = \text{number of days}$$

$$q_k = \text{number of local calls on day } k.$$

The foregoing model was applied by KP to data from a SLUS study on 1456 1MR and 1FR households for the eight months of June, September, October, November, and December of 1984 and January, February, and March of 1985. These records were matched with information on socio-demographical variables obtained from a household survey. Matches were obtained for 427 households. The dependent variable for the class-of-service choice is binary, with the values of 1 if a household has chosen measured service with a call allowance of 50 calls and 0 if the household has chosen flat-rate service. Usage is measured by the mean of calls per day per month over the eight months in the sample. Initial estimates of the parameters were obtained from two-stage least-squares estimation of linear probability specifications of both the class-of-service and usage equations. Final estimates were obtained by maximizing the likelihood function in expression (25) using the quadratic hill-climbing algorithm of Goldfeld, Quandt, and Trotter (1966).

The parameter estimates and their associated t-ratios are presented in Table 1.[12] Except for the constant in the choice of class-of-service, all of

---

[12] COSprice is a dummy variable which takes the value if respondents answered no to the question: Have you ever tried to determine if flat-rate or measured service would be more economical for your household? Income is a categorical variable where a household was placed in one of the 15 income categories. Race is a dummy variable with value 1 for black, 0 otherwise. Adults is the number of adults in the household in addition to the respondent and/or spouse. Seniors is the number of persons 65 or older residing in the household. Teens is the number of persons aged 13–20 residing in the household. Children is the number of persons aged 0–12 residing in the household. Distance is a dummy variable with value 1 if respondents indicated that most of their relatives or friends lived in the local-calling area, 0 otherwise. Busphone is a dummy variable with value 1 if respondent indicated that someone in the household uses the telephone for business, 0 otherwise.

TABLE 1

Kling-Van der Ploeg model coefficient estimates

Coefficient	Estimate	t-ratio
Gamma α_1	1.87	16.2
Gamma α_2	0.78	14.0
Beta v_1	4.10	20.0
Beta v_2	5.37	20.6
β_p	-2.79	-21.4
β_{logit}	0.23	2.2

Coefficients on Attributes and Demographic Variables

Class of Service Choice:

Ignorance	0.44	4.1
Constant (β_0)	0.09	0.6
COSprice	-0.66	-2.7
Income	-0.03	-3.0

Usage:

Race	0.18	17.9
Adults	0.21	48.2
Seniors	-0.35	-46.2
Teens	0.20	46.3
Children	0.04	12.2
Distance	-0.08	-7.8
Busphone	0.41	27.9

Source: Kling and Van der Ploeg (1990, Table 1)

t-ratios are greater than two (in absolute value); most are greater than 12. Of the usage parameters, black households make a larger number of calls than non-black house-holds,[13] the more adults the more calls, and the same is true for teens and children but not for seniors. Fewer calls are made if most of the household's acquaintances reside in the local-calling area, while more calls are made if someone in the household uses the telephone for business purposes.

Of the class-of-service parameters, π, the coefficient for the probability that a household is aware that a measured option exists, indicates that the

[13] Cf. Brandon and Brandon (1981).

opportunity to choose measured service is restricted to about 44% of the households in the sample. This represents a bias toward flat-rate service that can be attributed to ignorance or inertia. KP interpret the negative sign for COSprice as indicating that if a household has not explicitly examined the cost difference in the two classes of service, then it is more likely to choose flat-rate service. Households with higher incomes are also more likely to choose flat-rate service. Finally, the statistical insignificance of the constant indicates that most of the explicit preference for flat-rate service is reflected in the ignorance parameter, income, and COSprice.

The parameters of most interest are the logit parameter ξ and the coefficient for the price of usage β. Kling and Van der Ploeg note that the estimated value of 0.23 for ξ implies that the maximum probability of switching from flat-rate to measured service in response to a $1 change in the difference in fixed outlays between the two services is about 0.06. This probability is calculated for a probability of choice measured service of 0.5, assuming that the household has knowledge that both services are available. When the ignorance parameter of 0.44 is taken into account, the size of this probability response is reduced to about 0.025 for the sample as a whole.

Since the demand function is semi-logarithmic, the price elasticity is equal to βp. The estimated call price coefficient of -2.79 accordingly yields price elasticities that range from -0.03 for a price of one cent per call to -0.28 for a price of 10 cents per call. The details are given in Table 2. At the current Michigan Bell price (at the time of the sample) of $0.062 per call, the estimated price elasticity is -0.17. In addition to point elasticities, KP also calculate arc elasticities between points on the demand function $p = 0$ (which corresponds to flat-rate service) and $p = \$0.05$ and for $p = \$1.10$. The values are -0.07 and -0.21.

II. BYPASS VIA EAS: KRIDEL (1988)

As is well-known, the toll-to-local subsidy was "justified" historically by allocating a substantial portion of the costs of local plant to toll service. At the time of the AT&T divestiture, these non-traffic-sensitive "costs" totaled about $16 billion, of which about $9 billion was the inter-state portion and about $7 billion the intra-state portion. With divestiture, most of these non-traffic-sensitive costs were to be recovered through traffic-sensitive per minute charges at both ends of a toll call. Since these charges were seen as "payment" to the toll carrier's switch (or point-of-presence), those at the sending end could be avoided if the customer were to bypass the LEC by connecting

TABLE 2

Price elasticities of demand; Kling-Van der Ploeg study

Base Price	New Price	Elasticity of Demand
	0.01	-0.03
	0.02	-0.06
	0.03	-0.08
	0.04	-0.11
	0.05	-0.14
0.00	0.05	-0.07*
	0.06	-0.17
	0.07	-0.20
	0.08	-0.22
	0.09	-0.25
	0.10	-0.28
0.05	0.10	-0.21*

* Arc elasticities; other elasticities are point elasticities.

Source: Kling and Van der Ploeg (1990, Table 2)

directly with its toll carrier's point-of-presence.[14]

Since bypass facilities are not inexpensive, for direct bypass to pay requires a large volume of toll calling, and accordingly is not feasible for the vast majority of residential customers. However, in a circumstance in which there is a large volume of toll calling between adjacent regions, bypass could be effected by merging the regions into a local-calling area through Extended Area Service (EAS). Bedroom communities adjacent to large central cities provide cases in point, and in 1987–1988 several of these in Texas were using the regulatory forum to demand lower toll rates via optional calling plans (OCPs) or EAS.

EAS is typically flat-rate 2-way calling, in which subscribers may call into and be called from a given geographical area an unlimited number of times for a fixed monthly fee. Since the service is 2-way, a separate serving exchange (or NNX) must be established. As a result, network design engineers require accurate forecasts of the number of customers that will subscribe to the service and the associated increase in traffic volume. In order to properly design the

[14] For a discussion of this and related issues, see Wenders (1987), Brock (1984), Bell Communications Research (1984), and Egan and Weisman (1986).

plan and the rates, these forecasts are needed prior to offering the plan. The study now to be discussed describes the approach developed by Donald Kridel of Southwestern Bell (Kridel 1988) for making such forecasts.

The point of departure for Kridel is that standard utility maximization framework in which, given a choice between two calling plans (toll and EAS), the customer is assumed to choose the one which yields the greater utility (as measured by consumer surplus). More particularly, if the increase in consumer surplus from switching to EAS is greater than the subscription price, the customer will choose EAS. The increase in consumer surplus associated with EAS consists of two parts: (1) the toll savings due to the decrease to zero in the price of calls and (2) the benefits that arise from additional calling. The details are presented in Figure 6, where at a toll price of p_0, q_0 calls are purchased. The toll savings are represented by the rectangle labeled TS, while the benefits associated with the increase in the number of calls to q_n from q_0 is given by the area denoted by V_s. EAS will be purchased if

$$\Delta CS = TS + V_s > p_{\text{EAS}}, \tag{26}$$

where:

ΔCS = the increase in consumer surplus associated with the purchase of EAS

TS = toll savings

V_s = value of stimulated calls

p_{EAS} = the addition to the monthly service fee for EAS.

Since the increase in consumer surplus is not directly observable, Kridel reformulates the choice criterion in expression (26) in probability terms as:

$$\Delta CS = \Delta CS^* + u > p_{\text{EAS}}, \tag{27}$$

where ΔCS^* represents the observed or deterministic portion of the increase in consumer surplus and u is a well-behaved error term. The probability of a customer choosing EAS will then be given by

$$\Pr(\text{EAS}) = \Pr\left(u > \gamma(p_{\text{EAS}} - \Delta CS^*)\right), \tag{28}$$

where γ is a parameter that can be thought of as the inclination of a subscriber to take advantage of a given net benefit (or loss) resulting from the selection of EAS. This parameter will be discussed further below.

At this point, it should be noted that the analysis is *ex ante* to any observed market behavior. Survey-based purchase intentions form the basis for estimating the parameters of the model. As the ultimate subscription price was

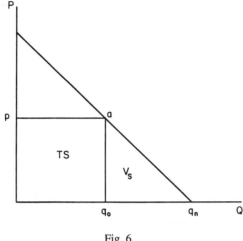

Fig. 6.

unknown at the time of the survey, customers were queried whether EAS would be purchased at a given subscription price, and this price was varied across respondents. This price variation allows for predictions to be made of take-rates at various subscription prices. The customer, when providing a rational response to the EAS purchase query, is (at least subconsciously) estimating the benefits to be derived from additional calling, for the customer was informed of his/her toll savings just prior to the purchase question. Since the benefit in question is directly related to the amount of usage stimulation, it is natural (as Kridel notes) to treat the customer's new usage level (q_N) as a parameter to be estimated.

For the choice model specified in expression (28) to be estimated, it is necessary that the ΔCS^* be specified in terms of observable quantities. To this end, Kridel assumes that the demand function for q is the "Perl" form:

$$q = Ae^{\alpha p}y^{\beta}, \tag{29}$$

where:

$$q \;=\; \text{minutes of toll usage into the EAS area}$$

$$p \;=\; \text{toll price}$$

$$y \;=\; \text{income}$$

$$A, \alpha, \beta \;=\; \text{parameters.}$$

With this functional form, the consumer surplus under each option will be as follows:

$$CS_0^* = \int_{p_0}^{\infty} e^{\alpha p} y^{\beta} \, \mathrm{d}p = q_0/\alpha \quad \text{non-EAS} \tag{30}$$

$$CS_N^* = \int_{0}^{\infty} e^{\alpha p} y^{\beta} \, \mathrm{d}p = q_N/\alpha \quad \text{EAS} \tag{31}$$

where:

p_0 = current price of toll

q_0 = observed toll usage at p_0

q_N = the satiation level of usage with EAS (since $p_N = 0$).

Using these two expressions, ΔCS^* will accordingly be given by

$$\Delta CS^* = CS_N^* - CS_0^* = (q_N - q_0)/\alpha. \tag{32}$$

Although the satiation level of usage q_N is unobserved, it can be calculated from the demand function in expression (28) as

$$q_N = q_0 e^{\alpha p_0} \tag{33}$$

At this point, the choice model is seen to involve two parameters, α and γ. The parameter α is related to the price elasticity of demand for toll, which is equal to $-\alpha p$, while γ (as noted earlier) can be thought of as the inclination of the subscriber to take advantage of a given net benefit (or loss) resulting from selection of EAS. The higher (in absolute value) is γ, the more likely (everything else remaining constant) a customer is to purchase EAS.

Kridel extends the model to allow for individual effects by assuming the parameters α and γ to be functions of income and subscriber demographics. This allows for all customers to have the same form of demand function, but to have different price elasticities and inclinations to purchase EAS. Demand-type variables (income, household size, etc.) are included in α, while choice-influencing variables (perceptions, education, etc.) are included in γ.

The equation specified for and are as follows:

$$\alpha = \alpha_0 \exp(\alpha_1 \ln y + \alpha_2 \text{INT}), \tag{34}$$

where:

y = customer's income

INT = customer's "interest" in EAS area[15]

and

$$\gamma = \gamma_0 \text{EXP}(\gamma \ln \text{TBILL} + \gamma_2 DM^* \text{EDUC} + \gamma_3 DH^* \text{EDUC}), \tag{35}$$

where:

$$
\begin{aligned}
\text{TBILL} &= \text{ customer's perceived total bill} \\
\text{DM} &= \text{ dummy variable for middle 50\% of users} \\
\text{DH} &= \text{ dummy variable for highest 25\% of users} \\
\text{EDUC} &= \text{ an education index.}
\end{aligned}
$$

The error term u is assumed to have a logistic distribution, so that the probability of a customer choosing EAS will be given by

$$
\begin{aligned}
\text{Pr(EAS)} &= \text{Pr}\left(u > \gamma(p_{\text{EAS}} - \Delta CS^*)\right) \\
&= \frac{1}{1 + \exp\left(\Gamma(p_{\text{EAS}} - \Delta CS^*)\right)},
\end{aligned} \tag{36}
$$

where γ and ΔCS^* are as defined above. The logarithm of the likelihood function is accordingly:

$$\text{LLF} = \sum_1 \left[C_i^* \ln \text{Pr}_i(\text{EAS} + (1 - C_i)^* \ln(1 - \text{Pr}_i(\text{EAS})\right], \tag{37}$$

where:

$$
C_i = \begin{cases} 1 & \text{if respondent says he/she will purchase EAS} \\ 0 & \text{otherwise.} \end{cases}
$$

The model is estimated by maximizing LLF for a sample of 840 households drawn at random from suburban communities in Texas using a hybrid Berndt-Hausaman-Hall-Hall and Quasi-Newton optimization routine. The estimates of the parameters, together with their associated asymptotic t-ratios, are given in Table 3.

As expected, income and the variable representing a customer's attachment to the area defining the EAS (INT) have positive effects on the choice of EAS, for both $\hat{\alpha}_1$, and $\hat{\gamma}_2$ are positive. Determining the effects of the total bill and education requires tedious calculation of partial derivatives. The

---

[15] "Interest" is an index for working, shopping, children in school, and family or friends in the EAS calling area. The index takes the value of 4 if all four hold, 3 if three of the four hold, etc.

TABLE 3

Coefficient estimates; Kridel study

Coefficient	Estimated Value	Asymptotic t-Ratio
α_0	10.081	7.2
α_1	0.521	5.6
α_2	0.319	2.4
γ_0	-0.046	-10.7
γ_1	-0.313	-7.4
γ_2	0.820	1.6
γ_3	0.104	2.1

Source: Kridel (1988, Table 1)

partial derivative of Pr(EAS) with respect to education (calculated for the large users, i.e., $DH = 1$ and $DM = 0$) is, for example:

$$\frac{\partial \Pr(\text{EAS})}{\partial \text{EDUC}} = \gamma \gamma_0 \gamma_3 \left(p_{\text{EAS}} - \Delta CS^* \right) \hat{p}(1 - \hat{p}), \tag{38}$$

where $\hat{p}$ denotes the probability of choosing EAS. Note that the sign of this derivative depends upon the size of the net benefit of EAS – i.e., on $p_{\text{EAS}} - \Delta CS^*$. Since $\hat{\gamma}_3$ this result implies the plausible result that higher education customers are more likely to choose EAS if the net benefit is positive than if it is negative.

Rather than pursuing the tedious calculation of partial derivatives, Kridel uses the estimated coefficients in Table 3 to simulate the effects on the probability of choosing EAS of changes in income and the demographical variables. The effects on usage are also calculated. The results are presented in Table 4 for a subscription price for EAS of $20. In the simulations: (1) income is increased by $1000; (2) the interest index (INT) is increased by one unit (but is not allowed to exceed four); (3) the perceived bill (TBILL) is increased by $1; (4) the education index is increased by one unit (but is not allowed to exceed its current maximum value).

Income and the perceived total bill (TBILL) have small positive effects on the probability of choosing EAS. Education has a somewhat larger effect. The largest effect is registered by INT, which is not surprising since this variable in essence is a direct measure of a customer's attachment to the area in question. The last column in Table 4 is of particular interest because it shows the estimated effect on usage for each of the cases. The numbers

TABLE 4

Comparative statics, Kridel model

Case	Penetration (%)	Stimulation (%)
Base case	58.0	72.5
Δ INCOME	58.2	72.6
Δ INT	61.2	76.5
Δ TBILL	58.1	72.5
Δ EDUC	59.2	74.0

Source: Kridel (1988, Table 2)

show that the average (arc) price elasticity $(-\alpha p)$ for the toll calls in question for the 840 households in the sample is about -0.75.[16] Kridel notes that individual values range from -0.1 to -1.5 depending upon the characteristics of the household.

The final exercise undertaken by Kridel is to predict the take-rate and usage stimulation corresponding to EAS subscription prices of $5, $20, and $25 per month. The results are tabulated in Table 5. At a subscription price of $5 per month, the model predicts a take-rate of nearly 76% and an increase of nearly 93% in usage. At a price of $25, the predicted take-rate is a little over 50% and an increase in usage of about 65%. The interesting (and significant) thing about the stimulation estimates is that they are about twice as large as would have been generated using Southwestern Bell's (then) existing price elasticities for toll.[17]

III. RESULTS FROM THE GTE MEASURED-SERVICE EXPERIMENT: PARK, WETZEL, & MITCHELL (1983)

The third study to be discussed in this chapter is by Park, Wetzel, and Mitchell (1983) – hereafter PWM – on the effects on local calling of a mandatory switch

---

[16] This is much larger than the values that have conventionally been viewed as holding for local and short-haul toll, but is in line with the recent estimates of Train, McFadden, and Ben-Akiva (1987) and Hobson and Spady (1988) of -0.45 and about -0.9, respectively.

[17] This should not be taken to mean that the existing elasticities are wrong, but only that they are not applicable to the question being asked. One can reasonably infer that the households whose data are being analyzed exhibit above-average price responses because they are drawn from suburban communities that were already petitioning for EAS. The price elasticities obtained by Kridel are applicable for such circumstances, but almost certainly not to short-haul toll calls in general.

TABLE 5

Predictions from Kridel model

Subscription price	Development (%)	Stimulation (%)
$5	75.7	92.8
$20	58.0	72.5
$25	51.6	64.9

Source: Kridel (1988, Table 3)

from flat-rate to measured local service. The PWM analysis is based on data that were generated in the well-known GTE local measured-service experiment that was conducted between 1975 and 1979 in three small exchanges in central Illinois – Clinton, Jacksonville, and Tuscola.[18] In May 1975, GTE began recording information on individual customers' telephone usage under the flat-rate tariffs that were in effect in those exchanges. On September 1, 1977, GTE switched to measured-service tariffs and continued to record usage information. In contrast with usual practice when measured-service plans are implemented, the experimental tariffs were non-optional and included no call allowance. The only way that residential subscribers could avoid paying for each outgoing call was by downgrading to multi-party service. A second measured-service tariff went into effect on June 1, 1979 and remained in effect through the end of the period spanned by PWM's data, which was December 1979. The tariffs for residential service are given in Table 6.

The data set analyzed by PWM consists of aggregate monthly usage for the 52 months from September 1975 through December 1979 for the three exchanges in the experiment. The model specified by PWM allows for measured service to have effects on usage: (1) a direct effect whereby, for those who remain with single-party service, usage is reduced in response to the non-zero price and (2) a substitution effect whereby (since multi-party service remains flat-rate) there is substitution of multi-party calls for single-party calls for those customers who downgrade from single- to multi-party service. The total effect is represented by the sum of the two.

The model that is specified allows for a monthly reference level of usage (μ_t) to be modified by a set of multiplicative factors which include the effects of exchange size (α_i), growth γ_{it}, repression η_{it}, and substitution (δ_{it}). The

[18] For a description of the GTE experiment, see Cohen (1977). Other studies that are based on the GTE data include Mitchell and Park (1981b), Park, Mitchell, Wetzel, and Alleman (1981), and Park, Mitchell, and Wetzel (1981).

TABLE 6

Tariffs in effect during the GTE local measured-service experiment

(residential telephone service)

	September '75–December '76			January '77–August '77			September '77–May '79			June '79–December '79		
	J	C	T	J	C	T	J	C	T	J	C	T
Single-party service												
Monthly service charge												
Urban areas	$ 7.95	$6.20	$5.90	$ 8.60	$6.60	$6.30	$3.15	$2.50	$2.50	$3.15	$2.50	$2.50
Suburban areas	10.50	8.80	8.45	11.30	9.35	9.00	5.70	5.10	5.05	5.70	5.10	5.05
Price per cell, P_c	–	–	–	–	–	–	0.02	0.00	0.00	0.025	0.025	0.025
Price per minute, P_M	–	–	–	–	–	–	0.01	0.015	0.015	0.01	0.01	0.01
Multi-party service												
Monthly service charge												
Urban areas (2-party)	6.70	5.10	4.85	7.25	5.45	5.15	7.25	5.45	5.15	7.25	5.45	5.15
Suburban areas (4-party)	8.80	7.10	6.75	9.50	7.55	6.75	9.50	7.55	7.20	9.50	7.55	7.20

Notes: J, C, and T indicate Jacksonville, Clinton, and Tuscola. There is a 20 percent discount on usage charges P_c and P_M evenings (5–11 p.m.) and Sunday and holidays (8 a.m.–11 p.m.); there is a 50 percent discount nights (11 p.m.–8 a.m.). There is a $19 per month ceiling on usage charges. Multi-party service has remained on flat rate throughout the experiment. Business service has been measured since September 1977, with the same usage charges as for residential service, but higher monthly charges.

Source: Park, Wetzel, and Mitchel (1983, Table IV)

model for single-party use can then be written as:

$$q^1_{it} = \mu_t \alpha_i \gamma_{it} \eta_{it} \delta_{it} + \varepsilon_{it}, \quad t = 1, \ldots, 52, \quad i = 1, \ldots 3, \tag{39}$$

where q^1 denotes single-party usage (either calls per main station or minutes per main station), t denotes monthly observations of the sample, i denotes the exchange, and ε is a random error term.

The monthly reference usage level μ_t is allowed to differ from one calendar month to another to account for seasonal influences. Let $m(t)$, $m = 1, \ldots,$ 12, denote calendar months. The first term, μ_t, can accordingly be written:

$$\mu_t = \mu M_{m(t)}, \tag{40}$$

where μ is a 12-element row vector of monthly reference levels of use, and $M_{m(t)}$ is a 12-element column vector whose elements are zero except for the $m(t)$th which is one.

The exchange factor α_i allows for the fact that usage per subscriber is generally greater in large exchanges than in small exchanges.[19] The factor is parameterized as

$$\alpha_i = \alpha D_i, \tag{41}$$

where α is a three-element row vector $(1, \alpha_c, \alpha_T)$ and D_i is a three-element column vector with all elements zero except the first equals one if the observation is for Jacksonville, the second equals one if the observation is for Clinton, and the third equals one if the observation is for Tuscola.

The growth factor γ_{it} accounts for any smoothly trended effects. PWM specify each growth factor as a linear trend with an initial value of 1 on September 1, 1975, and a change in slope at the introduction of single-party measured service on September 1, 1977. The trends are allowed to differ across the three exchanges. Formally, the growth factor is specified as[20]

$$\gamma_{it} = 1 + F_t \left[\gamma_1 D_i(t - 0.5)\right] + (1 - F_t)\left[24\gamma_1 D_i + \gamma_2 D_i(t - 24.5)\right], \tag{42}$$

where γ_1 and γ_2 are three-element row vectors of growth rates in each of the exchanges during flat-rate and measured-rate months, respectively, D_i is the column vectors of exchange dummies from above, and F_t is a dummy variable equal to one during flat-rate months ($t = 1, \ldots, 24$) and zero otherwise.

The repression factor η_{it} captures the reduction in use due to the experimental usage charges, excluding the reduction that is due to the substitution

---

[19] "... presumably because there are fewer people in the local area to call." (Park, Wetzel, and Mitchell 1983, p. 1715).

[20] The 0.5s appear in the equation because each monthly observation refers to the middle of the month, whereas the trend starts at the beginning of September, 1975.

of multi-party for single-party service. Both the per-call charge (P_c) and the per-minute charge (P_M) are expected to affect both calls per main station and minutes per main station. PWM specify γ_{it} as a negative exponential function of the two prices:

$$\gamma_{it} = \exp\left(-\zeta_C P_{C,it} - \eta_M P_{M,it}\right). \tag{43}$$

The substitution factor δ_{it} is assumed to have the same analytical form as the repression factor,

$$\delta_{it} = \exp\left(-\delta_C P_{c,it} - \delta_M P_{M,it}\right). \tag{44}$$

PWM note that the substitution and repression factors cannot be separately identified in the model for single-party service because they are identical functions of the same variables, P_C and P_M. The total reduction in single-party use can be estimated, but an extraneous estimate of the substitution factor is needed in order to obtain a separate estimate of repression. The needed extraneous estimate is provided in the multi-party part of the model.

The multi-party part of the model has the same form as for single-party use:

$$q_{it}^* = \mu_t \alpha_i \beta_i \gamma_i^* \delta_{it}^* + \varepsilon_{it}. \tag{45}$$

The monthly reference level of use μ_t and the exchange size factor α_i are assumed to have the same values as for single-party use. The fact that the multi-party use is generally observed to be less than single-party use when both are on a flat-rate tariff is taken in account in the multi-party factor, β_i. This factor is allowed to differ among exchanges as

$$\beta_i = \beta D_i, \tag{46}$$

where β is a three-element row vector and D_i is the column vector of exchange dummies defined earlier.

The growth factor γ_{it}^* is assumed to have the same form as for γ_{it} for single-party use, although the multi-party slopes γ_1^* and γ_2^* are allowed to differ from γ_1 and γ_2:

$$\gamma_{it}^* = 1 + F_t\left[\gamma_1^* D_i(t - 0.50)\right] + 1 - F_t\left[24\gamma_1^* D_i + \gamma_2^* D_i(t - 24.5)\right], \tag{47}$$

where F_t is the dummy variable for the introduction of measured service as defined earlier.

In specifying the substitution factor δ_{it}^*, PWM assume that all of the increase in multi-party use after imposition of the measured-service tariff is due to substitution from single-party to multi-party service. In terms of the factors in the model, this assumption can be written as:

$$N_{it} = \mu_t \alpha_i \gamma_{it}(1 - \delta_{it}) = N_{it}^* \mu_t \alpha_i \beta_i \gamma_{it}^* (\delta_{it}^* - 1), \tag{48}$$

where N_{it} and N_{it}^* denote the numbers of single- and multi-party main stations. Solving for δ_{it}^* yields:

$$\delta_{it}^* = 1 + (N_{it}/N_{it}^*)(\delta_{it}/\delta_{it}^*)(\eta_{it}/\beta_i)(1 - \delta_{it}). \tag{49}$$

The final estimating equation is obtained by combining expressions (38) and (43) using a dummy variable C_j to denote the class of service:

$$q_{ijt} = (1 - C_j)\mu_t \alpha_i \gamma_{it} \mu_{it} \delta_{it} + c_j \mu_t \alpha_i b_i \gamma_{it} \delta_{it}^*, \tag{50}$$

where $i = 1, 2, 3$ exchanges, $j = 1, 2$ classes of service, and $t = 1, \ldots, 52$ months. In terms of the full specification of each of the factors, this expression becomes:

$$\begin{aligned}
q_{ijt} = \ & (1 - C_j)\mu M_{m(t)} \alpha D_i (1 + F_t) \left[\gamma_1 D_i(t - 0.5)\right] \\
& + (1 - F_t) \left[24\gamma_1 D_i + \gamma_2 D_i(t - 24.5)\right] \\
& \times \exp\left(-\eta_c P_{c,it}\right) \exp(-\gamma_C P_{C,it} - \gamma_M P_{M,it} + C_j \mu M_{m(t)} D_i \beta D_i \\
& \times 1 + F_t \left[\gamma_1^* D_i(t - 0.5)\right] + (1 - F_t) \left[24\gamma_1^* D_i + \gamma_2 D_i(t - 24.5)\right] \\
& + C_j \mu M_{m(t)} D_i (N_{it}/N_t^*) 1 + F_t \left[\gamma_1 D_i(t - 0.5)\right] \\
& + (1 - F_t)[24\gamma_1 D_i] \\
& + \delta_2 D_i(t - 24.5) \exp(\eta_C P_{C,it} - \eta_M P_{M,it}) \\
& \times \left[1 - \exp(\gamma_C P_{C,it} - \delta_M P_{M,it})\right] \varepsilon_{ijt}. \tag{5}
\end{aligned}$$

Nonlinear generalized least squares estimates of the price effects in equation (52), both with and without the trend terms, for both calls per main station and minutes per main station are presented in Table 7. Signs are correct and, except for the substitution coefficients for the per-call charge, (asymptotic) t-ratios are large. And, as expected, minutes are more sensitive to price than calls and both are more sensitive to per-minute charges than to per-call charges. Price elasticities, for the model with trend terms calculated at the 1979 experimental prices of $P_C = 2.5$ and $P_M = 1$, are presented in Table 8. None of the values exceed 0.1 in absolute value, but would be proportionately higher at higher prices (since the price elasticity is equal to ηP).

IV. THE DEMAND FOR CUSTOM-CALLING FEATURES

The last topic to be examined in this chapter is the demand for custom-calling features, such as call-waiting and call-forwarding, that are supplied by local

TABLE 7

Estimated price effects in Park, Wetzel, and Mitchell model

Resulting from a 1-cent Increase in	Percent Change Due to			
	Repression		Substitution	
	Calls	Minutes	Calls	Minutes
Model with Trend Terms				
Per-call charge, P_c	-3.0	-3.4	-0.1	-0.2
	(0.5)	(0.9)	(0.1)	(0.2)
Per-minute charge, P_M	-5.5	-10.9	-1.4	-3.4
	(1.2)	(1.9)	(0.2)	(0.3)
Model without Trend Terms				
Per-call charge, P_c	-3.0	-2.6	-0.4	-0.6
	(0.4)	(0.7)	(0.1)	(0.1)
Per-minute charge, P_M	-5.2	-8.9	-1.6	-4.0
	)0.7)	(1.3)	(0.1)	(0.2)

Notes: The repression effects are estimates of η_c and η_M in equation (52) (expressed as negative per cent). The substitution effects are estimates of δ_c and δ_M. Effects on calls and effects on minutes are from separate regressions with, respectively, calls per main station and minutes per main station as dependent variables. Estimated asymptotic errors are in parentheses. Estimates of the other (nuisance) coefficients in the estimating equation (51) are not tabulated.

Source: Park, Wetzel, and Mitchell (1983, Table V)

exchange companies. These services can be subscribed to at the option of the customer on a monthly basis for a fixed monthly fee. They can be purchased individually or in packages that bundle two or more features together for a single fee. The price of a package is always less than the price that would be paid if the components were purchased individually. By offering packages that are priced in this way, it is possible for telcos to increase the overall demand for custom-calling features and to increase profits beyond what they would be if features were only sold individually.[21]

[21] See Adams and Yellen (1976), Spence (1980), and McAfee, McMillan, and Whinston (1989).

TABLE 8

Estimated price elasticities at December 1979 experimental prices[a]; Park, Wetzel, and Mitchell study

Charge	Repression Elasticity[b]		Substitution Elasticity[c]	
	Calls	Minutes	Calls	Minutes
Per-call charge, P_c	-0.076	-0.086	-0.02	-0.05
	(0.013)	(0.022)	(0.003)	(0.004)
Per-minute charge, P_M	-0.055	-0.109	-0.14	-0.034
	(0.012)	(0.019)	(0.002)	(0.003)

Note: Estimated asympotic standard errors are in parentheses.

[a] December 1979 experimental prices are $P_c = 2.5c$ and $P_M = 1c$.

[b] Elasticities with respect to P_c and P_M are calculated as $-P_c\eta_c$ and $P_M\eta_M$, respectively. Values for η_c and η_M are from Appendix A.

[c] Elasticities with respect to P_c and P_M are calculated as $-P_c\delta_c$ and $-P_M\delta_M$, respectively. Values for δ_c and δ_M are from Appendix A.

Source: Park, Wetzel, and Mitchell (1983, Table VI)

While bundling increase demand and profits, it complicates life for the demand analyst, for it can add greatly to the number of cross-price effects that need to be taken into account. Among other things, bundling can lead to two services, call-forwarding and speed-calling, for example, whose demands in the absence of bundling may be independent to behave with bundling as though they are complements. To see how this can arise, let us consider two goods, 1 and 2, that can be purchased either individually or as a bundle. Let p_1 and p_2 denote their prices if purchased individually and let $p_b = p_1 + p_2 - \varepsilon$, where $\varepsilon > 0$, denote their price if purchased as a bundle. Let v_1 and v_2 represent a consumer's willingness-to-pay for the goods. Only good 1 will be purchased if $v_1 > p_1$ and $v_2 < p_2 - \varepsilon$. Similarly, only good 2 will be purchased if $v_2 > p_2$ and $v_1 < p_1 - \varepsilon$. Both goods will be purchased if $v_1 + v_2 > p_b$, $v_1 > p_1$, and $v_2 > p_2 - \varepsilon$ or if $v_1 + v_2 > p_b$, $v_2 > p_2$, and $v_1 > p_1 - \varepsilon$. Finally, neither good will be purchased if $v_1 + v_2 < p_b$, $v_1 < p_1$, and $v_2 < p_2$.

These four cases are illustrated in Figure 7. Good 1 only will be purchased in region A, good 2 only in region B, both goods in region C, and neither good in region D. Figure 7 also illustrates the increases in demand that bundling permits. In the absence of bundling, both goods would be purchased only if $v_1 > p_1$ and $v_2 > p_2$, which is smaller than region C by the area marked with

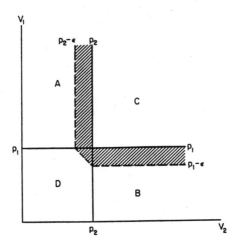

Fig. 7.

hatched lines. Note that the triangle lying to the southwest of the intersection of the lines corresponding to p_1 and p_2 represents a region wherein both goods will be purchased under bundling, but neither would be bought in its absence.

In order to deal with a population of consumers, it will be assumed that v_1 and v_2 are random variables with a joint density function $f(v_1, v_2)$. The probability that good 1 will be purchased will be given by:

$$\Pr(1 \text{ alone}) = \Pr(v_1 > p_1, v_2 < p_2 - \varepsilon)$$

$$= \int_{p_1}^{\infty} \int_{0}^{p_2-\varepsilon} f(v_1, v_2) \, dv_2 \, dv_1. \tag{52}$$

Similarly, for good 2:

$$\Pr(2 \text{ alone}) = \Pr(v_1 < p_1 - \varepsilon, v_2 > p_2)$$

$$= \int_{p_2}^{\infty} \int_{0}^{p_1-\varepsilon} f(v_1, v_2) \, dv_1 \, dv_2, \tag{53}$$

while for both goods:

$$\Pr(1 \text{ and } 2) = \Pr(v_1 + v_2 > p_b, v_1 > p_1, v_2 > p_2 - \varepsilon)$$

$$= \int_{p_1}^{\infty} \int_{p_2-\varepsilon}^{\infty} f(v_1, v_2) \, dv_2 \, dv_1 + \int_{p_1-\varepsilon}^{p_1} \int_{p_2+v_1}^{\infty} f(v_1, v_2) \, dv_2 \, dv_1. \tag{54}$$

The probability of purchasing good 1 either singly or in a package with good 2 will accordingly be equal to:

$$P(1) = \Pr(1 \text{ alone}) + \Pr(1\&2)$$

$$= \int_{p_1}^{\infty} \int_0^{p_2-\varepsilon} f(v_1, v_2) \, dv_2 \, dv_1 + \int_{p_1}^{\infty} \int_{p_2-\varepsilon}^{\infty} f(v_1, v_2) \, dv_2 \, dv_1$$

$$+ \int_{p_1-\varepsilon}^{p_1} \int_{p_2-v_1}^{\infty} f(v_1, v_2) \, dv_2 \, dv_1. \tag{55}$$

Similarly, for good 2:[22]

$$P(2) = \Pr(2 \text{ alone}) + \Pr(1\&2)$$

$$= \int_{p_2}^{\infty} \int_0^{p_1-\varepsilon} f(v_1, v_2) \, dv_1 \, dv_2 + \int_{p_2}^{\infty} \int_{p_1-\varepsilon}^{\infty} f(v_1, v_2) \, dv_1 \, dv_2$$

$$+ \int_{p_2-\varepsilon}^{p_2} \int_{p_1-v_2}^{\infty} f(v_1, v_2) \, dv_1 \, dv_2. \tag{56}$$

Equations (52)–(56) provide, in the abstract, expressions for determining the proportions of a population that will purchase the two goods, either individually or jointly in a package. To make the expression operational, it will be assumed that:

$$v_1 = \alpha' x + u_1 \tag{57}$$

$$v_2 = \beta' + u_2 \tag{58}$$

where x and z denote observable vectors of economic-socio-demographical factors and u_1 and u_2 are independently distributed random variables with means zero and variances σ_1^2 and σ_2^2. Independence of u_1 and u_2 implies independence of the demands for the two goods. With these assumptions, the probabilities in expressions (52) and (56) can be written as:

$$P(1 \text{ alone}) = \left[1 - \Phi(p_1 - \alpha' x)\right] \Phi(p_2 - \varepsilon - \beta' z) \tag{59}$$

---

[22] Pr(1&2) in this expression is calculated as $\Pr(v_1 + v_2 > p_b, v_2 > p_2, v_1 > p_1 - \varepsilon)$. In expression (55), Pr(1&2) is calculated as equivalently as $\Pr(v_1 + v_2 > p_b, v_1 > p_1, v_2 > p_2 - \varepsilon)$.

$$P(2 \text{ alone}) = \left[1 - \Phi(p_2 - \beta' z)\right] \Phi(p_1 - \varepsilon - \alpha' x) \tag{60}$$

$$
\begin{aligned}
P(1 \text{ and } 2) = {} & \left[1 - \Phi(p_1 - \alpha' x)\right]\left[1 - \Phi(p_2 - \varepsilon - \beta' z)\right] \\
& + \left[1 - \Phi(p_1 - \beta' z - \varepsilon/2)\right] \\
& \times \left[\Phi(p_1 - \alpha' x) - \Phi(p_1 - \varepsilon - \alpha' x)\right]
\end{aligned}
\tag{61}
$$

$$
\begin{aligned}
P(1) = {} & \left[1 - \Phi(p_1 - \alpha' x)\right]\Phi(p_2 - \varepsilon - \beta' z) \\
& + \left[1 - \Phi(p_1 - \alpha' x)\right]\left[1 - \Phi(p_2 - \varepsilon - \beta' z)\right] \\
& + \left[1 - \Phi(p_2 - \beta' z - \varepsilon/z)\right]\left[\Phi(p_1 - \alpha' x) - \Phi(p_1 - \alpha' x)\right] \\
= {} & 1 - \Phi(p_1 - \alpha' x) + \left[1 - \Phi(p_2 - \beta' z - \varepsilon/2)\right] \\
& \times \left[\Phi(p_1 - \alpha' x) - \Phi(p_1 - \varepsilon - \alpha' x)\right]
\end{aligned}
\tag{62}
$$

$$
\begin{aligned}
P(2) = {} & \left[1 - \Phi(p_2 - \beta' z)\right]\Phi(p_1 - \varepsilon - \alpha' z) \\
& + \left[1 - \Phi(p_2 - \beta' z)\right]\left[1 - \Phi(p_1 - \varepsilon - \alpha' x)\right] \\
& + \left[1 - \Phi(p_1 - \alpha' x - \varepsilon/2)\right]\left[\Phi(p_2 - \beta' z) - \Phi(p_2 - \varepsilon - \beta' z)\right] \\
= {} & 1 - \Phi(p_2 - \beta' z) + \left[1 - \Phi(p_1 - \alpha' x - \varepsilon/2)\right] \\
& \times \left[\Phi(p_2 - \beta' z) - \Phi(p_2 - \varepsilon - \beta' z)\right],
\end{aligned}
\tag{63}
$$

where Φ denotes the distribution function for u_1 and u_2 and where the integrals from $p_2 - \varepsilon - v_1$ to ∞ and $p_1 - \varepsilon - v_2$ to ∞ in expressions (62)–(64) are evaluated at v_1 and v_2 equal to $\varepsilon/2$.

We now extend the analysis to include a third good, and assume that the goods can be purchased individually, in packages of any two, in a package of all three, or none at all. For notation, let $p_{ij} = p_i + p_j - \varepsilon_{ij}$ denote the price of the package that includes goods i and j at a discount of ε_{ij} from their individual prices, and let $p_b = p_1 + p_2 + p_3 - \varepsilon$ denote the price of the package that includes all three goods at a discount of ε from their individual prices, where ε is greater than ε_{ij}.

Purchase of good 1 alone requires that the following conditions be satisfied:

(i) $v_1 > p_1$
(ii) $v_1 + v_2 < p_{12},\ v_1 + v_3 < p_{13}$
(iii) $v_1 + v_2 + v_3 < p_b.$

Condition (i) is obvious. Condition (ii) rules out purchase of either good 2 or good 3 in a package with 1, while condition (iii) rules out the purchase of all three goods. Conditions (i) and (ii) can also be written as:

(iv) $v_1 > p_1$, $v_2 < p_2 - \varepsilon_{12}$, $v_3 < p_3 - \varepsilon_{13}$,

which in turn implies that:

(v) $v_1 > p_1$, $v_2 + v_3 < p_2 + p_3 - \varepsilon_{12} - \varepsilon_{13}$.

Combining (i) and (iii) yields:

(vi) $v_1 > p_1$, $v_2 + v_3 < p_2 + p_3 - \varepsilon$.

From these last two expressions, we can conclude that (v) implies (vi) if $\varepsilon < \varepsilon_{12} + \varepsilon_{13}$, while (vi) implies (v) if $\varepsilon > \varepsilon_{12} + \varepsilon_{13}$. Consequently, it follows that the probability of purchasing good 1 alone will be given by:

$$P(1 \text{ alone}) = \int_{p_1}^{\infty} \int_{0}^{p_2 - \varepsilon_{12}} \int_{0}^{p_3 - \varepsilon_{13}} f(v)\, dv, \quad \varepsilon < \varepsilon_{12} + \varepsilon_{13} \tag{64}$$

$$= \int_{p_1}^{\infty} \int_{0}^{p_2} \int_{0}^{p_3 - \varepsilon} f(v)\, dv + \int_{p_1}^{\infty} \int_{p_2 - \varepsilon}^{p_2} \int_{p_3 - \varepsilon + p_2 - v_2}^{p_3} f(v)\, dv, \quad \varepsilon > \varepsilon_{12} + \varepsilon_{13} \tag{65}$$

where $f(v)[= f(v_1, v_2, v_3)]$ denotes the joint density function of v_1, v_2, and v_3.

Similar expressions obtain for the probabilities of purchasing goods 2 and 3 alone:

$$P(2 \text{ alone}) = \int_{p_2}^{\infty} \int_{0}^{p_1 - \varepsilon_{12}} \int_{0}^{p_3 - \varepsilon_{23}} f(v)\, dv, \quad \varepsilon < \varepsilon_{12} + \varepsilon_{23} \tag{66}$$

$$= \int_{p_2}^{\infty} \int_{0}^{p_1} \int_{0}^{p_3 - \varepsilon} f(v)\, dv + \int_{p_2}^{\infty} \int_{p_1 - \varepsilon}^{p_1} \int_{p_2 - \varepsilon + p_1 - v_1}^{p_3} f(v)\, dv, \quad \varepsilon > \varepsilon_{12} + \varepsilon_{23} \tag{67}$$

$$P(3 \text{ alone}) = \int_{p_3}^{\infty} \int_{0}^{p_1 - \varepsilon_{13}} \int_{0}^{p_2 - \varepsilon_{23}} f(v)\, dv, \quad \varepsilon < \varepsilon_{13} + \varepsilon_{23} \tag{68}$$

$$= \int_{p_3}^{\infty} \int_{0}^{p_1} \int_{0}^{p_2 - \varepsilon} f(v)\, dv + \int_{p_3}^{\infty} \int_{p_1 - \varepsilon}^{\infty} \int_{p_2 - \varepsilon + p_1 - v_1}^{p_2} f(v)\, dv, \quad \varepsilon > \varepsilon_{12} + \varepsilon_{23} \tag{69}$$

The conditions that must be fulfilled for the purchase of goods 1 and 2 in a package are $v_1 + v_2 > p_{12}$ and $v_1 + v_2 + v_3 < p_b$, or equivalently, $v_1 + v_2 > p_{12}$ and $v_3 < p_3 - \varepsilon + \varepsilon_{12}$. The first condition again is obvious, while the second condition rules out the purchase of all three goods. The probability of purchasing goods 1 and 2 will accordingly be given by:

$$P(1\&2) = \int_0^{p_3-\varepsilon+\varepsilon_{12}} \int_{p_1}^{\infty} \int_{p_2-\varepsilon-\varepsilon_{12}}^{\infty} f(v)\, dv$$

$$+ \int_0^{p_3-\varepsilon+\varepsilon_{12}} \int_{p_1-\varepsilon_{12}}^{p_1} \int_{p_2-\varepsilon_{12}+p_1-v_1}^{p_2} f(v)\, dv. \tag{70}$$

Similarly, for $P(1\&2)$ and $P(2\&3)$:

$$P(1\&3) = \int_0^{p_2-\varepsilon+\varepsilon_{12}} \int_{p_1}^{\infty} \int_{p_3-\varepsilon-13}^{\infty} f(v)\, dv$$

$$+ \int_0^{p_2-\varepsilon+\varepsilon_{13}} \int_{p_1-\varepsilon_{13}}^{p_1} \int_{p_3-\varepsilon_{13}+p_1-v_1}^{p_3} f(v)\, dv. \tag{71}$$

$$P(2\&3) = \int_0^{p_1-\varepsilon+\varepsilon_{23}} \int_{p_2}^{\infty} \int_{p_3-\varepsilon-23}^{\infty} f(v)\, dv$$

$$+ \int_0^{p_1-\varepsilon+\varepsilon_{23}} \int_{p_2-\varepsilon_{23}}^{p_2} \int_{p_3-\varepsilon_{23}+p_2-v_2}^{p_3} f(v)\, dv. \tag{72}$$

The conditions that must be satisfied for all three goods to be purchased are: $v_1 + v_2 + v_3 > p_b$, $v_1 > p_1 - \varepsilon$, $v_2 > p_2 - \varepsilon$, and $v_3 > p_3 - \varepsilon$. The probability that these conditions obtain will accordingly be given by:[23]

$$P(1\&2\&3) = \int_{p_1-\varepsilon}^{\infty} \int_{p_2-\varepsilon}^{\infty} \int_{p_3-\varepsilon}^{\infty} f(v)\, dv$$

$$- \int_{p_1-\varepsilon}^{p_1} \int_{p_2-\varepsilon+p_1-v_1}^{p_2} \int_{p_3-\varepsilon+p_1-v_1+p_2-v_2}^{p_3} f(v)\, dv. \tag{73}$$

[23] This probability can be viewed geometrically as the probability measured over the volume in the positive orthant defined at the point $(p_1 - \varepsilon, p_2 - \varepsilon, p_3 - \varepsilon)$ minus the volume of the cube defined by that point and the plane defined by $(v_1 - p_1) + (v_2 - p_2) + (v_3 - p_3) = \varepsilon$.

Finally, the probability that none of the goods will be purchased is given by:[24]

$$P(\text{none}) = 1 - P(1 \text{ alone}) - P(2 \text{ alone}) - P(3 - \text{alone}) - P(1\&2)$$
$$- P(1\&3) - P(2\&3) - P(1\&2\&3)$$

$$= \int_0^\infty \int_0^{p_2-\varepsilon} \int_0^\infty f(v)\, dv + \int_{p_1-\varepsilon}^\infty \int_{p_2-\varepsilon}^\infty \int_0^{p_3-\varepsilon} f(v)\, dv$$

$$+ \int_0^{p_1-\varepsilon} \int_{p_2-\varepsilon}^\infty \int_{p_3-\varepsilon}^\infty f(v)\, dv$$

$$+ \int_{p_1-\varepsilon}^{p_1} \int_{p_2-\varepsilon+p_1-v_1}^{p_2} \int_{p_3-\varepsilon+p_1-v+p_2-v_2}^{p_3} f(v)\, dv. \tag{74}$$

As before, let $v_1 = \alpha' x + u_1$, $v_2 = \beta' z + u_2$, and $v_3 = \gamma' w + u_3$, where u_1, u_2, and u_3 are independently distributed random variables with zero means and variances σ_1^2, σ_2^2, and σ_3^2. We once again assume that demands are independent. Let ϕ denote the distribution function for the u's. With these assumptions and notation, the probabilities in expressions (64)–(74) can be written as:

$$P(1 \text{ alone}) = [1 - \phi(p_1 - \alpha' x)]\, \phi(p_2 - \varepsilon_{12} - \beta' z)\phi(p_3 - \varepsilon_{13} - \delta' w),$$
$$\varepsilon < \varepsilon_{12} + \varepsilon_{13} \tag{75}$$
$$= [1 - \phi(p_1 - \alpha' x)]\, \phi(p_2 - \beta' z)\phi(p_3 - \varepsilon - \delta' w)$$
$$+ \phi(p_3 - \varepsilon/2 - \delta' w)\, [\phi(p_2 - \beta' z) - \phi(p_2 - \varepsilon - \beta' z)],$$
$$\varepsilon > \varepsilon_{12} + \varepsilon_{13} \tag{76}$$

$$P(2 \text{ alone}) = [1 - \phi(p_2 - \beta' z)]\, \phi(p_1 - \varepsilon_{12} - \alpha' x)\phi(p_3 - \varepsilon_{23} - \delta' w),$$
$$\varepsilon < \varepsilon_{12} + \varepsilon_{13} \tag{77}$$
$$= [1 - \phi(p_2 - \beta' x)]\, \phi(p_1 - \varepsilon_{12} - \alpha' x)\phi(p_3 - \varepsilon_{23} - \delta' w)$$
$$+ \phi(p_3 - \varepsilon/2 - \delta' w)\, [\phi(p_1 - \alpha' x) - \phi(p_1 - \varepsilon - \alpha' x)],$$
$$\varepsilon > \varepsilon_{12} + \varepsilon_{13} \tag{78}$$

---

[24] This probability can be viewed geometrically as the probability measured over the volume between two positive orthants, one with origin at $(0, 0, 0)$ and the other with origin at $(p_1 - \varepsilon, p_2 - \varepsilon, p_3 - \varepsilon)$, plus the volume of the cube defined in the preceding footnote.

$$P(3 \text{ alone}) = [1 - \phi(p_3 - \delta'w)] \, \phi(p_1 - \varepsilon_{13} - \alpha'x)\phi(p_2 - \varepsilon_{23} - \beta'z),$$

$$\varepsilon < \varepsilon_{13} + \varepsilon_{23} \tag{79}$$

$$= [1 - \phi(p_3 - \delta'w)] \, \phi(p_1 - \varepsilon_{13} - \alpha'x)\phi(p_2 - \varepsilon_{23} - \beta'z)$$

$$+ \phi(p_2 - \varepsilon/2 - \beta'z) \left[\phi(p_1 - \alpha'x) - \delta(p_1 - \varepsilon - \alpha'x) \right],$$

$$\varepsilon > \varepsilon_{13} + \varepsilon_{23} \tag{80}$$

$$P(1\&2) = \phi(p_3 - \varepsilon + \varepsilon_{12} - \delta'w) \left[1 - \phi(p_1 - \alpha'x) \right]$$

$$\times \left[1 - \phi(p_2 - \varepsilon_{12} - \beta'z) \right]$$

$$+ \left[1 - \phi(p_2 - \varepsilon_{12/2} - \beta'z) \right]$$

$$\times \left[\phi(p_1 - \alpha'x) - \phi(p_1 - \varepsilon_{12} - \alpha'x) \right] \tag{81}$$

$$P(1\&3) = \phi(p_2 - \varepsilon + \varepsilon_{13} - \beta'z) \left[1 - \phi(p_1 - \alpha'x) \right]$$

$$\times \left[1 - \phi(p_3 - \varepsilon_{13} - \delta'w) \right]$$

$$+ \left[1 - \phi(p_3 - \varepsilon_{13/2} - \delta'w) \right]$$

$$\times \left[\pi(p_1 - \alpha'x) - \phi(p_1 - \varepsilon_{13} - \alpha'x) \right] \tag{82}$$

$$P(2\&3) = \phi(p_1 - \varepsilon + \varepsilon_{23} - \alpha'x) \left[1 - \phi(p_2 - \beta'z) \right]$$

$$\times \left[1 - \phi(p_3 - \varepsilon_{23} - \delta'w) \right]$$

$$+ \left[1 - \phi(p_3 - \varepsilon_{23/2} - \delta'w) \right]$$

$$\times \left[\pi(p_2 - \beta'z) - \phi(p_2 - \varepsilon_{23} - \beta'z) \right] \tag{83}$$

$$P(1\&2\&3) = \left[\phi(p_1 - \varepsilon - \alpha'x) \right] \left[1 - \phi(p_2 - \varepsilon - \beta'z) \right]$$

$$\times \left[1 - \phi(p_3 - \varepsilon - \delta'w) \right]$$

$$+ \left[\phi(p_1 - \alpha'x) - \phi(p_1 - \varepsilon - \alpha'x) \right] \left[\phi(p_2 - \beta'z) \right]$$

$$\times \left[\phi(p_3 - \delta'w) - \phi(p_3 - \varepsilon/3 - \delta'w) \right] \tag{84}$$

$$P(\text{none}) = \phi(p_2 - \varepsilon - \beta'z) + \left[1 - \phi(p_1 - \varepsilon - \alpha'x) \right]$$

$$\times \left[1 - \phi(p_2 - \varepsilon - \beta'z) \right] \phi(p_3 - \varepsilon - \delta'w)$$

$$+ \phi(p_1 - \varepsilon - \alpha'x) \left[1 - \phi(p_2 - \varepsilon - \beta'z) \right]$$

$$\times \left[1 - \phi(p_3 - \varepsilon - \delta'w) \right]$$
$$+ \left[\phi(p_1 - \alpha'x) - \phi(p_1 - \varepsilon - \alpha'x) \right]$$
$$\times \left[\phi(p_2 - \beta'z) - \phi(p_2 - 2\varepsilon/3 - \beta'z) \right]$$
$$\times \left[\phi(p_3 - \delta'w) - \phi(p_3 - \varepsilon/3 - \delta'w) \right], \tag{85}$$

where in calculating (84) and (85) the lower limits for v_2 and v_3 in the last integrals in expressions (70) and (71) are assumed to be $p_2 - 2\varepsilon/3$ and $p_3 - \varepsilon/3$.

From the foregoing, it is evident that adding goods to the choice set leads to increasingly complex expressions for the purchase probabilities and that the expressions for four goods will be messy indeed. This being the case, we shall now turn to questions of estimation and the calculation of elasticities under the assumption of a choice set of three goods. Formally, the problem is a multinomial choice problem with choice probabilities given by expressions (75)–(85). From these expressions, it is seen that the parameters to be estimated include the vectors α, β, and γ, plus the three variances, σ_1^2, σ_2^3, and σ_3^2.

Estimation of models of this type is by the method of maximum likelihood. As preparatory to the writing of the likelihood function, define a set of of eight dummy variables as follows:

$$y_1 = \begin{cases} 1 & \text{if customer chooses good 1 only} \\ 0 & \text{otherwise} \end{cases}$$

$$y_2 = \begin{cases} 1 & \text{if customer chooses good 2 only} \\ 0 & \text{otherwise} \end{cases}$$

$$y_3 = \begin{cases} 1 & \text{if customer chooses good 3 only} \\ 0 & \text{otherwise} \end{cases}$$

$$y_4 = \begin{cases} 1 & \text{if customer chooses good 1 and 2} \\ 0 & \text{otherwise} \end{cases}$$

$$y_5 = \begin{cases} 1 & \text{if customer chooses good 1 and 3} \\ 0 & \text{otherwise} \end{cases}$$

$$y_6 = \begin{cases} 1 & \text{if customer chooses good 2 and 3} \\ 0 & \text{otherwise} \end{cases}$$

$$y_7 = \begin{cases} 1 & \text{if customer chooses all three goods} \\ 0 & \text{otherwise} \end{cases}$$

$$y_8 = \begin{cases} 1 & \text{if customer chooses none of the goods} \\ 0 & \text{otherwise} \end{cases}$$

Also, let

$$P(1) = P(1 \text{ alone})$$

$$P(2) = P(2 \text{ alone})$$

$$P(3) = P(3 \text{ alone})$$

$$P(4) = P(1\&2)$$

$$P(5) = P(1\&3)$$

$$P(6) = P(2\&3)$$

$$P(7) = P(1\&2\&3)$$

$$P(8) = P(\text{none})$$

With this notation, the likelihood function for a sample of N households will be given by:

$$L = \prod_{i=1}^{N} \prod_{j=1}^{8} P_i(j)^{y_{ij}}, \tag{86}$$

or in logarithms:

$$\ln L = \sum_{i=1}^{N} \sum_{j=1}^{8} y_{ji} \ln P_i(j). \tag{87}$$

Estimates of α, β and γ can be obtained from solving the set of eight non-linear first-order-condition equations that arise from taking the partial derivatives of $\ln L$ with respect to α, β and γ. As these expressions are lengthy and messy, they will not be presented here.[25]
As is usual with quantal choice models, elasticities are defined in terms of the impact on choice probabilities of a change in price. Their calculation will be illustrated for the purchase probabilities for good 1. From expressions (60), (66), (67), and (69), we will have:

$$\frac{\partial P(1)}{\partial p_1} = -f(p_1 - \alpha' x)\phi(p_2 - \varepsilon_{12} - \beta' z)\phi(p_3 - \varepsilon_{13} - \gamma' w) \tag{88}$$

---

[25] Estimation obviously requires specification of the distribution function ϕ. The standard procedure is to assume ϕ to be either normal or logistic, yielding either a probit or logit model. The empirical results to be reported assume a probit framework.

$$\frac{\partial P(4)}{\partial p_1} = -\phi(p_3 - \varepsilon + \varepsilon_{12})f(p_1 - \alpha' x)\left[1 - \phi(p_2 - \varepsilon_{12} - \beta' z)\right]$$

$$- \left[1 - \phi(p_2 - \varepsilon_{12}/2 - \beta' z)\right]\left[f(p_1 - \alpha' x) - f(p_1 - \varepsilon_{12} - \alpha' x)\right] \quad (89)$$

$$\frac{\partial P(5)}{\partial p_1} = -\phi(p_2 - \varepsilon/2)f(p_1 - \alpha' x)\left[1 - \phi(p_3 - \varepsilon_{13} - \gamma' w)\right]$$

$$- \left[1 - \phi(p_3 - \varepsilon_{13}/2 - \gamma' w)\right]\left[f(p_1 - \alpha' x) - f(p_1 - \varepsilon - \alpha' x)\right] \quad (90)$$

$$\frac{\partial P(7)}{\partial p_1} = -f(p_1 - \varepsilon)\left[1 - \phi(p_2 - \varepsilon)\right]\left[1 - \phi(p_3 - \varepsilon)\right]$$

$$- f(p_1 - \alpha' x) - f(p_1 - \varepsilon - \alpha' x) \times \left[\phi(p_2 - \beta' z)\right.$$

$$\left. -\phi(p_2 - 2\varepsilon/3 - \beta' z)\right]\left[\phi(p_3 - \gamma' w) - \phi(p_3 - \varepsilon/3 - \gamma' w)\right]. \quad (91)$$

Consequently, for good 1 purchased wither singly or in packages with good 2 and 3:

$$\frac{\partial P(\text{good}1)}{\partial p_1} = \frac{\partial P(1)}{\partial p_1} + \frac{\partial P(4)}{\partial p_1} + \frac{\partial P(5)}{\partial p_1} + \frac{\partial P(7)}{\partial p_1}. \quad (92)$$

An elasticity can then be defined by:

$$\eta_{11} = \frac{\partial P(1)}{\partial p_1} \cdot \frac{p_1}{P(1)} + \frac{\partial P(4)}{\partial p_1} \cdot \frac{p_1}{P(4)}$$

$$+ \frac{\partial P(5)}{\partial p_1} \cdot \frac{p_1}{P(5)} + \frac{\partial P(7)}{\partial p_1} \cdot \frac{p_1}{P(7)}. \quad (93)$$

We now report the results of an application of the foregoing undertaken by Kridel and Taylor (1993) to a sample of about 9000 households drawn from the data base of the National Telecommunications Demand Study. The application is to two custom-calling features, call-waiting and call-forwarding. In the sample analyzed, which was collected in the first quarter of 1989, approximately 75% of the customers purchased neither service, about 20% purchased call-waiting alone, 1% call-forwarding alone, and the remaining 4% purchased the package.[26]

In the discussion that follows, CW and CF will be denoted by subscripts 1 and 2, respectively. The probability functions corresponding to expressions (59)–(61) specified by Kridel and Taylor (KT) are as follows:

$$P(1 \text{ alone} = \left[1 - \phi(\gamma_1 p_1 - \tilde{\alpha}' x)\right]\phi(\gamma_2\{p_2 - \varepsilon\} - \tilde{w}' z) \quad (94)$$

---

[26] The sample used in estimation is stratified by package: only those households that purchase CW or CF alone or packaged with each other are included.

$$P(2 \text{ alone} = \left[1 - \phi(\gamma_2 p_2 - \tilde{w}'z)\right] \phi(\gamma_1\{p_1 - \varepsilon\} - \tilde{\alpha}'w) \tag{95}$$

$$
\begin{aligned}
P(1\&2) = {} & \left[1 - \phi(\gamma_1\{p_1 - \varepsilon\} - \tilde{\alpha}'x)\right] \left[1 - \phi(\gamma_2\{p_2 - \varepsilon\} - \tilde{w}'z\right] \\
& + 0.5 \left[\phi(\gamma_1\{p_1 - \varepsilon\} - \tilde{\alpha}'x) - \phi(\gamma_1 p_1 - \tilde{\alpha}'x)\right] \\
& \times \left[\phi(\gamma_2\{p_2 - \varepsilon\} - \tilde{w}'z) - \phi(\gamma_2 p_2 - \tilde{w}'z)\right],
\end{aligned} \tag{96}
$$

where:

ϕ denotes the standard normal distribution function

$\gamma_i = 1/\sigma_i$

$\tilde{\alpha} = \alpha/\sigma_1$

$\tilde{w} = w/\sigma_2$

$\varepsilon = $ the discount

$\sigma_1, \sigma_2 = $ standard deviations of u_1, u_2.

The systematic parts of the willingness-to-pay (v_1 and v_2), $\tilde{\alpha}'$ and $\tilde{w}'$, are specified as follows:

$$
\begin{aligned}
\tilde{\alpha}'x = {} & \tilde{\alpha}_0 + \tilde{\alpha}_1 \text{HHSIZE} + \tilde{\alpha}_2 \text{LINC} \\
& + \tilde{\alpha}_3 \text{MARRIED} + \tilde{\alpha}_4 \text{URBAN} + \tilde{\beta} \text{SALESOPP}
\end{aligned} \tag{97}
$$

$$\tilde{w}' = \tilde{w}_0 + \tilde{w}_1 \text{LINC} + \tilde{w}_2 \text{MARRIED} + \tilde{\beta} \text{SALESOPP}, \tag{98}$$

where:[27]

HHSIZE = household size

LINC = logarithm of household income

MARRIED = indicator for married households

URBAN = indicator for households in urban areas

SALESOPP = sales opportunity index, defined as 1 for customers who have had account activity since 1958, -1 with no activity since 1980, and 0 otherwise

$\tilde{\alpha}_i, \tilde{w}_i, \tilde{\beta}_i = $ parameters to be estimated.

[27] Income and the demographical variables in the NTDS data base are matched with households at the block level. Hence, the data in the sample, except for the individual account and the account activity, are block group aggregates (e.g., MARRIED is the proportion of married households within the block group in which the household lives).

In addition to the model just presented, which assumes that the error terms for the two services are independent, Kridel and Taylor also estimate a model in which independence is not assumed. Independence is almost surely violated for call-waiting and call-forwarding, for the unobservables that make a household likely to purchase CW are likely to be correlated with the unobservables that make a household likely to purchase CF. The unobservables in both cases may, for example, reflect a taste for "high-tech" services.

Non-independence leads to some complications in evaluating the integrals in expressions (95)–(97) and requires some respecification as follows:[28]

$$P(1 \text{ alone}) = \phi(\gamma_1 p_1 - \tilde{\alpha}'x, \infty, \rho)$$
$$- \phi(\gamma_1 p_1 - \tilde{\alpha}'x, \gamma_2\{p_2 - \varepsilon\} - \tilde{w}'z, \rho) \quad (99)$$

$$P(2 \text{ alone}) = \phi(\infty, \gamma_2, p_2 - \tilde{w}'z, \rho)$$
$$- \phi(\gamma_1\{p_1 - \varepsilon\} - \tilde{\alpha}'x, \gamma_2 p_2 - \tilde{w}'z, \rho) \quad (100)$$

$$P(1\&2) = P(\text{both anyway}) + P(2 \text{ anyway and 1 with } \varepsilon)$$
$$+ P(1 \text{ anyway and 1 with } \varepsilon) + P(\text{both due to } \varepsilon), \quad (101)$$

where:[29]

$$P(\text{both anyway}) = 1 - \phi(\gamma_1 p_1 - \tilde{\alpha}'x, \gamma_2 p_2 - \tilde{w}'z, \rho) \quad (102)$$

$$P(2 \text{ anyway and 1 with } \varepsilon) = \phi(\gamma_1\{p_1 - \varepsilon\} - \tilde{\alpha}'x, \infty, \rho)$$
$$- \phi(\gamma_1 p_1 - \tilde{\alpha}'x, \gamma_2 p_2 - \tilde{w}'z, \rho) \quad (103)$$

---

[28] The complications arise because of the need to evaluate integrals in which the inequalities go in different directions, as in $P(u_1 < k_1, u_2 > k_2)$. With independence, this probability is simply $[1 - \phi(k_1)]\phi(k_2)$ and is straightforward to evaluate. With non-independence case, this is no longer the case, but requires rewriting the integrals so that the inequalities all go in the same direction. Johnson and Kotz (1972) provide a discussion of what is involved. Note: $\phi(k_1, k_2, \rho)$ in the equations that follow now refers to the distribution function for the bi-variate unit normal with correlation ρ.

[29] These four probabilities correspond to the four disjoint areas of buying both services in Figure 7: "both anyway" represents the households that would buy both services in the absence of a discount, "2 anyway and 1 with ε" represents the households that are induced to buy CF with CW because of the discount, "1 anyway and 2 with ε" represents the households that are induced to buy CW with CF because of the discount, while "both due to ε" represents the households that would buy neither service in the absence of the discount.

$$P(1 \text{ anyway and } 2 \text{ with } \varepsilon) = \phi(\infty, \gamma_2\{p_2 - \varepsilon\}, \tilde{w}'z, \rho)$$
$$- \phi(\gamma_1 p_1 - \tilde{\alpha}'x, \gamma_2 p_2 - \tilde{w}'z, \rho) \qquad (104)$$

$$P(\text{both due to } \varepsilon) = 0.5 \left[\phi(\gamma_1\{p_1 - \varepsilon\} - \tilde{\alpha}'x) - \phi(\gamma_1 p_1 - \tilde{\alpha}'x)\right]$$
$$\cdot \left[\phi(\gamma_2\{p_2 - \varepsilon\} - \tilde{w}'z) - \phi(\gamma_2 p_2 - \tilde{w}'z)\right]. \qquad (105)$$

The estimation results for the two models are provided in Table 9.[30] All coefficients are significant and have the theoretically expected sign.[31] Except for the constant ($\tilde{w}_0$) and the price coefficient (γ_2) for CF, the coefficient estimates are not materially affected as the independence assumption is relaxed. (Note, however, the substantial decrease in the t-ratio for γ_2). In both models, the coefficient on the price of CF (γ_2) is much larger than the corresponding coefficient for CW (γ_1). The correlation coefficient is seen to be very significant and its inclusion leads to a 1.3% improvement in the likelihood function at convergence.

The impacts of customer contact are interesting as well. Not surprisingly, customers who have had a recent contact with the telephone company (SALEOPP) are more likely to have purchased a CCS feature. In contrast, those who have not had account activity in the last decade are less likely to have any CCS feature. Although it affects the probability of purchasing a CCS feature, account activity does not significantly influence the type of service chosen.

Figure 8 compares actual penetration levels with those predicted by both models. As is evident, the model that assumes independence performs poorly (over-predicting CW by nearly 6%, CF by 114%, and under-predicting the package by 29%). On the other hand, the model that allows for dependence predicts reasonably well (over-predicting CW by less than 0.5%, CF by 10% and under-predicting the package by under 3%). This difference in predictive ability, coupled with the statistical improvement in the model, clearly favors the model allowing dependence. All subsequent discussion will accordingly be based on the model that allows dependence.

A more stringent test of the predictive ability is to consider customer segments instead of aggregate predictions. Figure 9 provides a visual comparison of actual and predicted values across the 4 income quartiles. On the whole, the model appears to fit the observed data quite well. As can be observed,

---

[30] All estimation was performed utilizing PERM. The optimization algorithm – a hybrid BHHH/Quasi-Newton – was originally developed by Richard Spady at Bell Communications Research.

[31] Notice the way the prices enter the probabilities that a positive coefficient implies a negative impact on choice.

TABLE 9

Coefficient estimates; Kridel-Taylor study

Variable	Independent Errors		Dependent Errors	
	Estimate	t-statistic	Estimate	t-statistic
constant ($\tilde{\alpha}_0$)	-11.46	-21.3	-11.320	-21.0
$P_{cw}(\gamma_1)$	0.059	8.1	0.054	7.5
HHSIZE ($\tilde{\alpha}_1$)	0.772	17.0	0.739	16.6
LINCOME ($\tilde{\alpha}_2$)	1.023	17.7	1.011	17.7
MARRIED ($\tilde{\alpha}_3$)	-0.029	-15.9	-0.028	-15.9
URBAN ($\tilde{\alpha}_4$)	0.005	8.0	0.005	7.9
SALES OPP (β)	0.096	5.4	0.111	5.3
constant ($\tilde{\omega}_0$)	-4.930	-6.4	-7.280	-9.4
$P_{cf}(\gamma_2)$	0.956	21.1	0.444	7.3
LINCOME ($\tilde{\omega}_1$)	0.598	7.3	0.724	9.1
MARRIED ($\tilde{\omega}_2$)	-0.010	-5.6	-0.011	-6.3
correlation	NA	NA	0.458	13.3
Likelihood at convergence		-6164.97		-6082.57

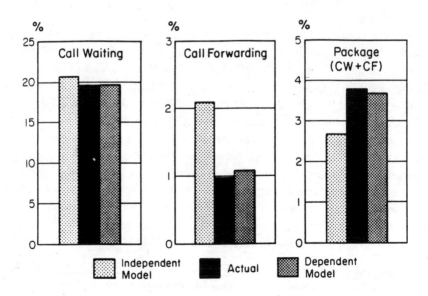

Fig. 8.   Actual vs. predicted levels (%).

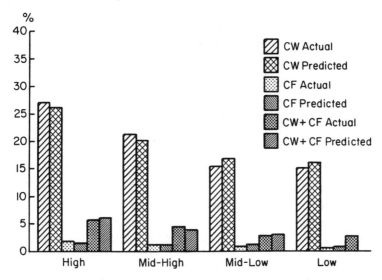

Fig. 9.   Penetration (%) by income quartile actual vs. predicted.

both CW and CF over-predict at the lower end of the income distribution and under-predict at the upper end. This is consistent with an underestimation of the income coefficient.[32] For CW, however, the errors are not serious (the largest being about 8%). While the errors are much larger for CF (the largest being about 92%), these errors seem acceptable given the relatively low penetration of CF singly. The errors for the package show no consistent pattern as income is increased, suggesting that bias in the income coefficient does not extend to the package.

Simulation of the model obtained above (at current price and income levels) yields the following results:

1. The price elasticity of demand for CW individually is about -0.14;
2. The price elasticity of demand for CF individually is about -2.5;
3. The income elasticities of demand for the features are: 1.1 for CW, 0.7 for CF, and 1.9 for the package;
4. Of those that buy the package, approximately 58% would have bought both services even without the discount, 40% are induced to buy CF because it is discounted, just over 1% are induced to buy CW along with CF because CW is discounted, and the remaining 1% (that would have bought neither service) are induced to buy both services because of the discount.[33]

---

[32] This could reflect a censoring bias induced by the stratification of the sample.

[33] We are describing these probabilities loosely. In fact, for each individual we calculate the probability of falling in each cell. We then aggregate across individuals in the standard way

5. Approximately 58% of those that buy both services, would have bought both services even without the discount;
6. Virtually no customers (1%) are induced to buy CW along with CF because CW is discounted and very few customers (< 1%) are induced to buy both services because of the discount.

To illustrate the comparative statics, the model was simulated for three hypothetical changes in the discount (ε) and the price of call waiting: (1) the discount is set to zero: (2) the price of CW is increased by 25%; and (3) the price of CW is increased 25% simultaneously with a 50% increase in the discount (ε). The results show that eliminating the discount reduces revenue by approximately 2%. In addition to the decline in revenue, the results indicate that the proportion of customers predicted to purchase both services would fall over 40% (from approximately 3.7% to 2.1%) as a result of the elimination of the discount.

Increasing the price of CW 25% would generate approximately 17% more revenue, while the proportion of customers without either CCS feature would only increase from 75.6% to 76.4%. Finally, simultaneously increasing the discount (ε) by 50% and the price of CW by 25% would increase revenue by just over 17%, while the number of customers predicted to purchase the package would increase from 3.6% to 4.7%. Relative to the changing of only the price of call waiting, the results indicate that the joint change of the discount and the CW price would reduce the number of subscribers by 0.4%.

The Kridel-Taylor study illustrates the feasibility of applying standard quantal-choice methodology to the demand for commodity bundles. The study will obviously not be the last word on the subject because of its restriction to packages of two services. Extension to packages of three or more services is reasonably straight-forward in the case of independence, but not (as the Kridel-Taylor results suggest to be the case) in the event of non-independence. Current plans are to approach estimation in this case using a simulated-methods-of-moments framework,[34] and also in a non-parametric framework.

(simple enumeration) to estimate the probability that an individual would fall in any one cell.
[34] See McFadden (1989) and Pakes and Pollard (1989).

CHAPTER 8

BUSINESS TELEPHONE SYSTEM DEMAND, TOTAL-BILL, AND SOCIO-DEMOGRAPHIC EFFECTS

This chapter completes the review of the empirical literature on telecommunications demand by collecting together several miscellaneous topics, all of interest but none with a literature large enough to warrant a separate chapter. The topics to be discussed include the business demand for telephone systems, total-bill effects, and socio-demographic effects.

I. BUSINESS TELEPHONE SYSTEM DEMAND

In this section, we will take a look at a recent study by Ben-Akiva and Gershenfeld (1989) that focuses on business choice of a telephone system. As discussed in Chapter 4, a major difference between business and residential demands for access is that business access demand is much more intertwined with the demand for customer-premise equipment. The governing factor is the large number of lines that, small retail establishments aside, the typical business requires and the consequent needs for internal communication. Small numbers of lines can be handled through a key system, but large numbers require much larger capacity to switch, in which case the question becomes whether to do the switching on premise through the purchase or lease of a PBX or to switch off premise through the purchase of centrex service. Households and small businesses whose usage needs require just a few lines do not face this choice.[1]

Previous studies of business access demand have been time-series (or combined time-series/cross-section) models which focus on the demand for business access lines, where lines are defined in terms of single-line equivalents. Centrex lines are counted, one-for-one, as regular lines, whereas PBX

---

[1] Recent advances in centrex offerings now make centrex feasible for four lines or less, especially when packaged with custom- or class-calling features.

193

trunks are typically counted as eight regular lines.[2] The information provided by such studies is useful in terms of the volume of access that is driven by usage, but no information is provided on the choice among alternative telephone systems. The Ben-Akiva/Gershenfeld study is the first to focus on this choice.

The framework employed by Ben-Akiva and Gershenfeld (BG) is a nested conditional logit model in which the decision to acquire a particular telephone system is pursued in two stages. In the first stage, the firm decides whether to change telephone systems, while in the second stage, which is conditional on the decision to switch, the firm decides upon which new system to acquire. The model, accordingly, has the same form as the one used in the study of Train, McFadden, and Ben-Akiva (1987) that is discussed in Chapter 5: the probability of the joint event to switch to a new system and the choice of a particular system is decomposed into the product of the unconditional probability of switching to a new system with the conditional probability of purchasing a specific system given the decision to switch to begin with. Logit models are specified for the probabilities at the two stages (or levels).

The upper-level model relates the decision to switch to a new telephone system to the firm's demand for access lines and the transaction costs that would be involved in replacing the existing system. As transaction costs are for the most part firm-specific, they are measured by a variety of firm characteristics. These include:

1. The change in the number of lines from the previous to the current year;
2. The number of centrex equivalent lines;
3. Multiple rather than sole occupancy of the building;
4. Rental of the firm's premises rather than ownership;
5. The existence of plans for the firm to move to a different location;
6. The number of years that the firm has been at the current location.

In the lower-level model (i.e., the model describing the choice of type of new telephone system, given that a new system is to be purchased), the choice probabilities are related to system costs as well as firm characteristics. Three categories of costs are included in the model: non-recurring charges, monthly recurring charges, and equipment costs. The non-recurring and recurring monthly charges are those that are paid to the local telephone company. Equipment costs include estimates of installation and wiring costs in addition

---

[2] Attempts, as at Bell Canada, to estimate separate time-series models for PBX trunks have not been particularly successful. The major problem in doing so is the deregulation in both the U.S. and Canada of the terminal equipment market and the general lack of price indices for terminal equipment that adequately account for technological change. The inability to date to account, in a time-series context for substitution between PBX and Centrex is also a factor.

to equipment charges. Equipment and installation costs are assumed to be zero for standard service. Since firms vary in size, the prices included in the model are expressed on a per-line basis, calculated by dividing total cost by centrex line equivalents.

The choice set of telephone systems is assumed to consist of standard service, key, PBX, and centrex service. No system at all is included implicitly as the initial condition for new customers. A decision to purchase a new system is defined as including not only a switch from one system to another (as in the replacing of a key system with a PBX), but also the replacement of a key system with another key system and the same for a PBX. Retaining standard or centrex service, however, is treated as no change.

The data analyzed in the study consist of a sample of 1000 business customers drawn from the customer list of a Bell Operating Company. The sampling unit is the business establishment or location. In order to get a sample with a reasonable number of observations in each of the categories of interest, the sample design was a stratified sample enriched with a sample of switchers. Telephone company records for the units sampled was augmented by customer-specific information obtained by telephone interviews. Data on business customer telephone systems were collected during August and September 1987. Firms provided information about the type of telephone systems that were currently being used, the date of acquisition of the system, the type of system that had been used previously, and other firm characteristics. A firm was designated a "switcher" for model estimation if it had acquired a new telephone system within the previous 18 months. Telephone company records for the customers provided data on the number of lines, distance from central office, and other information.

The empirical results for the lower-level model (choice of system type) show that the primary driving variables are the system costs. With inclusion of cost variables, other variables related to firm characteristics have little influence on the choice of system type. The relative values of the price coefficients seem to indicate that customers are most sensitive to monthly recurring charges and are considerably less sensitive to one-time charges. Examination of the coefficients in present value terms, however, reveals high implicit discount rates, which is to say that there is a large disutility in paying now rather than later. Interestingly, of the one-time charges, customers appear to be more sensitive to non-recurring telephone company charges than to equipment costs.

The firm-specific variables in the model indicate that, *ceteris paribus*, centrex, PBX, and key systems are less favored in relation to standard service in retail and wholesale trade, while the reverse is true for firms in manufacturing. This is consistent with manufacturing firms being larger and having a greater need for internal communication between employees, therefore requiring more sophisticated telephone systems. The results also indicate a system inertia, in which everything else being constant firms tend to replace a key system with another key system and the same for PBXs.

In the upper-level model (the switch/no switch decision), the results show that as a firm grows (as represented by the change in the number of access lines demanded), the probability of switching to a new telephone system increases as well. A larger total number of lines (as opposed to the change), however, leads to larger transaction costs and decreases the probability of switching. The probability of switching is also decreased by the longer that the firm has been at the same location and, not surprisingly, by expressed plans to move to a new location within the next three years.

The inclusive-value variables that are included in the upper-level model (as measured by the logarithm of the denominator of the lower-level choice model) represent the net gain by a switch from one system to another. These variables are introduced in the model specific to previous system type, as are all of the variables in the upper-level model. If the coefficient of the inclusive-value variable is zero or insignificant, the implication is that the attributes of potential new systems do not have a significant effect on the decision to switch to a new system. The results show significant coefficients for the inclusive-value variable for firms with previous centrex and standard systems, but insignificant coefficients for firms with previous PBX and key. Ben-Akiva and Gershenfeld interpret these results as indicating that firms with PBX and key systems who have ties to their equipment or who have made capital investments in their systems are *pushed* into switching by the conditions of their current system. In contrast, centrex and standard customers who are not physically tied to their existing systems may be *pulled* into switching by the attributes of a new system.[3]

The BG models are developed at the customer level and predict individual customer behavior. Market behavior is analyzed by Ben-Akiva and Gershenfeld through the microsimulation technique known as sample enumeration. In this procedure, choice probabilities are calculated for the firms in the sample based on the estimated choice equations. The values of the independent variables in the models can be modified to reflect changes in tariffs, equipment costs, and the availability of centrex service. Each firm in the sample is assigned an expansion factor (or weight) that is applied to the calculated choice probabilities. The weighted probabilities are then summed across the sample to produce estimates of market demands.

The BG results for the market demands for centrex and dial-tone lines

[3] Ben-Akiva and Gershenfeld (1989, p. 23).

TABLE 1

Demand Effects

Ben-Akiva/Gershenfeld Study

Due to 1 Percent Increase in:	Percent Change In:			
	Number of Centrex Lines	Number of Dial Tones Lines	Number of Centrex Customers	Number of Dial Tone Customers
Centrex	−0.38	0.04	−1.36	0.02
Dial Tone Charges	0.27	−0.05	1.18	−0.02
Equipment Costs	0.95	−0.10	2.19	−0.03

Source: Ben-Akiva and Gershenfeld (1989, Table 4–3).

and centrex and dial-tone customers from applying this technique to one-percent increases in centrex charges, dial-tone charges, and equipment costs are presented in Table 1.[4] The percent increases in centrex and dial-tone rates represent an increase in the entire tariff, that is, both recurring and non-recurring charges. The table shows much larger numbers for centrex lines and customers than for dial-tone lines and customers. This reflects the much smaller base of centrex lines. The value of −0.05 for dial-tone lines is consistent with most other estimates of the price elasticity for standard forms of access.

Of particular interest is the difference in the estimates between lines and customers. For centrex service, the number of customers is much more sensitive to price changes than the number of lines, while the opposite is true for regular dial-tone service. The latter is clearly to be expected, since for multi-line customers, adjustment will be in terms of the volume of access, rather than access *per se*. Also, since key and PBX systems are represented in terms of centrex line equivalents, the only substitution reflected in Table 1 is between centrex and "regular" dial-tone. Any substitution between standard access and key and between key and PBX triggered by an increase in dial-tone rates will be washed out.

The situation is different with centrex. The typical centrex customer will have a large number of lines and the only really relevant substitution is between centrex and a PBX. In contrast to dial-tone, an increase in centrex

[4] Ben-Akiva and Gershenfeld emphasize that the numbers in this table represent predicted changes in demand over an 18-month period.

TABLE 2

Own Elasticities
Ben-Akiva/Gershenfeld Study

Centrex: Total	−0.44
Line Size Group*	
1 (smallest)	−1.02
2	−1.74
3	−0.17
4 (largest)	−0.23
Dial Tone: Total	−0.10
Line Size Group*	
1	−0.06
2	−0.40
3	−0.03
4	−0.02

*   All line size Categories are in terms of Centrex line equivalents.
Source: Ben-Akiva and Gershenfeld (1989, Table 4–4).

rates is much more likely to affect the *type* of access rather than the *volume* of access. As the base of centrex customers is small in relation to the number of lines, a switch to a PBX from centrex will have a larger percentage effect on the number of customers than on the number of lines.[5]

Estimates of the own-price elasticities calculated from the conventional elasticity formula for probabilistic choice models are presented for the BG models in Table 2. Estimates are calculated for four different line size-groups for both centrex and dial-tone. The estimates are calculated at the weighted sample means. Examination of the elasticities by line size-group indicates that demand is least elastic for large customers, presumably because large firms face high transaction costs in switching to a new telephone system. Therefore, they are not likely to be able to react to price changes as quickly as

[5] The substantial cross-price effect on centrex demand of a change in PBX and key system equipment costs should be noted. This cross-elasticity indicates a high degree of substitutability between centrex service and competing CPE technologies. As noted in footnote 2 above, the inability to take this substitutability into account has plagued efforts to model business access demand using aggregate time-series data.

smaller firms would be able to.[6] Large firms also have the smallest number of alternatives available to them, since standard service is not an option and key systems are infeasible beyond a certain size. Demand is accordingly most elastic in line size group 2, for medium-sized firms have the largest number of alternatives available to them.

Ben-Akiva and Gershenfeld summarize the implications of their empirical results as follows:[7]

> Short-run price response varies by size of firm: The heterogeneity of firms with respect to their telecommunications needs has been acknowledged previously. Our model indicates that their heterogeneity applies to price sensitivity as well. Therefore, the effects of changes in rates should be analyzed by line size segment rather than in the aggregate.
>
> Firms' implicit discount rates are high: Non-recurring charges tend to discourage firms from switching to a new service and should therefore be kept low. This strategy of reducing or waiving the one-time charge for a service has already been used to several cases by telecommunications firms to attract new customers to the service.
>
> A high degree of substitutability exists between Centrex and competing CPE: Centrex demand is therefore vulnerable to price changes in the equipment market. Service providers should monitor the developments in the equipment market and analyze the potential response of firms to changes in the market.

The Ben-Akiva/Gershenfeld study makes an important contribution to empirical knowledge of the business demand for access and customer-premise equipment. The models employed are consistent with the theoretical structure of business telecommunications demand that was presented in Chapter 4, and the results confirm the heterogeneous nature of business demand that chapter emphasizes. The price elasticities that are obtained are consistent with the best existing estimates of the price elasticity for standard dial-tone and they provide the first defensible estimates of the own-and cross-price elasticities for centex service. The study is a solid piece of research and merits extension to the demand for private-line services.[8]

---

[6] Since the analysis covers an 18-month horizon, the elasticities should be interpreted as essentially short-run elasticities.

[7] Ben-Akiva and Gershenfeld (1989, p. 28).

[8] Nieswiadomy and Brink (1990) is the only recent private-line demand study of which I am aware. The model is point-to-point (LATA-to-LATA) for 57 LATAs using AT&T data for 1983–1987.

II. TOTAL-BILL EFFECTS

We now turn to an often recurring question in analyzing telephone demand, namely, whether households approach their expenditures for telecommunications services in terms of a total bill. The usual assumption in demand analysis – and the one that has been implicit throughout this book – is that telephone services – local, long distance, features, etc. – compete along with all of the other goods and services in the household's market basket for the household's income. In this framework, short-haul toll calls can be either complements or substitutes for long-haul calls and an increase in access charges need not impinge upon either. An alternative view, is that households budget for a total amount to be spent on telecommunications services so that an increase in access charges (say) will necessarily lead to less being spent on usage.

At one level, the debate can be cast in terms of what is the appropriate budget constraint to be used in telecommunications demand functions: income or a budgeted total expenditure for telecommunications? Should the household's preferences be appropriately separable (whether weakly or strongly need not concern us), the two approaches are of course equivalent, for the optimization problem can be formulated in terms of a two-stage budgeting. In the first stage, the household decides how to allocate its income between telecommunications and all other goods and services, while in the second stage it allocates the total telecommunications expenditure determined in the first stage optimally among the different telecommunications services (including access).

Whether a household's preferences are appropriately separable is ultimately an empirical question, and until recently has not been addressed in a systematic fashion. Among some, however, there appears to be an even stronger assumption than separability, namely, the view that all that matters to the consumer is the total bill.[9] Households are assumed to alter their demands in response to changes in telephone prices to keep the total bill unchanged. The practical difference between this assumption and separability (or two-stage budgeting) is in the total-bill response to price changes in individual telephone services. With two-stage budgeting, a household would reassess its total phone bill in response to a price change, whereas with the second assumption, the phone bill would not be reassessed, but demands would be altered so that total spending remains the same.

In the paper now to be discussed, Zona and Jacob (1990) examine the Doherty-Oscar Total Bill hypothesis *vis-à-vis* the two stage budgeting hypothesis using data for United Telecommunications. As Zona and Jacob (ZJ) note, the hypotheses impose different structures on cross-price elasticities. Two-

---

[9] See Doherty and Oscar (1977).

stage budgeting implies that a consumer's demand response for a good in one group for a price change in another group is independent of the specific price that is changed. A targeted total bill, in contrast, implies that own-and cross-price elasticities within the group within which there is a price change must compensate for one another.

The vehicle employed by Zona and Jacob to test the hypotheses is the Almost Ideal Demand System (or ALIDS) of Deaton and Muellbauer (1980). The ALIDS is a budget share model, which relates expenditure shares to prices and the level of total expenditure. The ALIDS specification involves flexible functional forms and does not limit substitution, but it easily allows in estimation for the restrictions on cross elasticities that are imposed by the two hypotheses. The ZJ procedure is to estimate three models, an unrestricted model, in which the budget constraint is income and no restrictions are imposed on the cross elasticities, and two restricted models, one corresponding to the Two-Stage Budgeting hypothesis and the other corresponding to the Total-Bill hypothesis.

The unrestricted model has four share equations, for each of interLATA toll, intraLATA toll, local service (access, custom calling features, inside wiring, etc.), and all other goods. For good i, the ALIDS specification is given by

$$w_i = \alpha_i + \sum_j \gamma_{ij} \ln P_j + \beta_i \ln(x/P). \tag{1}$$

where w_i denotes the budget share, p_i is the price of good j, x is income, and P is the quadratic price deflator defined by Deaton and Muellbauer. Certain restrictions on the parameters are imposed across equations in order to ensure consistency (adding up, symmetry, etc.) with standard demand theory.[10] The price elasticities for the model are given by

$$\eta_{ij} = \frac{1}{w_i} \left(\gamma_{ij} - \beta_i d_j - \beta_i \frac{\Sigma}{k} \gamma_{jk} \ln P_k \right) - \delta_{ij}, \tag{2}$$

where $\delta_{ij} = 1$ if $i = j$ and 0 otherwise.

Under the Two-Stage Budgeting hypothesis, the second stage conditional budget share will be given by

$$w_i^* = \alpha_i^* + \sum_j \gamma_{ij}^* \ln P_j + \beta_i^* \ln(B/P^*), \tag{3}$$

where w_i^* is the bill share for service i, B is the total phone bill, and P^* is a suitably defined quadratic price deflator. Conditional price elasticities are

---

[10]   See Deaton and Muellbauer (1980, p. 316).

given by the same formula as in expression (2), except that B is substituted for x and the parameters are replaced by the ones appearing in expression (3):

$$\eta_{ij}^G = \frac{1}{w_i^*}\left(\gamma_{ij}^* - \beta_i^*\alpha_j^* - \beta_i^*\sum_k \gamma_{jk}^* \ln P_k\right) - \delta_{ij}. \tag{4}$$

In the first stage, households are assumed to allocate income (or total expenditure) between telecommunications and all other goods. Zona and Jacob again assume an ALIDS specification:

$$w^G = \alpha + \gamma \ln(P_B/\text{CPI}) + \beta \ln(x/P^{**}), \tag{5}$$

where w^G is the telecommunications budget share, P_B is the telecommunications group price index, CPI is the price of other goods, and P^{**} is a suitably defined quadratic price deflator. The group price elasticity is given by

$$\eta^G = \left[\frac{x}{B}\gamma - \beta\alpha - \beta\gamma\ln(P_B/\text{CPI})\right] - 1. \tag{6}$$

Unconditional elasticities are obtained in the two-stage budgeting model by combining the group elasticities with the conditional elasticities. These are given by

$$\eta_{ij} = \eta_{ij}^G + \eta_i^G w_j^*(1 + \eta^G), \tag{7}$$

where η_i^G represents the conditional expenditure elasticity for good i. This expression can be interpreted as the conditional price elasticity plus a bill effect (η_i^G) times the percent change in the bill due to a change in the price of a telephone service.[11]

Under the Targeted-Bill hypothesis, the group price elasticity must be equal to -1 since the bill does not change when there is a change in the group price. This implies, accordingly, that the first term in the parenthesis on the right-hand side in expression (7) must be equal to zero, or equivalently that

$$\gamma - \beta\alpha - \beta\gamma\ln(P_B/\text{CPI}) = 0. \tag{8}$$

The data used by Zona and Jacob in estimation are from four distinct areas served by the United Telecommunications System. Each area is located in a different state and face different local tariffs. The time frame of the data used in the analysis was June–December 1989. All billed residential recurring revenues were recorded. For toll, information on minutes, messages, and recurring revenues was collected by jurisdiction at the LATA level for message telephone service. The local portion of the bill consisted of all access lines

---

[11] See Zona and Jacob (1990, p. 7).

TABLE 3

Own & Cross Price Elasticities
Zona–Jacob Study

Model		Price Elasticity		
		Interlata	Intralata	Local Service
Unrestricted	Interlate	−0.49	0.07	0.005
	Intralata	0.08	−0.47	0.005
	Local Service	0.02	0.01	−0.15
Two-Stage Budgeting	Interlata	−0.41	0.09	−0.06
	Intralata	0.10	−0.47	−0.07
	Local Service	0.07	0.06	−0.15
Bill-Targeting	Interlata	−0.79	−0.21	−0.39
	Intralata	−0.30	−0.79	−0.42
	Local Service	0.04	0.04	−0.17

Source: Zona and Jacob (1990, Tables 1–3)

reported as residential and their associated recurring billed revenues, and included recurring charges for custom-calling features, touch tone, inside wiring, the subscriber line charge, and other items that are billed on an ongoing basis. As local exchange and interexchange companies are increasingly billing separately for their services, the four areas included in the study were areas where equal access had not yet been implemented. This was done in order to increase the likelihood that United was the billing agent for all telecommunications services.

The telephone data are aggregated to the three services noted earlier, local, intraLATA toll, and interLATA toll. The variables developed include the average total bill (total revenue divided by estimates of the numbers of households in the areas), bill shares for the three services, price indices for the three services (defined as average revenue per unit), a state-specific consumer price index, and estimates of average household income. The unit of observation is a month, so that the data set consists of 28 observations (7 months, 4 areas). A fixed-effects (i.e., least-squares dummy-variable) pooled time-series/cross-section framework was used in estimation.

The estimates of the own-and cross-price elasticities for telephone services for the three ZJ models are tabulated in Table 3. The results show little difference in the own and cross elasticities for inter-and intraLATA toll for the unrestricted and two-stage budgeting models, but a big difference in the estimates between those models and the bill-targeting model. Lagrange multiplier tests fail to detect a difference between the unrestricted and two-stage budgeting models,[12] but reject the bill-targeting model in favor of two-stage budgeting. The ZJ results thus support two-stage budgeting, but not bill-targeting.

The size of the estimated price elasticities in the unrestricted and two-stage budgeting models are in general consistent with estimates obtained elsewhere. The value for interLATA toll is somewhat smaller than most estimates for the U.S., but this could reflect a shorter length-of-haul for United's toll traffic in comparison with estimates based upon interstate data. The value of –0.15 for local service seems high at first glance, but not when it is considered that local service in this context includes custom-calling features and other recurring non-access local charges.

The Zona-Jacob study is a valuable addition to the telecommunications demand literature and in my view provides rather compelling evidence against the Bill-Targeting hypothesis. This does not mean, however, that the issue should be considered closed. Further investigation using micro-based household survey data is in order.

III. Socio-Demographic and Other Characteristics of Telecommunications Demand

In this section, we shall take a brief look at some of the non-price characteristics of telecommunications demand. Except for the strong interest in how various minority/disadvantaged groups might be affected by rising local-service rates, the 1980s saw little research that focused on structural characteristics *per se*. Much of the following discussion, accordingly reproduced from the 1980 book (specifically, from the end of Chapter 1).

1. Socio-Demographic Characteristics

Four studies in the Bell System in the 1970s focused on socio-demographic characteristics of residential customers.[13] The study analyzed data for Cincinnati Bell, Illinois Bell, Pacific Telephone and Telegraph Co., and Southern

---

[12] For a description of Lagrange multiplier tests, see Judge *et al.* (1985, pp. 182–187).

[13] The motivation for these studies was largely to collect information in anticipation of the implementation of local measured-service.

New England Telephone Co.[14] The Cincinnati Bell study was conducted between March 1975 and January 1976 on a sample of 731 households served by eight wire centers in Cincinnati. Data were obtained on the average number of local calls per line, and socio-demographic information was solicited in a mail questionnaire. Two hundred ninety-three households responded fully to the questionnaires. The Illinois Bell study relates both toll and non-toll calling characteristics for a sample of Chicago households to several socio-demographic factors. Data on telephone usage (number of calls, duration, time-of-day, and length-of-haul) were collected between October 1972 and April 1974 for 849 households attached to 11 wire centers. Socio-demographic data for the households were obtained in a mail/telephone/in-person questionnaire in March 1973. Six hundred twenty-three households responded to the questionnaire.

The data for the Pacific Bell study were collected from a sample of 1719 households served by 10 wire centers in or near Los Angeles and San Francisco between May 1972 and September 1973. Information was obtained on the number of calls per account per day as well as on socio-demographic characteristics in a mail questionnaire. Seven hundred five households responded fully to the questionnaire. Finally, the SNET study obtained data on daily minutes of use for 1748 households served by nine wire centers in Connecticut between November 1974 and October 1975. Socio-demographic information was obtained in a mail questionnaire, to which 1168 households responded.[15]

One of the principal findings of these studies is an indication that local-calling behavior of nonwhite households differs from that of white households.[16] Specifically, nonwhite households appear to make more local calls (all four studies), to speak longer (Illinois Bell), and to make fewer calls to the suburbs (Illinois Bell), which suggests a tighter community-of-interest on the part of nonwhite households. The higher calling frequency of nonwhite households shows up at all levels of income in the Illinois Bell study, but only for households with less than $10,000 income in the SNET study. The Illinois Bell study also indicates that the peak calling frequency is in the evening for nonwhite households, while for white households there are twin

[14] The Cincinnati Bell study is described in Collins and Infosino (1978), the Illinois Bell study in Brandon (1981), the Pacific Bell study in Infosino (1976), and the Southern New England study in Southern New England Telephone Co. (1977c).

[15] The socio-demographic information obtained in the mail questionnaire was augmented by data from the 1970 Census in all of the studies except in the one by Illinois Bell.

[16] Nonwhite in the Illinois Bell and Cincinnati Bell studies refer specifically to blacks. In the other two studies, nonwhites includes hispanics and orientals as well as blacks. The Illinois Bell study (Brandon 1981) provides by far the most detailed analysis of black/white differences.

peaks: one in mid-afternoon and the other at the same time in the evenings as for nonwhite households.

Another finding is that local telephone usage is directly related to the size of the household (Cincinnati, Illinois Bell, and Pacific), and the same three studies also indicate that local usage is lower in households headed by a person aged sixty-five or more. Finally, the Cincinnati and Pacific studies taken together suggest that regional differences in local-calling behavior exist that cannot be accounted for by race, income, or household age or size, or by other variables used in individual studies, such as telephone density, sex of household heads, and so on.[17]

2. Time, Duration, Distance, and Customer Characteristics

Telephone companies view a telephone call as having five dimensions:[18]

- The time-of-day and day-of-week that the call is made;
- The type of call (DDD, person-to-person, etc.);
- Duration of the call;
- Length-of-haul of the call;
- Customer class making the call.

Six studies, Garfinkel (1977a, 1977b, 1979a), Pavarini (1976a), and Gale (1971, 1973), have examined the distribution of calls along these dimensions. Both Garfinkel and Pavarini focus on local use, while Gale focuses on interstate toll demand.[19]

[17] As has been noted, much of the motivation for the 1980s studies of residential access demand [particularly, those of Perl (1983) and Taylor and Kridel (1990) for the U.S. and Bodnar *et al.* (1988) for Canada] was to find out how certain socio-demographic groups would be affected by rising local-service rates. Generally, what the results show is that low-penetration is a low income/poverty phenomenon that is exacerbated for households that are nonwhite, non-urban, and male-headed.

[18] The price of a long-distance call varies according to the time-of-day and day-of-week, duration, and length-of-haul, but not by class of customer. In general, the price of local calls does not vary by time-of-day or day-of-week, but may vary by duration and length-of-haul, depending upon whether the price of local service is flat-rate or measured-rate.

[19] The data reported on in the Garfinkel studies were collected during the last seven months of 1972 in ten #1 ESS exchanges in California. Two thousand four hundred forty-one accounts were represented in the data analyzed, 2,292 residential accounts and 1,149 business accounts. Both flat-rate and measured-service accounts are represented in the sample. The data analyzed by Pavarini were collected in sampling studies conducted in seventy-nine Bell System wire centers in ten states between June 1972 and December 1975. A total of 7,253 flat-rate local-service accounts, both residence and business, are represented in the sample. The data analyzed in both the Garfinkel and Pavarini studies were mostly collected by the Subscriber Line Use Study (SLUS) System, which was a mechanized data collection system developed

The structural characteristics associated with local use reported in the Garfinkel and Pavarini studies include:

— Business customers make more local calls per account per day than residential customers; business customers also have more account-to-account variation in calling rates.

— Holding times (i.e., call durations) are longer for residential accounts than for business accounts.

— Flat-rate business classes have higher calling rates, in the same area, than measured-rate business classes.

— A gamma distribution (or a power-transformed normal distribution in the case of Pavarini) provides a reasonable description of local-calling rates within each class of service.[20]

— Mean local-calling rates for both business and residential customers appear to be distributed normally across wire centers.

Gale, in contrast with Garfinkel and Pavarini, focuses on the structural characteristics of toll use. The data analyzed by Gale were obtained from the Bell System MASP data files and were collected between 1966 and 1971. Most of Gale's emphasis is on interstate messages, but some intrastate messages were also analyzed. Some of the more interesting of Gale's findings regarding the distribution of toll messages by time-of-day (Gale 1973) are as follows:[21]

— The percentage of calls for a typical weekday by residential customers that are made in the "daytime" as opposed to "nighttime", decreases with mileage.[22]

— The day of the week makes a large difference in the distribution of calls by time-of-day for business traffic, but only a moderate difference for residence traffic. The typical business weekday traffic has a morning peak between 10:00 and 11:00 A.M. and an afternoon peak between 2:00 and 3:00 P.M. The morning peak is also the day's peak. Saturday has a morning peak virtually identical to the weekday morning peak, but no

at Bell Laboratories and offered to the Bell System operating telephone companies by AT&T. Finally, the data analyzed by Gale were obtained from the Bell System MASP data files. For a description of the MASP data, see AT&T (1978).

[20] The gamma distribution is a two-parameter distribution that is unimodal and skewed to the right. A power-transformed normal distribution simply means that a random variable raised to some specified power (which may be fractional) has the normal distribution.

[21] Many of these findings are confirmed in the data collected in the GTE measured-service experiment in Illinois. See Park, Mitchell, Wetzel, and Alleman (1983).

[22] Since the differential between daytime and nighttime rates increases with mileage, this result probably reflects a price effect.

afternoon peak. Sunday has only a small morning peak, and an evening peak.

— For residence traffic, there is always a morning peak, an afternoon dip, and the day's peak in the evening. The magnitude and location of the morning peak changes between weekdays and the weekend, and the magnitude of the evening peak decreases on the weekend, although the peak hour remains 7:00 to 8:00 P.M.

— Collect calls were distributed much like paid calls, but billings to third parties show unusual patterns for both business and residence. Third-party billings for business customers show a secondary evening peak, which suggests that much of this traffic may be personal rather than commercial. On the other hand, third-party billings to residential accounts show the typical business pattern of morning and afternoon peaks, which suggests that much of this traffic may be commercial.[23]

— Finally, person-to-person calls show a more businesslike pattern than do station-to-station calls. For business traffic, the daytime peaks are more pronounced for person-to-person than for station-to-station calls, while for residence traffic person-to-person calls follow the business pattern of morning and afternoon peaks.

In his 1971 paper Gale examines the variation in the average length of calls with respect to such factors as mileage, class of customer, and time-of-day. The data analyzed refer to interstate toll calls for March 1969, and the findings include:

— The mean duration of a call is longer, other things being constant, the more distant is the call – or, "the longer-the-haul, the longer-the-call," as the Bell System saying goes.

— The mean duration of a toll call from residential accounts is longer than from business accounts. The same is true, it will be recalled, for local calls.

— Weekday calls are shorter, on the average, than weekend calls.

— Calls between 7:00 P.M. and midnight are longer, on the average, than during the daytime.[24]

— The mean duration of person-to-person calls is longer than station-to-station calls.

— Collect calls and calls billed to third parties are longer, on the average, than paid calls.

---

[23] Third-party billings are now virtually nonexistent.

[24] Since nighttime rates are lower than daytime rates, this difference will also contain a price effect.

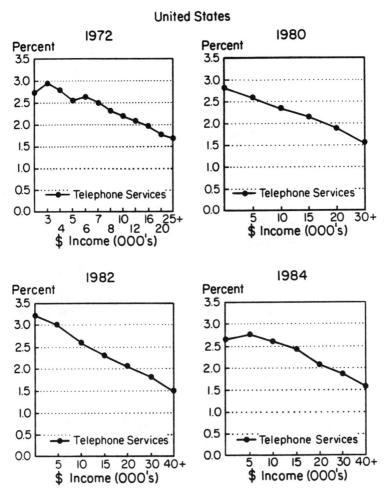

Telephone Spending by Income Group

Fig. 1.

3.Consumption/Income Relationships

We will now examine briefly several graphs showing the relationship between expenditures for telecommunications services and income for U.S. and Canadian households for selected years between 1972 and 1985. Graphs for the U.S. are presented in Figure 1 for 1972, 1980, 1982, and 1984, while graphs for Canada are presented in Figure 2 for 1972, 1978, 1984, and

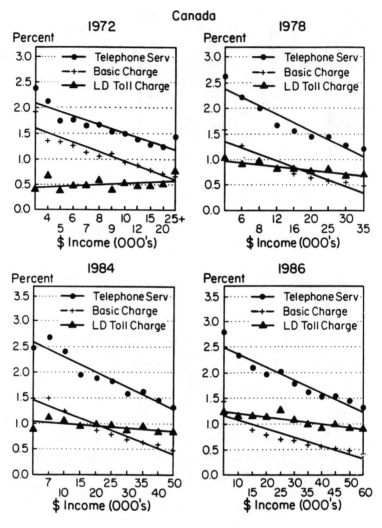

Spending on Telephone Services as % of Average Current Consumption

Fig. 2.

1986.[25] Expenditures for telecommunications as a percent of total consumption expenditure is on the vertical axes in these graphs, while income is on the horizontal axes. The data for Canada are broken down into expenditures

[25] I am grateful to Gerald W. Wall for providing these graphs. For a more detailed discussion of them, see Taylor, Waverman, and Wall (1990).

for local service (which includes all vertical services) and expenditures for long-distance, while the data for the U.S. refer just to the aggregate.

The story that these graphs relate can be summarized as follows:

1. In general, telecommunications expenditures as a percentage of total consumption expenditure decreases steadily with rising income. This is true for both the U.S. and Canada and for all years considered. This is also true for expenditures for local service. These results are consistent with income elasticities for households that are less than 1.

2. Long-distance expenditures as a proportion of total expenditure were essentially flat in 1972 and 1978, but show a mild decrease with rising income in 1984 and 1986. This suggests that the income elasticity for toll calling may also now be less than 1.

3. In 1984, expenditures for toll calling in Canada began to exceed expenditures for local services at an income level between $15,000 and $20,000 per year. In 1986, the income level at which this occurred had fallen to less than $10,000 per year.[26]

---

[26] For the implications of this result for welfare-pricing of telecommunications services, see Taylor, Waverman, and Wall (1990).

CHAPTER 9

CONSUMPTION EXTERNALITIES

The focus in this chapter will be on the network and call externalities. Little in telecommunications demand has attracted as much attention as the network externality, yet empirically we know little more about this externality than we did 10 years ago. As described in Chapter 2, the idea underlying the network externality is a simple one, that a new subscriber joining the network will confer a benefit on existing subscribers because one more telephone can be reached. This creates a divergence between the private and social benefits of subscription. The private benefits are simply the benefits to a new subscriber, while the social benefits are these plus the enhanced value to existing subscribers. A network whose size were determined by equating private benefits with marginal cost would accordingly be too small from a social point of view. A subsidy would seem in order.

While it might seem straightforward to test for a network externality, such has not been the case. The standard approach has been to relate the penetration rate with aggregate data, or the probability of a household having a telephone with individual household data, to the number of telephones that can be reached. Empirical results are mixed. As we have seen, Perl (1983) and Taylor and Kridel (1990), among others, find some evidence of an externality, but the impact is tiny in magnitude and frail statistically.

Part of the problem in attempting to isolate the network externality has been a failure of theory. The statement of the externality given above is straightforward and noncontroversial. I know no one who would take serious exception to it. Yet as a guide to empirical research, the statement is not particularly helpful. Among other things, its focus is on access. Access to a large network will be more valuable than access to a small network. But what about usage? A large network will clearly have greater usage than a small network simply because it is larger, but will it also have greater usage per telephone? And, if so, is this a reflection of the network externality? Also, does it matter whether an additional telephone results from an increase in the penetration rate, population remaining constant, or an increase in population, penetration remaining constant.[1] Finally, precisely how are network externalities to be defined? As the impact on social welfare, as theorists seem to prefer? Or in terms of the number of subscribers who might be forced to give up telephone service if local rates should be increased to costs, as policymakers seem to prefer? These and related questions are the focus in this chapter. The first four sections of the chapter are purely formal and have two concerns: (1) to develop measures of the network externality that can be useful for policy discussions and (2) to examine the implications of the network externality for the (Ramsey) optimal pricing of telecommunications services.

The call externality is discussed in Section V. In contrast with the network externality, the call externality (which to recall from Chapter 2 is rooted in the fact that a completed call affects the welfare of a second party) has never received much attention, probably because of the view (also noted in Chapter 2) that over time the effects of the externality are internalized. The results of the point-to-point toll demand models that were reviewed in Chapter 6 suggest, however, that this is too narrow and static a view. In these models, calling appears to give rise to further calling which cannot be attributed either to the network externality or to just the unpaid-for benefits of incoming calls. On the other hand, to identify all of these "call-back" effects with the call externality seems contrived. An endogenous factor appears to be present that was referred to in Chapter 6 as the "dynamics of information exchange."

In Section VI, we turn to a brief review of the empirical evidence on the consumption externalities. With one exception, the evidence that will be reviewed is from studies discussed in earlier chapters. The exception is a paper by Breslaw (1985), which provides an extensive analysis of the implications of the network externality for the elasticities for price and market size. Breslaw's study is discussed in Appendix 3.

I. THE NETWORK EXTERNALITY AND OPTIMAL PRICING OF TELECOMMUNICATIONS SERVICES

In order to keep the analysis as simple as possible, only two services will be considered, access and usage, all usage will be assumed to be toll, and all subscribers will be viewed as residential. The focus throughout this section will be on the determination of prices for access and usage which maximize a social welfare function subject to a profit constraint for the serving telco.

---

[1] Cf. de Fontenay and Lee (1983).

For notation, let:

$$Q \; = \; \text{aggregate usage of network}$$

$$p \; = \; \text{price per unit of usage}$$

$$\pi \; = \; \text{price of access}$$

$$M \; = \; \text{number of subscribers}$$

$$N \; = \; \text{population of potential subscribers}$$

$$B \; = \; \text{telco profit constraint}$$

$$C(Q, M) \; = \; \text{telco cost function}$$

$$CS \; = \; \text{aggregate consumers' surplus from use of network}$$

$$W \; = \; \text{CS} - \pi M \; \text{(social welfare)}$$

Per usual, the optimization problem is taken to be to find prices of access and usage that maximize social welfare W, defined as aggregate *net* consumers' surplus of subscribers,[2] subject to the profit constraint for the serving telco. The maximand is accordingly:

$$Z \; = \; W - \lambda[pQ + \pi M - C(Q, M) - B]$$

$$= \; CS - \pi M - \lambda[pQ + \pi M - C(Q, M) - B] \tag{1}$$

where λ is a LaGrangian multiplier associated with the telco profit constraint:

$$pQ + \pi M - C(Q, M) = B. \tag{2}$$

Together with (2), the first-order conditions will be given by:

$$\frac{\partial CS}{\partial p} - \pi \frac{\partial M}{\partial p} - \lambda \left[Q + p \frac{\partial Q}{\partial p} + \pi \frac{\partial M}{\partial p} - \frac{\partial C}{\partial Q} \frac{\partial Q}{\partial p} - \frac{\partial C}{\partial M} \frac{\partial M}{\partial p} \right] = 0 \tag{3}$$

$$\frac{\partial CS}{\partial \pi} - M - \pi \frac{\partial M}{\partial \pi} - \lambda \left[p \frac{\partial Q}{\partial \pi} + M + \pi \frac{\partial M}{\partial \pi} - \frac{\partial C}{\partial Q} \frac{\partial Q}{\partial \pi} - \frac{\partial C}{\partial M} \frac{\partial M}{\partial \pi} \right] = 0. \tag{4}$$

In the absence of network externalities, $\partial CS/\partial p$ could be replaced by $-Q$[3] and we could replace $\partial CS/\partial \pi$ by $-Q(\partial Q/\partial y)$, where Y denotes income,

---

[2] This social welfare function differs from the one usually posited in that, in line with Chapter 2, it is assumed that benefits arise only from usage and that access is demanded only if the consumer surplus from usage exceeds the price of access. Klein and Willig (1977), for example, define aggregate consumers' surplus to encompass consumer surplus for both access and usage. Option demand and benefits from incoming calls (except in so far as they are reflected in the network externality) will be ignored.

[3] See Section V in Chapter 2.

since $\partial Q/\partial \pi = -\partial Q/\partial Y$. Network externalities complicate things, in that we have to allow for the change in the value of belonging to the network caused by changes in the number of subscribers. Accordingly, for $\partial CS/\partial p$ and $\partial CS/\partial \pi$, we can write

$$\frac{\partial CS}{\partial p} = \frac{\partial CS}{\partial p}\bigg|_{M^0} + \frac{\partial CS}{\partial M}\frac{\partial M}{\partial p} \tag{5}$$

$$\frac{\partial CS}{\partial \pi} = \frac{\partial CS}{\partial \pi}\bigg|_{M^0} + \frac{\partial CS}{\partial M}\frac{\partial M}{\partial \pi}. \tag{6}$$

The first terms in these expressions represent the change in consumers' surplus holding the number of subscribers constant, while the second terms allow for changes in the number of subscribers which in turn affects the value of belonging to the network because of the network externality. As just noted, the first terms can be replaced by $-Q$ and $-Q(\partial Q/\partial Y)$, respectively, so that expressions (5) and (6) can be written as:

$$\frac{\partial CS}{\partial p} = -Q + \frac{\partial CS}{\partial M}\frac{\partial M}{\partial p} \tag{7}$$

$$\frac{\partial CS}{\partial \pi} = -Q\frac{\partial Q}{\partial Y} + \frac{\partial CS}{\partial M}\frac{\partial M}{\partial \pi}. \tag{8}$$

We now turn to the first-order conditions in (3) and (4), which can now be rewritten as:

$$-(1+\lambda)Q + (CS_m - \pi)\frac{\partial M}{\partial p}$$
$$- \lambda\left[p\frac{\partial Q}{\partial p} + \pi\frac{\partial M}{\partial p} - c_q\frac{\partial Q}{\partial p} - c_m\frac{\partial M}{\partial p}\right] = 0 \tag{9}$$

$$-Q\frac{\partial Q}{\partial Y} - (1+\lambda)M + (CS_m - \pi)\frac{\partial M}{\partial \pi}$$
$$- \lambda\left[p\frac{\partial Q}{\partial \pi} + \pi\frac{\partial M}{\partial \pi} - c_q\frac{\partial Q}{\partial \pi} - c_m\frac{\partial M}{\partial \pi}\right] = 0, \tag{10}$$

where (to simplify notation) $CS_m = \partial CS/\partial M$ and $c_q = \partial C/\partial Q$ and $c_m = \partial C/\partial M$, the marginal costs of usage and access, respectively. If we now divide (9) by Q, (10) by M, and replace partial derivatives by equivalent elasticities, (9) and (10) become:

$$-(1+\lambda) + (CS_m - \pi)\frac{M\varepsilon_{mp}}{pQ}$$
$$- \lambda\left[\varepsilon_{qp} + \frac{\pi M}{pQ}\varepsilon_{mp} - \frac{c_q}{p}\varepsilon_{qp} - \frac{c_m M}{pQ}\varepsilon_{mp}\right] = 0 \tag{11}$$

$$-(1+\lambda) - \frac{Q^2}{Y}\varepsilon_{qy} + (CS_m - \pi)\frac{\varepsilon_{m\pi}}{\pi}$$

$$-\lambda\left[\frac{pQ}{\pi M}\varepsilon_{q\pi} + \varepsilon_{m\pi} - \frac{c_q Q}{\pi M}\varepsilon_{q\pi} - \frac{c_m}{\pi}\varepsilon_{m\pi}\right] = 0, \tag{12}$$

or

$$-(1+\lambda) + \frac{[CS_m + \lambda c_m - (1+\lambda)\pi]M\varepsilon_{mp}}{pQ}$$

$$-\lambda\left(\frac{p - c_q}{p}\right)\varepsilon_{qp} = 0 \tag{13}$$

$$-(1+\lambda) - \frac{Q^2}{Y}\varepsilon_{qy} + \frac{CS_m - \pi}{\pi}\varepsilon_{m\pi}$$

$$-\frac{\lambda(p - c_q)Q\varepsilon_{q\pi}}{\pi M} - \lambda\left(\frac{\pi - c_m}{\pi}\right)\varepsilon_{m\pi} = 0, \tag{14}$$

where ε_{mp} denotes the elasticity of M with respect to p and similarly for ε_{qp}, $\varepsilon_{q\pi}$, and ε_{qy}. Dividing (14) by (13) yields (after some rearrangement):[4]

$$\frac{\frac{\pi - c_m}{\pi}}{\frac{p - c_q}{p}} = \frac{1 + \lambda - \frac{(CS_m - \pi)\varepsilon_{m\pi}}{\pi}}{1 + \lambda - \frac{[CS_m + \lambda c_m - (1+\lambda)\pi]M\varepsilon_{mp}}{pQ}} \cdot \frac{\varepsilon_{qp}}{\varepsilon_{m\pi}}. \tag{15}$$

The left-hand side of expression (15) is the familiar Ramsey ratio of proportional departures from marginal cost. The right-hand side is seen to consist of a complicated factor times the ratio of the usage to access elasticities. In the absence of network externalities and a cross elasticity between access and the price of usage (i.e., both CS_m and ε_{mp} zero), equation (15) would reduce to:[5]

$$\frac{\frac{\pi - c_m}{\pi}}{\frac{p - c_q}{p}} = \frac{1 + \lambda + \varepsilon_{m\pi}}{1 + \lambda} \cdot \frac{\varepsilon_{qp}}{\varepsilon_{m\pi}}. \tag{16}$$

Whether network externalities exist is an empirical question, but this is not the case for the cross-price elasticity, ε_{mp}. This is because the condition for demanding access is that consumer surplus from usage be at least as great as the price of access. As consumer surplus depends upon the price of usage,

---

[4] As Q^2/Y and $\varepsilon_{q\pi}$ will both be small, the terms involving these factors in expression (14) are excluded.

[5] Because of the presence of $\varepsilon_{m\pi}$, equation (16) does not reduce to the well-known inverse-elasticity rule (cf. Baumol and Bradford 1970).

so too must M. Consequently, ε_{mp} cannot be zero. Thus, for a network with CS_m equal to zero, but $\varepsilon_{mp} \neq 0$, the Ramsey ratio would be:

$$\frac{\frac{\pi-c_m}{\pi}}{\frac{p-c_q}{p}} = \frac{1+\lambda+\varepsilon_{m\pi}}{1+\lambda - \frac{[\lambda c_m-(1+\lambda)\pi]M\varepsilon_{mp}}{pQ}} \frac{\varepsilon_{qp}}{\varepsilon_{m\pi}}. \tag{17}$$

Expression (17) [as is also expression (15)] is complicated by the presence of p and π in the factor on the right-hand side, so that it does not yield an explicit solution for the optimal tax ratio. Examination of this factor, however, does suggest some important conclusions. Let the factor in question be denoted by

$$\Phi = \frac{1+\lambda+\varepsilon_{m\pi}}{1+\lambda - \frac{[\lambda(c_m/\pi)-(1+\lambda)]\pi M\varepsilon_{mp}}{pQ}} \tag{18}$$

which, since $\varepsilon_{mp} \cong \varepsilon_{m\pi}(pQ/\pi M)$,[6] can be rewritten as

$$\Phi = \frac{1+\lambda+\varepsilon_{m\pi}}{1+\lambda - [\lambda(c_m/\pi) - (1+\lambda)]\varepsilon_{m\pi}}. \tag{19}$$

From expression (19), it is evident that, since λ must be less than -1,[7] the sign of Φ depends upon the sign of the denominator. For Φ to be negative (i.e., for π to be less than c_m), the denominator must be positive. However, it is easy to show that this would require c_m/π to be less than 1, which is an obvious contradiction. In the absence of externalities, we can accordingly rule out a price for access that is less than marginal cost.

We now consider the size of Φ in relation to 1. From expression (19), we see that Φ will be greater or less than 1 depending upon whether $-[\lambda(c_m/\pi) - 1 + \lambda)]$ is less or greater than 1. It is straightforward to show that, for this latter term to be less than 1, c_m/π would have to be greater than 1, but this would contradict the condition that Φ is positive. Consequently, Φ is less than 1, which means that the Ramsey tax ratio will be less than what is implied by the simple inverse-elasticity rule.

With network externalities present, the factor on the right-hand side of expression (15) becomes:

$$\Phi = \frac{1+\lambda - \frac{(CS_m-\pi)\varepsilon_{m\pi}}{\pi}}{1+\lambda - [(CS_m - \lambda c_m)/\pi - (1+\lambda)]\varepsilon_{m\pi}}. \tag{20}$$

---

[6] Again, see Section VI of Chapter 2.

[7] λ measures the cost in consumers' surplus of a dollar increase in the telco profit constraint. Since the demand function for usage is almost certainly inelastic, λ is necessarily less than -1.

Let us consider first the condition under which Φ will be less than 1. Since we can reasonably assume that $CS_m > \pi$, we see from expression (20) that $\Phi < 1$ requires

$$\frac{CS_m - \pi}{\pi} > \frac{CS_m + \lambda C_m}{\pi} - (1 + \lambda). \tag{21}$$

After some manipulation, this reduces to simply $\pi > c_m$, which is the same condition as in the case of no network externalities. The conclusion, accordingly, is that network externalities cannot lead to a Ramsey price for access that is less than marginal cost.

We should expect, however, that network externalities lead to a reduction in the Ramsey tax ratio, and comparison of expressions (18) and (19) shows that this is indeed the case. Also, inspection of expression (20) shows that, again as we should expect, the size of the reduction varies directly with the size of CS_m.

The conclusion that emerges from this section is that network externalities lead to Ramsey prices for access and usage for which the ratio of proportional departures from marginal costs is less than that implied by the simple inverse-elasticity rule. The optimal tax ratio is a decreasing function of the strength of the externality, so that the stronger the externality, the smaller will be the burden on access. In no situation, however, would access ever be priced below marginal cost.[8]

II. AN ALTERNATIVE MEASURE OF THE NETWORK EXTERNALITY

To this point, the network externality has been defined in terms of the effect on aggregate consumers' surplus of the addition or exit of a marginal subscriber to the telephone network. The conventional wisdom in the telephone industry has been that a network externality can justify continuation of a subsidy to residential subscribers. We have just seen, however, that a subsidy to access cannot be justified on Ramsey grounds. While this might seem to dispense with the matter, such is not really the case, for Ramsey pricing assumes that everyone pays the same prices. The preceding section would seem to rule out a subsidy to everyone, but leaves open the possibility of a subsidy to

---

[8] The most extensive analyses of the welfare implications of network externalitites for the pricing of local service are Rohlfs (1978) and Griffin (1982). Both use assumed values for the size of the externality, measuring it in terms of the divergence of social and private benefits of an additional subscriber. Griffin concludes that even a strong externality would make little difference in the welfare issue created by the toll-to-local subsidy (at 1975 prices) in the U.S. because of the small price elasticity for local service.

those for whom the benefits of calls to them were they on the network (i.e., $\partial CS/\partial M$) outweighs the shortfall between their willingness-to-pay and the price of access. Identifying these marginal few will be the focus of this section.

The question that will concern us is whether a network externality leads to a telephone network with a suboptimal (i.e., too few) number of subscribers. By too few in this context, we shall mean the following: Let p and π (however arrived at) continue to denote the price of usage and access, respectively, and let M be the resulting size of the network. Let cs_j denote the consumer surplus from usage for the jth nonsubscriber. Since j is a nonsubscriber, $cs_j < \pi$. Order the nonsubscribers in terms of decreasing cs_j and consider the first $j = 1, \ldots, k$ of these as determined by $cs_1 > cs_2 > \ldots > cs_k$. Let CS_j represent the aggregate consumers' surplus that would be gained by the M subscribers on the network if the jth nonsubscriber were in fact a subscriber. If $CS_j > \pi - cs_j$, then the M existing subscribers should in principle be willing to pay a tax of $\pi - cs_j$ to subsidize j's subscription to the network. Next, let CS_k denote the aggregate consumers' surplus that the M subscribers would gain if the first k nonsubscribers were in fact subscribers. Let k be determined such that:

$$CS_k > \sum_{j=1}^{k}(\pi - cs_j), \quad CS_{k+1} < \sum_{j=1}^{k+1}(\pi - cs_j). \tag{22}$$

In this situation, the M existing subscribers should in principle be willing to pay a tax equal to $\sum_{j=1}^{k}(\pi - cs_j)$ to subsidize the subscription of these k nonsubscribers. In the absence of the tax and subsidy, the network can be said to be k subscribers too small. That is what shall be meant by suboptimal.

The important question, obviously, is, for given p and π, what is the size of k – i.e., how many nonsubscribers would existing subscribers be willing to subsidize in order to have them on the network? Several comments are in order at this point. Note, to begin with, that there is no supposition of optimal pricing; p and π can represent real-world prices and M can be the resulting market-determined size of the network. This is in keeping with what seems to be the current view as to what constitutes universal service – i.e., universal service is what presently exists. Note, also, that the issue is not one of a subsidy to everyone, but only to a targeted few, namely, the first k extramarginal subscribers. The M existing subscribers would pay the access price of π for these k nonsubscribers. This contrasts with conventional theoretical treatments of the network externality in which the value of the externality is subtracted from (private) marginal cost, thereby providing a

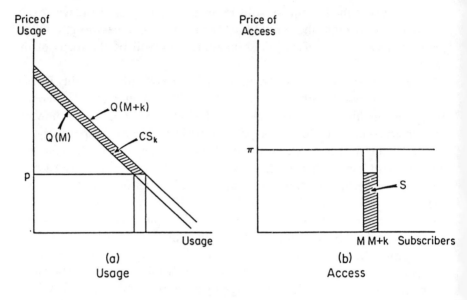

Fig. 1.

subsidy to everyone.[9]

The tax subsidy involved is described graphically in Figure 1. Panel a in the figure refers to the usage market, while panel b refers to the access market. In panel a, $Q(M)$ represents the demand for usage for the network of M subscribers; $Q(M + k)$ represents the demand for usage by these M subscribers if the first k extramarginal subscribers were also on the network. CS_k accordingly measures the consumers' surplus associated with the calls that the M subscribers would make to the k extramarginal subscribers.

Turning now to panel b, consider the points M and $M+k$ on the horizontal axis. M represents the number of households demanding access at the access price of π. $M + k$ includes the first k extramarginal subscribers for which, by definition, $cs_j < \pi$. The area labeled S measures the shortfall in willingnesses-to-pay for these k households. If $CS_k > S$, then the M subscribers (for whom $cs > \pi$) should in principle be willing to contribute collectively at least S in order to attract these k households onto the network. If k is the largest number for which $CS_k \geq S$, then $M + k$ represents, for

---

[9] See Wenders (1987). The view that is adopted in this section is that the network externality creates a problem that is internal to subscribers on the network and is to be solved, at least in principle, by potential gainers compensating the extramarginal subscribers whose presence would be group beneficial but whose private willingnesses-to-pay are less than the price of access. The result would be Pareto-improving but not necessarily Pareto-optimal.

prices p and π, the optimal size of the network.

CS_k in panel a of Figure 1 in Chapter 10 has been drawn exaggeratedly large in order to make the graph legible. The algebraic condition that must be satisfied in determining the number of extramarginal subscribers to be subsidized is as follows:

$$\sum_{m=1}^{M} \int_{p}^{\infty} \left[q_m(z; M+k) - q_m(z; M) \right] \, dz \geq k\pi - \sum_{j=1}^{k} \int_{p}^{\infty} q_j(z; M+k) \, dz. \quad (23)$$

CS_k is given by the left-hand side of this inequality, while S is given by the right-hand side. The largest k which satisfies the inequality is the value of k desired.

The useful thing about the inequality in expression (23) is that it translates the network externality (measured in terms of consumers' surplus) into the number of households that are potentially affected. A statement that a network is k households too small because of a network externality is much more meaningful in everyday discourse than a statement that consumers' welfare is Z dollars too low. The important question, of course, is the size of k and whether it can be estimated, and it is to this question we now turn.

To begin with, it is clear that, for given p and π, the size of k is going to be determined by (1) how badly existing subscribers wish to communicate with nonsubscribers (the size of CS_k in panel a of Figure 1 and (2) how near nonsubscribers are to being subscribers on their own (the size of S in panel b of Figure 1). My own view is that, as a practical matter, neither of these factors is of much significance. As regards the size of CS_k, it would seem that private subsidies are already provided in situations in which the desire to communicate with a potential nonsubscriber is large. Obvious examples are parents who pay for their childrens' telephones at school and children who pay for the telephones of aged/infirm parents or other close relatives. A large residual value for CS_k accordingly seems unlikely.[10]

As regards to the size of S, it must be kept in mind that its value will depend upon the level of penetration, being much smaller at low and intermediate levels than at high levels. At current levels of penetration in the U.S. and (especially) Canada, it might be more accurate to say that households without telephone service have reasons for not wanting a telephone as opposed to wanting a telephone but being unable to afford it.[11]

---

[10] Note that we are taking M to be whatever is observed at prices p and π. Private subsidization that has already taken place will already be reflected in M.

[11] Information on the characteristics of nonsubscribers is generally sparse. Both the decennial census and the Current Population Survey (which is the source for the ongoing FCC

As noted in footnote 8, a thrust of this section is that a network externality creates a tax/subsidy problem that is *internal* to the subscribers and near-subscribers of a telephone network. Subsidies should be financed by existing subscribers because they are the ones who benefit.[12] This leaves unanswered, however, the question of how a tax/subsidy scheme might be effected in practice. The telco is the obvious place to look. Economists usually argue against telephone companies being required to engage in social-welfare programs, but this case is different because it involves transfers between existing and potential subscribers.

The telco is clearly in the best position to collect fees from existing subscribers, and the only question, really, is how to identify the group to be subsidized. Ideally the group would be identified exactly as the first k extramarginal households and a subsidy of $\pi - cs_j$ offered to the jth of these. Obviously, this is impossible. Even if the information needed to identify these households at a particular time were available, the transaction costs of keeping the group current would be overwhelming. Several alternatives could be considered. One would be to define a target group in terms of a set of socio-economic-demographic criteria and provide subsidized access to all who qualify. A second alternative, far superior in my view, would be to offer a "budget" measured-service, that is available to everyone, but would be uneconomic to all but moderate users. This may already be operative in many existing lifeline plans.[13]

III. DISTRIBUTIONAL EQUITY[14]

Thus far in this chapter, social welfare has been defined in terms of a function in which a unit of welfare is a unit of welfare no matter who receives it. In this section, we shall consider a modification of the welfare function which involves weighting the consumers' surplus of different individuals according to the marginal social utility of income. This offers one way of incorporating considerations of distributional equity directly into the welfare function. The model to be discussed was introduced by Feldstein in 1972 for the purpose of determining the optimal prices of two public goods that are consumed in

informative recent study of which I am aware is by Bell Canada (1986a, 1986b; Bodnar and Lefebvre 1992a, 1992b). Some information from the 1950s is given in a survey undertaken by the Survey Research Center at the University of Michigan (Adelson *et al.* 1956).

[12] I emphasize again that the focus here is on the network externality. If society should decide, for other reasons that access warrants subsidization, society at large should bear the costs. This will be discussed below.

[13] The literature on lifeline rates is extensive. See, in particular, Perl (1983).

[14] This section is based in great part on Taylor, Waverman, and Wall (1990).

different proportions by high- and low-income households.[15] Treating access and local service as a necessity and toll as a luxury, Breslaw and Smith (1982) used the Feldstein model to derive socially optimal access and toll prices for Bell Canada's service territory in Ontario and Quebec.

Assume that a public enterprise produces two goods that are sold at prices p_1 and p_2. Let $S(p_1, p_2, y)$ denote the consumers' surplus of a household with income y from consuming q_1 and q_2 at prices p_1 and p_2. Let $u(y)$ denote the *social* utility of income y and let $u'(y)$ represent the corresponding marginal social utility. Finally, let N denote the number of households and let $f(y)$ denote the density function of income. $Nf(y)\,dy$ then represents the number of households with income y.

The social welfare function is defined as a weighted sum of consumers' surpluses as follows:

$$W = N \int_0^\infty u'(y) S(p_1, p_2, y) f(y)\,dy. \tag{24}$$

W is to be maximized subject to the profit constraint for the public enterprise:

$$p_1 Q_1 + p_2 Q_2 - C(Q_1, Q_2) = B, \tag{25}$$

where $C(Q_1, Q_2)$ is the cost function and:

$$Q_1 = N \int_0^\infty q_1(p_1, p_2, y) f(y)\,dy \tag{26}$$

$$Q_2 = N \int_0^\infty q_2(p_1, p_2, y) f(y)\,dy. \tag{27}$$

The Lagrangian is accordingly:

$$Z = N \int_0^\infty u'(y) S(p_1, p_2, y) f(y)\,dy$$

$$+ \lambda[p_1 Q_1 + p_2 Q_2 - C(Q_1, Q_2) - B], \tag{28}$$

where λ is the Lagrangian multiplier associated with the profit constraint.[16]

---

[15] Feldstein (1972a).
[16] As I am using Feldstein's notation at this point, λ will be positive rather than negative as in Section I.

The first-order conditions for maximizing Z are given by:

$$-N \int_0^\infty u'(y)q_1(y)f(y)\, \mathrm{d}y$$

$$+ \lambda \left[Q_1 + p_1 \frac{\partial Q_1}{\partial p_1} + p_2 \frac{\partial Q_2}{\partial p_1} - m_1 \frac{\partial Q_1}{\partial p_1} - m_2 \frac{\partial Q_2}{\partial p_1} \right] = 0 \qquad (29)$$

$$-N \int_0^\infty u'(y)q_2(y)f(y)\, \mathrm{d}y$$

$$+ \lambda \left[p_1 \frac{\partial Q_1}{\partial p_2} + Q_2 + p_2 \frac{\partial Q_2}{\partial p_2} - m_1 \frac{\partial Q_1}{\partial p_2} - m_2 \frac{\partial Q_2}{\partial p_2} \right] = 0 \qquad (30)$$

where we have used the fact that $\partial S/\partial p_i = -q_i(y)$ and where $m_i = \partial C/\partial Q_i$, the marginal cost of good i.

At this point, Feldstein introduces the notion of the distributional characteristic of a good, defined for good i as

$$R_i = \frac{N}{Q_i} \int_0^\infty u'(y)q_i(y)f(y)\, \mathrm{d}y. \qquad (31)$$

R_i represents a weighted average of the marginal social utilities, the marginal social utility attaching to each household weighted by that household's consumption of good i. The conventional assumption that $u'(y)$ decreases as y increases implies that R_i will be greater for a necessity than for a luxury. More precisely, the higher the income elasticity for a good, the lower will be the value of R_i.[17]

Using expression (31) to define R_1 and R_2, equations (29) and (30) become:

$$-Q_1 R_1 + \lambda \left[Q_1 + p_1 \frac{\partial Q_1}{\partial p_1} + p_2 \frac{\partial Q_2}{\partial p_1} - m_1 \frac{\partial Q_1}{\partial p_1} - m_2 \frac{\partial Q_2}{\partial p_1} \right] = 0 \quad (32)$$

$$-Q_2 R_2 + \lambda \left[p_1 \frac{\partial Q_1}{\partial p_2} + Q_2 + p_2 \frac{\partial Q_2}{\partial p_2} - m_1 \frac{\partial Q_1}{\partial p_2} - m_2 \frac{\partial Q_2}{\partial p_2} \right] = 0 \quad (33)$$

Replacing partial derivatives by elasticities and assuming negligible income effects so that $\varepsilon_{ij} = \varepsilon_{ji}(p_j Q_j/p_i Q_i)$, equations (28) and (29) can be rewritten (after some manipulation) as:

$$R_1 = \lambda \left[1 + \varepsilon_{11} \left(\frac{p_1 - m_1}{p_1} \right) + \varepsilon_{12} \left(\frac{p_2 - m_2}{p_2} \right) \right] \qquad (34)$$

---

[17] The higher the income elasticity, the larger will be q_i/Q_i for higher income households, and therefore the lower will be $u'(y)$.

$$R_2 = \lambda \left[1 + \varepsilon_{21} \left(\frac{p_1 - m_1}{p_1} \right) + \varepsilon_{22} \left(\frac{p_2 - m_2}{p_2} \right) \right]. \tag{35}$$

Equations (34) and (35) can be solved for the Ramsey "tax rates" to yield:

$$\frac{\frac{p_1 - m_1}{p_1}}{\frac{p_2 - m_2}{p_2}} = \frac{\varepsilon_{22}(R_1 - \lambda) - \varepsilon_{12}(R_2 - \lambda)}{\varepsilon_{11}(R_2 - \lambda) - \varepsilon_{21}(R_1 - \lambda)}. \tag{36}$$

When distributional characteristics are irrelevant (i.e., $R_1 = R_2$), equation (34) reduces to the basic Ramsey rule with non-zero cross elasticities:

$$\frac{\frac{p_1 - m_1}{p_1}}{\frac{p_2 - m_2}{p_2}} = \frac{\varepsilon_{22} - \varepsilon_{12}}{\varepsilon_{11} - \varepsilon_{21}}. \tag{37}$$

The familiar inverse-elasticity rule emerges if, additionally, the cross elasticities are zero:

$$\frac{\frac{p_1 - m_1}{p_1}}{\frac{p_2 - m_2}{p_2}} = \frac{\varepsilon_{22}}{\varepsilon_{11}}. \tag{38}$$

Finally, when cross elasticities are zero but distribution characteristics are relevant (i.e., $R_1 = R_2$), equation (36) becomes:

$$\frac{\frac{p_1 - m_1}{p_1}}{\frac{p_2 - m_2}{p_2}} = \frac{\varepsilon_{22}(R_1 - \lambda)}{\varepsilon_{11}(R_2 - \lambda)}. \tag{39}$$

Equations (36) and (39) show how introduction of distributional considerations into the welfare function leads to modifications in the Ramsey taxation rules. In the case of zero cross elasticities, we see from the right-hand side of equation (39) that the simple Ramsey inverse-elasticity rule is adjusted by the factor $(R_1 - \lambda)/(R_2 - \lambda)$. Since λ represents the reduction in social welfare per unit of increase in the public enterprises' profit (i.e., $\partial Z/\partial B = -\lambda$), λ must be positive. The size of $(R_1 - \lambda)/(R_2 - \lambda)$ relative to one will accordingly depend upon the sizes of R_1 and R_2 in relation to λ. If $R_2 < R_1 < \lambda$, $(R_1 - \lambda)/(R_2 - \lambda)$ will be less than 1, so that the "equity adjustment" leads to a reduction in the simple Ramsey tax ratio. In other words, equity considerations lead to a lower relative tax on the good with the lower income elasticity.[18]

[18] While this is the expected result, it does depend upon R_1 and R_2 being less than λ. Unlike in previous sections in which the welfare function is measured in terms of dollars of consumers' surplus, the welfare function in this section is measured in units of marginal utility. All our assumptions really require, however, is that $u'(y) \geq 0$. Utility units can accordingly be scaled so that $0 \leq u'(y) \leq 1$, in which case we will have from expression (34) $R_i < 1$. On the other hand, λ must necessarily be greater than 1 because of downward sloping demand functions whose elasticities are greater than -1.

As mentioned earlier, the Feldstein model was first applied to telecommunications pricing by Breslaw and Smith (1982), specifically in the form of equation (39). Access and local service were identified with good 1 (the necessity), toll with good 2 (the luxury), and cross elasticities were assumed to be zero. This is a tempting scenario, but there is a major problem with it, for the Feldstein model, at least in the form that Feldstein presented it, is really not applicable to telecommunications. The welfare function has to be modified to take into account the direct connection between access and usage and also to allow for the network externality.

The counterpart for telecommunications of the Feldstein welfare function in expression (24) will be

$$W = N \int_{y^*}^{\infty} u'(y)[S(p, y, M) - \pi]f(y)\, dy, \tag{40}$$

where $S(p, y, M)$ denotes the consumer's surplus from $q(p, y, M)$ units of telephone usage at a price p per unit of usage for a household with income y on a network with M subscribers. As before, π denotes the price of access, and y^* denotes the threshold value of income for which $S \geq \pi$ (the condition required for access being demanded). The Lagrangian function is accordingly:

$$Z = N \int_{y^*}^{\infty} u'(y)[S(p, y, M) - \pi]f(y)\, dy$$

$$+ \lambda[pQ + \pi M - C(Q, M) - B]. \tag{41}$$

The first-order conditions for maximizing this function will be given by:

$$N \int_{y^*}^{\infty} u'(y) \left[\left.\frac{\partial S}{\partial p}\right|_M + \frac{\partial S}{\partial M}\frac{\partial M}{\partial p} \right] f(y)\, dy$$

$$+ \lambda \left[Q + p\frac{\partial Q}{\partial p} + \pi\frac{\partial M}{\partial p} - c_q\frac{\partial Q}{\partial p} - c_m\frac{\partial M}{\partial \pi} \right] = 0 \tag{42}$$

$$N \int_{y^*}^{\infty} u'(y) \left[\frac{\partial S}{\partial M}\frac{\partial S}{\partial \pi} - 1 \right] f(y)\, dy + \lambda \left[M + \pi\frac{\partial M}{\partial \pi} - c_m\frac{\partial M}{\partial \pi} \right] = 0. \tag{43}$$

Network externalities are allowed for through the terms involving $\partial S/\partial M$ in the brackets within the integrals in these equations. Note also that it is assumed, as in the discussion leading to equation (15), that the terms involving $\partial S/\partial \pi$ and $\partial Q/\partial \pi$ are zero.[19]

Following Feldstein, define distributional characteristics, R_q and R_m, as:

$$R_q = -\frac{N}{Q} \int_{y^*}^{\infty} u'(y) \left[\left.\frac{\partial S}{\partial p}\right|_M + \frac{\partial S}{\partial M} \frac{\partial M}{\partial p} \right] f(y)\, dy \tag{44}$$

$$R_m = -\frac{N}{M} \int_{y^*}^{\infty} u'(y) \left[\frac{\partial S}{\partial M} \frac{\partial M}{\partial \pi} - 1 \right] f(y)\, dy, \tag{45}$$

so that (42) and (43) become:

$$-R_q Q + \lambda \left[Q + p\frac{\partial Q}{\partial p} + \pi\frac{\partial M}{\partial p} - c_q\frac{\partial Q}{\partial p} - c_m\frac{\partial M}{\partial p} \right] = 0 \tag{46}$$

$$-R_m M + \lambda \left[M + \pi\frac{\partial M}{\partial \pi} - c_m\frac{\partial M}{\partial \pi} \right] = 0. \tag{47}$$

Dividing (46) by Q, (47) by M, and replacing partial derivatives by elasticities yields:

$$-R_q + \lambda \left[1 + \varepsilon_{qp} + \frac{\pi M}{pQ}\varepsilon_{mp} - \frac{c_q}{p}\varepsilon_{qp} - \frac{c_m M}{pQ}\varepsilon_{mp} \right] = 0 \tag{48}$$

$$-R_m + \lambda \left[1 + \varepsilon_{m\pi} - \frac{c_m}{\pi}\varepsilon_{m\pi} \right] = 0. \tag{49}$$

Rearranging:

$$\lambda \left(\frac{p - c_q}{p} \right) \varepsilon_{qp} = R_q - \lambda - \lambda \left[\frac{(\pi - c_m)M}{pQ} \right] \varepsilon_{mp} \tag{50}$$

$$\lambda \left(\frac{\pi - c_m}{p} \right) \varepsilon_{m\pi} = R_m - \lambda. \tag{51}$$

Dividing (50) into (51), replacing ε_{mp} by $(pQ/\pi M)\varepsilon_{m\pi}$, and then multiplying by $\varepsilon_{qp}/\varepsilon_{m\pi}$ finally yields:

$$\frac{\frac{\pi - c_m}{\pi}}{\frac{p - c_1}{p}} = \frac{R_m - \lambda}{R_q - \lambda - \lambda[(\pi - c_m)/\pi]\varepsilon_{m\pi}} \frac{\varepsilon_{qp}}{\varepsilon_{m\pi}}. \tag{52}$$

[19] The terms involving $\partial y^*/\partial p$ and $\partial y^*/\partial \pi$ are zero as well because they appear as products with net consumer surplus (i.e., $S - \pi$) which is zero at y^*.

The left-hand side of this expression is the Ramsey tax ratio, which we see differs from the simple inverse-elasticity rule by the factor:

$$\theta = \frac{R_m - \lambda}{R_q - \lambda - \lambda[(\pi - c_m)/\pi)]\varepsilon_{m\pi}}. \tag{53}$$

Before attempting to sign and size this expression, it will be useful to rewrite R_q and R_m as:[20]

$$R_q = R_q^* - \varepsilon_{m\pi} R, \tag{54}$$

$$R_m = R_m^* - \varepsilon_{m\pi} R, \tag{55}$$

where:[21]

$$R_q^* = \frac{N}{Q} \int\limits_{y^*}^{\infty} u'(y)q(y)f(y)\,dy \tag{56}$$

$$R_m^* = \frac{N}{M} \int\limits_{y^*}^{\infty} u'(y)f(y)\,dy \tag{57}$$

$$R = \frac{N}{\pi} \int\limits_{y^*}^{\infty} u'(y)S_m(y)f(y)\,dy. \tag{58}$$

Expressions (54) and (55) allow for explicit treatment of network externalities through the terms in R. If externalities are absent ($S_m = 0$), R is zero, and R_q and R_m reduce to their "Feldstein" form [cf. expression (31)]:

$$R_q = \frac{N}{Q} \int\limits_{y^*}^{\infty} u'(y)q(y)f(y)\,dy \tag{59}$$

$$R_m = \frac{N}{M} \int\limits_{y^*}^{\infty} u'(y)f(y)\,dy. \tag{60}$$

With $S_m > 0$, R will be positive, as will also $-\varepsilon_{m\pi} R$ (since $\varepsilon_{m\pi}$ is negative), so that network externalities increase both R_q and R_m and by the same amount.

---

[20] Note that we once again use the fact that $\varepsilon_{mp} \cong (pQ/\pi M)\varepsilon_{m\pi}$.

[21] We use $\partial S/\partial p|_M = -q$ in expression (56) and denote $\partial S/\partial M$ by $S_m(y)$ in (58).

Unlike in the "pure" Feldstein model, for which R_q and R_m must both be less than 1, so that $R_q - \lambda$ and $R_m - \lambda$ are both negative, in the present situation both R_q and R_m can be greater than 1. Indeed, inspection of expression (45) shows that R_m can be greater than 1 even in the absence of externalities. This allows for the possibility of a Ramsey price for access that is less than marginal cost. This would require λ in expression (54) to be negative, which for $R_m - \lambda > 0$ would require

$$R - \lambda - \lambda[(\pi - c_m)/\pi]\varepsilon_{m\pi} < 0. \tag{61}$$

Manipulation of this inequality reduces it to the following condition on π and c_m:

$$\frac{c_m}{\pi} < \frac{R_q - \lambda}{\lambda \varepsilon_{m\pi}} + 1. \tag{62}$$

From this expression, we can conclude that π can be less than c_m so long as the externality does not cause R_q to be greater than λ. In short, a large value for R_m can justify a Ramsey price for access that is less than marginal cost.

This is about the only conclusion that can be reached. Clearly, one expects that inclusion of distributional considerations in the welfare function would reduce the relative tax burden on access (or even hasten a subsidy), but the expressions (20) and (52) are simply too complicated to establish analytically that this is in fact the case.

At this point I want to take up the more fundamental question of whether the Feldstein model is in principle even applicable to telecommunications. The Feldstein model is intended for circumstances in which one of two goods is consumed primarily by low-income households and the second good is consumed primarily by high-income households. The goods can be related in consumption, but strong complementarity would seem to be ruled out. Beer and spirits seem a good example, for (at least on the popular view) beer is the drink of the poor and spirits the drink of the wealthy. But telecommunications does not fit into this mold, for access and usage are functionally connected complements. For most households, access is something that once demanded is purchased in equal amounts by poor and rich alike. Since usage requires access, rich households do not substitute usage for access as they might spirits for beer. Moreover, while it is true that the largest toll users tend to be high-income households, it is not necessarily the case that the income elasticity for usage is higher for high-income households than for low-income households.

Data for Canadian households between 1978 and 1983 show that toll takes a declining proportion of income at all but the lowest levels of income and that the point at which toll expenditures exceed expenditures for access and local service was below the mean level of income by 1978.[22] In the circumstances, an across-the-board subsidy to access would benefit rich households as much as poor. What the Canadian data show is that a tax on toll to subsidize access would essentially be a tax on where a household lives. The tax would bear most heavily on households living in rural and small urban areas to the benefit of households living in large urban areas. As incomes are lower in the former, a Feldstein-type distributional tax subsidy would be a regressive tax on income, hardly the result envisioned!

IV. SOME REMAINING QUESTIONS

Two questions that were raised in the introduction have not yet been addressed. These are:

1. Whether the network externality is different depending upon whether an increase in network size arises from an increase in population, penetration remaining constant, or from an increase in penetration, population remaining constant? (Type I versus Type II externalities.)
2. Whether the greater usage per telephone that might be observed in a large system as opposed to a small system is a reflection of the network externality.

Nothing that has been said to this point suggests that there are any inherent differences between an increase in network size that arises from an increase in population as opposed to an increase that arises from an increase in the penetration rate. Either event leads to one more telephone that existing subscribers can reach. The only point that occurs to me is that someone coming onto the network through a population increase is likely to have a higher income than someone who has previously just been on the margin of subscribing. Higher income should in general be associated with a larger externality, that is, $\partial S/\partial M$ should be expected to be larger the higher is the level of income of the marginal subscriber. However, this seems a slender reed on which to hang a distinction between Type I and Type II externalities.

Turning now to usage per telephone, there seems little question that a large system confers more benefits to subscribers than a small system. This may not be true for every subscriber, but it is almost certainly true on the average. Consequently, we should probably expect, everything else being constant, to observe greater usage per telephone in a large system. The question is, is this a reflection of network externalities? The answer would seem pretty clearly to be yes, but the externalities are global rather than individual-specific, for

[22] See Taylor, Waverman, and Wall (1990). See also Section 8.3.2.

what is being reflected is the fact that, for whatever reason, the willingness-to-pay to belong to a large network is greater than the willingness-to-pay to belong to a small network.[23]

The only way that any of this would seem to have any social implications would be if the individual externalities, as they have been defined in this chapter, are larger in a large system than in a small system, that is, if $\partial S/\partial m$, where m denotes the first extramarginal subscriber, were larger in a large system than in a small system. If this were the case, an argument could be made for larger systems having larger targeted subsidies. However, I see no reason for thinking $\partial S/\partial m$ would in fact be larger in a larger system.

V. CALL EXTERNALITIES

Unlike network externalities, call externalities have never received much attention, almost certainly because they have never been seen as posing a problem for pricing. The view has been that, since people in general make about as many calls as they receive, the unpaid-for benefits attending the receipt of calls balance out over time.

Information exchange is a complex process, however, and recent research suggests that call externalities may play a role larger than simply helping to determine who pays for a call. In particular, there is accumulating evidence that calling is a reciprocal process not only in terms of "taking turns", but also in terms of call stimulation. Simply put, calling appears to give rise to further calling. Toll models that are specified on a point-to-point, bi-directional basis, in which calling from A to B is distinguished from calling B to A, indicate that a call in one direction gives rise to half to two-thirds of a call in the opposite direction.[24] The purpose of this section is to examine the role (or roles) that call externalities might be playing in this phenomenon.

1. Formal Statement of the Call Externality

As discussed in Chapter 2, the point of departure for defining the call externality is the fact that a completed telephone call requires the participation of a second party whose welfare is thereby affected. The gratuitous effect which falls on the second party represents the call externality. Assuming, as is the usual presumption, that the externality is positive, recipients of calls (since most calls are paid for by the originator) receive unpaid-for benefits. The

---

[23] Option demand and call externalities can also be factors in this. Call externalities are discussed in the next section.

[24] See Larson, Lehman, and Weisman (1990) and Appelbe *et al.* (1988).

existing view in the literature pretty much has been that, since most calling is bi-directional, the externality is internalized over time as today's recipients of calls are tomorrow's originators. This balances out obligations *vis-à-vis* one another. For the system as a whole, the benefits from incoming calls can be seen as increasing willingness-to-pay to have a telephone, both individually and in the aggregate, which means that a telephone system will be larger when call externalities are present than what it would be in their absence.[25]

The foregoing is the conventional view of the call externality and is uncontroversial. But it is also not very useful empirically for its only implication is that a telephone system will be bigger with call externalities than without. It is a statement about size, not usage. Nothing is said or implied about usage, which seems strange since the source of the call externality is in fact usage. The implications of the call externality for usage have been overlooked in the literature, and it is to these that we will now turn.

To begin with, let us consider two individuals, A and B, who regularly communicate with one another by telephone and for each of whom the call externality is positive in the sense that each looks forward to receiving a call from the other. Two circumstances can be identified, one in which the number of calls between A and B is determined "exogenously" as a function (say) of their respective incomes and the price of calls and a second circumstance in which the number of calls between A and B depends not only on incomes and price, but also on the number of calls that A makes to B and the number of calls that B makes to A. Calling is clearly endogenous in the second circumstance.

In the first circumstance, one could easily imagine the appearance of an implicit contract in which A calls B half of the time and B calls A the other half.[26] This is the situation envisioned in the conventional interpretation of the call externality and simply involves the internalization of the externality through an implicit contract. The total number of calls is determined by income and price and the only effect of the externality is to help determine how the cost of the calls is divided.

The second circumstance is clearly much more complex, because not only can there be an implicit contract defining "turn" but it is a situation in which a call can create the need for a further call. The call externality in this situation not only helps to determine who pays for the calls but also leads to an actual stimulation of calling. This to me is the missing ingredient in existing discussions (including my own in the 1980 book) of the call externality, and it is clear that modeling it requires the specification of a two-equation, point-to-point bi-directional model in which calling from A to B depends upon the

---

[25] Cf. Squire (1973) and Littlechild (1975).
[26] See Larson and Lehman (1986).

reverse-calling from B to A and vice-versa.

2. The Dynamics of Information Exchange

To this point, it has been assumed that calls giving rise to further calling is rooted in the call externality. This would be the case in a situation in which A's call to B increased B's utility so much that he called A back to tell him so or else called C to tell her that there has been a call from A. This is probably a common event in real life, but there is another situation that is probably even more common (especially among business users) in which calling triggers further calling but which is not rooted in the call externality (as conventionally defined). This is the situation in which the exchange of information *creates the need* for further exchange. Several authors collaborating on a paper provides an obvious example. For lack of a better term, this situation will be referred to as the dynamics of information exchange.

The dynamics of information exchange may not only involve B returning a call to A as the result of an initial call from A, but may create a need for B to call C to corroborate something that A had told B, which in turn may lead to C calling D, and so on. Essentially the same dynamics can operate when, for whatever reason, a piece of information is injected into a group that forms a community of interest. An obvious example is the death of one of the members of the group. A learns that B had died, calls C, and the grapevine kicks into operation.

3. Empirical Modeling of Call Externalities

We now turn to an empirical model of toll demand that allows for the considerations just described. The discussion will revolve around the generic form of the model, discussed in Chapter 6, that was applied by Telecom Canada to analyze toll traffic among the member companies of Telecom Canada and toll traffic between Canada and the U.S.

For notation, let Q_{AB} denote the toll traffic from area A to area B, and similarly for Q_{BA}. Also, let Y_A denote the income in A, P_{AB} the price of a call from A to B, T_A the number of telephones in A, and similarly for Y_B, P_{BA}, and T_B. For Q_{AB} and Q_{BA}, it is postulated:

$$\ln Q_{AB} = \alpha_0 + \alpha_1 \ln Y_A + \alpha_2 \ln P_{AB}$$
$$+ \alpha_3 \ln T_A + \alpha_4 \ln T_B + \alpha_5 \ln Q_{BA} \tag{63}$$

$$\ln Q_{BA} = \beta_0 + \beta_1 \ln Y_B + \beta_2 \ln P_{BA}$$
$$+ \beta_3 \ln T_B + \beta_4 \ln T_A + \beta_5 \ln Q_{AB}. \tag{64}$$

These equations form a simultaneous system in which toll traffic from one area to another is assumed to be a double-logarithmic function of income and the number of telephones in the sending area price, the number of telephones in the receiving area, and the amount of reverse traffic. The effects of call externalities are reflected in the reverse-traffic variables, Q_{BA} in equation (63) and Q_{AB} in equation (64). Network externalities are allowed for through inclusion of the number of telephones that can be reached in the receiving areas, T_B in equation (63) and T_A in equation (64).

The reduced forms for the two models are as follows:

$$\ln Q_{AB} = \frac{\alpha_0 + \alpha_5 \beta_0}{\theta} + \frac{\alpha_1}{\theta} \ln Y_A + \frac{\alpha_5 \beta_1}{\theta} \ln Y_B + \frac{\alpha_2}{\theta} \ln P_{AB}$$

$$+ \frac{\alpha_5 \beta_2}{\theta} \ln P_{BA} + \frac{\alpha_3 + \alpha_5 \beta_4}{\theta} \ln T_A + \frac{\alpha_5 \beta_3}{\theta} \ln T_B \qquad (65)$$

$$\ln Q_{BA} = \frac{\beta_0 + \beta_5 \alpha_0}{\theta} + \frac{\beta_1}{\theta} \ln Y_B + \frac{\beta_5 \alpha_1}{\theta} \ln Y_A + \frac{\beta_2}{\theta} \ln P_{BA}$$

$$+ \frac{\beta_5 \alpha_2}{\theta} \ln P_{AB} + \frac{\beta_3 + \beta_5 \alpha_4}{\theta} \ln T_B + \frac{\beta_5 \alpha_3}{\theta} \ln T_A, \qquad (66)$$

where $\theta = 1 - \alpha_5 \beta_5$.

With reverse-calling in the picture, calling from A to B will be affected by changes in price and income in B as well as in A. In view of this, it is necessary (and useful) to distinguish among uni-directional and bi-directional elasticities for income and price. The uni-directional own-elasticity with respect to P_{AB}, for example, will be given by α_2, while the bi-directional elasticity will be given by $\alpha_2/(1 - \alpha_4 \beta_4)$. Similar elasticities apply for income. The necessity for this is most apparent in a situation, as with interprovincial calling in Canada and calling between Canada and the U.S., for which traffic from A to B and from B to A is handled by different telcos. Traffic carried by Telecom Canada between Ontario/Quebec and the U.S. northeast, for example, can be stimulated by a decrease in the rate charged by U.S. carriers even though there is no change in the rates charged by Telecom Canada.

While of interest in its own right, the foregoing digresses from our present focus, which is on the implications of call externalities on the demand for usage. As noted, call externalities are allowed for in equations (63) and (64) through the reverse-traffic variables. Positive coefficients for these variables would be consistent with call externalities having a positive effect on usage. Existing empirical studies with models of the type described by equations (63) and (64) yield strong reverse-traffic (or call-back) effects.[27] Coefficients

---

[27] See Larson, Lehman, and Weisman (1990) and Appelbe *et al.* (1988).

for the reverse-traffic variables are usually of the order of 0.4 to 0.6 and are highly significant statistically. The evidence is thus consistent with a call in one direction giving rise to half or two-thirds of a call in return. This is a strong effect, and one has to question whether it can be attributed exclusively to call externalities. This is a difficult question to answer, for neither theory nor experience offers much guidance.

Two things, in particular, need to be considered. The first relates to a possible identification problem, while the second relates simply to interpretation. The identification problem arises in connection with the possibility of not being able to distinguish between the effects of call externalities and the effects of network externalities. Network externalities in equations (63) and (64) are represented in the number of telephones that can be reached, $\ln T_B$ in equation (63) and $\ln T_A$ in equation (64). However, apart from the contribution to usage of realized option demand, what really matters in connection with network externalities is communities of interest. But the problem with communities of interest is measurement.

In equations (63) and (64), $\ln T_B$ and $\ln T_A$ are measures of communities of interest, but so too are the reverse-traffic variables. Indeed, for a large system, reverse-traffic is probably a much better measure of community of interest than simply the number of reachable telephones. The consequence is an identification problem, for network externalities will be reflected in the coefficient for reverse-traffic as well as call externalities.[28] In view of this, it is not surprising that strong collinearity between T_B and Q_{BA} and between T_A and Q_{AB} generally precludes estimation of the model in equations (63) and (64). The Telecom Canada models, for example, exclude altogether the number of telephones in receiving areas, which means that any effects of network externalities will be reflected in the coefficient for reverse-traffic.

Turning now to the matter of interpretation, a substantial part of the reverse-traffic effect, it seems to me, can be attributed to what has just been described as the dynamics of information exchange, wherein the exchange of information in a call creates the need for a further exchange of information. Although this arises from the interaction of two (or more) individuals, it seems to me to stretch the point to identify this effect with the call externality. In my view, it is best to restrict the call externality to the unpaid-for benefits

[28] There would be no problem if reachable telephones were a perfect measure of community of interest, for reverse-traffic would then provide a clean measure of the effects of call externalities on usage. But this is clearly not the case, for in a large system individual communities of interest will be small fractions of the total system. Aggregation over telephones in the sending area will alleviate the problem somewhat because every telephone in the receiving area should with high probability be in the community of interest of at least one telephone in the sending area. Reverse-traffic, on the other hand, will almost certainly provide a tighter measure.

conferred on the receiving party of a call and to stop short of identifying the call externality with the endogenous stimulation of calling that arises from information exchange. This means, of course, that there is yet another identification problem, for the calling that is associated with the call externality cannot be distinguished empirically from the calling that is associated with the dynamics of information exchange.

V. EMPIRICAL EVIDENCE REGARDING CONSUMPTION EXTERNALITIES

We now turn to a brief review of the empirical evidence on consumption externalities. The focus in this section will be on the network externality, and specifically on the network externality as it affects the demand for access. As has just been noted, recent experience in modeling toll demand on a point-to-point basis indicates the existence of substantial call-externality effects, but identification problems preclude attributing these effects solely to the unpaid-for benefits from incoming calls.

Two studies, Perl (1983) and Taylor and Kridel (1990), were noted in Chapter 6 as providing evidence that access demand is positively related to system size. Both studies focus on the residential demand for access using data from the 1980 U.S. Census. Perl, it will be recalled, uses a national sample of individual households, while Taylor and Kridel use data at the Census tract level in the states served by Southwestern Bell. Perl uses a logit model, Taylor and Kridel a probit model. Perl uses two measures of system size in testing for the network externality, the number of telephones in the local calling area and the number of telephones per square mile in the local-calling area. Taylor and Kridel use just the former.

The number of telephones in the local-calling area has a positive effect on the probability of a household demanding access in Perl's model, while the effect of density is positive up to 2000 telephones per square mile, but negative for densities greater than 2000 telephones per square mile.[29] Perl uses his estimated coefficients to calculate the value to a typical household of belonging to networks ranging in size from 25,000 subscribers to 250,000.

---

[29] The coefficients for Perl's model are given in Table 1 of Chapter 6. Perl cautions that one should not conclude from the negative effect of density for densities beyond 2000 that there is no externality or a negative externality at higher densities: It is just that phone density is an imperfect proxy for network size. Where phone density is very high, population density is also high. As population density rises it becomes increasingly easier to reach people by means other than a phone. In very dense cities, for example, most people live very close to people they know and can easily reach those people by visiting instead of phoning them. Since phone density and population density are very closely correlated, the phone density variable provides a statistically biased measure of the network externality [(Perl 1983), pp. 31–32)].

TABLE 1

Value of Telephone Service to the Average
Household at Various Local Network Sizes
Perl Study

Network Size (Number of Subscribers	Phone per Square Mile	Value of Telephone Service
25,000	100	$ 56.02
50,000	200	60.38
100,000	400	61.55
500,000	2,000	68.40

Source: Perl (1983, Figure 16)

The results are given in Table 1. The number for each network size was derived by calculating the area beneath the demand curve for that network size for access charges ranging between infinity and zero. The calculations assume a calling area of fixed geographic size, small enough to ensure that density would not exceed 2000 telephones per square mile. This means, therefore, that increases in network size are achieved through an increasing population density or an increasing proportion of subscribing households.

The results imply that in 1980 the value of telephone service for a typical household was $56 per month for a network of 25,000 subscribers, about $60 per month for a network of 50,000 subscribers (an increase of about 8%), about $62 per month for a network of 100,000 subscribers (an increase of another 2%), and about $68 per month for 500,000 subscribers. Doubling network size is thus seen to increase the value of telephone service, but at a sharply diminishing rate.

Using these results as a measure of the network externality, Perl estimates the extent to which access prices would need to be set below cost if the objective were to optimize network size. This was done by setting a price which maximizes the sum of consumer and producer surplus. With a $20 access cost, the prices implied are between $13 and $18 depending upon density. At a $30 access cost, the optimal prices range between $23 and $28. Averaged across all density bands, the optimal access prices are about $14 below cost. The results are summarized in Table 1.

Perl notes that the welfare gains from setting access prices below cost appear to be modest:

At a $20 access cost, they range from about 1.0 cents to 10.2 cents per household per month. At the $30 access cost, the gain ranges from 1.4 cents to 16.2 cents per household per month. Averaged across all density bands, the gains were about 5.0 cents and about 7.0 cents when costs were $30. These gains may simply not justify the administrative burdens associated with subsidizing access. (Perl 1983, p. 35).[30]

The coefficients for the Taylor-Kridel model are given in Table 6 of Chapter 6. The number of telephones that can be reached in the local calling area has a positive effect on residential access demand, but the impact is small. At the mean values for all of the variables, a 10% increase in the number of lines implies an increase of 0.027 in the percentage of households that would demand access. Unfortunately, calculations similar to Perl's were not made at the time that Kridel and Taylor did their study, and at this later date it has not been possible to retrieve the information that is needed to do the calculations. I would be surprised, however, if the numbers were much different from Perl's.[31]

VI. CONCLUSIONS

A common view in the telephone industry is that the presence of a network externality can justify an access price to residential subscribers that is below marginal cost. The conclusion of the chapter is that, in general, this view lacks both theoretical and empirical justification. We have seen that the existence of an externality leads to a reduction in the Ramsey tax rate on access in relation to the tax rate on usage, but that access would never be priced below marginal cost. Distributional equity considerations of the type suggested by Feldstein in which consumer surplus is weighted by marginal social utility is sometimes offered as a second justification for pricing access below marginal cost. The earlier conclusion is not materially affected. Equity considerations lead to a reduction in the Ramsey-optimal tax rate on access, but the access price would remain above marginal cost except in the event of a large externality or a counterfactual concentration of toll usage among high-income households. More fundamentally, it is questionable whether the Feldstein framework is even applicable to telephone services in the way that has been suggested. Access and demand are functionally related complements, not goods (such as beer and spirits) for which one is substituted for the other as the level of income increases.

---

[30] The calculations assume that the subsidy is financed by a lump sum tax on all individuals.

[31] For additional efforts to quantify network externalities, see Perl (1986).

A final conclusion relates to the question of who should be taxed in the event that network externalities should justify the paying of a subsidy to a group of extramarginal non-subscribers. The conventional view of economists has usually been that subsidies for access should ideally be paid from general tax revenues. However, there are really two issues involved here, and care must be taken not to confuse them. The first issue, which is the one focused on in this chapter, relates to the possible distortions caused by network externalities, while the second issue relates to access to the telephone network being seen (especially by regulators) as a social-merit good (in the sense of Musgrave 1959).

Let s denote the subsidy as seen by regulators that should be paid to the "meriting" group and let s_1 denote the part of s that can be attributed to network externalities; $s - s_1$ accordingly represents the social-merit component of s. (In present circumstances, s_1 is almost certainly small in relation to $s - s_1$.) The thrust of this chapter is that, since network externalities are internal to the telephone network and therefore benefit existing subscribers rather than society at large, s_1 should in principle be financed by existing subscribers (through preferably through a tax on access rather than on toll). The social-merit portion, on the other hand, since it benefits society at large, should be financed from general tax revenues.[32]

With regard to call externalities, existing discussions of telephone consumption externalities have tended to focus on network externalities because of the problems that network externalities pose for the optimal social pricing of access. Call externalities have never been viewed as posing such a problem. While the benefits associated with incoming calls lead to an increase in the willingness-to-pay to have a telephone, the benefits are individual-specific and, since most people receive about as many calls as they make, tend to be internalized for a system as a whole. This being the case, there is no divergence, as with network externalities, between the private and social benefits of a marginal subscriber.

The foregoing, however, is a static view which concentrates on usage. What the literature has tended to overlook is the dynamical effects of the call externalities on usage. The utility that is conferred on the recipient of a call can lead to a call in return, which in turn can lead to yet another call in return, etc. This type of call stimulation can unambiguously be attributed to the call externality. But this is only part of the story. Another stimulation to calling can arise out of the interaction of the parties to a call. The exchange

---

[32] I say "in principle" in connection with the financing of s_1 because, with more than 93% of U.S. households having a telephone, there is not much difference between existing subscribers and society at large. Consequently, there would be little efficiency loss if s_1 were financed out of general tax revenues as well. I am grateful to Dennis Weisman for discussions on this point.

of information in a call can stimulate the need for a further call (or calls) either between the original parties or with third parties. This stimulation seems inherent in the dynamics of information exchange and should not, in my view, be attributed to the call externality.

Interest in call externalities has been spurred by recent application of point-to-point toll demand model which allow for bi-directional traffic to be simultaneously determined.[33] The results suggest that a call in one direction gives rise to about half to two-thirds of a call in return. This is strong evidence, in my view, of the phenomenon just discussed, that calling is inherently self-stimulating.

Although most of the focus in this chapter has been on statics, the central message is really one of dynamics. We have seen, especially in connection with the toll models of Bell Canada and Telecom Canada, how usage tends to stimulate further usage, which would seem to be a dynamical aspect of the call externality that has not previously been identified. While this represents endogenous growth of a sort, it is a sort that is akin to a multiplier process initiated by changes in income, population, and prices, rather than of the self-sustaining variety identified by Rohlfs (1974) and Van Rabenau and Stahl (1974) involving movement from a low-equilibrium user set to a high-equilibrium user set.

Self-sustaining endogenous growth of this last type, if it ever occurred, is almost certainly many years in the past in the U.S. and Canada, but this is not the case in many parts of the world, particularly in countries whose telecommunications systems are underdeveloped in relation to the rest of their economies. France in the 1970s may have experienced endogenous growth of this sort, while all of the Eastern European countries may currently be poised for it to occur.

---

[33] These models were reviewed in Chapter 6.

CHAPTER 10

PRICE ELASTICITIES IN THE HEARING ROOM: THE PROMISE AND
LIMITS OF ECONOMETRIC ANALYSES OF
TELECOMMUNICATIONS DEMAND

My initiation to using econometric demand models in a serious way in the telephone industry was with a telephone call in late 1975 from Edward D. Lowry, then at State Regulatory at AT&T in New York. Mountain Bell had just had its nose bloodied in a rate hearing before the Public Utility Commission in New Mexico. An intervenor with some econometric sophistication had raised some embarrassing questions about Mountain's method of calculating the repression effects of some proposed new toll rates. The request for repression was denied, and Mountain had appealed to State Regulatory at AT&T for help.

Within a fairly short period of time, a demand analysis district was established at Mountain Bell's corporate headquarters in Denver. Workshops and seminars on applied econometric demand analysis were held, and computers began to hum with the estimation of intrastate toll demand models for the seven states in Mountain Bell's service territory. Mountain Bell was not alone in doing this. With active encouragement from AT&T, demand analysis districts were set up in most of the other Bell Operating Companies, and by 1978 econometric models for intrastate toll demand had been used in regulatory proceedings in at least 34 states.[1]

The motivation for the econometric models was the estimation of price elasticities that could be used to calculate the price effects of proposed new rates. The procedure was first to calculate for some test year "repriced" revenues by multiplying test-year quantities by the new rates. The repriced revenues were then adjusted for non-zero price elasticity using elasticity estimates derived from the econometric models. Sometimes the telco estimates of repression were accepted as presented, sometimes not, depending upon the sophistication of intervenors and the credibility of their witnesses.

The purpose of this chapter is to step back from the details of theory, models, and estimation and to examine what it is that econometric demand

---

[1] Cf. Table 1 in Appendix 2.

modeling is capable of accomplishing and what (at least in the present state of the art) it cannot accomplish. The point of departure, and also the organizing framework, for the discussion will be an overview of the formal structure of an econometric study.[2] In Section II, the discussion will turn to the formulation of a set of principles and precepts that (in my view, anyway) ought to guide the development of econometric models of telecommunications demand and their use in regulatory proceedings. Finally, Section III will focus on a number of questions and issues whose poor understanding and treatment often leads to confusion and the drawing of unwarranted conclusions.

I. THE STRUCTURE OF AN ECONOMETRIC STUDY[3]

Econometrics as a formal discipline came into being in the early 1930s with the founding of the Econometric Society and publication of its affiliated journal, *Econometrica*. In the words of one of its founders, Ragnar Frisch, the Econometric Society is ". . . an international society for the advancement of economic theory in its relation to statistics and mathematics." The fledgling discipline achieved early prominence, despite a critical review by Keynes, with publication of Tinbergen's *Business Cycles* which involved an attempt to test empirically various theories of the business cycle using the statistical tools of multiple correlation and regression. Many of the issues raised by Keynes were addressed by Haavelmo in his famous 1944 monograph, *The Probability Approach to Econometrics*, and subsequently by researchers at the Cowles Commission, who developed the equations-system approach to estimation and inference in a system of simultaneous equations.[4]

1. The Textbook Paradigm for Econometrics

The Haavelmo and Cowles Commission monographs had such tremendous impact that by 1960 an accepted paradigm of an econometric study had emerged and was widely disseminated through the influential textbooks of Johnston (1962) and Goldberger (1964). In the words of Johnston (1962, p. 6):

---

[2] As methodology discussions are inherently controversial, I hasten to say that the overview in question represents my own views on how an econometric study should be structured. The influence of Haavelmo's well-known 1944 *Econometrica* monograph will be evident, as will also the recent reformulation of Haavelmo by Spanos (1989).

[3] This section draws heavily on Spanos (1989).

[4] See Koopmans (1950) and Hood and Koopmans (1953).

... The essential role of econometric modeling is the estimation and testing of economic models. The first step in the process is the specification of the model in mathematical form ... Next, we must assemble appropriate and relevant data or sector that the model purports to describe. Thirdly, we use the data to estimate the parameters of the model in an attempt to judge whether it constitutes a sufficiently realistic picture of the economy being studied or whether a somewhat different specification has to be estimated ...

The textbook paradigm can be summarized in three words: Specification, Estimation, and Testing. Specification, in the textbook paradigm, consists of three steps:

1. A statement as to which variables are endogenous and which variables are exogenous;
2. Specification of the functional forms of the relationships;
3. Specification of the statistical properties of the error terms.

Estimation involves the use of a set of appropriate and relevant data to establish values for the parameters of the model. Finally, testing refers to the use of appropriate procedures of statistical inference to test how well the postulated model conforms with the reality that it purports to explain.

2. Problems with the Textbook Paradigm

There are two practical problems with the textbook paradigm. The first problem is that as a prescription for practice, the paradigm almost always founders on ignorance. The validity of the paradigm requires that one arrive at the testing with the following view intact: that the parameters of the model have been estimated from a data set that can be interpreted as having arisen as a sample drawn at random from the universe described by the specification of the model. The problem is that models as initially specified almost never pass muster, and the model that is ended up with is seldom the one specified at the start. Variables may be added or deleted, functional forms may be changed, dynamics may be respecified, and the underlying theory may even be reformulated. All of these modifications are standard in practice, but since they involve interactions between specification and data, the preconditions for statistical testing are obviously violated.

The second problem is related to the first and involves the fact that the textbook paradigm does not allow for the data that are to be used in estimation and testing also to be used in formulating the model to begin with. The problem is that specification in the textbook paradigm is an inclusive process that does not distinguish among theoretical, statistical, and empirical models.[5] By failing to do so, it is not recognized that many of the problems that are encountered in applied econometrics relate to the specification of an adequate statistical model rather than to the specification of the underlying theoretical model. (An adequate statistical model in this context refers to a statistical model whose underlying assumptions are valid for the data that are being used in estimation and testing of the theoretical model.)[6] As will be discussed in the next section, separating the specification of the statistical model from the specification of the theoretical model allows for "fiddling" with the former not to contaminate statistical inference in relation to the latter.

3. A Reformulation of the Textbook Paradigm

The purpose of this section is to suggest a reformulation of the textbook paradigm for an econometric study that is based upon the distinction among theoretical, statistical, and empirical models. The framework that is developed accommodates much of current practice in applied econometrics and will provide a vehicle for reducing the confusing debate that has marked the use of econometric models in regulatory proceedings.

A schematic overview of the reformulated paradigm is given in Figure 1. The point of departure for an econometric study is the question to be investigated, depicted by the square box at the top of the figure. Two arrows run from this box, one to the left which ends in a box labeled "theory" and one to the right which ends in a box labeled "data." The role of the theory side is to formulate the question to be investigated in a meaningful way and to provide a framework for relating the relevant facts to one another. The role of the data side is to identify a data set that is germane to the question being investigated and to formulate a statistical model that adequately accounts for the probabilistic character of the data.

The first step on the theory side is to specify a theoretical model that represents in abstract terms the question to be investigated. The theoretical model defines the variables of interest and describes the relationships among them in the form of mathematical equations. This is depicted in Figure 1 by the box labeled "theoretical model". Theoretical models in this framework

---

[5] As 'model' can have several different meanings, it is important that it be understood what I mean by these concepts. A *theoretical model* is a formal structure that describes in abstract terms the phenomena that are being investigated. An *empirical model* is a translation of the theoretical model into a form which allows for empirical testing. A *statistical model* describes in statistical terms the particular body of real-world data that are to be used in testing the theoretical model.

[6] The concept of statistical adequacy can be traced to R.A. Fisher. See Koopmans (1937).

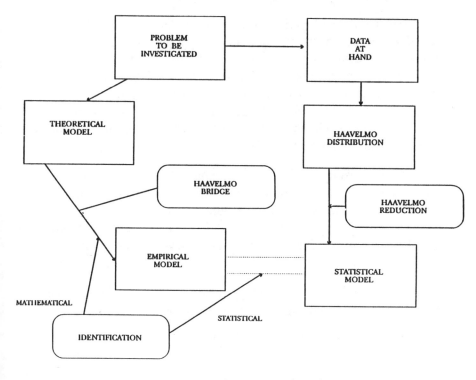

Fig. 1.   Structure of an econometric study.

are viewed as human constructs rather than hidden truths.[7] Underlying the analysis on the data side is an *assumption* that the data to be analyzed have been generated by a probabilistic process. The first step on the data side, then, is to specify the *Haavelmo distribution*, by which is meant the joint distribution of all of the observable random variables for the whole of the sample period. The Haavelmo distribution represents the most general description of the sample information and demarcates the relevant variables for modeling purposes. The second step on the data side is the *Haavelmo reduction*,[8] which involves particularizing the Haavelmo distribution to a specific distri-

---

[7] "It is not to be forgotten that they [theoretical relationships] are all our own artificial inventions in a search for understanding of real life; they are not hidden truths to be 'discovered'." (Haavelmo 1944, p. 3.)

[8] The terms Haavelmo distribution and Haavelmo reduction are taken from Spanos (1989). These terms as well as other terms used in this section, such as theoretical, estimable, statistical, and empirical models and the Haavelmo bridge, are not yet established terminology. Hendry and Mizon (1987), for example, use Haavelmo distribution and Haavelmo reduction differently, although they attribute the concepts to Spanos. Accordingly, all of these terms as I use them are defined in the text. I am grateful to Aris Spanos for bringing this to my attention.

bution (such as the multivariate normal) and making assumptions concerning the independence, invariance, and memory properties of the process which generated the data. Before discussing what is meant by these terms, the sampling frame-of-reference needs to be addressed. The essence of the probability approach to econometric modeling is that a theoretical model acquires empirical meaning only when accompanied with some form of "experiment" which describes the circumstances under which the theoretical relationships are measurable. In the words of Haavelmo (1944, p. 6):

> ... when we set up a system of theoretical relationships and use economic names for the otherwise purely theoretical variables involved, we have in mind some *actual experiment*, or some *design of an experiment*, which we at least imagine arranging, in order to measure those quantities in real economic life that we think might obey the laws imposed on their theoretical namesake ... (Italics in original.)

The notion of an actual or designed experiment can be illustrated using the classic example of demand and supply schedules:

$$q_t^d = \alpha_0 - \alpha_1 p_t \tag{1}$$

$$q_t^s = \beta_0 + \beta_1 p_t. \tag{2}$$

The experiment that we could imagine that would give empirical meaning to this theoretical model would be for somebody to call a sequence of prices within a certain range p_{it}, $i = 1, \ldots, N$, and buyers and sellers register their intentions which when added up yield the series q_t^d and q_t^s.

Although actual experiments of the type just described are now common in the study of a wide variety of markets,[9] the fact is still that most data that are available to economists are nonexperimental in origin. Again, in the words of Haavelmo (1944, p. 6):

> [The economist] is presented with some results which, so to speak, Nature has produced in all their complexity, his task being to build models that explain what has been observed ... one should study very carefully the actual series considered and the conditions under which they were produced, before identifying them with the variables of a particular theoretical model.

An obvious question at this point is whether the fact that data are generated nonexperimentally precludes treating them for practical purposes as if they

---

[9] See Smith (1982).

were. The validity of econometrics as it has been practiced for nearly 50 years requires that this question be answered in the affirmative. For this is the vital condition that enables statistical methods to be applied to economics. We now turn to the considerations that lead to the condition being accepted as fulfilled.

Most of the time, the economic question that is being investigated can be reduced to the sign and size of a particular partial derivative. Examples: What is the effect on toll calling of a change in toll rates? What is the effect on investment of a change in the rate of interest? If economists could study these questions under laboratory conditions, experiments could be designed in which all factors that impinge upon toll calling or investment, except for toll rates and the rate of interest, were either held constant or randomized. Toll rates and the rate of interest would be varied and measurements made on toll calling and investment. In this case, only the simple two-variable regression model would be needed to estimate the partial derivatives in question, for the effects of the factors held constant would be reflected in the constant terms and the other factors would be orthogonal to toll rates or the rate of interest through randomization.

The problem with data from Natural experiments is that Nature is under no constraint to provide a well-designed experiment. Factors like income and the stage of the business cycle are not held constant, and their variation in relation to toll rates and the rate of interest (to continue the examples) is not one of orthogonality. This is where the multiple regression model comes into play, for it provides a conceptual vehicle for holding the effects of these nonorthogonal factors constant. The variation that remains is channeled into an unobservable error term, which is viewed as a random variable. The Natural data are then viewed as having arisen from an experiment whose design consists of the X matrix and the random error term. An observation (or data point) is seen as consisting of two components, a systematic component which is determined by the values taken by the variables in X which are viewed as being under the control of a fictive experimenter, and a random component consisting of a particular realization of the error term. If the Natural data set consists of T data points, the T random components are viewed as constituting a sample of size T drawn at random from the distribution describing the error term.

The foregoing provides the probability basis for the standard multiple regression model and opens the door for hypothesis testing and other forms of statistical inference. It is important to recognize, however, that most of the variables included in X are there for reasons of control. They are included explicitly as predictors only because History does not provide experiments in which their effects are either not constant across observations or not random with respect to the variables whose partial derivatives are the parameters of interest. This means, accordingly, that the variables to be included as controls usually cannot be specified on purely theoretical grounds, for whether or not they belong in a model depends on vagaries of History and their identification requires knowledge of the historical and institutional circumstances which defined the Natural experiment. Econometric analysis of Natural data thus necessarily involves a historical dimension.

The textbook paradigm does not recognize this historical dimension, for specification is treated inclusively. There is no distinction within the paradigm between specification of the relationships that are of theoretical interest and identification of controls. Any "fiddling" with the model that is related to the acquisition of knowledge of the circumstances which defined the Natural experiment is seen, within the textbook paradigm, as constituting contamination. Since such fiddling in applied econometrics is, and always has been, nearly universal, the textbook paradigm is simply not useful as a practical guide.

Modeling the historical circumstances which defined a Natural experiment is represented on the data side of Figure 1. The data at hand represent the data generated by the experiment. As noted earlier, underlying the modeling procedure is an assumption that the Natural experiment can be modeled as a particular statistical process. The first step is to specify the Haavelmo distribution, which involves the specification of the joint distribution of all of the sample period. The second step is the Haavelmo reduction, which involves a particularization of the Haavelmo distribution to an operational distribution which defines the statistical model. The statistical model is the statistical representation of the Natural experiment.

For the representation to be valid, however, the statistical model must be statistically adequate. A statistical model is *statistically adequate* when its underlying assumptions are valid for the data at hand. A lot of testing is in principle required at this stage, and it is clear that much of the "fiddling" referred to earlier really entail attempts to test for or to achieve statistical adequacy. Tests at this stage cannot (and should not) be viewed as contaminating, for the validity of the inference which is of primary concern, namely, that involving the partial derivatives of interest, requires statistical adequacy of the statistical model. Valid tests at this stage include tests for normality (if normality is being assumed), stationarity, invariance, and the autocorrelation structure of error terms. Co-integration should be tested for, as should structural stability of parameters through time.

This is also the stage where the question of the variables to be included for statistical control is addressed: what variables belong in the model for historical or institutional reasons (i.e., because of an ill-designed experiment), although they are of no theoretical interest? While this can involve considerable searching for variables which "belong" in a model,[10] it should not be confused with methods of building an econometric model that involve statistical searches over a large set of possibly relevant independent variables.[11] The motivation at this stage is to seek out variables that belong in the statistical model as controls because to exclude them would result in problems of bias and inconsistency as a result of non-orthogonality with the variables that are of theoretical interest. When done carefully, empirical tests of this type are also non-contaminating.

This completes discussion for the moment of the data side of Figure 1. We now return to the theoretical side. Once the problem to be investigated is articulated, the first step on the theoretical side is to formulate a theoretical model. A theoretical model is an abstract representation of reality and provides a framework for studying and analyzing the problem that is of interest. The variables of interest are defined and the relationships connecting them are specified in mathematical terms. The second step on the theoretical side is the translation of the theoretical model into an empirical model. This is labeled the Haavelmo bridge in Figure 1 and involves identifying each of the constructs in the theoretical model with a measurable real-world counterpart. If, for example, the question being asked is how does toll-calling vary in response to changes in price and income, three theoretical constructs have to be identified with real-world quantities: toll-calling, price, and income.

The empirical model represents an estimable form of the theoretical model. For the theoretical model to have empirical content, the model must impose some restrictions on real-world behavior. The empirical model must reflect these restrictions as well. A tenet of standard economic theory, for example, is that demand functions are homogeneous of degree zero in income and prices. The empirical model can reflect this restriction either in the form of a maintained hypothesis to be imposed in estimation or as a hypothesis to be tested.

The empirical model is shown on the same level in Figure 1 as the statistical model, for this is the point at which the theoretical and data sides come together. Estimability requires that the empirical model be embeddable in the statistical model. This means that the two models have equivalent

---

[10] It must be emphasized that the focus at this point is on the statistical model, not the theoretical model. Empirical analysis is often instrumental to the construction of theoretical models, but interaction between a theoretical model and the particular data set that is to be used in testing that theoretical model is improper.

[11] One such method that was current at the time I was a graduate student was to specify a large list of independent variables and then to instruct the computer to select the subset which maximized the corrected R^2.

functional forms and that all of the variables in the empirical model also be in the statistical model. Generally, however, the statistical model will include, for reasons of statistical control, variables that are not in the empirical or theoretical models. Also there is no need for the time-series structures of the two models to be the same. The equations in the empirical model can represent, as will often be the case, equilibrium relationships, while the equations in the statistical model (since the real-world is almost always perpetually in disequilibrium) will usually be stochastic difference or integral equations. The implied equilibrium relationships in the two models must be the same, however. Of course, the theoretical model can specify dynamics, in which case the empirical model must be dynamical as well. In this case, the dynamical structure implied by the theoretical model can be treated as a hypothesis to be tested.[12]

We now turn to the concept of identification, which plays a dual role in the reformulated paradigm. One role is mathematical and the other is statistical. The mathematical role refers to the relationships that connect the parameters in the theoretical model with the parameters in the empirical model. The theoretical model is identified if all the parameters in the theoretical model can be solved for in terms of the parameters in the empirical model. This is identification as it has always appeared in the econometrics literature and is the identification of the textbook paradigm.

Statistical identification, in contrast, refers to the relationships between the parameters in the empirical model and the parameters in the statistical model, and involves mathematical identification as well as the ability to estimate. Not only must the parameters be estimable in principle, but in fact as well. The latter is not always possible because of ill-designed Natural experiments. Statistical identification is the concept of identification usually used by time-series analysts and operations researchers.

The message which emerges from this section is that a properly executed econometric study involves the development of three distinct models:

1. A theoretical model which describes in abstract terms the relationships among the variables of interest;
2. A statistical model which describes the Natural experiment which generated the data to be used in estimation and testing;
3. An empirical model which is an estimable form, embeddable in the statistical model, of the theoretical model.

An important implication of the reformulated paradigm is that, unlike in the textbook paradigm (which combines all three modeling efforts in one

---

[12] The focus in this paragraph has been on time-series data. The same principles apply to cross-sectional data, although questions involving dynamics usually take a different form.

operation, specification), tests relating to the adequacy of the statistical model do not contaminate inference concerning the theoretical model. In short, certain types of data analysis are not only necessary, but legitimate.

II. ECONOMETRICS IN THE HEARING ROOM: SOME GUIDING PRECEPTS

We now turn our attention to the development of a set of precepts for guiding the use of econometric demand models in regulatory proceedings. The question that we shall focus on is what can reasonably be expected of an econometric model in the hearing room, both in terms of a model's development and presentation and in terms of the questions that a model can reasonably be expected to answer. In general, the discussion in this section will not be about the role of the econometrician or statistician as an expert witness. This is treated admirably by Cooter and Rubinfeld (1989), Daggett and Freedman (1985), Fisher (1980, 1986), Rubinfeld (1985), and Rubinfeld and Steiner (1983), and the material here is intended as complementary to the discussions of those writers.

What follows is a list of the needs and concerns that any applied econometric study, and its developers, should address:

1. Is the question being asked reasonable in the circumstances and are the data relevant to answering the question?
2. Does the theoretical model that is selected provide a coherent framework for explaining the phenomenon under investigation? Is the theoretical structure state-of-the-art and is its relevance convincingly justified?
3. Is the statistical model that is used to describe the data sample statistically adequate? Is statistical adequacy tested for using state-of-the-art techniques?
4. Does the empirical model (i.e., the estimable form of the theoretical model) provide a bridge to the theoretical model that is reasonable and convincing? Are the parameters of the theoretical model identified? If not, does this affect the conclusions that can be drawn concerning the question (or questions) under investigation?
5. Are state-of-the-art techniques employed in estimation? Are the parameters of interest statistically identified? – i.e., can they actually be estimated in the context of the statistical model?
6. Is the statistical inference concerning the parameters of interest conducted in proper fashion using state-of-the-art procedures? Are the conclusions that are drawn on the basis of the inferences justified and reasonable?
7. Are the procedures and results of the analysis presented in a consistent way and in a manner that inspires confidence that the analysts know what

they are doing? Econometrics and statistics are inherently technical, but explanations need not be and can (and should) be made understandable to a general audience.

8. Are the procedures, results, and data underlying the analysis available in some acceptable form for inspection?

The forgoing checklist, which is largely procedural, provides what, in my view, is to be expected of an econometric study in a regulatory proceeding. The requirements extolled are practical and feasible and can be put simply: that analysts know what they are doing and put forth their best efforts using state-of-the-art theory, data, and statistical techniques. Consistent with this, it is important that the view not be conveyed that the econometric model being presented embodies final truth. What may be seen as true today may not be seen as being true tomorrow. The credibility of results depends upon the integrity and legitimacy of the process that produces the results, but the process itself is inherently evolutionary. The emphasis in the process is on state-of-the-art, and the state-of-the-art in theory, data, and statistical techniques is constantly evolving and improving.

To give some examples, at the time of the 1980 book:

1. The use of discrete choice models in analyzing the demand for various types of access was in its infancy. Now the use of these models is standard.
2. The analysis of toll demand on a point-to-point basis that allows for call-back features had not yet been contemplated.
3. Little use had been made in using data of the "what if" type. Now their use is common-place in forecasting the demands for new services.
4. Co-integration analysis had not been developed,[13] nor had the diagnostics of Belsley, Kuh, and Welsch for testing for the harmful effects of multicollinearity.[14] The 1980s have also seen considerable progress in the development and refinement of non-nested hypothesis testing.[15]

III. SOME PITFALLS IN USING ECONOMETRIC MODELS

Demand analysts, as well as regulators and intervenors, have to be reasonable as to what an econometric model is capable of accomplishing. For example,

---

[13] See Engle and Granger (1987).

[14] See Belsley, Kuh, and Welsch (1980) and Belsley (1982).

[15] See, among others, Davidson and MacKinnon (1981) and Judge *et al.* (1985), and Sands and Trosset (1990). For an excellent survey of recent advances in econometrics see Pagan and Wichens (1989).

econometric models of demand, although they provide point estimates of price and income elasticities, cannot ascertain the precise values of these elasticities. The best that econometric models can do in this regard is to provide ranges within which "true" elasticities are likely to lie. For example, one cannot state on the basis of existing evidence that the price elasticity for toll calling in Ontario and Quebec is -0.4 as opposed to -0.5. The evidence (at least in my opinion) does support the conclusion, however, that this price elasticity, whatever its actual value, is smaller (in absolute value) than the -1.34 proposed by CNCP in the Interexchange Hearings before the Canadian Radio-television and Telecommunications Commission in 1984.[16]

Another area in which there has been abuse in the use of econometric telecommunications demand models in the regulatory area is in the forecasting of revenues. The abuse is in the tendency on the part of regulators to use the estimated repression effects of proposed new rates as forecasts of the actual revenue effects. The observed revenue effects of new rates are often much smaller than the estimated repression effects, and this "over-estimate" is used to discredit the model. The problem with this procedure is that, estimates of repression are made on a *ceteris-paribus* basis, whereas actual revenues reflect changes in income, population, other prices, etc. Econometric models can certainly be used to forecast revenues, but the forecasting must be done properly, which includes obtaining accurate forecasts as possible of all the independent variables.

Yet another pitfall to be avoided is the use, as was done in both the U.S. and Canada in the 1980s, of econometric models of residential access demand to estimate the dropoff from the network that would occur in the event of a doubling or tripling of local-service rates. By all accounts, the residential access price elasticity is small – of the order of -0.05 at most – but small elasticities applied to huge price changes and a large base of subscribers imply large numbers of dropoff. As an example, mechanical application of a price elasticity of -0.05 to a doubling of local service rates in the U.S. would seem to imply a dropoff of upwards of 5 million households. Needless to say, such numbers are political lightning rods, and their blind and unthinking acceptance by many has impeded the elimination of the toll-to-local subsidy in both the U.S. and Canada.

On the surface, such dropoff numbers seem to be clear implications of the econometric models involved. To begin with, however, they cannot pass the test of common sense. No telephone demand analyst with whom I am familiar would have supported the argument that a doubling of local-service rates from $10 to $20 per month in the U.S. in the early 1980s would have

---

[16] See Taylor (1984).

caused upwards of five million U.S. households to give up telephone service. The following considerations argue against an exodus of this magnitude:[17]

1. The data that the models are based on do not distinguish between single-line households and households with multiple lines. Some of the impact would take the form of multiple-line households giving up one or more of their extra lines.

2. In principle, the coefficients upon which access price elasticities are based refer to decisions to purchase on the margin. The implicit assumption is that a household already on the telephone network but whose net benefits from usage are just equal to the price of access would give up telephone service if the price of access were increased in the same way that a household not on the network but whose benefits from usage (if they were to have a telephone) would also just equal the price of access would acquire telephone service if the price of access were reduced. Such symmetry is almost certainly not present in real life. Many households with telephone service, who by otherwise objective criteria would appear to be candidates for giving up telephone service, will not in fact do so because of the attachment to having a telephone that has been built up from experience.[18]

3. Pursuant to the asymmetry just noted is a likelihood that much of the effect will be to repress new connections. The effect will occur over time through what F.D. Orr of Bell Canada has called "a failure to drop-in" rather than existing subscribers dropping off.

The foregoing represent just a few of the pitfalls of the use of econometrically based telecommunications price elasticities in the regulatory arena. Econometric modeling has progressed markedly in the telephone industry during the last 10 years, and although the resources that are devoted to demand modeling have decreased, the sophistication of the researchers has increased and the quality and credibility of the results are much improved. Ten years ago, a regulatory proceeding devoted entirely to procedural questions related to econometric estimation of telecommunications price elasticity, such as the one before the Canadian Radio-Television and Telecommunications Commission in early 1989, would have been unthinkable.[19] That such as hearing took place is a tribute to the econometric maturity of all concerned – telephone companies, regulators, and intervenors.

---

[17] For an interesting airing of confusion in a hearing room regarding these points, see the cross-examination of Bruce L. Egan, witness for Southwestern Bell, in Texas Docket 4545, November 1982, at pp. 7132–7155.

[18] Existing models of access demand do not reflect this phenomenon.

[19] See Canadian Radio-television and Telecommunications Commission (1990).

CHAPTER 11

EVALUATION AND CONCLUSIONS

We are finally at a point to bring the discussion of telecommunications demand
to a close. Unlike in the 1980 monograph, I have not attempted in this book to
provide an exhaustive exposition of the literature. My approach, rather, has
been to review a selection of post-1980 studies, some of which I have been
personally involved with, which in my view particularly add to our empirical
understanding of the structure of telecommunications demand or involve the
development or application of new theoretical models.

The 1980s saw both advances and retreats. There was notable progress
in filling-in missing entries in the price elasticity matrix and in firming up
existing entries. There was also notable progress on the theoretical front, both
in the development of appropriate models and in the sophistication of their
estimation. An important start has been made in estimating the structure of
business demand, and several new and useful data sets were collected. One
of the most promising of these is the data set being organized in connection
with the National Telecommunications Demand Study (NTDS). The data set
from this on-going study is now more than two million observations on both
business and residential customers, and its potential for analysis has scarcely
been tapped.[1]

Yet, the 1980s also saw some retreats, mainly because of competition and
the divestiture. Access to data has been greatly restricted, reflecting both the
proprietary nature of much of the data and the fragmentation of its collection.
As a consequence, it is accurate to say that a comprehensive industry study
was much easier to undertake 10 years ago than would be the case now.
A related casualty of competition (and deregulation) has been the resources
within the industry that are devoted to demand analysis. These have been
greatly reduced at the Bell Operating Companies, and this would appear to
be the case at AT&T and Bell Canada as well. An implication of this is that
models are being used in some jurisdictions that are simply out of date.

---

[1] Among other things, data sets of this size offer opportunities for applying semi-and non-
parametric regression procedures, for which there is a burgeoning literature. Manski (1991)
provides an excellent introduction to this literature.

In the remainder of this concluding chapter, the format is first to provide a summary view of the state of knowledge regarding the structure of telecommunications demand as of early 1993. This will be followed in Section II by an evaluation of the current state of telecommunications demand analysis and list the areas which in my view are in need of continued or expanded research. Some final observations concerning the role of demand analysis in a competitive/partially regulated environment conclude the book in Section III.

I. What We Appear to Know about the Structure of Telecommunications Demand

At the time of the 1980 book, we knew a lot more about the demand for usage than the demand for access, a lot more about toll usage than local usage, a lot more about residential demand than about business demand, and we probably had more precise knowledge about price elasticities than about income elasticities. There was some knowledge of international demand, a little about business MTS demand, even less about business WATS and private-line demands, and virtually nothing about business demand for terminal equipment. Also, virtually nothing was known regarding cross-elasticities between local and toll usage or between other categories of service. We knew that network and call externalities were important conceptual elements of telephone demand, but there was little empirical information as to their magnitudes. Option demand was also known to be a potentially important component of access demand, but again virtually nothing was known of its empirical importance.

A continuum of price elasticities emerged, with access at the bottom (in terms of absolute value) and long-haul toll and international calls at the top. Price elasticities clearly appeared to increase with length-of-haul. There was some evidence of an elastic demand in the longest-haul toll and international markets, but there seemed little question that the toll market in general was inelastic. Income elasticities, for the most part, appeared to be in excess of 1.

What about research during the 1980s? How has it contributed to our knowledge of telecommunications demand? In my view, the research of the 1980s has:

1. Added greatly to our knowledge of the demand for residential access. The small, but nevertheless nonzero, access elasticities obtained by Perl (1978) have been confirmed and sharpened in the studies of Cain and MacDonald (1991), Perl (1983), and Taylor and Kridel (1990) for the U.S. and Bodnar *et al.* (1988) for Canada.

2. Made a significant start in quantifying the structure of business demand, especially with regard to standard access and the demands for key, PBX, and centrex systems. I particularly have in mind here the studies of Ben-Akiva and Gershenfeld (1989) and Watters and Roberson (1992).

3. Confirmed and sharpened previous estimates of the price elasticities for medium- to long-haul toll usage. Studies that come to mind in this connection include Gatto, Kelejian, and Stephan (1988), Gatto *et al.* (1988), Larson, Lehman, and Weisman (1990), Zona and Jacob (1990), the Bell-Intra models of Bell Canada (1984, 1989), and the Telecom Canada models (Appelbe *et al.* 1988).

4. Added to and greatly sharpened previous estimates of the price elasticities for short-haul toll. The studies that have contributed to this include Kling and Van der Ploeg (1990), Kridel (1988), Train, McFadden, and Ben-Akiva (1987), Train, Ben-Akiva, and Atherton (1989), and Zona and Jacob (1990).

5. Made an important start on providing estimates of cross-price elasticities between measured- and flat-rate local service, local service and toll, local use and toll, and key, PBX, and centrex systems. Contributing studies include Ben-Akiva and Gershenfeld (1989), Kling and Van der Ploeg (1990), Kridel (1988), Train, McFadden, and Ben-Akiva (1987), Train, Ben-Akiva, and Atherton (1989), Watters and Roberson (1992), and Zona and Jacob (1990).

6. Made a start (Kridel and Taylor 1992) in analyzing the demand for custom-calling features, both singly and in bundles.

On the modeling front, three innovations stand out, in my view, in the literature of the 1980s: (1) the widespread use of quantal-choice models, (2) the analysis of toll demand on a point-to-point basis, and (3) application of a full-blown random-coefficients methodology to a system of interstate toll demand equations. With the much greater emphasis on access demand in post-1980 research, it is natural that quantal-choice models would find much greater use. In the pre-1980 literature, the only study that used a quantal-choice framework was Perl (1978). In the 1980s, studies using a quantal-choice framework include Ben-Akiva and Gershenfeld (1989), Kling and Van der Ploeg (1990), Kridel (1988), Kridel and Taylor (1993), Perl (1983), Taylor and Kridel (1990), Train, McFadden and Ben-Akiva (1987), Train, Ben-Akiva, and Atherton (1989), and Bodnar *et al.* (1988). The most sophisticated application is by Train *et al.* where a quantal-choice framework is used to analyze the choice among standard flat-rate, EAS, and measured services and the choice of a particular portfolio of calls by time-of-day and length-of-haul.

At the time of the 1980 book, only two studies had analyzed toll demand on a point-to-point basis, Larsen and McCleary (1970) and Deschamps (1974). Both are reviewed in Appendix 1. Nine years elapsed between Deschamps and the next point-to-point study, which was undertaken by Pacey (1983), using a sample of city-pair data from Mountain Bell. The real impetus to point-to-point modeling, however, came in 1985 with the appearance of the point-to-point demand study at Southwestern Bell (Larson, Lehman, and Weisman 1990), again using city-pair data. The innovation in this model is that it allows for a reverse-traffic effect, whereby the volume of calling in one direction affects the volume of calling in the reverse direction. As discussed in Chapter 6, the Southwestern Bell model has subsequently been applied to the demand for interprovincial toll in Canada and Canada-U.S. calling by Telecom Canada (Appelbe *et al.* 1988) and to international calling by Acton and Vogelsang (1992).

The study of Gatto, Kelejian, and Stephan (1988) is of interest because not only does it mark the first application of a full-blown random-coefficients methodology to a large system of toll demand equations using a pooled time-series/cross-section data set, but it also introduces two new concepts into applied demand analysis: stochastic symmetry and stochastic weak separability. The model is the latest in a distinguished line of interstate toll demand models at AT&T. Interstate toll demand is approached in a multi-equation framework in which toll demand is disaggregated by mileage bands, time-of-day, and non-operator/operator handled calls. The model is estimated in a random-coefficients, variance-components format using a pooled data set consisting of quarterly observations for the 48 continuous states plus the District of Columbia.[2] Stochastic symmetry in the model means that the Slutsky symmetry conditions across commodities in a cross-section are only satisfied stochastically, while stochastic weak separability means that the price elasticities in a cross-section are stochastically proportional to the income elasticity.

Progress was also made in the 1980s in clarifying understanding of the network and call externalities. In great part, this occurred as a result of protracted debates before the Canadian Radio-television and Telecommunications Commission concerning the size of the coefficients for market size in Bell Canada's toll demand models.[3] While precise empirical estimates of the magnitudes of the externalities are unfortunately still lacking,[4] the relevant

---

[2] The data set ends with the fourth quarter of 1983! – an interesting data consequence of the divestiture.

[3] See Bell Canada (1984, 1989), Breslaw (1985), Globerman (1988), and Taylor (1984). See also de Fontenay and Lee (1983).

[4] See, however, the discussion in Section V of Chapter 9 and the studies referred to there.

questions have been greatly sharpened. In 1980, the biggest concern regarding the consumption externalities was whether the network externality might be large enough to justify continuing the large toll-to-local subsidy. Little attention was paid to the call externality because it was thought that, even if one of any magnitude existed, it would be internalized between calling parties within reasonable periods of time.

What such a view appears to have overlooked is the possibility – or indeed the likelihood – that calls give rise to further calls, quite independently of price and income. Strong empirical evidence in support of this is given in the point-to-point toll demand models of Southwestern Bell and Telecom Canada just mentioned, which indicate that a call in one direction stimulates about one-half to two-thirds of a call in return. The call externality thus seems to have a dynamic dimension that goes beyond a simple cost sharing of the calls between two parties. As suggested in Chapter 9, it is best in my opinion not to attribute all of the call-back effect to the call externality, but to see part of it as reflecting an independent phenomenon, what I termed there "the dynamics of information exchange". But whatever, it is clear that the call externality is a much more complicated phenomenon than was thought to be the case 10 years ago.

An obvious question to ask is whether there were structural changes in telecommunications demands during the 1980s. In my view, there is little evidence that this was the case, at least for the large categories like residential and business access and medium-to long-haul toll.[5] I find no evidence that the toll market as a whole has become either more or less elastic than in 1980. Residential access price elasticities, in contrast, appear to have gotten smaller[6], but this is a consequence of higher residential penetration rates.[7]

One of the most interesting results emerging from the 1980s research

---

[5] This is for the industry as a whole. Price elasticities for individual interexchange carriers are another matter,(as are also elasticities for certain submarkets within a given market). Because of a decrease in market share, the price elasticities that AT&T faces are clearly larger now than in 1980. For MCI and Sprint, they are almost certainly smaller.

[6] Cf., however, Cain and MacDonald (1991), who obtain access price elasticities about double Perl's, especially at very low-income levels. As their results are based upon data from the mid-1980s, Cain and MacDonald interpret their higher elasticities as reflecting structural change. Whether this represents genuine structural change or arises from sharp shifts in the ethnic and social composition of households, however, is not clear.

[7] Price elasticities calculated from the probit/logit models that are used in estimating access demand vary inversely with the level of penetration. A point that is worthy of mention is that, in comparing the results with data from the 1980 Census with his earlier results with data from the 1970 Census, Perl (1983) found an upward shift in the willingness-to-pay on the part of households to have telephone service that could not be attributed to income or changes in other socio-demographic factors. It will be interesting to see whether the 1990 Census show the same phenomenon *vis-à-vis* 1980.

relates to the price elasticity for short-haul toll call of (say) 15 to 40 miles. In 1980, the view was that this elasticity was quite small, of the order (say) of -0.2. There was no real evidence for this number; it simply fit in with the flow of elasticities as one went from shorter to longer lengths-of-haul. The evidence now points to a larger value for this short-haul price elasticity, in the range of -0.25 to -0.5.[8] I wish to emphasize, however, that this should not be viewed as an instance of structural change, but rather the emergence, for the first time, of credible evidence as to what the value of the short-haul price elasticity is.

As has just been noted, post-1980 results confirm – indeed, strengthen – the earlier finding that the absolute value of the toll price elasticity increases with length-of-haul. All considered, this probably represents the best-established empirical regularity in telecommunications demand. Interestingly, however, no convincing explanation has ever been offered as to why this ought to be the case. There have been some suggestions that the empirical regularity primarily reflects a price phenomenon: that since price elasticities (for non-constant elasticity demand functions) in general vary with the level of price, price elasticities for longer-haul calls will be larger than for shorter-haul calls simply because they cost more.[9] On the other hand, an argument can also be made that the regularity represents a distance effect, in that (for whatever reason) calls with a longer-haul are simply more price-elastic.

Strong evidence against the price-elasticity/length-of-haul relationship being just a price phenomenon is provided by results from the AT&T Interstate Access Minutes model of Gatto *et al.* (1988).[10] The price elasticity obtained in that model, -0.723, agrees closely with the pre-1980 price elasticities for long-haul toll calls that are discussed in Appendix 1,[11] but it is estimated from a data set in which the real price of toll calling was sharply lower (because of competition) than the levels of the 1970s. If the positive relationship between the size of the toll price elasticity and length-of-haul were due just to price, then the price elasticity obtained by Gatto *et al.* should be smaller than the price elasticities obtained in the pre-1980 models. This follows because length-of-haul is effectively held constant. Since the elasticity obtained by Gatto *et al.* is not smaller, the conclusion, accordingly, has to be that the relationship in question is not a matter of price, but reflects a positive relationship between the size of the toll price elasticity and length-of-haul.

---

[8] See Hausman (1991), Kling and Van der Ploeg (1990), Kridel (1988), Train, McFadden, and Ben-Akiva (1987), Train, Ben-Akiva, and Atherton (1989), and Zona and Jacob (1990).

[9] This follows from the definition of price elasticity as $(\partial q/\partial p)(p/q)$, where q and p denote quantity and price, respectively.

[10] This model is discussed in Section III of Chapter 6.

[11] See Table 5 of Appendix 1. Cf., also, Table 1 of Appendix 2.

We now turn to the factors that might account for this relationship. Unfortunately, surprisingly little is known about either the characteristics or motivations associated with calls to different distances. The only study that I am aware of that provides much in the way of useful information in this regard is from a household survey in Los Angeles and Orange Counties in California that was undertaken by GTE of California in the mid-1980s.[12] From the 680 households that participated in the survey, information was collected from a log of calls made by the households during a two-week period. The information collected included date, time of call, length of call, where the call went, person making the call, the party called, purpose of the call, and importance of the call.

Summary physical characteristics of the 22,351 calls that were analyzed include:[13]

1. A high degree of skewness in the distribution of distance; half of all calls terminated within six miles of the calling party.
2. A high degree of skewness in the distribution of duration; half of all calls lasted four minutes or less.
3. A significant day-to-day variation of calls:

   - calls more frequent on weekdays than on weekends;
   - calls on weekdays less frequently to longer distances than is the case on weekends;
   - calls on weekdays shorter in duration than is the case on weekends (mean 6.1 minutes vs. 7.2 minutes).

4. A significant variation in the rate periods of calls:

   - 48 percent of calls during business day; remainder nearly evenly split between evening (28 percent) and night/weekend (24 percent);
   - mean call length-of-haul steadily increases from business day (33.4 miles) to evening (67.6 miles) to night/weekend (105.2 miles);
   - mean call duration increases from business day (5.6 minutes) to over 7 minutes in evening and night/weekend periods;
   - mean cost of calls increases from business day ($0.361) to night/weekend ($0.446) to evening ($0.496).

Summary attitudinal characteristics of calls include:

1. Significant variations in call purposes:

   - greatest proportion of calls (33.8 percent) are to friends, followed by calls to relatives (26.6 percent);

[12] See Mead (1985).
[13] See Mead (1985, Executive Summary).

- calls to friends were to shorter distances, similar duration (8.1 minutes), less costly and of lesser importance than calls to relatives;
- work-related calls are less frequent (10.5 percent), shorter, less costly, and more important than social calls.

2. Differentiation of calls by callers:

- two-thirds of calls are by wives;
- calls by teenage girls are longest (mean 9.1 minutes vs. 6.7 minutes);
- husbands are most likely to make calls to work; childrens' calls are predominantly to friends.

With foregoing physical and attitudinal characteristics of calling behavior as background, I believe that it is now possible to put together a convincing story that can account for the observed positive relationship between the size of toll price elasticities and length-of-haul. The point of departure will be to remind ourselves of a point that is probably often forgotten: that price elasticity consists of two components, an income effect and a substitution effect. The substitution effect is a measure of the extent to which goods or services can substitute for one another when there is a price change without making the consumer any worse off in terms of consumer welfare. The income effect, on the other hand, is a measure of the extent to which the consumer's real income is changed when there is a change in price. Ordinarily, the importance of the income effect is represented by the importance of the good whose price has changed in the consumer's budget. Goods whose expenditures account for a small proportion of the consumer's total expenditure will have a small (or even tiny) income effect, while a good whose expenditures account for a large proportion of total expenditure will have a possibly large income effect. Goods that in ordinary discourse are seen as necessities (such as heating fuel and telephone service) will also have relatively larger income effects the lower the level of income.

In assessing income effects, however, a point that is usually overlooked is the effect on the consumer's welfare of not consuming a good because of a price increase. In the case of making or not making a phone call because it has become more expensive, the question that needs to be asked is what are the consequences (not necessarily in monetary terms) of not making the call. For residential consumers, this cost is usually cast in terms of the utility (or satisfaction) that is given up by the call not being made. For many calls, however, this is not the correct measure of cost, for the call may be important to the *earning* of income, rather than being simply a way of *consuming* it. In this case, the actual income effect of not making a telephone call may be large, although the decrease in real income, (as customarily measured), occasioned by the price increase may be extremely small. Note that what is being discussed here is a negative income effect that arises from a call *not* being made, in contrast with the small negative income effect that arises from the actual making of a now more expensive call. The relevance of this will become clear in a moment.

Let us now consider the communities of interest that are associated with calls of different lengths-of-haul. Although the length-of-haul for a call can vary continuously, it will be assumed for simplicity that there are only four lengths-of-haul, local calls, short-haul toll calls, medium-haul toll calls, and long-haul toll calls. For concreteness, these can be identified with local calls, intraLATA toll, interLATA intrastate toll, and interstate toll calls. In terms of numbers, the communities of interest for most people will be largest for the local-calling area and then decrease progressively with length-of-haul. The GTE survey, as well as common sense, suggests that the community of interest for local calls, again for most people, will consist of friends and relatives and people and acquaintances associated with work, shopping, and recreation. Friends and relatives become progressively more important in relative terms as the communities of interest become increasingly more distant. Interestingly, the GTE California survey suggests that friends are relatively more important than relatives in the community of interest for local and short-haul toll calls, but the reverse is true for medium and long-haul toll calls.

What, then, are the implications of this changing composition in the community of interest for the size of price elasticities? To begin with, it seems clear that calls which are related to work, shopping, and commercial recreation will be less sensitive to price than calls that are to friends and relatives. A major reason for this is the contingency noted earlier regarding the cost of not making a call. Almost certainly, this cost (whether psychic or monetary) will be higher for a call related to work, shopping, or commercial recreation, than a call to a friend or relative. The former are simply of greater urgency (in the sense that their primary purpose is information exchange, rather than chatting and recreation), and there may be no feasible substitute for a telephone call (such as waiting for the friend or relative to call instead). For shopping and commercial recreation, the price of the phone call is probably treated as part of the price of the good or activity in question, and the price of a phone call will not in general loom large. This is a strong argument as to why calls of less than six miles are most numerous, shortest in duration (in terms of mean holding time), and have the smallest price elasticity of demand.

As we move to longer-haul calls, the relative importance of these two generic types of calls changes, as the communities of interest come to consist more and more of friends and relatives and less and less of people associated with work, shopping, and commercial recreation. For short-haul toll calls, these latter characteristics of the community of interest will obviously still be a factor, but not to the extent as for local calls. Since the opportunity cost of not making a call will in general be of less consequence, calls and calling will become more sensitive to price, which in turn implies a larger price elasticity.

The GTE California survey shows that the calls in the mileage bands constituting medium- and long-haul toll categories are predominantly to relatives. These calls tend to be concentrated in the evening and night/weekend time periods, and are significantly longer in duration than local or short-haul toll calls. In general, urgency is less critical, and substitute forms of communication are much more feasible. As noted in Chapter 3, for someone with several relatives or friends in a distant city or locale, a lengthy call to one can serve to communicate with all via subsequent local calls being made by the one that is called to begin with. All of these factors auger for a greater sensitivity of the volume of toll usage to price for longer-haul calls, and thus to a higher price elasticity.[14]

Let me now turn to some areas for which little or no new information was forthcoming in the 1980s. As in 1980, the structure of business demand heads the list. The study of Ben-Akiva and Gershenfeld (1989) provides an important start, but is restricted to access/usage of the public switched network.[15] Egan and Griffin (1983) represents the only attempt (at least in the open literature) to estimate cross-price elasticities among WATS, Private Line, and MTS,[16] but their analysis is based on aggregate data, focuses only on usage, and provides no information on how the demands for WATS, PL, and MTS interact with the demand for terminal equipment or vary with size, type, or organizational structure of a business.

International calling is a second area for which little new information has been forthcoming. The only new studies of international demand that I have seen in the open literature is the study by Telecom Canada (Appelbe *et al.* 1988) of Canada-U.S. calling, a recently completed study by the Rand Corporation (Acton and Vogelsang 1992), and another recent study by Hackl and Westlund (1992). The price elasticities obtained in the Telecom

---

[14] Preliminary results (as of January 1993) from a study by Paul Rappoport, Don Michels, and myself using data from the NTDS data base in which distance and price are separated confirm that this is indeed the case for intraLATA toll.

[15] Some interesting results concerning the input intensity of telecommunications across manufacturing industries in Italy is provided by Antonelli (1990). Antonelli's procedure is to relate industry telecommunications coefficients in an input/output table to structural characteristics of the industry. As no price variation is reflected in the data, price elasticities are not estimated.

[16] Hausman (1991), using a two-level budgeting framework and data from the NTDS data base, estimates cross-price elasticities between WATS and MTS for intraLATA toll.

Canada study are based on a point-to-point model and are reported only on a uni-directional basis (that is, for a change in Canada-U.S. rates only). The elasticities are estimated to be of the order of -0.5, which (since they are uni-directional) is consistent with existing (generally bi-directional) estimates of -0.9 or larger.

The Rand study (Acton and Vogelsang 1992) is based upon annual data for minutes of calling between the United States and 17 Western European countries from 1979 to 1986. The volume of calling both originating and terminating in the United States was examined as a function of the price in the country of origin and the price in the country of termination together with economic and conditioning variables such as the volume of trade between the countries, the structure of employment, the number of telephones, and the price of telex services. Models are estimated for 1979–82 and 1983–86. Estimates of uni-directional price elasticities vary from insignificant to nearly -1.0.[17]

A third area for which little new information was forthcoming in the 1980s relates to the duration and time-of-day dimensions of calling. Indeed, I am not aware of any 1980s study that focuses explicitly on duration. Brandon (1981) examined the effects on duration of income and socio-demographical factors, but there was no variation in the price in the data that he analyzed. On the time-of-day front, a number of studies of toll demand [e.g., the Bell Canada and Telecom Canada models and Gatto, Kelejian, and Stephan (1988)] disaggregate according to rate periods – i.e., weekday peak and evening and night time discount – but none of these (except possibly for Gatto *et al.*) estimate cross elasticities between the different periods. The only new information concerning time-of-day tradeoffs that I am aware of is for short-haul toll calls in Train, McFadden, and Ben-Akiva (1987), and Train, Ben-Akiva, and Atherton (1989).

Before leaving this section, a few comments regarding income elasticities are in order. In the 1980 book, I concluded that income elasticities (on a total, as opposed to a per-capita, basis) were probably greater than 1 for all markets except for access. The evidence from the 1980s suggest that income elasticities for toll usage may be lower now than 10 years ago. Indeed, the evidence from 1980s research [e.g., Gatto, Kelejian, and Stephan (1988), Gatto *et al.* (1988) Bell Canada (1984, 1989), Appelbe *et al.* (1988), Train, McFadden, and Ben-Akiva (1987)] is essentially uniform in suggesting this. Nevertheless, it remains my view that the income elasticity in the longest

---

[17] The models estimated by Acton and Vogelsang allow for arbitrage and call externalities, but not for reverse-traffic effects of the type analyzed in the Southwestern Bell and Telecom Canada studies. Also, the models include the number of telephones in the European countries, but not the number of telephones in the U.S.

haul toll and international markets is at least 1. Also, an income elasticity less than 1 for the toll market overall should not be interpreted to mean that the toll market will not expand in line with the overall economy, *for usage per telephone is clearly increasing faster than the increase in income.* This is most evident in the Bell Canada and Telecom Canada models which have rather modest income elasticities but substantial elasticities with respect to market size (as measured by potential toll connections), or alternatively with respect to reverse traffic. Delving into the behavioral relationships involved represents one of the modeling challenges for the 1990s.

In the 1980 book, I included a table which summarized my own subjective views concerning a number of telecommunications demand price and income elasticities. While I believe that this on the whole served a useful purpose, both the literature and practice have matured a lot since 1980 and I now feel that researchers and those interested in particular elasticities will be better served by a handy summary and guide to the post-1980 literature organized in terms of residential and business access, short-and long-haul toll, customer-premise equipment, etc. This is provided in Table 1.

II. PROBLEM AREAS

This section lists what in my view are the areas of telecommunications demand that are most in need of research. Several of these are evident from previous discussion.

1. Business Demand

Ten years ago, little was known about the structure of business telecommunications demand. Thanks to the study of Ben-Akiva and Gershenfeld (1989), there is now some knowledge of the key own- and cross-price elasticities for business-telephone systems, but this information refers only to the public switched network. There is still precious little known regarding the tradeoffs among WATS, private line, and MTS, and how these relate to the organizational and structural characteristics of firms.[18]

---

[18] In my view, telecos (both local and interexchange) should organize their business demand analysis around data bases that consist of information for their largest (say) 1000 customers. These data bases would draw not only from telcos own records, but from Census and Surveys of Manufacturers, the SEC, Moodys and Standard and Poors, Dun and Bradstreet, etc. Data obtained directly from customers would also be included. Such data bases would not only serve demand analyses, but would be invaluable for marketing as well.

TABLE 1

Abridged guide to post-1980 research on telecommunications demand

Residential Access Demand	Network Externalities
Bodnar *et al.* (1988)	Perl (1983)
Bodnar & Lefebvre (1992a)	Taylor & Kridel (1990)
Bodnar & Lefebvre (1992b)	
Cain & McDonald (1991)	Peak/Off Peak
Kling & Van der Ploeg (1990)	Appelbe *et al.* (1988)
Park *et al.* (1983)	Bell Canada (1984, 1988)
Perl (1983)	Colias & Maddox (1990)
Taylor & Kridel (1990)	Gatto, Kelejian & Stephan (1988)
Train *et al.* (1987)	
Train *et al.* (1989)	International
	Acton & Vogelsang (1992)
Business Access Demand	Appelbe *et al.* (1988)
Ben-Akiva & Gershenfeld (1989)	Hackl & Westlund (1992)
Local Calling	Extended-Area Service
Colias & Maddox (1990)	Kridel (1988)
Hobson & Spady (1988)	Martins-Filho & Mayo (1993)
Kling & Van der Ploeg (1990)	
Train *et al.* (1987)	Optional Calling Plans
Train *et al.* (1989)	Watters & Roberson (1992)
Short-Haul Toll	Bypass
Duncan & Perry (1992)	Watters & Grandstaff (1988)
Hausman (1991)	
Kling & Van der Ploeg (1990)	WATS
Nall & Ronayne (1986)	Griffin & Egan (1985)
Train *et al.* (1987)	Hausman (1991)
Train *et al.* (1989)	
Zona & Jacob (1990)	Private Line
	Nieswiodomy & Brink (1990)
Medium-Haul Toll	Watters & Grandstaff (1988)
Bell Canada (1984, 1989)	Watters & Roberson (1991)
Larson *et al.* (1990)	
Zona & Jacob (1990)	Custom-Calling Features
	Kridel & Taylor (1993)
Long-Haul Toll	
Appelbe *et al.* (1988)	Customer-Premise Equipment
Appelbe *et al.* (1992)	Ben-Akiva & Gershenfeld (1989)
Gatto, Kelejian & Stephan (1988)	
Gatto *et al.* (1988)	Directory Assistance
	Daly & Mayor (1980)
	Williamson and Chen (1991)

2. Residential Cross-Price Elasticities

The research of the 1980s made some progress in providing information on cross-price elasticities among local usage and short-and long-haul toll calling. Gaps still remain and existing estimates need to be firmed up.

3. Separability

Closely related to the foregoing is a need for further analysis of separability between telecommunications and other goods and services in households' budgets. The study of Zona and Jacob (1990), which casts doubt on the Targeted-Bill Hypothesis, suggests that separability exists, but the analysis is based upon aggregate data, and it would be useful to see whether separability obtains with data for individual households. The BLS Consumer Expenditure Surveys, which are now conducted on an on-going quarterly basis, provide an obvious data base to analyze, as does also the data base of the National Telecommunications Demand Study.

4. Dynamics of Information Exchange

One of the most interesting results to emerge from the research of the 1980s, especially in the context of the Bell Canada and Telecom Canada models (Bell Canada 1984, 1989; Appelbe *et al.* 1988), is the finding that usage stimulates further usage. How this phenomenon relates to income and market size (as measured by the number of telephones that can be reached) and whether there is a calling dynamic that operates outside of the normally thought-of call externality are questions clearly in need of research.[19]

5. Option Demand

In the real world of uncertainty, the purchase of access, as noted in Chapter 2, is really the purchase of the option of making calls on demand. That there is a value attaching to this option which increases the willingness-to-pay to have a telephone has long been recognized, but devising a way of estimating this value has been another matter. Some evidence that the magnitude of option value may be significant is provided in Kridel (1988).[20]

---

[19] Related to these questions is a continuing need to understand how communities-of-interest form.

[20] See also three papers presented by D. Kridel, D. Lehman, and D. Weisman, K. Train, and T. Tardiff at the 1990 Hilton Head Conference sponsored by Bell Canada and BELLCORE.

Two areas have emerged for which a better understanding of option demand is relevant. The first of these relates to the option value associated with "carrier-of-last-resort" obligations. A large industrial firm, headquartered in St. Louis (say), sets up its own private networks for internal communication, but uses the public facilities of Southwestern Bell when its internal system periodically crashes. Clearly, there is a value to the firm for having the option of using Southwestern's facilities. How should this option be priced?[21]

The second area relates to the proliferation of optional calling plans (OCP), such as AT&T's "Reach Out America" and "Pro-America" and Bell Canada's "Between Friends" and "Teleplus Canada". OCPs provide telephone companies a vehicle for segmenting customers with particular demand characteristics and do so in a way that makes both the telcos and the customers better off. Subscribers to such plans will have essentially the same demand characteristics as customers who migrate between competitive suppliers in response to discounts, that is, large users with inelastic demands.[22] Subscribers will also tend to have demand characteristics that give rise to certain types of option values. Portions of these option values are garnered by the up-front charges in the OCPs.[23]

6. Firm-Specific Elasticities

As was noted in Section VI of Chapter 3, as entry occurs in markets that have been previously supplied by a single firm the price elasticities faced by that firm cease being the market elasticities and become firm-specific. The price elasticity faced by AT&T is now larger than when it was the monopoly supplier of toll. Similarly, the price elasticities faced by Bell Canada and B.C. Telephone will increase with the entry of Unitel into the Canadian toll market. For obvious reasons, companies facing competition are not about to publish their firm-specific elasticities, but even if they were so inclined the estimation of firm-specific demand functions is anything but straightforward. The problem, among other things, is that the price reaction functions between firms must themselves be represented in the specification of the demand functions, and executing this in a realistic, tractable manner still

---

[21] For discussions of this and related questions, see Weisman (1987) and Kridel, Lehman, and Weisman (1991). See also Kahn (1966).

[22] See Section V of Chapter 3.

[23] The only econometric study that I have seen that analyzes the demand for OPCs is Watters and Roberson (1992), who look at the demand for intraLATA MTS pricing plans.

awaits development.[24] Moreover, there is some question whether incumbent demand functions in the circumstances can even be identified.[25]

III. DEMAND ANALYSIS IN A COMPETITIVE/PARTIALLY REGULATED ENVIRONMENT

One of the failings of the traditional corporate decision-making structure in the telephone industry has been that demand analysis has always played a spot role, used and useful for calculating repression/stimulation effects of proposed tariff changes in regulatory proceedings, but never employed in a systematic way in budgeting, forecasting, and marketing.[26] Its home in Bell Operating Companies has been in Revenue Requirements, and as deregulation and competition in recent years have forced telcos to slim down, demand analysis has tended to be treated as regulatory overhead, no longer necessarily necessary.

In truth, some slimming-down is probably in order, but to allow demand analysis to languish because of the advent of competition and incentive regulation would be a mistake. The challenge for demand analysis in the telephone companies in the years ahead is to forge links with marketing departments and to become integrated into company budgeting and forecasting processes. Applied demand analysis has a strategic role to play in a competitive environment, ranging from the conventional types of elasticity estimation in traditional markets to the identification of new markets.[27] The possibilities are vast. It only requires imagination, hard work – and some humility – on the part of economists and demand analysts.

---

[24] My own efforts to estimate demand functions for AT&T and the OCCs as a group for interLATA MTS toll have so far been singularly unsuccessful. See Taylor and Taylor (1993).

[25] See Breshahan (1989).

[26] The reference here is to U.S. telephone companies. Demand analysis and forecasting has been integrated into the corporate decision-making process at Bell Canada for years.

[27] A device that I particularly have in mind here is a linking, as in the on-going National Telecommunications Demand Study, of traditional econometric demand modeling with market segmentation defined in terms of a host of socio-demographic factors. Each observation in the NTDS residential data base, for example, is assigned a particular "lifestyle" code that corresponds to a particular socio-demographic lifestyle (such are "Urban Gentry" or "Empty Nesters"). Demand equations can then be estimated for each of the customer segments. If a telco finds that an important customer segment in its service territory has low penetration, relative to the national average, of a particular service (call waiting, for example), then that customer segment can be targeted for a special marketing effort. This provides a prime example of how demand analysis and marketing can be joined.

THE PRE-1980 EMPIRICAL LITERATURE ON TELEPHONE DEMAND: ACCESS, LOCAL SERVICE, AND INTERSTATE TOLL

Chapters 3 and 4 of the 1980 book provided a survey of the empirical literature on telecommunications demand as of mid-1979. While dated, the studies described in those chapters still have relevance, and in some cases remain the only game in town, and for this reason, the chapters are reproduced with only minor editing in Appendices 1 and 2.

The organization of these appendices is as follows: This appendix and the first five sections of Appendix 2 summarize models and results for domestic demand. Section VI of Appendix 2 does the same for international demand, while Section VII focuses on the demand for yellow-pages advertising. Finally, Section VIII of Appendix 2 provides a brief survey of time-series approaches to analyzing telephone demand.

I. THE DEMAND FOR ACCESS

Despite its importance to an understanding of telephone demand, the demand for access has not received much empirical attention. I found only eight pre-1980 studies – Alleman (1977), Feldman (1976), Davis *et al.* (1973), Perl (1978), Pousette (1976), Rash (1971), Southern New England Telephone Co. (1977a), and Waverman (1974) – that contain equations for the demand for access. Alleman, Perl, Rash, and SNET focus on the residential market, while Feldman, Pousette, and Waverman estimate equations for residence and business telephones separately. Pousette also has an equation for the telephones in the public sector, and, finally Davis *et al.* estimate an equation for the total number of main stations. The focus is the United States as a whole for Alleman, Davis *et al.*, Feldman and Perl; Connecticut for SNET; Canada for Rash; Canada and Sweden for Waverman; and Sweden for Pousette. Davis *et al.*, Pousette, Rash, SNET, and Waverman all employ aggregate time-series data, while Alleman, Feldman, and Perl use cross-section data. The observations are cities for Alleman, states for Feldman, and households for Perl.

271

The Perl study provides by far the most intensive study of access demand in the literature. Data for individual households from the 1970 Census are used to analyze the economics and demographic determinants of telephone availability in the residential sector. Perl's study has a number of interesting results, and will be described in detail below. Alleman's analysis is also quite intensive, but the focus is on the pricing of local service, rather than on access per se. Alleman devotes an entire chapter in his study (which was his Ph.D. dissertation at the University of Colorado) to the theory of telephone demand. Following Squire (1973), Alleman relates the demand for access, in a consumer's surplus framework, to the demand for use. Alleman's analysis, however, is disappointing, for the theoretical structure that is carefully built up in the early chapters of the study is ignored almost entirely in the empirical chapters.

The Feldman study is the most comprehensive analysis of telephone demand in the literature.[1] Thirty-six categories of service provided by the pre-divestiture Bell System are analyzed, including residence and business main stations and business WATS lines (both inward and outward). As noted above, the analysis is cross-sectional, with states (the Bell Systems parts thereof) as observations. In the equation for main stations in the residential sector, main stations are assumed to be a function of the price of basic service (measured by average local-service revenues per main station), Bell area population, per-capita personal income, and a set of regional dummy variables that allows the constant term to vary among regions. The population is intended as a measure of market size, but population will also be a proxy for system size, and its coefficient will therefore reflect the access externality. The equation for business main stations is similar, except that local revenue per main station (as a measure of the price of access) is omitted.

A major shortcoming of the Feldman study is the absence of a well-defined theoretical framework. An excellent data base was constructed, and, as we shall see throughout these two appendices, a number of interesting and useful results have been obtained. However, the results lack the crispness and precision of interpretation that a well-articulated theoretical structure would have provided. The study's methodology clearly distinguishes between access and use (since access and use are modeled separately), but one is left with the impression that the dependence of access on the benefits generated by use and the conditionality of use on access are not fully appreciated. Another shortcoming of the study is in the measures of price that are used. Average revenue per unit (of whatever that is being explained) is used for the price variable, but this can lead to problems that are potentially serious.

---

[1] This was the case prior to 1980; it remains the case today.

In the equations for main stations, for example, defining the price of access as local revenues divided by the number of main stations has three problems: (1) With main stations as both the dependent variable and in the denominator of the price variable, a negative relationship between the number of main stations and the "price" of access is necessarily established; (2) variations in service quality (single-party versus two-party, etc.) will be reflected in local revenues, and these, in turn, will be reflected in average revenue per main station; (3) in areas with measured service, average revenue per main station will reflect charges for local use, as well as the price of access. In this case – as indeed in all cases – the measure of price that is used should only record *shifts* in the underlying tariff schedule, not *movements along it*.[2]

Let me now take up a more detailed discussion of the study of Perl. The questions addressed in Perl's study can be summarized as follows:

1. How is the demand for basic telephone service influenced by characteristics of the household?
2. How is the demand for basic telephone service influenced by the price charged for telephone service?
3. Does the price elasticity of demand vary with income and age?

The determinants of telephone availability are explored using data contained in the household and individual records of the 1/1000 Public Use Sample from the 1970 Census. The sample actually used contains data on 36,703 households in the United States in 1970. In the 1970 Census, respondents were asked whether or not there was "a telephone on which people in your living quarters can be called." The answer to this question, coded as a dichotomous, (0,1) variable, defines access (availability) in Perl's study.[3] Three forms of models are estimated, linear, logit, and probit. In the linear model, the probability of a household having access to a telephone conditional on a particular set of economic and demographic characteristics is assumed to be a linear function of those characteristics. Let x a denote vector of economic and demographic characteristics and let $P(T|x)$ denote the probability that a household has access to a telephone conditional on x. Then, in the

---

[2] I do not mean to single out Feldman's study as the only transgressor in the use of average revenue as the price variable. Many other studies do it – including Dobell, Taylor *et al.* (1972)! For a more detailed discussion of the econometric problems involved, and the procedures that have evolved for mitigating them (such as instrumental variable estimation and two-level budgeting), see Section I of Chapter 3.

[3] Since some households which do not subscribe to telephone service may nevertheless have access to a telephone (at a nearby coin station or a neighbor's telephone) and some which do subscribe may indicate otherwise (because the number is unlisted, for example), a positive response to the Census question unfortunately cannot be precisely equated with subscription.

model,

$$P(T|x) = x\beta + \varepsilon, \tag{1}$$

where β is a vector of coefficients and ε is a random error term.

The virtue of the linear model is that it can be estimated conveniently and inexpensively as a linear regression model. However, it has the drawback that the "conditional probabilities" estimated are not necessarily bounded between 0 and 1.[4] The logit and probit models do not have this defect but they are also much more expensive to estimate.[5] The logit model takes the form

$$\frac{P(T|x)}{1 - P(T|x)} = e^{x\beta + \varepsilon}, \tag{2}$$

while the probit model is defined by

$$P(T|x) = \frac{1}{\sqrt{2\pi}} \int_x^\infty e^{-z^2/2} \, dz. \tag{3}$$

Perl estimates the linear model by ordinary least squares and the logit and probit model by maximum likelihood techniques. In each case, individual households provide the unit of observation, so that the data set used in estimation contains 36,703 observations.

Three price variables are included in the models as predictors, the monthly service charge, the service-connection charge for a new subscriber, and a dummy variable that distinguishes whether or not a household resides in an area with measured local service.[6] The monthly service charged used by Perl is adjusted for the level of income in order to approximate the minimum

---

[4] Perl notes that another drawback of the linear model is that the least squares estimates of the coefficients in (1) are inefficient because the variance of the error term ε depends on the values taken by x. However, in this case, a generalized least squares estimator can be used that is asymptotically efficient. See Goldberger (1964, pp. 248–50).

[5] See McFadden (1974) for a discussion of conditional logit models, and their estimation by maximum likelihood methods. See also Train (1986), Ben Akiva and Lehrman (1985), and Amemyiya (1981). The standard reference on the probit model is Finney (1971); see also Amemyiya (1985).

[6] The price data are based on information from AT&T's Market Research Information System (MRIS), which contains billing records and household data for 30,000 residential subscribers located in each of one hundred Bell System Revenue Accounting Office (RAOs). (An RAO is a collection of exchanges, usually contiguous, that have been grouped together for accounting purposes.) The MRIS data on monthly service charges were linked to Census data by identifying the RAO in which each Census household was located.

charge at which a household can obtain telephone service.[7]   The dummy variable for the presence of measured service is intended to allow for the lower monthly service charge that is likely to result from local use (or at least a part thereof) being charged for directly.

Besides the three price variables, the other predictors in Perl's models include household income, age of household head, years of schooling of household head, size of household, and dummy variables indicating whether the head of the household is employed; the household is headed by a male, no spouse present; one-person household, male; one-person household, female.

Perl finds that the demand for basic telephone service is significantly influenced by both the monthly service charge and the service-connection charge. His estimates of the average elasticity of demand with respect to the monthly service charge vary from -0.067 to -0.091 and from -0.016 to -0.022 with respect to the service-connection charge. Further, the price elasticity of demand is found to be quite sensitive to the level of household income and to the age of the head of the household.[8] The logit and probit models appear to perform somewhat better than the linear model.   The average impact of specific variables is similar in the logit and probit models. The percentage of households with basic telephone service is found to be positively related to income, age, and education, and inversely related to the number of persons in the household. This percentage is also higher for households with its head employed, higher in urban than in rural areas, lower in the South than elsewhere, and lower for nonwhite households.   Finally, the percentage of households with basic telephone service is lower among single-person households (both male and female) and lower also for male-headed households with spouse absent than for other household types.

[7] See Perl (1978, pp. 10–11) for details. The purpose of this adjustment is to neutralize the positive correlation between income and the monthly service charge. This positive correlation reflects the fact that as income rises, families often choose a more enriched grade of basic service, such as one-party service as opposed to two- or four-party service. As a consequence of this positive correlation between income and the basic service charge, average charges are likely to appear higher in high income areas than in low income areas. Since high income areas are also likely to have higher telephone availability, this – as Perl noted in an earlier version of his paper – would tend to bias the relationship between telephone availability and telephone charges toward zero. Perl also analyzed two other measures of the basic monthly service charge, the average monthly service charge in the RAO in which the household was located and the average monthly charges paid by households with annual incomes under $5,000. However, of these three measures of price, Perl concludes (correctly, in my opinion) that the income-adjusted measure is the most appropriate, and bases most of his analysis on this measure.

[8] For example, for households with a twenty-year old head and income of $1,500, Perl's estimates of the price elasticity with respect to the monthly service charge range from -0.173 to -0.422 – three to four times the average elasticity for all age groups and income levels.

In general, the Perl study is an important contribution to the empirical analysis of access demand. It utilizes a rich data and the findings are interesting and useful. As in the Feldman study, however, the analysis is weakly motivated theoretically. Perl does an excellent job in identifying the charges corresponding to access and then relating the demand for basic service to them, but once again the dependence of the demand for access on the benefits conferred by use is ignored. The impact of system size is also ignored. However, since Perl distinguishes between urban and rural households, and since urban exchanges are larger than rural exchanges, the system externality is reflected, at least to some extent, in the higher demand by urban households.

The final study to be reviewed in this section is by Pousette (1976). Pousette estimates access and use equations for residence, business, and public sector customers in Sweden using aggregate time-series data for the period 1949–1974. Pousette does not explain the number of subscribers directly, but rather specifies separate equations for new connections and disconnections.[9] The "stock" of telephones is then calculated as last period's stock plus new connections minus disconnections. Pousette's overall model therefore consists of behavioral equations for telephone use, new connections, and disconnections, plus the stock identity.

To illustrate Pousette's analysis, we shall present his equations for residence new connections and disconnections. The equation for new connections is as follows (*t*-ratios appear in parentheses):[10]

$$CT_R = \frac{-20.77}{(-0.22)} + \frac{0.09}{(3.00)} (H - ST_R) + \frac{3.78}{(1.26)} \left(\frac{C}{H}\right)$$

$$- \frac{0.50}{(-2.78)} \left(\frac{P_u}{P_C}\right) - 1.24 \, (-9.54) \left(\frac{P_I}{P_C}\right) + \frac{1.57}{(7.58)} AUT_L$$

$$\bar{R} = 0.970, \tag{4}$$

where:

$$CT_R = \text{number of new residence connections ordered (in thousands)}$$

$$H = \text{number of households (in thousands)}$$

$$ST_R = \text{stock of telephones in residence (in thousands)}$$

[9] In the telephone industry in the United States, reconnections and new connections and disconnections are referred to as inward and outward movement. Since I shall be using Pousette's notation in presenting his equations, it is convenient to keep his terminology.

[10] Because there was an installation backlog during the sample period in Sweden, new connections refer to telephones ordered rather than actual installations. Disconnections also refer to orders, although in this case queuing was not a problem.

$$C = \text{private consumption (in thousands of 1968 kronor)}$$
$$P_U = \text{weighted sum of subscription charge and call charge}$$
$$P_C = \text{implicit deflator for private consumption}$$
$$P_I = \text{service-connection charge index}$$
$$AUT_L = \text{index for the automation of local calls.}$$

For residence disconnections, Pousette obtains:[11]

$$DT_R = \frac{-165.53}{(-6.30)} + \frac{3.50}{(4.58)} D + \frac{1.62}{(5.40)} E + \frac{0.26}{(3.25)} CT_R$$

$$+ \frac{21.75}{(5.28)} D4960 + \frac{14.45}{(2.90)} D61$$

$$\bar{R}^2 = 0.924, \tag{5}$$

where:

DT_R = number of disconnections ordered (in thousands)

D = number of deaths, not married, twenty years or over (in thousands)

E = number of emigrants, twenty years and over (in thousands)[12]

CT_R = number of residence new connections ordered (in thousands)

$D4960$ = dummy variable for incorrect data (1 for 1949–1960, 0 otherwise)

$D61$ = dummy variable for incorrect data (1 for 1961, 0 otherwise).[13]

Income is represented in the equation for new connections by private consumption, and is the only predictor with a t-ratio less than 2 (in absolute value). The term $H - ST_R$, which denotes the number of households without a telephone, is included as a measure of market potential. The service-connection charge is the most significant predictor, followed by the index for the automation of local calls. The highly significant positive coefficient on

---

[11] While Pousette uses both ordinary least squares and three-stage least squares in estimation, only the OLS results are reported here.

[12] The number of married emigrants is divided by 2.

[12] The two dummy variables correct for a change in definition in the time series for disconnections in 1961. The dummy variable for 1961 is, of course, equivalent eliminating that year from the analysis (except that the zero residual for the year goes into the calculation of the R^2).

this variable attests that service-quality is an important factor and that Swedes place a positive value on their time. The price index for subscription and call charges on new connections is less than that of the service-connection charge. In terms of elasticities (which Pousette unfortunately does not provide), it would appear that the elasticity with respect to the subscription and use charges is about half the elasticity for the service-connection charge.

In the equation for disconnections, deaths and emigration are the most important predictors.[14] The number of new connections is included in the equation as a measure of the "potential" for disconnections. Pousette observes that the longer that a household has had a telephone, the more difficult it is likely to be to get along without the service. The best candidates, therefore, for disconnecting are those that have just recently become subscribers. The positive, and highly significant, coefficient on new connections supports this view.

Pousette's study is of a great deal of interest because it, along with Waverman (1974), comes closest (of the pre-1980 studies) to utilizing the access/use framework outlined in Section III of Chapter 2.[15] Pousette recognizes that the demand for access depends on the price of use, as well as the subscription fee and the service-connection charge, although it is unfortunate that the subscription fee and the price of use are combined in a single index. Pousette also departs from the model suggested in Chapter 2 in that the focus is on the change in access demand, as opposed to the level of access demand. But by specifying separate equations for new connections and disconnections, Pousette is able to focus more explicitly on socio-demographic factors. Interestingly enough, though, this is probably of greater relevance in the U.S. market, where changes in address are frequent and there is substantial seasonal "churning".

Pousette's specifications do have some problems, however, in that the dependent variables are changes, while the independent variables are levels. Of course, it may be that the relationship between the stock of telephones and price and income is quadratic, in which case Pousette's specifications are appropriate. I doubt, though, that this is what Pousette had in mind. Also, Pousette does not make any allowance for the access externality in his equation for new connections. The existing number of subscribers does appear in the market potential term $H - ST_R$, and one might interpret the

---

[14] Swedes do not change residences with anything approaching the frequency of Americans. The coefficient for the number of deaths, it will be noted, is 3.50, which seems high.

[15] Waverman analyzes data for Canada and the U.K., as well as for Sweden. Waverman's analysis differs from Pousette's in that the stock of telephones is explained directly, and local calls are distinguished from intercity calls. Waverman's equation for local use will be discussed in the next section.

negative coefficient on ST_R (-0.09) as reflecting a non-linearity in the access externality. But this would seem to be pushing the point. Pousette interprets $H - ST_R$ as a measure of nonsaturation, and the empirical results have to be viewed as bearing this out.

In Table 1, I have listed the price and income elasticities of the demand for access that have been estimated in the empirical studies. The conclusion that emerges is that the price elasticity, calculated with respect to the price of basic service, appears to be in the neighborhood of -0.1, while the income elasticity appears to be in the neighborhood of 0.5. Waverman's results for residence main stations in Ontario and Quebec and Perl's results for the United States suggest that the income elasticity may be smaller than 0.5, but these are the only exceptions.[16] A very small price elasticity and a moderate, but yet decidedly inelastic, income elasticity is precisely what one should expect for basic telephone service: Access to the telephone system is not a plaything of the rich (at least in the developed countries), but has become a basic necessity for virtually all income groups.

Perhaps the most important finding is that the price elasticity of the demand for access is in fact different from zero. The results of Perl are especially strong in this regard, and while one might question certain aspects of Perl's models, his price results will almost certainly hold up to respecification. As one should expect, the elasticity with respect to the service-connection charge is smaller than the elasticity with respect to the subscription fee. Perl's estimate of this elasticity is -0.02, while Waverman's estimate is -0.04. In neither case is the estimate strong statistically, which contrasts sharply with the results of Pousette. Pousette found [cf. equation (4)] the service-connection charge to be considerably stronger statistically than the subscription fee. And while Pousette's actual elasticities are not available, it is clear from the regression coefficients that the elasticity for the connection charge is at least double the elasticity for the subscription fee.

For Perl and Waverman, however, the quantity being explained is either telephone availability or the number of subscribers, while for Pousette, the quantity being explained is the number of new subscribers. Because the service-connection charge is faced only once – at a time of connection – we should naturally expect this charge to have more of an impact on additions to the stock of telephones than on the stock itself.[17] Thus, that the service-

---

[16] In both cases, the estimate of the income elasticity is 0.15. Perl's elasticity (calculated from his logit equation) is estimated with a model in which other factors such as education, which is highly correlated with income, are taken into account. Thus a smaller income elasticity is probably to be expected.

[17] It has been suggested by Paul Brandon that the service-connection charge should be amortized over several years as part of the subscription fee. Edward Lowry of AT&T has

TABLE 1

Estimates of price and income elasticities of the demand for access to the telephone system

Class of Customer and Study	Dependent Variable	Price Elasticity		Income Elasticity	Type of Data
		Service-Connection Charge	Basic Service Charge		
Residential					
Alleman	main stations	NE	-0.17	0.56	CS: Cities, U.S.
Feldman	main stations plus extensions	NE	-0.05	0.54	CS: States, U.S.
Perl	telephone availability	-0.02	-0.08	0.15	CS: Households, U.S.
Rash	main stations	NE	-0.11	0.61	TS: A, Ontario and Quebec
Waverman	main stations	NE	-0.12	0.15	TS: A, Ontario and Quebec
Business					
Waverman	main stations	NE	-0.09	NE	TS: A, Ontario and Quebec
Residential & Business Combined					
Davis *et al.*	total telephone less residence main stations	NE	-0.08	0.39	TS: A, Bell System, U.S.
Waverman	main stations	-0.04	-0.06	0.56	TS: A, Sweden

Symbols: NE: not estimated; CS: cross-section; TS: time series; A: annual.

connection charge shows up much stronger in Pousette's equation than in the equations of Perl and Waverman is to be expected. Moreover, that the elasticity for the service-connection charge is larger than the elasticity for the subscription fee suggests that, even in Sweden, there may be a population of "churners" whose turnover of main stations can be dampened by higher charges for reconnection.

In closing this review of access demand, I would like to reproduce, in Table 2, a part of the table from Perl's study that shows the dependence of the estimated elasticity with respect to the price of basic service on the level of income and the age of the head of household. Perl calculated these estimates for all three of his models, linear, logit, and probit, but, since the three models yield similar results, Table 2 contains only the estimates from the logit model.

Table 2 tells an interesting story. The estimated elasticity of demand for basic service with respect to the monthly charge for that service varies directly with the size of the charges, inversely with the level of household income, and inversely with the age of the household head.[18] The first two results are really a reflection of the same thing, namely, the importance of the income effect in the overall price elasticity for access demand. Let us concentrate for a moment on households whose heads are thirty-five years of age. The value of -0.013 – the estimated price elasticity for a monthly service charge of $4.00 for a household income of $17,500 – should lie reasonably close to the pure substitution elasticity (i.e., the Slutsky, income-compensated price elasticity) for a household with this age of head. Compare this number to the value of -0.340 for the elasticity for a household with head of age thirty-five, income only $1,500, and facing a monthly service charge of $7.50. The income effects are relatively very large.

When substitution effects are large relative to income effects, consumers can substitute away from goods whose prices have risen with little loss in utility. However, when income effects are large relative to substitution effects, an increase in price means a relatively large decrease in utility. Since the income effect is indicated to be large relative to the substitution effect in the price elasticity of demand for access for households with low income, particularly if they are young, the welfare of these households may be significantly decreased by increases in the price for basic service. The results of Perl thus suggest that the telephone companies may encounter spirited customer opposition to moves to bring the price of access for residential customers into line with the cost of supply. Events of the early 1980s bear this out.

taken a few tentative research steps in this direction as part of his PH.D. dissertation, but the results so far are not very encouraging. Neither are the results of Fask and Robinson (1977).

[18] The interaction terms upon which the estimates of Table 2 are based are all highly significant statistically.

TABLE 2

Estimated price elasticity of demand with respect to the
income-adjusted basic monthly service charge logic model;
1978 Perl study

Age of Household Head and Household Income	Income-Adjusted Monthly Service Charge		
	$4.00	$5.75	$7.50
20 Years of Age			
$1,500	-0.168	-0.282	-0.422
$4,500	-0.128	-0.220	-0.337
$7,500	-0.093	-0.161	-0.251
$10,500	-0.064	-0.113	-0.178
$17,500	-0.026	-0.045	-0.074
35 Years of Age			
$1,500	-0.0131	-0.223	-0.340
$4,500	-0.096	-0.165	-0.258
$ 7,500	-0.064	-0.112	-0.177
$10,500	-0.042	-0.074	-0.119
$17,500	-0.013	-0.023	-0.037
55 Years of Age			
$1,500	-0.089	-0.154	-0.242
$4,500	-0.062	-0.109	-0.171
$7,500	-0.040	-0.071	-0.114
$10,500	-0.026	-0.046	-0.074
$17,500	-0.010	-0.018	-0.029
70 Years of Age			
$1,500	-0.066	-0.116	-0.184
$4,500	-0.043	-0.075	-0.120
$7,500	-0.027	-0.049	-0.080
$10,500	-0.017	-0.031	-0.051
$17,500	-0.008	-0.014	-0.023

Source: Perl (1978, Table 7)

II. The Demand for Local Use

We shall now turn our attention to the demand for local use. Unfortunately, local use is difficult to analyze empirically because its price is usually rolled into the monthly service charge. As a consequence, much of the empirical literature on local demand involves the analysis of local revenues, which is not coextensive with local use. However, there are a few (pre-1980) studies – Beauvais (1977), New York Telephone Co. (1976a, 1976b), Pavarini (1975, 1979), and Waverman (1974) – that have been able to analyze the demand for local use directly. Most of this section will be devoted to discussion of these studies.

We begin with the Beauvais study, which provides an interesting contrast of innovations and problems. Beauvais is concerned with estimating the demand for outgoing local calls by residential customers under flat-rate pricing, with the view of being able to estimate the impact on residential customers of a move to measured service from flat-rate service. Beauvais's analysis is based on data from GT&E's measured service trial in three exchanges in Illinois. The data represent a one-month (August 1976) cross-section of observations from a sample of about 1,000 residential subscribers in these three exchanges.

Beauvais assumes that the number of outgoing local calls is a function of income, the marginal price of a local call, and the average price of a local call. The actual level of a household's income was not collected, but only the interval within which the household's income fell. Income is accordingly represented by a set of dummy variables. The average price of a local call is measured by the monthly service charge divided by the number of outgoing local calls. Defining the average price in this way unfortunately involves a serious error, and undermines Beauvais's empirical results. But, more about this below.

The marginal price of a local call is measured by the opportunity cost of the time spent by a caller in making a call. Beauvais measures this opportunity cost as the amount of time spent on a call (by all subscribers in the sample) multiplied by the subscriber's wage rate. While one may question whether this is the appropriate way of defining the opportunity cost of a call, the recognition that the price of a call involves more than just the out-of-pocket expense of the call (which, in this case, is zero) is a major innovation.

But, while the introduction of the opportunity cost of time represents a major innovation, defining the average price as the monthly service charge divided by the number of outgoing calls creates a major problem. As Beauvais himself notes, in having the dependent variable (i.e., the number of out-going local calls) in the denominator of the average price, a negative relationship between the number of calls and the average price is necessarily established, which implies that the estimate of the coefficient on the average price will be biased downward. The strength of this bias will depend, in great part, upon the variance of the monthly service charge in relation to the variance of the number of calls. If the latter is large relative to the former (as is almost certainly the case), the bias *can* be substantial. And, if the number of calls is only weakly correlated with the monthly service charge, the bias *will* be substantial.

In the data analyzed by Beauvais, it is unlikely that there is much variation in the monthly service charge, but it is very likely that there are a few households that make a very large number of calls.[19] The presence of just a few outliers of this type is sufficient to impact a substantial negative bias to the estimate of the coefficient on the average price.[20] What Beauvais might have done was to include the monthly service charge as a predictor without dividing it by the number of outgoing calls. This would yield a model that would be in keeping with the treatment of two-part tariffs discussed in Section VII of Chapter 2, but with the added feature that the opportunity cost of a caller's time is explicitly taken into account.

Let me now turn to Waverman's study. Waverman analyzes the demand for local use in Sweden in a framework that draws on the access/use distinction discussed earlier. The model postulated for explaining local usage is

$$\ln\left(\frac{Q}{T}\right)_t = b_0 + b_1 \ln\left(\frac{Q}{T}\right)_{t-1} + b_2 \ln X_t + b_3 \ln P_t + u_t, \tag{6}$$

where:

Q = number of local "pulses"[21]

T = number of telephones (main stations)

X = real gross domestic product/household

P = marginal price per pulse

u = random error term.

As an alternative to the model in (6), Waverman also estimates

$$\ln Q_t = b_0 + b_1 \ln Q_{t-1} + b_2 \ln X_t + b_3 \ln P_t + b_4 \ln T_t + u_t. \tag{7}$$

---

[19] Cf. Garfinkel (1977a, 1977b).

[20] One is alerted of this problem in Beauvais's analysis by the size of the t-ratio for the coefficient on the average price. Its value is 67.6, while the next largest t-ratio is 10.9.

[21] Many European telephone companies use a pulse system for measuring holding time, so that the number of pulses for a call represents the holding time (or length) of the call. For a discussion, see Mitchell (1978b).

Waverman estimates his model using annual time-series data for the period 1949–1969. The results obtained for the two local-usage equations are as follows (t-ratios are in parentheses):

$$\ln\left(\frac{Q}{T}\right)_t = \underset{(3.50)}{1.15} + \underset{(1.43)}{0.294} \ln\left(\frac{Q}{T}\right)_{t-1} + \underset{(3.32)}{0.832} \ln X_t$$

$$- \underset{(-1.50)}{0.097} \ln P_t \qquad R^2 = 0.971 \qquad (8)$$

$$\ln Q_t = \underset{(-1.32)}{-4.17} + \underset{(1.45)}{0.286} \ln Q_{t-1} + \underset{(0.54)}{0.228} \ln X_t$$

$$- \underset{(-2.33)}{0.272} + \underset{(3.36)}{1.19} \ln P_t \qquad R^2 = 0.997. \qquad (9)$$

To begin with, it will be noted that the coefficient on $\ln T_t$ in equation (9) is greater than 1 (although not significantly so). This result suggests that, *ceteris paribus*, more calls are made per telephone in a large system, which would seem to be consistent with a positive access externality.[22] Secondly, it is somewhat surprising to find that, with the stock of telephones held constant, habit formation (or inertia) in local calling is modest. That this is so is reflected in coefficients on the lagged dependent variable in equation (8) and (9) that are closer to 0 than to 1, and, indeed, by conventional criteria, not significantly different from 0. Finally, it is seen that GDP/household is statistically significant in equation (8) but not in equation (9). This no doubt reflects a collinearity between GDP/household and the number of main stations.

The final study of local-service demand to be given detailed review is Pavarini (1975).[23] Pavarini is concerned with analyzing the impact of local calling of a conversion from flat-rate to measured service. The focus is on data taken from customers subscribing to METROPAC, an optional extended area service offered in some exchanges bordering the Denver metropolitan area. METROPAC was converted from flat rate to measured rate in January 1971. Pavarini's data set consists of observations on a sample of 387 residential customers and eighty business customers for three different four-month periods: April–July 1970, August–November 1970, and April–July 1971. The purpose of the study is to quantify the impact of METROPAC conversion to local usage.

---

[22] However, see the discussion in Chapter 9 and Appendix 3.
[23] See also Pavarini (1979).

Ordinarily, one uses a standard demand model to estimate price and income effects, but in this case, the variation in price is too limited for a conventional demand model to be of much value. Pavarini uses, instead, a model that relates the number of calls after the conversion to measured service to the flat-rate demand and the measured-service price per call. The flat-rate demand is viewed as providing the base from which the impact of measured service is estimated. The standard formulation of this model would be to regress the number of calls after the conversion on the number of calls before the conversion and the price per call after the conversion. However, the conventional regression model is not really appropriate in this situation because of the fact that the flat-rate demand is itself subject to random variation. The independent variable is thus measured with error, and, as is well known, ordinary least squares applied to such a model will yield biased and inconsistent estimators. An errors-in-variables model is called for.

Pavarini does in fact adopt an errors-in-variables framework, although it is not of the form traditionally employed in econometrics, and Pavarini does not even refer to it as an errors-in-variable model. Briefly stated, Pavarini's methodology consists of estimating the "normal" variation in usage between the period August–November and April–July 1971 that would be expected to occur in the absence of the rate conversion. The difference between the estimated normal usage and that which was actually observed is then attributed to the rate conversion.[24]

We shall begin with a description of Pavarini's method for estimating variation in normal usage. Suppose that there are two periods, and assume that a household's usage in each of the periods is a random variable. Let X and Y denote usage in the two periods, and let f_{XY} denote their joint distribution. Let $f_{Y|X}(y|x)$ denote the conditional distribution of y given x.[25] Finally, let $f_X(x)$ and $f_Y(y)$ denote the marginal distributions. By definition, $f_Y(y)$ will be given by

$$f_Y(y) = \int_x f_{(Y|X)}(y|x) f_X(x)\, \mathrm{d}x. \tag{10}$$

In the present context, however, our interest is confined to the conditional distribution $f(y|x)$.

Let us assume that we observe a particular value of usage in period 1, say $X = x^*$. What can we say about the value of y, which is yet to be observed? Clearly, the natural quantity to consider is the expected value of Y conditional

---

[24] Pavarini's approach is similar in spirit to one developed in an article by Blomqvist (1977).
[25] It is assumed that $f_{Y|X}(y|x)$ is the same for all households.

on $X = x^*$. If the form of the conditional distribution $f(y|x)$ is known, this conditional mean can be calculated as

$$E(Y|x^*) = \int_y y f_{Y|X}(y|x^*)\, dy. \tag{11}$$

Now, let:

U_{f1} = usage (measured as the number of minutes/month) in the period August–November 1970

U_{f2} = usage in the period April–July 1970

U_m = usage in the period April–July 1971.

In line with equation (11), Pavarini seeks to estimate the expected value of U_m given u_{fl} (i.e., given the observed amount of usage in the period August–November 1970) and given the conversion to measured service in January 1971. However, in order to allow for normal customer volatility, the period April–July 1970 is used as an intermediate step in the estimation.

Pavarini postulates that the conditional density of U_{f2} given u_{f1} [$f_{Y|X}(y|x)$] in the previous notation] will be lognormal with mean $\alpha(u_{f1})$ and variance σ^2. [26] Further, it is assumed that the mean of $(U_{f2}|u_{f1})$ will be given by

$$E(U_{f2}|u_{f1}) = s u_{f1}^q \tag{12}$$

and that

$$\text{VAR}(U_{f2}|u_{f1}) = w^2 (s u_{f1}^q)^2, \tag{13}$$

where s, q, and w^2 are constants. It then follows from the properties of the lognormal distribution that the mean and variance of $\ln(U_{f2}|u_{f1})$, $\alpha(u_{f1})$ and σ^2, will be equal to

$$\alpha(u_{f1}) = \ln s + q \ln u_{f1} - \frac{\ln(w^2 + 1)}{2} \tag{14}$$

$$\sigma^2 = \ln(w^2 + 1). \tag{15}$$

It will be useful to rewrite expression (14) as

$$\alpha(u_{f1}) = \theta_1 + \theta_2 \ln u_{f1} \tag{16}$$

[26] $(U_{f2}|u_{f1})$ being lognormal means that $\ln(U_{f2}|u_{f1})$ is normal with mean $\alpha(u_{f1})$ and variance σ^2. The standard reference on the lognormal distribution is Aitchison and Brown (1957). Pavarini cites Johnson and Kotz (1970).

where

$$\theta_1 = \ln s - \frac{\ln(w^2 + 1)}{2} \tag{17}$$

and

$$\theta_2 = q. \tag{18}$$

Since $\ln(U_{f2}|u_{f1})$ is assumed to be normally distributed with mean equal to $\theta_1 + \theta_2 \ln u_{f1}$ and variance equal to σ^2, estimates of θ_1, θ_2 and σ^2 can be obtained from a least-squares regression of $\ln u_{f2}$ on $\ln u_{f1}$. From these estimates, it is possible to derive estimates of the parameters w^2, s, and q.[27] One can then obtain an estimate of the expected value of $(U_{f2}|u_{f1})$ from

$$E(U_{f2}|u_{f1}) = s u_{f1}^q. \tag{19}$$

Pavarini notes that the foregoing, which provided a methodology for forecasting variation in "normal" usage under a flat-rate tariff, feeds in to the larger problem of estimating the impact of conversion to measured service as follows:

> Instead of interpreting the price response as the transformation of U_{f1} to U_m, let us isolate the pure price response by considering that each customer gets from u_{f1} to u_m in two discrete steps. First, his usage changes to *what it would have been* had there been no price change. This is normal usage variation. Then, consider that it is this usage level that he adjusts so as to arrive at u_m. This second movement is the price effect. In the absence of any strong evidence of long-term growth in METROPAC usage, we will use U_{f2} (usage in the same period one year before) as a surrogate for the results of movement from U_{f1} due to normal usage variation. That is, U_{f2} will be the prediction of what usage would have been in the April–July 1971 period had there not been a price change. This is *not* to say that we will simply compare the values of u_{f2} and u_m for each customer, for such a comparison would still be "noise" contaminated. Rather, for customers who showed a specific value of usage just previous to the rate change (u_{f1}), a prediction is made of the probability density of their usage $(U_{f2}|u_{f1})$ in the absence of price change and this density is transformed

---

[27] Since $\sigma^2 = q$, θ_2 will provide an unbiased estimator of q. However, since s and w^2 are nonlinear, functions of θ_1 and θ_2 the estimators of s and w^2 obtained directly from θ_1 and θ_2 will, in general be biased. Pavarini obtains asymptotically unbiased estimators of s and w^2 by utilizing the asymptotic distributions of $\ln s$ and $\ln(w^2 + 1)$.

to the conditional density of $(U_m|u_{f1})$ via a price relation that has u_{f2} as its usage argument. (Pavarini 1975, pp. 16–17), italics in original.)[28]

We now bring the conversion to measured service into the picture. Let $g(x, p)$ denote the number of calls made by customers with flat-rate demand x after they are charged a price of p per unit of usage. The transformation from U_{f1} to U_m, under Pavarini's assumptions, will therefore be given by

$$(U_m|u_{f1}) = g[(U_{f2}|u_{f1}), p].$$ (20)

Pavarini considers two representations of the function g that preserves the lognormality of $(U_m|u_{f1})$,[29] one deterministic and the other stochastic. For the deterministic representation, it is assumed that

$$u_m = c(p)u_{f2}^{d(p)},$$ (21)

while, for the stochastic representation, it is assumed that

$$(U_m|u_{f2}) = e^{A(p)}U_{f2}^{b(p)},$$ (22)

where $A(p)$ is a random variable with mean $\mu_a(p)$ and variance $\sigma^2(p)$.

In equation (21), the functional forms of $c(p)$ and $d(p)$ cannot be specified because their values can only be estimated at $p = 0$, which corresponds to $c(o) = 1$ and $d(o) = 1$, and at the METROPAC price. However, since

$$(U_m|u_{f1}) = g[U_{f2}|u_{f1}), p] = c(p)(U_{f2}|u_{f1})^{d(p)},$$ (23)

and because $(U_{f2}|u_{f1})$ is lognormal with mean αu_{f1} and variance σ^2, it follows that $(U_m|u_{f1})$ will be lognormal with mean $d(p)(u_{f1}) + \ln c(p)$ and variance $[d(p)]^2\sigma^2$.

Since we have estimates of αu_{f1}, estimates of $c(p)$ and $d(p)$ can be obtained from the coefficients in a least-square regression of $\ln u_m$ on (u_{f1}),

$$\ln u_m = \eta_1 + \eta_2\alpha u_{f1} + \varepsilon,$$ (24)

where

$$\eta_1 = \ln c(p),$$ (25)

[28] As Pavarini observes (p.17), the validity of this analysis requires that the conditional distribution describing the movement in usage from the period August–November 1970 to April–July 1970 also describes the movement (in the absence of rate change) from August–November 1970 to April–July 1971. This requires (1) that there be no year-to-year trend in usage, (2) that any seasonal component be stable and represented in the parameters θ_1 and θ_2 and (3) that σ^2 be constant through time.

[29] Pavarini establishes (by analysis of the residuals in a least-square regression of $\ln u_m$ on $\ln u_{f1}$) that the conditional density of $(U_m|u_{f1})$ can in fact be considered to be lognormal.

$$\eta_2 = d(p), \tag{26}$$

and ε is a random error term. Estimation of equation (24) will also yield an estimate of the variance of $\ln u_m$, say δ^2. However, from equation (21), it follows that

$$\alpha^2 = [d(p)]^2 \sigma^2 \tag{27}$$

Consequently, since we already have an estimate of σ^2, we have three equations [(25), (26), (27)] in two unknowns $c(p)$ and $d(p)$. This provides a check on the consistency of the deterministic specification in (21).

In both the residence and business samples, Pavarini finds $\hat{\eta}_2 = \hat{d}(p) < 1$ and $\hat{\alpha}^2 > \sigma^2$. Pavarini notes (p. 21): "Aside from the obvious inconsistency, this is a clear indication that the variance of the conditional densities is greater than one would expect if the price relations [were] deterministic. The results indicate that part of the observed variance is due to the different price-related reactions of customers at the same flat-rate usage level." Pavarini accordingly turns his attention to the stochastic relation in expression (22).

In (22) Pavarini assumes that, for fixed p, $A(p)$ is normally distributed with mean $\mu_a(p)$ and variance $\sigma_a^2(p)$. $A(p)$ is assumed to be independent of U_{f1}, and $b(p)$ is a constant. For $p = 0$, both $\mu_a(o)$ and σ_a^2 are assumed to be 0, and $b(o)$ is assumed to be 1. Since[30]

$$e^{A(p)} \sim \Gamma\left[\mu_a(p), \sigma_a^2(p)\right] \tag{28}$$

and

$$\left(U_{f2}|u_{f1}^{b(p)}\right) \sim \Gamma\left[b(p)\alpha(u_{f1}), [b(p)]^2\sigma^2\right], \tag{29}$$

it follows that

$$(U_m|u_{f1}) \sim \Gamma\left[\mu_a(p) + b(p)\alpha(u_{f1}), \sigma_a^2(p) + [b(p)]^2\sigma^2\right]. \tag{30}$$

The unknown parameters in this expression $\mu_a(p)$, $b(p)$, and σ_a^2, can be estimated, as before, from a least-squares regression [cf. equation (24)] of $\ln u_m$ on $\hat{\alpha}(u_{f1})$. The estimates obtained by Pavarini together with estimated standard errors, at the METROPAC price are given in Table 3.[31]

At this point, Pavarini is able to estimate the portion of the observed variation in usage between August–November 1970 and April–July 1971

---

[30] The notation $x \sim \Gamma(\mu, \sigma^2)$ means that x is distributed lognormally with mean μ and variance σ^2.

[31] In interpreting his results, Pavarini assumes that αu_{f1} is measured without error.

TABLE 3

Estimates of the parameters in equation
(30)

	$\hat{b}(p)$	$\hat{\mu}_a(p)$	$\hat{\sigma}_a^2(p)$
Residence	0.41	2.08	0.28
	(0.06)	(0.30)	(0.02)
Business	0.80	0.87	0.06
	(0.10)	(0.60)	(0.04)

Source: Pavarine (1975, p. 23)

induced by the conversion to measured service in January 1971. The price-affected portion, considered as the movement from u_{f2} to u_m, is found from the relation,

$$(U_m|u_{f1}) = e^{A(p)} u_{f2}^{b(p)}, \tag{31}$$

using estimated values of μ_a, σ_a^2, and b. In particular, since $(U_m|u_{f2})$ is distributed lognormally, we will have

$$(U_m|u_{f2}) \sim \Gamma \left[\mu_a(p) + b(p) \ln u_{f2}, \sigma_a^2(p) \right]. \tag{32}$$

The expected value of $(U_m|u_{f2})$ as a function of flat-rate usage will then be equal to

$$E(U_m|u_{f2}) = \exp \left[\mu_a(p) + \sigma_a^2(p)/2 \right] \mu_{f2}^{b(p)}, \tag{33}$$

while the variance of $(U_m|u_{f1})$ will be equal to

$$\text{VAR}(U_m|u_{f2}) = [E(U_m|u_{f2})]^2 [\exp(\sigma_a^2(p)) - 1]. \tag{34}$$

A point estimate of the change in usage induced by the rate conversion can be obtained from expression (33) using the estimated values of μ_a, σ_a^2, and b from Table 3.

The variation in usage that is actually observed (U_m versus U_{f1}) is specified by "adding" the normal variation in usage (U_{f2} versus U_{f1}) to the price-induced variation (U_m versus U_{f2}). Since the price relation specifies u_m as a function of u_{f2}, an estimate of u_{f2} is required as an input to the price model. Alternatively, to predict the distribution of usage following a rate change, both a price model (U_m versus u_{f2}) and knowledge of the distribution of U_{f2} are required.

Pavarini illustrates his errors-in-variables framework by comparing the predicted impact on the number of "measured" calls using his model, which allows for normal variation in the flat-rate demand, with the predicted impact from a model which does not allow for such variation. Briefly summarized, his results indicate that

> ... the existence of normal usage variation causes the mean *total* response to be higher (lower) than the *pure* response at low (high) flat rate levels. The price effect shows, for example, that customers with a flat rate demand of 200 minutes per month exhibit a mean measured usage of 82.6. However, had one interpreted the total effect as purely price-related, the estimate of the mean price response would have been some 7% higher (88.3). In this case, the 7% difference is "small" considering that movement was from the 200 level. However, as usage reduction due to price becomes less than the 59% reduction here (200 to 82.6), the contamination due to normal usage variation becomes more significant. In the limiting case when usage reduction due to price is *zero*, the total effect model would show a usage *increase* from the 200 level to a new mean level of 248. (Pavarini 1975, p. 26, italics in original.)

Measured local service is increasingly discussed these days, and Pavarini's model provides a vehicle for predicting what its impact on usage might be. It is for this reason that I have described his methodology in detail.[32] Also, one can also see Pavarini's methodology being used in analyzing the data being generated in the time-of-day electricity pricing experiments sponsored by the Department of Energy.[33] I mention this because price variation is at a premium in most of these experiments, and Pavarini's methodology provides a useful alternative to the conventional regression model.[34]

[32] In his 1976 paper, Pavarini estimates the impact on local usage of the METROPAC rate conversion for each of the three Denver exchanges separately (Erie, Ft. Lupton, and Longmont). Differences in estimated parameters across exchanges are then related to differences in income. In attempting this, Pavarini embeds his model in a utility-maximization framework. Readers interested in Pavarini's methodology should read *both* Pavarini (1975) and Pavarini (1976b). See also Pavarini (1979).

[33] For a description of these experiments, see Hill *et al.* (1978).

[34] Before moving on to the studies that analyze the demand for basic service, I should mention briefly the studies done by the New York Telephone Co. In the areas served by NYT, a specified number of local message-units are included in the monthly service charge, but message-units beyond the allowance cost the subscriber so much per message unit. The NYT studies analyze the demand for additional message units for residential customers, business customers, and for residential and business customers combined. The price and income

So far, our focus in this section has been on the few studies that have analyzed the demand for local use per se. A number of other studies have looked at local service, but they have taken price-deflated local revenues as the dependent variable. What is being analyzed in these studies is a category of demand that combines access with local use. The models estimated may be useful for explaining real expenditures for local service, but since the distinction is blurred between access and use, little or no information is conveyed about the demand for local use.[35]

The studies that estimate equations for price-deflated local revenues include Davis *et al.* (1973), Dobell *et al.* (1972), New York Telephone Co. (1976a, 1976b), and Southern New England Telephone Co. (1977a). Davis *et al.*, as part of the FORECYT model, have an equation for local service for residence and business combined that is estimated with aggregate quarterly time-series data for the Bell System. Dobell *et al.* employ annual time-series data, but the geographical entity is Canada. Equations for local-service revenues are estimated for residence and business customers combined using data for all of Canada, and residence customers and business customers separately using Bell Canada data for Ontario and Quebec. The SNET study uses quarterly time-series data for Connecticut and estimates separate equations for residence and business. Finally, the NYT study estimates equations for residence and business, both separately and combined, using quarterly time-series data for New York.

In Table 4, I have tabulated the estimated price and income elasticities of demand from the studies that have been discussed in this section. However, of the studies that focus explicitly on local use, only the estimates obtained by Waverman are included in the table. Pavarini's model does not readily allow for the calculation of a price elasticity, and I have omitted Beauvais' result because of the problem, noted earlier, with his definition of the average price of a local call. Dynamic models, usually of the Houthakker-Taylor or Koyck distributed-lag variety, are employed in all of the studies, so that both short-run and long-run elasticities have been estimated.

The estimated price elasticities are typically small, which is to be expected. The price elasticity for local use should be expected to be larger than the price elasticity for access, but it should not be too much larger because of the importance attached to the making and receiving of local calls. There is only one estimated price elasticity in the table that seems seriously open to question, namely, the Dobell *et al.* long-run price elasticity using data for

elasticities estimated in these studies are tabulated in Table 4.

[35] Since in most exchanges local calls are free (not counting the opportunity cost of a caller's time), the demand for local service should more properly be interpreted as primarily a demand for access.

TABLE 4

Estimates of price and income elasticities of the demand for the local use and local service

Type of Demand	Service	Price Elasticity		Income Elasticity		Type of Data
		SR	LR	SR	LR	
Residential						
Dobell et al.	basic	NE	NE	0.42	2.38	TS: A, Ontario and Quebec
NYT (1976a)	basic + terminal equipment	-0.10	-0.14	0.10	0.14	TS: Q, New York
NYT (1976a)	AMU	-0.35	NE	0.25	NE	TS: Q, New York
SNET (1977)[a]	basic	-0.02	-0.21	NC	0.16	TS: Q, Connecticut
Residential–Business						
Davis et al.	basic	-0.21	-0.27	0.25	0.33	TS: A, Bell System
Dobell et al.	basic	-0.20	-0.70	0.38	2.16	TS: A, Canada
NYT (1976b)	basic	-0.03	-0.17	0.07	0.40	TS: Q, New York
NYT (1976b)	AMU	-0.17	NE	0.29	0.67	TS: Q, New York
Waverman	basic	-0.27	-0.38	0.23	1.25	TS: A, Sweden
Business						
Dobell et al.	basic	NE	NE	0.99	1.55	TS: A, Ontario and Quebec
SNET (1977)[a]	basic	-0.03	-0.07	NE	NE	TS: Q, Connecticut
NYT (1976a)	basic + terminal equipment	-0.08	-0.15	0.10	0.19	TS: Q, New York
NYT (1976a)	AMU	-0.18	NE	0.13	0.24	TS: Q, New York

[a] The long run in the SNET study refers to the elasticities calculated after the lapse of one year.

Symbols: TS: time series; AMU: additional message units; CS: cross-section; NE: not estimated; A: annual; NC: not calculated; Q: quarterly.

all of Canada. The estimated value of -0.7 seems implausibly high, and is also completely out of line with the value of 0 found in their residence and business equations for Ontario and Quebec.

Apart from the Dobell *et al.* equation, the estimated elasticities in the equations for local service (in which price-deflated local revenue is the dependent variable) are generally in line with the price elasticities for access that are tabulated in Table 1. This provides support for the earlier observation that the demand for local service is primarily to be identified with the demand for access. The most interesting entry in the table, in my opinion, is Waverman's study, since it is the only one that focuses explicitly on the demand for local use. The price elasticity is estimated to be -0.27 in the short-run and -0.38 in the long-run. While I do not know at this point whether these elasticities are too large, too small, or just right in absolute value, they are larger than the price elasticities for access, and this provides some reassurance.[36]

The estimates of income elasticity in Table 4 are much more varied than the estimates of price elasticity. Most of the estimated long-run income elasticities are less than 0.5, but the three equations of Dobell *et al.* all have long-run values in excess of 1.5. Once again, I feel that Waverman's results are to be given the most weight because of the explicit focus on local use. Waverman's estimate of the long-run income elasticity is 1.25, so that the estimates of Dobell *et al.* may be closer to the mark than those of the other studies.[37]

III. Long-Haul (Interstate) Toll Demand

We now turn to a discussion of toll demand, which constitutes by far the largest component of the empirical literature on telephone demand. The format will be to discuss interstate and intrastate toll separately. In classifying the literature on toll demand, I have defined interstate toll to include all studies of interstate toll in the United States and all studies of toll demand within national boundaries in other countries. Although the distinction between interstate and intrastate toll is artificial from the point of view of demand,[38] it

---

[36] These words were first written in mid-1978. The absolute and relative sizes of local price elasticities in light of current research is discussed in Chapter 11.

[37] Since Waverman's equation for local use is embedded in an access/use framework, the long-run thus allows for a change in income to affect the number of telephones. The estimated income elasticity in Waverman's equation for the number of telephones is 0.56. The value of 1.25 is then obtained [from the coefficients in equation (9) as $[0.228 + 1.19 (.056)/(1 - 0.286)]$].

[38] What matters is price and length-of-haul, not that a state boundary is crossed.

has been retained because it assists materially in organizing the literature.[39] Only the most common form of toll service, namely, message toll service (or MTS), will be discussed in this section.

1. Interstate (Long-Haul) Toll Demand

The literature that we shall review under interstate toll includes AT&T Long Lines (Betteridge 1973), Davis *et al.* (1973), Deschamps (1974), Dobell *et al.* (1972), Khadem (1973a), Kwok, Lee, and Pearce (1975), Larsen and McCleary (1970), Pousette (1976), Rash (1972), Waverman (1974), and Wert (1976). As with local-service demand, our procedure will be to describe briefly the main features of these studies and to tabulate the estimates of the price and income elasticities of demand. Five studies will be reviewed in detail.

A wide range of models and data are represented in the interstate toll studies. The extreme of both size and disaggregation is provided by the pioneering Long Distance Interstate (LDI) model of AT&T Long Lines, which disaggregates toll volume to 6750 different cells and offers the facility for predicting the impact on each of a change in the interstate toll schedule. Indeed, in comparison with the LDI model, the rest of the models in the literature are highly aggregated. The level of aggregation employed in the other studies is as follows: Davis *et al.*, Deschamps, and Pousette all focus entirely on total toll volume. Dobell *et al.*, Larsen and McCleary, and Waverman estimate models for residence and business customers separately, as well as for total toll. Finally, Khadem, Rash, and Wert restrict their attention to residential customers. Larsen and McCleary use cross-sectional data in estimation exclusively, while Deschamps and Wert use both time-series and cross-sectional data. The remaining studies all rely entirely on time-series data.

In general, the models that have been used for toll demand are similar to those that have been used for local service, and two broad classes of models can be identified. The first class approaches the dependence of toll volume on the stock of telephones in a distributed-lag framework. With these models, the stock of telephones appears in the analysis only implicitly. The models of Dobell *et al.*, Khadem, and Rash fall into this category. With the second class of models, the stock of telephones appears explicitly, either as a deflator of toll volume or directly as an independent variable. The models of Davis *et al.*, Pousette, and Waverman are of this type.[40]

---

[39] Most of the literature on toll demand relates to intrastate toll, which, in great part, reflects the widespread use after the mid-1970s of intrastate toll demand models in rate filings before state regulatory commissions.

[40] The models of Davis *et al.*, and Waverman employ a distributed-lag framework as well.

Most of the focus in the interstate studies is on estimating price and income elasticities of demand for rather broadly defined customer classes. Nevertheless, some interesting twists are to be found. Wert, for example, is concerned with estimating the impact of day/night differentials in price on the day/night distribution of toll traffic. His conclusion is that, on the whole, given the time span investigated, changes in day/night price differentials lead to only minor shifts in traffic. Larsen and McCleary, on the other hand, are concerned with modeling interstate toll demand on a point-to-point basis. The dependent variable in their analysis is the directional traffic between state pairs. Finally, Deschamps focuses on toll demand in Belgium, using traffic volume by mileage bands as the dependent variable. As we shall see below, Deschamps' study is especially interesting in the way it treats price.

The estimated price and income elasticities of demand obtained in the interstate studies are tabulated in Table 5. The elasticities listed for the LDI model are calculated with reference to a typical long-distance interstate call. As mentioned earlier, Pousette does not present sufficient information to calculate the elasticities implied in his toll equation. The elasticities appearing in Table 5 are, on the whole, fairly substantial, and this is true for price as well as for income. Toll price is missing from only one model in the table (the business equation of Dobell *et al.*), while income is omitted from two (Deschamps and Larsen-McCleary). In general, the evidence otherwise suggests long-run elasticities of at least 1 for income and in the neighborhood of -1 for price. The estimated price elasticities are substantially smaller than 1 (in absolute value) in the LDI model and in the residential-business equations of Deschamps for Belgium and Kwok *et al.* for Ontario and Quebec. However, Deschamps' model is static rather than dynamic – a dynamic model would almost certainly yield a larger long-run price elasticity – and Kwok *et al.* find much larger price elasticities using TransCanada data.[41] In view of the extensive and generally successful forecasting experience of the LDI model, the LDI price elasticity of -0.4 to -0.5 has to be taken seriously. However, as will be discussed below, most of the parameters in the LDI model are underidentified and have been estimated on the basis of simulation and expert judgment.

As noted earlier, five toll demand studies have been selected for detailed review, namely, Deschamps, Larsen and McCleary, the LDI model of AT&T Long Lines, Pousette, and Waverman. The LDI model will be discussed first.

Allowance is thereby made for inertia in adjusting the volume of toll calling, for a given stock of telephones, to a change in price or income.

[41] The price elasticity estimated by Wert is also fairly small. However, the dependent variable in Wert's analysis is the day time proportion of toll volume, and the price elasticity estimated is with respect to day/night price differentials.

TABLE 5

Estimates of price and income elasticities of demand for long-haul toll calls for the United States and other countries

Study and Type of Demand	Dependent Variable	Price Elasticity		Income Elasticity		Type of Data
		Short-Run	Long-Run	Short-Run	Long-Run	
Residential						
Dobell et al. (1972)	PDR	-0.30	-1.90	0.20	1.27	TS: A, Ontario and Quebec
Khadem (1973)	PDR	-1.28	-2.58	0.40	0.84	TS: Q, Trans-Canada
Larsen and McCleary (1970)	messages	NE	-1.01	NE	NE	CS: M, States
Rash (1972)	PDR	[a]	-0.94	[a]	1.53	TS: M, Ontario and Quebec
Waverman (1974)	PDR/T	NE	-1.16	NE	1.03	TS: A, Ontario and Quebec
Wert (1976)	daytime calls (%)	(-0.29)		(1.06)		TS-CS: M, Bell System
Business						
Dobell et al. (1972)	PDR		NE	0.19	2.76	TS: A, Ontario and Quebec
Larsen and McCleary (1970)	messages	NE	-0.98	NE		CS: M, States
Waverman (1974)	PDR/T	-1.20	-1.35	0.45	0.51	TS: A, Ontario and Quebec
Residential–Business						
AT&T (LDI)	messages	NE	-0.4 to -0.5	NE	≈ 1.00	TS: Bell System
Davis et al. (1973)	PDR	-0.88	-1.03	0.83	0.96	TS: Q, Bell System
Deschamps (1974)	messages	(-0.24)		NE		TS: M, Belgium
Dobell et al. (1972)	PDR	-0.11	-2.57	0.08	1.90	TS: A, Canada
Kwok, Lee and Pearce (1975)	messages	-0.18	-0.41	0.51	1.15	TS: Q, Ontario and Quebec
Kwok, Lee and Pearce (1975)	messages	-1.70	-2.71	0.83	1.32	TS: Q, Trans-Canada
Waverman (1974)	PDR/T	-0.72	-1.12	1.00	1.56	TS: A, Great Britain
Waverman (1974)	messages/T	-0.41	-0.72	0.56	0.99	TS: A, Great Britain
Waverman (1974)	pulses/T	-0.51	-1.08	0.23	0.50	TS: A, Sweden
Waverman (1974)	messages/T	-0.29	-0.58	0.19	0.38	TS: A, Sweden

[a] Cannot be calculated.

Symbols: PDR: price-deflated revenue; M: monthly; T: number of main-station telephones; TS: time series; A: annual;

Development of the LDI model was begun in April 1966, and an operational version was available by midsummer 1967.[42] The model is a computerized mathematical model that simulates the generation of domestic message toll service (MTS) messages, conversation, minutes, and revenues. The market considered by the model is interstate MTS messages within the forty-eight contiguous states.

The LDI model simulates one month's (October) MTS message volume in great detail. The primary objective in developing the model was to provide management with a "flexible, consistent, accurate, and improvable system" for estimating the impact of a wide range of possible MTS rate schedules on the domestic interstate MTS market. Secondary objectives of the model included evaluating the impact of nonrate factors on MTS volumes and the composition of volumes by time-of-day, type-of-traffic, and so on. However, the secondary objectives were given weight in developing the model only to the extent that they were consistent with the primary objective. The disaggregation in the model is as follows:

1. Three customer classes (business, residential, and coin);
2. Fifteen lengths-of-haul (starting with one to eight miles, then nine to thirteen, fourteen to eighteen, and so on, up to 2,301 to 3,000 miles);
3. Two types of call (station-to-station and person-to-person);
4. Three types of day (weekdays, Saturday, and Sunday);
5. Twenty-five times of day (twenty-three one-hour periods and two half-hour periods).[43]

The model is thus seen to include 6,750 sectors (or cells). Each of the cells is postulated to have a "message generator" equation of the form

$$M_i = a_0 \left[X_{1i}^{a_1} X_{2i}^{a_2} X_{3i}^{a_3} X_{4i}^{a_4} a_6^{x_{6t}} a_8^{x_{8t}} X_{7i} \right] + X_{3i}^{a_3} \sum X_{60ij}. \qquad (35)$$

In this equation,

predicted messages in a sector of the market for a given October (M_i) are initially defined as being equal to a multiplicative function of several variables. On the right-hand side of the equation, each of the X's represents the value of a variable for a certain October (i). The appropriate weighting for that variable in that sector of the market is indicated by the

---

[42] The full name of the model is the Long Lines' Long Distance Interstate MTS Demand Model. The development of the LDI model was carried on under the direction of Robert Auray, with major contributions from Kendall Murphy and Howard Whitmore. The discussion that follows is based upon the description of the LDI model presented in Betteridge (1973). While the LDI model has been superseded at AT&T by more up-to-date econometric models, its impact on modeling telephone demand was sufficient to make its study still relevant.

[43] The divided hour is 4:00–5:00 A.M.

associated coefficient (a). In the equation X_1 is the military variable, X_2 is the economic variable, X_3 is the price (stimulation) variable, X_4 is a composite of the competitive effects plus shocks variable, X_6 and X_8 are representations of time, and X_7 is the equivalent business days (or trading days) variable. The symbol a_0 represents messages in that sector of the market during a base period (October 1960). Observe, therefore, that the model defines estimated messages in period "i" in terms of *changes from the 1960 situation*, due to the fact that time, rates, economic conditions and other enumerated factors may be different than the values prevailing in 1960. All variables in October 1960 are defined such that in October 1960 their value is 1.000; that is, each variable is measured in ratio or index form, with October 1960 equal to 1.000. (Betteridge 1973, pp. 18–20, italics in original.)

The second term on the right-hand side in (36), $X_{3i}^{a_3} \Sigma X_{60ij}$, represents the cross-elasticity, or the volume of messages "shifted or reclassified" from one cell to another when there is a change in price.[44] The summation in this term is over 150 separate cells, and reflects the fact that the model allows for shifting or reclassification from potentially 150 other sectors of the market into the given sector (literally only 149, excluding the given sector). The 150 sectors include the three groupings by type of day, two groupings by type of call, and twenty-five groupings by time of day. The possibility of shifting between mileage bands or class of customer is excluded.

The variable X_{60ij} thus represents the number of messages shifted from the jth cell to the ith cell as a result of a change in price in the ith or jth cell. The sum ΣX_{60ij} then measures the total number of messages shifted into ith cell from the 149 other cells. This total is then adjusted for price effects (i.e., multiplied by $X_{3i}^{a_3}$) just as if the shifted messages had been originally included in the sector. The model then assumes that when messages are shifted on balance from one sector to another, the customers shifting will generate additional calls (if the new cell has experienced a rate reduction) in the same proportion as those generated by customers already in that cell.

The value of X_{60ij} is determined according to the following "shift and reclassification" models:

$$X_{60ij} = \left[a_{0j} X_1^{a_{1j}} X_2^{a_{2j}} X_3^{a_{3j}} X_4 a_{6j}^{x_6} a_{8j}^{x_8} X_7 \right] \left[X_{5ji}^{a_{5ji}} - 1 \right]. \tag{36}$$

The point of departure in the model is the number of messages that initially

---

[44] As used by the LDI authors, "shift" means the rate-response transfer of calls from one hour of the day to another or from one day of the week to another, while "reclassification" denotes the transfer of calls from one type of traffic to another type (person-to-person to station-to-station, for example).

exist in cell j. This number is given by the first expression in brackets, and is simply the first term n the "message generator" [i.e., equation (35)] for cell j. The second expression in brackets measures the proportion of cell j's messages that are shifted to cell i. The variable X_{5ji} in this expression represents the ratio of the rate index (1960 = 100) in cell j to the rate index (1960 = 100) in cell i. If the rate indexes in the two cells are the same, X_{5ji} is equal to one, and there will be no shift of messages. However, if the indexes differ, messages will shift between the two cells, with the proportion being shifted depending on the value of the cross-elasticity a_{5ji}.

The cross-price elasticity between cells j and i is a composite quantity that is assumed to depend, among other things, on the distance in time between cells j and i and the "relative desirability" of calling at the time in cell i as opposed to the time in cell j. Specifically, it is assumed that

$$a_{5ji} = k_1 \frac{D_{ji}}{(1 + W_{ji})k_2},$$ (37)

where:

k_1 = propensity to shift *anywhere* from cell j

W_{ji} = distance in time between cells j and i

k_2 = scaling factor for $(1 + W_{ji})$

D_{ji} = relative desirability of calling at the time
of cell i versus the time of cell j.

Before describing the procedure by which the parameters in equation (35) to (37) were adduced, several variables in equation (35) remain to be discussed. Economic activity (X_2) is measured either by real disposable personal income (DPI) from the National Income Accounts (used for residence and coin markets) or by a weighted average of DPI and the Index of Industrial Activity constructed by AT&T. Each of these variables is measured as a ratio to its underlying trend. The price variable (X_3) is measured as a weighted average toll price for messages in a given market sector, defined as the charge to the customer plus applicable federal excise tax. X_3 for period i is then expressed as the toll price for i divided by the toll price for October 1960.[45] Substitute telecommunications service (X_4) is represented by a composite variable that reflects the impact of WATS and private line offerings and nonrecurring "shocks" on business MTS volume.

The variables X_6 and X_8 represent the "basic growth" in a sector. Specifically, the coefficient a_6 represents the growth rate of the given sector of the

---

[45] X_3 is not deflated by the CPI. The effects of general inflation are reflected in a trend term.

market prior to 1960, and a_8 represents the growth rate of that sector after 1960.[46] The military variable, X_1, is included in order to avoid confusing the impact of message volumes of the Korean War manpower buildup with the impact of the concurrent surge in economic activity. Specifically,

> when a substantial buildup in the armed forces occurs, it creates a new demand for telephone communication which did not previously exist. Large numbers of men are moved to locations remote from their former residences, leaving behind a number of relatives and friends with whom communication is desirable. (Betteridge 1973, p. 12.)

Estimates of the number of messages for a sector from equation (35) are converted to revenue by multiplying by the average price of a call in the sector. However, since most rate structures involve a fixed charge for a specified initial period of time plus an additional charge for each subsequent period of the call, the average price of a call clearly depends on the distribution of calls with respect to duration. In general, these distributions vary over time, and this variation has to be taken into account. Specifically, it is assumed that the distribution of calls by length of conversation is lognormal. The parameters of the distribution – namely, the mean and standard deviation – were then estimated as coefficients in a least-squares regression equation using data for October. Equations were estimated for each sector for each of the Octobers for which data were available. From these, it was possible to estimate how the length-of-conversation distributions vary over time.[47]

The length-of-conversation distributions are used to calculate for each sector, the weighted average number of overtime periods for the "typical" call in the sector. This number is multiplied by the appropriate rate per overtime period, and to this is added the initial fixed charge. The resulting average price of a message in a sector is then multiplied by the number of messages for the sector estimated from equation (35) to yield an estimate of the revenue that is generated in the sector.

Because of the large number of cells, values for the parameters in equation (35) and (37) had to be obtained in stages. Initial estimates of the parameters in equation (35) were derived by conventional multiple regression methods using aggregate time-series data for Octobers over the period 1948–1965. The

---

[46] This "split trend" approach is included in order to reflect a noticeable change in growth rates, particularly between station and person traffic, which occurred around 1960 in most sectors of the market. (See Betteridge 1973, pp. 20–21).)

[47] The results indicated that the mean lengths of calls vary with time, but that standard deviations do not. Trend rates of change in sector mean lengths-of-conversation were calculated from the estimated October means, and these were used in extrapolating the sector distributions forward or backward in time, taking October 1965 as the base.

coefficients obtained from these regressions were then used as benchmarks in a series of simulations of the disaggregated data, from which estimates of "shift and reclassification" effects were obtained. In this stage, time-series data which had been aggregated in the first stage were once again disaggregated into their original components (by type of call and rate period). The disaggregated model was then "calibrated" in a simulation framework. The coefficients estimated in the first stage served as points of departure in this calibration. Deviations of the actual number of messages from their simulated values were taken as estimates of shift and reclassification. From these estimates of shift and reclassification for 1963 and 1965, initial estimates of the parameters in equations (36) and (29) were derived.[48] Repeated simulation, with the residuals from a just completed simulation being used to modify the parameters used in the next simulation, eventually yielded the "final" model.

The parameter estimates obtained by this procedure can be briefly summarized as follows:[49]

1. Price elasticity coefficients [a_3 in equation (35)] range from about -0.10 to about -0.70. Small negative values are typical for short-haul, low-rate traffic, with progressively larger negative values being found for longer lengths of haul. Another generally consistent pattern is that the price elasticities for daytime traffic are noticeably smaller than for evening traffic.

2. The coefficients for economic activity [a_2 in equation (35)] vary from close to zero to as high as 2.5. Low values are associated with short-haul traffic, and higher values are generally associated with longer haul traffic.

3. A wide range of results were found for the "pure" growth rates [a_6 and a_8 in equation (35)]. With an average growth of about 10 percent per year for the period over which the model was calibrated, individual sector growth rates vary from -5 percent per year to over 30 percent per year. Again, there is a noticeable tendency for the coefficients to increase with length of haul. Growth rates of business and residence sectors are roughly equal, but both are consistently higher, other things being equal, than those for coin traffic.

---

[48] This was done initially at high levels of aggregation (e.g., daytime traffic versus nighttime traffic; or station-to-station traffic versus person-to-person traffic) to obtain estimates of total shift/reclassification. Then the data were further disaggregated to allocate and analyze the distribution of the shift by successively smaller and smaller time periods. Using the resulting detailed distribution or allocation of shifted and reclassified messages based on 1963 and 1965 experience, repeated simulations were made using the shift/reclassification model (see Charts 5 and 6) to develop coefficients for this model which approximated the actual distributions of "shift and reclassification" (Betteridge 1973, pp. 41–42).

[49] See Betteridge (1973, pp. 42–45).

4. The coefficient a_5 in the shift and reclassification model [equation (36)] is determined by the coefficients in equation (37). The "propensity to shift" coefficient [k_1 in equation (37)] varies between -0.002 and -0.65. *Ceteris paribus*, business k_1 coefficients tend to be smaller (in absolute value) than corresponding resident k_1 's and the latter tend to be lower than those for coin customers. Moreover, the absolute value of k_1 tends to increase with length of haul – that is, the longer the haul (and the larger the cost of the call), the greater is the propensity to shift the call. There does not appear to be any difference between the propensity to shift (i.e., to change the time of calling but not the class of call) and the propensity to reclassify from person-to-person to station-to-station.

5. The final coefficient determining the value of a_5 is k_2, the scaling factor for "waiting time" in equation (37). The values for k_2 range from 0.6 to 1.2. In general, the value of k_2 decreases as length of haul increases, and, other things being constant, are larger for business than for either residence or coin.[50]

During the 1970s, the LDI model was the most detailed model of toll demand in existence, and, according to its proprietors it fulfilled its mission well. After becoming operational, the model quickly came to be relied on by AT&T Long Lines and AT&T management as a tool of internal analysis and planning. Also, the model was used in rate filings with the FCC, as well as in the number of intrastate toll filings before state regulatory commissions. The simulation framework of the LDI model allowed it in certain circumstances to be easily modified without throwing the model out of balance, and this was done occasionally in order to take into account breaks in underlying structure or to adjust parameters in sectors in which the model was not tracking well.[51]

However, the strengths of the LDI model – namely, immense detail and a simulation framework that allows parameters to be modified without difficulty – are also it weaknesses. The detail available in the LDI model provides temptation for the model to be employed in circumstances for which it was not designed. Its use in intrastate toll filings are cases in point. The parameters of the LDI model were calibrated to interstate toll data for the continental United States. The LDI model is therefore a model of interstate toll demand for the entire continental United States, rather than being a model of intrastate toll demand for a specific state. And, while it is unlikely (at least in my opinion) that, *ceteris paribus*, intrastate and interstate toll demands are markedly

---

[50] The LDI model authors refer to k_2 as the "propensity not to wait," since the higher its value, the lower the value of a_5. Thus, *ceteris paribus*, the larger the propensity not to wait, the lower the propensity to shift or reclassify.

[51] See Betteridge (1973, pp. 47–49).

different, toll demand per se may very well differ between states or regions of the country.

If this is the case, then the structure reflected in the LDI model represents, in effect, a mean for the forty-eight contiguous states as a whole, but will not, in general, mirror the toll demand behavior for any particular state.[52] That this is a real possibility rendered the LDI model vulnerable in intrastate toll findings. The LDI model was also vulnerable in regulatory proceedings because of its simulation framework. Since the parameters in the model are calibrated by trial and error, rather than being estimated by econometric techniques, the model is open to charges that it is ad hoc and unscientific.[53] I want to emphasize, however, that these remarks are not directed at the integrity of the model. Given the disaggregation that was desired, there was no way to obtain values of the parameters other than the technique that was used, since the data available could not support estimation by econometric methods.[54] Still, science and the realities of the marketplace required that the LDI model eventually be replaced by a model whose parameter values are arrived at by more objective procedures.

The next model to be discussed is Deschamps (1974). Deschamps' focus is on the demand for toll calls in Belgium during the period 1961–1969. The data employed consist of observations on toll traffic within and between districts of forty districts for one day for each nine years, 14,400 observations in all. Deschamps estimated his models in the variance-components framework pioneered by Balestra and Nerlove (1966). The dependent variable in the analysis is the number of calls between district i and district j at time t. The logarithm of this quantity is then related to:

$D_k, k = 1, \ldots, 10$:   a dummy taking the value of 1 if the distance in kms between i and j lies in the interval $(10(k-1)), 20k)$;[55]

N_{it}, N_{jt}:   the logarithm of the number of subscribers in district i or j at time t;

R_{it}:   the logarithm of the income per capita in district i at time t;

---

[52] That toll demand is homogeneous across states or regions is a hypothesis that needs testing.

[53] Unscientific in the sense that the parameter values finally arrived at are probably not reproducible, even by the same investigators.

[54] Calibration of the LDI model illustrates in an instructive way how expert judgment and limited data can join in estimating underidentified parameters.

P_{ij}:	an index of sociological proximity, defined as the sum of the number of commuters from i to j and from j to i, and dividing by the aggregated population of districts i and j;[56]
L_{ij}:	a dummy variable taking the value of 1 if districts i and j speak the same language, 0 otherwise;
t:	a time trend;
$T_k, k = 1, \ldots, 9$:	a dummy variable taking the value of 1 in sample year 60 + k, 0 otherwise;
Q_{ij}:	a dummy variable taking the value of 1 if $i = j$, 0 otherwise.

The price variables considered by Deschamps were defined as follows:

P_{ijt}^1:	lump price per call, where applicable, 0 otherwise;
P_{ijt}^2:	the price of an additional minute beyond the first;
P_{ijt}^3:	the minimum price per call, where applicable, 0 otherwise;
P_{ijt}^4:	$\max(0, P_{ijt}^3 - P_{ijt}^2)$;
P_{ijt}^5:	the logarithm of a price index obtained by taking a weighted mean of the consumer costs of calls falling in different length classes (with weights independent of i, j, t);
P_{ijt}^6:	the price of the first minute of call (all i, j, t).

In selecting these definitions of price, Deschamps is clearly aware of the fact that a telephone call is charged for on a two- or multi-part tariff.[57] The hypotheses considered by Deschamps are as follows:

One may assume that (a) the length of a call is somewhat beyond the caller's control once the connection is established, and that (b) the marginal utility of the next minute is not known with certainty by the caller. If this is so, it would seem appropriate to assume that the caller decides, before lifting the receiver, whether he will make the call or not; this on the basis of the mathematical expectation of the call's length, from which an expected cost can be derived. Quantities demanded here are numbers of calls. This leads to the inclusion of a *price index* (weighted mean) in the regressors.

One may instead conduct a traditional analysis in terms of the marginal utility of an additional minute and its marginal cost. This leads to a specification where the *price of an additional minute* appears as an independent

---

[55] Distance is calculated as the distance between the towns (or cities) giving names to the districts.

[55] This matrix was computed from data in the 1961 Census.

[57] Cf. Chapter 3, Section I.

variable, along with the eventual *fixed part of the tariff.* The quality of service could also be introduced as an explanatory variable, since an increase in the average number of attempts has formally the same effect as an increase in the connection charge. (Deschamps 1974, pp. 2–3, italics added.)

Deschamps examined eight different specifications of his model. For each specification, the 14,400 observations in the data set were "stacked," and then estimated by the variance-components technique of Balestra and Nerlove. The eight specifications considered by Deschamps involved alternative representations of toll price, distance, and time. The distance dummy variables, D_k, were included in the model directly and also interacted with the number of subscribers in the district called. Time was represented by the linear trend, t, and the dummy variables, T_k. The best results obtained with distance interacted with the number of subscribers in the called district and the time dummy variable.

Deschamps tested five different price formulations, namely:

I. P^1, P^2, and P^3
II. P^1, P^2, and P^4
III. P^2 and P^6
IV. $Q_{ij}P^6$, $\bar{Q}P^6$, and P^2
V. P^5.

Formulations I–III reflect the multi-part tariff pricing of a telephone call; of these, specification II is most in keeping with the Deschamps' second hypothesis (and with the discussion in Section I of Chapter 3). Use of the price index in specification IV, in contrast, reflects the view expressed in Deschamps' first hypothesis. Finally, specification V is intended as a limited test of the hypothesis that the price elasticity of demand varies with distance.

The results obtained by Deschamps can be briefly summarized as follows:[58]

1. Specifications I and II are practically equivalent. Both yield better results, although not drastically so, than specification III. "The price the consumer has to pay for the first minute indeed appears to be the major and most reliable determinant of the number of calls. This can be explained by the high percentage of short calls, a phenomenon apparent even when the price of an additional minute is zero."
2. The sign for the coefficient of $Q_{ij}p^6$ in specification IV is positive. Deschamps notes that this variable relates to intradistrict calls, varies

---

[58] See Deschamps (1974, pp. 15–16).

almost exclusively with duration, and therefore probably does not display sufficient independent variation to identify its coefficient.[59]

3. Specification V gives the best results of all.[60] However, as Deschamps mentions, this may be due, at least in part, to the fact that p^5 is included as a logarithm.

Deschamps' results for specifications II and IV are presented in Table 6. In both of these equations, distance is represented by the distance dummy variable directly, rather than interacted with the number of subscribers in the district called. Also, time is represented by the linear time trend, t, instead of by the time dummy variables, T_k. Finally, income is absent altogether. In the models in which income is included, the sign is always negative and statistically insignificant.

The most important predictors, it will be noted, are the dummy variables for distance, the number of subscribers, and whether or not the districts in question have a common language. The "sociological proximity" index (P_{ij}) is also highly significant. This variable and the dummy variable for common language (L_{ij}) are clearly very closely associated with the "community of interest" of the callers. Note, also, that the elasticity with respect to the number of subscribers in the calling district is smaller than the elasticity of the number of subscribers in the district called (0.75 versus 0.99). Deschamps mentions that this may reflect the presence of coin telephone, since calls can be made at coin stations, but, in general, are not received at them.

Although the price variables in specification II are not as strong statistically as the distance, system size, or community-of-interest variables, signs are right, and the t-ratio for P^1, which represents the fixed charge for the first minute is greater than 3 (in absolute value). In specification IV, in which toll price is represented by a price index, price is highly significant. But Deschamps notes that it may be that the superior performance of P^5 vis-à-vis P^1, P^2, and P^4 reflects nothing more than the fact that P^5 is included as a logarithm. Clearly, it would have been of interest to have estimated specification II with P^1, P^2, and P^4 in appropriate logarithmic form.

We now turn to the study of Larsen and McCleary (1970), which focuses on point-to-point demand for interstate toll calls. Larsen and McCleary would appear to be the first to model interstate toll demand on a point-to-point basis. Their study predates the study of Deschamps, which we just discussed and which also focuses on point-to-point traffic, by several years, and, in all

---

[59] It is not clear why Deschamps did not test some models in which price was interacted directly with distance (unless, of course, distance and price are completely collinear).

[60] The price elasticity from this equation is the one tabulated in Table 5.

TABLE 6

Two equations from Deschamps' study of demand for calls in Belgium

Independent Variable	Specification II		Specification IV	
	Coefficient	t-ratio	Coefficient	t-ratio
constant	-3.62	-20.49	-3.51	-20.95
D_2	-0.98	-14.54	-0.92	-15.01
D_3	-1.64	-23.03	-1/52	-23.34
D_4	-1.97	-27.57	-1.84	-28.06
D_5	-2.18	-30.43	-2.05	-31.15
D_6	-2.22	-30.82	-2.10	-31.58
D_7	-2.34	-31.99	-2.21	-32.93
D_8	-2.38	-32.19	-2.25	-33.19
D_9	-2.40	-31.62	-2.27	-32.69
D_{10}	-2.42	-32.16	-2.29	-33.25
N_{it}	0.75	19.29	0.75	20.36
N_{jt}	0.99	75.18	0.99	83.49
t	-0.0073	-4.56	-0.097	-8.81
L_{ij}	0.38	27.81	0.38	30.64
C_{ij}	0.047	1.16	0.41	1.13
P_{ij}	1.58	6.67	1.47	6.89
P^1	-0.0031	-3.10	–	–
P^2	-0.0047	-1.68	–	–
P^4	-0.0053	-1.83	–	–
P^5	–	–	-0.24	-9.05
R^2	0.643		0.680	

[a] The dependent variable in both equations is the logarithm of the number of calls from district i to j.

The dependent variables are defined in the text.

likelihood, was unknown to Deschamps.[61]

Larsen and McCleary are concerned with explaining the volume of toll traffic flowing between individual pairs of states in the continental United

[61] Discussions with people at Bell Canada reveal that point-to-point toll demand modeling had also been undertaken at Bell Canada during the period in question. Point-to-point demand received considerable attention in Chapters 6 and 9.

States. Their procedure is to relate the volume of toll calls between state i and state j to income, price, and variables representing the "community of interest" between the states. A number of variables were considered as measures of community of interest, but the quantity receiving the most attention is the volume of mail (first-class and air mail) from state i to state j.

The model postulated by Larsen and McCleary has the form

$$\ln V_{ij} = + \ln M_{ij} + \ln P_{ij} + \ln Y_i + u_{ij}, \tag{38}$$

where

$$V_{ij} = \text{ the number of toll calls from state } i \text{ to } j$$

$$M_{ij} = \text{ mail volume (first-class and air) from state } i \text{ to } j$$

$$P_{ij} = \text{ the price of a call from state } i \text{ to } j$$

$$Y_i = \text{ income per capita in state } i$$

$$u_{ij} = \text{ random error term.}$$

The data used in estimation consists of observations on directional traffic for all distinct state pairs for the forty-eight contiguous states and the District of Columbia. The model is estimated for business and residential traffic separately, as well as for total traffic consisting of business plus residence plus coin. Data were available for two four-month periods, October 1966 through January 1967 and March through June 1968.[62] Two definitions of price are considered, the average *initial* charge for a call between state i and state j and the average *total* charge for a call between the two states.[63]

The major findings of Larsen and McCleary are as follows:

1. The equations for business and residence customers are very similar, although the fit for residence is inferior to that for business.
2. Mail volume is the most significant predictor. For all practical purposes, toll volume and mail volume are proportional.
3. The coefficient of income is negative and significantly different from zero. The authors are unable to offer any explanation for this apparent anomaly.
4. Price is also highly significant statistically. Average total charge yields smaller estimated elasticities and somewhat lower R^2's than average initial price. With average initial price, the estimated price elasticity is in the neighborhood of -1.

[62] Estimates of V_{ij} for these two periods were obtained from the Message Analysis Sampling Plan (MASP).

[63] See Larsen and McCleary (1970, pp. 10–12) for definitions of these variables.

5. There appears to be some inhomogeneity between bordering state pairs and nonbordering state pairs. The model appears to be most applicable to bordering state pairs. Washington, D.C., because of the large number of government calls is a definite outlier.

The following equation for total toll traffic using October 1966 data on all state pairs and average initial price typifies the results obtained by Larsen and McCleary:

$$\ln V_{ij} = \underset{(95.71)}{2.01} + \underset{(127.5)}{1.02} \ln M_{ij} - \underset{(-25.95)}{1.09} \ln P_{ij} \qquad R^2 = 0.912 \; (39)$$

Although it is not referred to as such, it is clear that the model used by Larsen and McCleary can be interpreted as a gravity model. "Mass" is measured by the volume of mail and income (although income has the wrong sign) and "distance" by price. Noteworthy, too, is the emphasis that is given to the community of interest of the calling parties. Larsen and McCleary measure community of interest by mail volume, and, given its importance as a predictor [cf. the t-ratio of $\ln M$ in equation (39)], the authors must be applauded for their choice.

All in all, the Larsen-McCleary study must be considered a good first effort at modeling interstate toll demand on a point-to-point basis, and it is unfortunate that it has not received a wider readership. Nevertheless, the study has some limitations. The perverse importance of income requires explanation, as does also (at least in my opinion) the weak showing of the number of telephones.[64] Preferably, too, toll price should be represented by the average charge for overtime periods, as well as by the average initial charge. Finally, in using state pairs as the unit of observation, the Larsen-McCleary analysis is at a very high level of aggregation. Among other things, the notion of community of interest is clearly much more ambiguous for a state than for a city or town.[65]

The final study to be discussed is Waverman (1974). Waverman estimates equations for toll (or trunk) demand in Canada, Great Britain, and Sweden,

---

[64] The culprit in both cases may be mail volume in that mail volume may be a good proxy for income and system size, as well as being an excellent measure of community of interest. Larsen and McCleary do not include the correlation matrix of the variables, so it is not possible to deduce the extent of multicollinearity among the predictors.

[65] Paul Brandon has pointed out that there will be a bias in the estimate of the price elasticity in the Larsen-McCleary study if there is a residual effect of distance that is not reflected in the mail volume. Both the probability of sending a letter and the probability of making a call will decrease with distance. However, if these probabilities do not decrease at the same rate, there will be a residual distance effect that, since the price of a call increases monotonically with distance, will be reflected in the estimate of price elasticity.

using dynamic models of the Houthakker-Taylor variety. Time-series data are utilized in all cases. For Canada, equations are estimated for total inland trunk demand for deflated toll revenue and the number of calls as dependent variables. The dependent variable in the equations for Sweden is the number of trunk "pulses," or alternatively the number of trunk calls, for business and residential customers combined. For Great Britain, Sweden, and residential demand for Bell Canada, equations are estimated both on a per-capita and per-telephone basis. For business demand for Bell Canada, equations are estimated for deflated toll revenue and deflated toll revenue per telephone.

The following equations illustrate Waverman's results:[66]

CANADA

Residence

$$\ln(R/T)_t = \underset{(-8.20)}{-4.65} + \underset{(4.35)}{1.03} \ln X_t - \underset{(-8.01)}{1.16} \ln P_t \tag{40}$$

Business

$$\ln(R/T)_t = \underset{(-3.21)}{-2.24} + \underset{(2.83)}{0.11} \ln(R/T)_{t-1}$$

$$+ \underset{(3.67)}{0.45} \ln X_t - \underset{(-3.53)}{1.20} \ln P_t \tag{41}$$

R = real toll revenue

T = number of telephones

X = real personal disposable income

P = average toll price/implicit deflator for GNP.

GREAT BRITAIN

$$(R/T)_t = \underset{(1.05)}{12.82} + \underset{(3.45)}{0.51} (R/T)_{t-1}$$

$$+ \underset{(2.06)}{0.0017} (X_t + X_{t-1}) - \underset{(-2.82)}{0.041} (P_t + P_{t-1})$$

$$= -0.051(d_t + d_{t-1}) \quad R^2 = 0.986 \tag{42}$$

[66] Waverman (1974, pp. 33, 36, 13, 43). The elasticities from these equations are tabulated in Table 5. Waverman does not include R^2 's for his equations for Bell Canada.

$$(C/T)_t = \frac{83.50}{(1.84)} + \frac{0.56}{(2.58)} (C/T)_{t-1}$$

$$+ \frac{0.0064}{(2.64)} (X_t + X_{t-1}) - \frac{0.15}{(-3.59)} (P_t + P_{t-1})$$

$$= -0.30(d_t + d_{t-1}) \quad R^2 = 0.997 \tag{43}$$

R = real revenue from inland trunk calls

C = number of inland trunk calls

T = number of telephones

X = real personal consumption expenditures

P = average price for trunk call/implicit deflator for personal consumption expenditures

d = percentage of trunk calls dialed by operator.

SWEDEN

$$\ln PU_t = \frac{-3.86}{(1.10)} + \frac{0.53}{(4.91)} \ln PU_{t-1} + \frac{0.23}{(0.52)} \ln X_t$$

$$- \frac{0.51}{(-4.10)} \ln P_t + \frac{0.89}{(2.87)} \ln T_t$$

$$R^2 = 0.998 \tag{44}$$

$$\ln C_t = \frac{-3.56}{(-1.20)} + \frac{0.51}{(3.80)} \ln C_{t-1} + \frac{0.19}{(0.45)} \ln X_t$$

$$- \frac{0.29}{(-2.43)} \ln P_t^* + \frac{1.20}{(3.63)} \ln T_t$$

$$R^2 = 0.998 \tag{45}$$

PU = number of trunk "pulses"

C = number of trunk calls

X = real Gross Domestic Product per household

P = marginal pulse rate/consumer price index

P^* = average price of a trunk call/consumer price index.

Waverman's results for Sweden are especially interesting, for the elasticity with respect to the number of telephones is less than 1 in equation (44), but greater than 1 in equation (45). Since the dependent variable in equation (44) is the number of pulses (which measure holding time), while the dependent variable in (45) is the number of calls, and since a coefficient greater than 1 on the number of telephones would seem to be consistent with a positive externality associated with system size,[67] this result suggests that the number of calls responds to this externality, but not the duration. Interesting, also, is the fact that the price elasticity in the equation for pulses is larger than in the equation for calls. This implies that duration is more responsive to price than is the number of calls.

This last result is corroborated in Waverman's equations for Great Britain. In equation (40), the dependent variable is average real trunk-call revenue per telephone, while in equation (42), the dependent variable is the average number of trunk calls per telephone. Thus the average duration of a call is reflected in equation (42), but not in equation (43). In Table 5, we see that the price elasticities are larger in the equation explaining real revenue per telephone than in the equation explaining the number of calls per telephone. Consequently, once again we can conclude that the duration of calls is more responsive to a price change than the number of calls. Moreover, the same conclusion holds for the income elasticities. In both Great Britain and Sweden, the duration of long-distance calls is more responsive to income changes than the number of calls.

---

[67] Once again, however, see the discussion in Chapter 9 and Appendix 3.

THE PRE-1980 EMPIRICAL LITERATURE ON TELEPHONE DEMAND: INTRASTATE TOLL, WATS AND PRIVATE LINE, COIN, ETC.

In this appendix, we continue to review the pre-1980 telephone demand literature, beginning with intrastate toll demand. The intrastate models that are discussed were organized and tabulated for the first edition of this book by Catherine Martin, then at AT&T in New York. The tabulation was kept current for several years, but not surprisingly was a casualty of divestiture. 'Tis a pity.

I. INTRASTATE TOLL DEMAND

Studies of intrastate message toll demand comprise a lion's share of the total literature on telephone demand. This attention reflected the increasingly common practice in the mid-1970s of utilizing an econometric model in estimating the impact on revenue of proposed changes in tariffs in rate filing before U.S. state regulatory commissions. The various state modeling efforts, for the most part, employed the common framework of relating a physical measure of intrastate message toll activity to a measure of economic activity, the relative price of MTS calls, the size of the market, and "habit". In all cases, MTS activity is measured by the number of intrastate toll messages or by intrastate toll revenues deflated by an MTS price index. Economic activity is usually measured by real personal income or real disposable personal income, but other measures of economic activity are used as well. These include Gross State Product and bank debits. MTS price is usually measured by a Laspeyres price index that aggregates over mileage bands, time of day, and class of customer.[1] For two states, interstate rates are represented as well.

Market size is usually represented in the models by the number of telephones less residence extensions or by the number of main stations, either explicitly as a predictor or implicitly as a deflator of toll activity. In the

---

[1] For more than a third of the states, a chain index is used instead of a Laspeyres index.

model for nine states, market size is measured (explicitly or implicitly) by population or the number of households. Finally, in all cases but one in which "habit" is represented, it is measured by the lagged value of the dependent variable.

As already noted, personal income (or disposable income) is expressed in real terms, usually on a per-capita or per-household basis. Where local deflators are not available, the national CPI is usually used as a surrogate. In nearly all cases, the CPI is used to deflate the toll price index, so that toll price is measured relative to the cost of other goods and services. Quarterly time-series data are used in estimation of the models, with one exception where monthly data are used.

Most of the intrastate toll models are variations on the following logarithmic Koyck distributed-lag model:

$$\ln M_t = \alpha_1 \ln M_{t-1} + \alpha_2 \ln X_t + \alpha_3 \ln P_t + \alpha_4 \ln T_t + u_t, \qquad (1)$$

where

M = number of intrastate toll messages in a state[2]

X = real personal income per capita in the state

P = toll price index for the state divided by the CPI

T = number of telephones in the state less the number of residence extensions

u = random error term.

Included among the variations of this model, one finds:

1. Restricting α_4 to equal 1. In this case, the dependent variable is $\ln M/T$.
2. Specifying the equation as linear rather than double logarithmic.
3. Restricting α_1 to equal 0, in which case $\ln M_{t-1}$ is omitted as a predictor.[3]
4. Use of a chain index for toll price rather than the Laspeyres index.
5. Including prices of substitute forms of communications as predictors.[4]
6. Finally, since quarterly (or monthly) data are used in estimation, some form of seasonal adjustment is required. Dummy variables are used in about half of the models, and the Shiskin (Census X–9 or X–11) method in the rest.

---

[3] The model may still be dynamic depending on the presence or absence of the number of telephones as a predictor. If the number of telephones is present, then the model is dynamic since the number of toll calls is *conditional* on the stock of telephones.

[4] One model includes a price index for other telephone services; the first-class letter rate appears as a predictor in two others.

The price and income elasticities of demand from the state models are tabulated in Table 1.[5] As mentioned, the models are estimated from quarterly data except for one estimated from monthly data. Typically over ten years of data are used in estimation. Also, all of the models are multiplicative except for three which are linear. The lagged dependent variable is absent from four of the models.[6] However, of these, only one model is truly static. The other three are conditional on the stock of telephones, or included lagged price and income terms.

The estimates of the price elasticities in Table 1 vary from -0.03 to -0.44 in the short run and from -0.22 to -1.04 in the long run. The mean of the short-run estimates is -0.21, while the mean of the long-run estimates is -0.67. There is greater variation in the estimates of the income elasticities, but here, too, there is substantial agreement among the estimates. The estimates range from 0.05 to 1.08 in the short run and from 0.28 to 2.72 in the long run, with means of 0.39 and 1.33, respectively.[7]

Thus, the evidence on price and income elasticities from the intrastate toll demand models indicates:

1. That intrastate toll demand is more responsive (measured in terms of elasticity) to changes in income than to changes in toll prices;
2. That intrastate toll demand is inelastic with respect to both price and income in the short run;
3. That intrastate toll demand, broadly but not everywhere, remains inelastic with respect to price in the long run, but is elastic in the long run with respect to income.

It will be noted that toll price appears in all of the models in Table 1 of Chapter 5 and that income (or some other measure of economic activity) also appears in all of the models. Further, signs are correct in every case, and, in general, *t*-ratios are impressive (at least for time-series data). For the majority of models, the *t*-ratio for toll price is at least 3 (in absolute value). The smallest *t*-ratio for toll price is 0.99, and the next smallest is 1.99. For

---

[5] I am grateful to the Demand Analysis Group, Tariffs and Costs Department, at AT&T for undertaking a detailed tabulation of the state models. Edward Dinan of New England Telephone worked on this study while a participant in the Internship Program sponsored by the Demand Analysis Group. The state models reviewed in this section were completed in 1976 through mid-1978, and represent, in many cases, the initial efforts of the Bell System operating telephone companies to build aggregate MTS demand models.

[6] The elasticities for these models appear in parentheses in Table 1 in order to emphasize that, since the models do not allow for habit formation, they will, in general, be intermediate between short-run and long-run elasticities.

[7] The estimates from the four models that do not allow for habit formation are excluded in calculating mean values of the price and income elasticities.

TABLE 1

Estimates of price and income elasticities of demand for intrastate toll calls (Bell system)

State	Dependent Variable	Price Elasticity		Income Elasticity		Form of Model	Remarks
		Short-Run	Long-Run	Short-Run	Long-Run		
State A–1	M	(-0.16)		(0.92)		Linear	Total toll includes interstate; estimated by Durbin Two-Stage Method; chain toll price index
State A–2	M/MT	-0.15	-0.2	0.58	0.86	Log Koyck	CPI separate variable; chain toll price index
State A–3	M/MT	(-0.12)		(0.88)		Linear	Total toll includes interstate estimated by Durbin Two-Stage Method; chain toll price index
State B–1	M/T	-0.32	-0.60	0.63	1.18	Log Koyck	Chain toll price index
State C–1	M	-0.07	-0.14	0.24	0.53	Log Koyck	Average number of telephones less residential extension included as predictor
State D–1	PD	-0.35	-0.45	0.31	0.40	Log Koyck	Chain toll price index time included as predictor
State E–1	M/MT	-0.03	-0.85	0.05	1.40	Log Fl-Adj	
State E–2	M/MT	-0.21	-0.73	0.19	0.65	Log Koyck	
State E–3	M/MT	-0.17	-1.04	0.09	0.55	Log Fl-Adj	
State E–4	M/T	-0.26	-1.04	0.14	0.56	Log Koyck	
State E–5	M/MT	-0.13	-0.81	0.21	1.28	Log Koyck	
State F–1	PDR/POP	-0.14	-0.62	0.21	0.91	Log Koyck	Main telephones per capita included as predictor
State G–1	PDR/POP	-0.16	-0.56	0.80	2.71	Log Koyck	Telephones less residential extensions per capita included as predictor
State H–1	PDR	-0.37	-0.50	0.63	0.88	Log Koyck	Time and price of other telephone services included as predictors; chain toll price index
State I–1	M/T	-0.44	-0.84	0.19	0.36	Log Koyck	Chain toll price index
State I–2	PDR/POP	-0.29	-0.64	0.24	0.54	Log Koyck	Chain toll price index; telephone less residential extensions per capita included as predictor

Table 1 (continued)

State	Dependent Variable	Price Elasticity		Income Elasticity		Form of Model	Remarks
		Short-Run	Long-Run	Short-Run	Long-Run		
State I-3	M/T	-0.35	-0.96	0.31	0.81	Log Koyck	Chain toll price index
State I-4	M/T	(-0.59)		(0.52)		Double Log	Chain toll price index; estimated by Cochrane-Orcutt
State J-1	PDR/POP	-0.14	-0.23	0.24	0.58	Log Koyck	Telephone less residential extensions per capita included as predictor; also weather
State K-1	PDR/T	-0.21	-0.91	0.39	1.70	Log Koyck	
State L-1	M	-0.20	-0.39	0.45	0.85	Log Koyck	Households included as predictor
State L-2	M	-0.23	-0.43	0.59	1.12	Log Koyck	Households included as predictor
State M-1	PDR/POP	-0.12	-0.69	0.47	2.77	Log Koyck	First class postal rate included as predictor
State M-2	PDR/POP	-0.17	-0.83	0.46	2.23	Log Koyck	First class postal rate included as predictor
State N-1	PDR/POP	-0.14	-0.82	0.33	2.01	Log Koyck	Change in
State N-2	PDR	-0.24	0.86	0.60	2.10	Log Koyck	insured unemployment
State N-3	PDR/POP	-0.15	-0.79	0.44	2.35	Log Koyck	rate included
State N-4	PDR/POP	-0.13	-0.91	0.36	2.52	Log Koyck	as predictor
State O-1	PDR/POP	-0.07	-0.84	0.23	2.65	Log Koyck	First order transformation; unemployment rate included as predictor
State R-1	PDR/POP	(-0.21)		(0.59)		Linear	Dependent variable first difference
State Q-1	PDR	-0.31	-0.37	1.08	1.32	Log Koyck	Dependent variable includes private line & WATS; second order GLS transformation; chain total toll price index

Symbols: M: messages; MT: main telephones; T: telephones less residential extensions;
PDR: price-deflated revenues; POP: population; Fl-Adj: Houthakker-Taylor flow adjustment model.

income, t-ratios are frequently 4 or more. The smallest t-ratio for income is 0.95, while the next smallest is 1.48.[8] Thus, it has to be concluded that both toll prices and income are major determinants of intrastate toll traffic.

The number of telephones (main stations or total telephones less residence extensions) appears in eighteen of the state models, either as a deflator of the dependent variable (thirteen models) or as an independent variable (five models). In the generic model, the stock of telephones is included, as noted, as a measure of market size.[9] Naturally, we expect more intrastate toll calls to be made in a state with a larger number of telephones, and this is presumably what the term "market size" is meant to convey. In the thirteen equations in which the number of telephones appears only as a deflator of the dependent variable, the assumption, clearly, is that, *ceteris paribus*, toll activity increases at the same rate as the size of the system. However, in Chapter 2, we emphasized the externalities that are associated with the telephone. The access externality makes belonging to a larger system more valuable than belonging to a smaller system, and this may be reflected in more calls per telephone being made in a larger system than in a smaller system.[10] It was suggested that the strength of the call externality may also be measured by system size. Thus, if access and call externalities are present, the increase in toll activity case, *ceteris paribus*, be faster than the increase in system size.

However, the empirical evidence for these externalities is mild.[11] Seven states have market-size variables included as predictors, and the coefficients of interest are tabulated in Table 2. The only states with the coefficient on the market-size variable greater than 1 are the two with market size measured by the number of households.

Some of the more individual features of the state toll demand models include

1. As already noted, the toll price index in two of the state models is a combined index that reflects interstate tariffs as well as intrastate. Implicit in these models is a "total bill" concept, which reasons that subscribers,

[8] Interestingly, there are more cases of t-ratios less than 2 for income than for price (6 versus 2). The model for State E–1 has the smallest t-ratio for both price and income. These poor results most certainly reflect data problems caused by extensive conversion to EAS in that state's largest metropolitan area in the 1960s and early 1970s. Because of this, it is difficult, if not impossible, to get a consistent time series for the number of toll calls.

[9] For States L–1 and L–2, market size is measured by the number of households.

[10] As noted in Chapter 2, the access externality, because of increased option demand, can lead to an increased willingness-to-pay to belong to a large telephone system; caller per telephone may be increased as well, but there is not necessity that this be the case. This is discussed in detail in Chapter 9.

[11] Empirical evidence for the call and access externalities were discussed in Chapters 5, 6, and 9.

TABLE 2

Coefficients of market-size variable (Bell system
intrastate toll demand models)

State	Coefficient	t-Ratio
Telephone as measure of market size		
State C–1[a]	0.93	3.90
State F–1[b]	0.46	2.08
State G–1[c]	0.53	2.96
State J–1[c]	0.97	3.03
State J–2[c]	0.92	2.67
Households as measure of market size		
State L–1	1.29	7.91
State L–2	1.39	7.59

[a] Total telephones less residence extensions.
[b] Main stations per capita.
[c] Total telephones less residence extension
   per capita.

especially residential subscribers, budget for interstate and intrastate toll
calls jointly. This is an interesting idea, but it cannot be readily tested
using aggregate data.[12]

2. In the models for nineteen states, the toll price index includes the Federal
excise tax. While there does not appear to exist any difference in results
that can be attributed to this adjustment, it is an appropriate adjustment
in principle to make. In five models, local sales taxes are included in
addition to the federal excise tax.

3. Although personal income (or disposable income) is typically used as
the measure of economic activity, there is some variation across the
states. Personal income is augmented by changes in the rate of insured
unemployment in the models for States N–1, N–2, N–3, N–4, and 0–1.
Gross State Product is used in place of personal income in the model for
State A–1. Finally, bank debits is used in lieu of income in the model for

---

[12] For a discussion of the "total bill" concept applied to all telephone related expenditures,
see Doherty and Oscar (1977). (See also Section II of Chapter 8). Alternatively, one can
interpret the use of a combined index as a reflection of consumers confusing intrastate and
interstate tariffs.

State I–4.[13]

4. Three state models include price variables in addition to toll price and the CPI (or other general deflator). State H–1 includes a price index (deflated by the CPI) reflecting the costs of basic service, additional message units, and interstate toll. In this case, inclusion of the costs of these other services is derived from the "total bill" concept. The sign of the variable is negative, in line with the hypothesis advanced, and its t-ratio is -1.97. The additional price variable in models for State M–1 and M–2 is the first-class letter rate (also deflated by the CPI). Its sign is positive, as expected, but its t-ratio is only 1.76 and 1.42, respectively.

5. A final term of interest is the finding in the model for State J–1 that toll activity is sensitive to inclement weather.

Thus far, the focus in this section has been on models of individual states developed by pre-divestiture Bell System operating companies. In all cases, the models refer to residence and business MTS messages combined and are estimated with time-series data. We now turn to two other analyses of intrastate toll, the cross-sectional study of Feldman (1976) and a combined time-series/cross-sectional study conducted by Stuntebeck (1976).

For both business and residence subscribers, the Feldman study (which was also discussed in connection with the demand for access in Section I of Appendix 1) specifies models for the following categories of MTS demand:

Number of Messages

    Operator-Handled
    Person-to-Person
    DDD

Number of Messages/Main Station

    Operator-Handled
    Person-to-Person
    DDD

Number of Minutes/Message

    Operator-Handled
    Person-to-Person
    DDD

---

[13] This substitution was prompted by the erratic behavior in the personal income series occasioned by sharp swings in agricultural prices. In this connection, it is interesting to note that measures of "permanent" income, constructed from moving averages of personal income, are used in the models for States B–1, D–1, I–3, and Q–1.

In the equations with messages as the dependent variable, the independent variables are toll price, the price of alternatives, price of local service, population (Bell-served area), per-capita personal income, a proxy for the size of the exchange area,[14] and regional dummy variables.[15] In the equations for average length-of-conversation, the independent variables are toll price, average length-of-haul, per-capita personal income, and regional dummy variables. The equations, double-logarithmic in all cases, are estimated for business and residence subscribers separately, using cross-sectional data for the fourth quarter of 1973.

The price and income elasticities obtained in the eighteen categories listed above are tabulated in Table 3. In general, the price elasticities in the equations for messages are consistent with those obtained in the state studies, but this is not the case for the income elasticities. Income is absent from all but one of the residence message equations, and from four of the business message equations. In contrast, income appears in all of the equations for average length-of-conversation.

Feldman's results will be illustrated in detail with the equations for messages per main station and average length-of-conversation for DDD calls by residential customers. The equations are as follows (t-ratios are in parentheses):

$$\ln(M/T) = \underset{(9.81)}{4.85} - \underset{(-4.31)}{0.58} \ln P_{DDD} - \underset{(-1.02)}{0.18} \ln L$$

$$+ 0.04 \ln(POP/P_{DDD}) + 0.02 \ln(P_{PER}/P_{DDD})$$

$$+ \underset{(5.94)}{0.13} \ln POP - \underset{(-10.94)}{0.62} \ln EA$$

$$+ \text{ regional dummy variables} \quad R^2 = 0.88 \tag{2}$$

$$\ln ALCO = \underset{(3.01)}{0.60} - \underset{(-2.45)}{0.14} \ln POP + \underset{(4.24)}{0.13} \ln ALOH + \underset{(4.37)}{0.25} (PI/POP)$$

$$+ \text{ regional dummy variables} \quad R^2 = 0.69, \tag{3}$$

---

[14] This variable is intended to take into account variation in exchange areas across states. It is measured by the ratio of local calls to intrastate toll calls. Feldman also experimented with a "call-preference" proxy, defined as the ratio of intrastate toll calls to interstate calls, as a measure of community of interest. However, multicollinearity prevented using both variables at the same time.

[15] The average length-of-haul is an additional predictor in a few of the message equations.

TABLE 3

Estimates of price and income elasticities for intrastate toll demand (Feldman study)

Dependent Variable	Residence		Business	
	Price Elasticity	Income Elasticity	Price Elasticity	Income Elasticity
Messages				
Station-to-station (operator handled)	-0.31	–	-0.38	1.02
Person-to-Person	-0.75	–	-1.31	–
DDD	-0.53	0.20	-0.49	0.74
Messages/Main Station				
Station-to-station (operator handled)	-0.40	–	-0.46	–
Person-to-person	-0.70	–	-0.58	–
DDD	-0.64	–	-0.53	–
Minutes/Message				
Station-to-station (operator handled)	-0.004	0.24	–	0.19
Person-to-person	-0.17	0.35		0.06
DDD	-0.14	0.25	–	0.10

Source: Feldman (1976)

where:

$$
\begin{aligned}
M &= \text{number of residence DDD intrastate MTS messages} \\
T &= \text{number of residence main stations} \\
L &= \text{local revenue per main station (residence)} \\
POP &= \text{population} \\
EA &= \text{local messages/intrastate MTS messages (residence)} \\
ALOC &= \text{average length-of-conversation (residence DDD MTS messages)} \\
P_{DDD} &= \text{average revenue per minute (residence DDD MTS messages)} \\
P_{OP} &= \text{average revenue per minute (residence operator-handled messages)} \\
P_{PER} &= \text{average revenue per minute (residence person-to-person messages)}
\end{aligned}
$$

ALOH = average length-of-haul (residence DDD MTS messages)

PI = personal income.

In the equation for DDD messages per main station, it is interesting to note the importance of toll price (measured by average revenue per message),[16] population, and the exchange area proxy. The price elasticities for both residence and business messages and messages per main station in Table 3 show that the elasticity for station-to-station calls is smaller than for DDD calls, which is smaller than for person-to-person calls. The negative coefficient for the exchange area proxy, with its large t-ratio, suggests an inverse relation between the sizes of local and "foreign" communities of interest.[17] In the equation for average length-of-conversation, we find, as expected, a positive (and significant) coefficient for the average length-of-haul. Price (now measured by average revenue per minute) continues to be important, although it is not as strong as in the equation for messages per main station. Note, however, that personal income, which is absent altogether from the message equation, is the strongest predictor in the duration equation.

The focus in Stuntebeck's study is on the relationship between day/night message distributions and day/night rate structures for residence weekday intrastate toll calls. The model specified relates the ratio of daytime to nighttime message volume in a mileage band to the ratio of the daytime to nighttime price,[18] personal income per capita, percentage of the population under eighteen years of age, percentage of the population over sixty-five,[19] and the average distance of a call in the mileage band. A double-logarithmic equation is estimated for three mileage bands, 25–50, 51–100, and 101–200 miles. State cross-sectional data for October–December 1968, March and April 1969, October–December 1970, March and April 1971, October 1972, and March 1973 are used in estimation.[20] A set of equations is estimated

---

[16] The estimates of 0.04 and 0.02 for the cross-price elasticities are taken from the equations for residence operated-handled and person-to-person messages, respectively. This is done in order to impose consistency in the cross-price elasticities across equations.

[17] However, one must be somewhat skeptical of this result because of the fact that the sum of total MTS and WATS messages appears in the denominator of EA. This can set up a spurious negative relationship, and the substantial t-ratio for EA may be a reflection of this. Still, the idea that there is a trade-off between local and "foreign" communities of interest is worthy of further study.

[18] Daytime is counted as 8:00 A.M. through 4:59 P.M., and nighttime as 5:00 P.M. through 7:59 A.M.

[19] The age variables are included to reflect "daytime opportunity".

[20] The data for 1969–1971 are from the Message Analysis Sampling Plan (MASP), while the data for 1972–1973 are from the Centralized Message Data System (CMDS).

TABLE 4

Estimates of day/night price and income elasticities (Stuntebeck study, cross-section sample

Mileage Band	Price Elasticity	Income Elasticity
25–50 miles	-0.11	0.56
51–100 miles	-0.27	0.58
101–200 miles	-0.59	0.18
Weighted mean	-0.21	0.52

Source: Stuntebeck (1976, p. 20)

using the data for October–December 1970, and another set is estimated pooling the observations for three of the six years.[21]

The price and income elasticities estimated by Stuntebeck in the cross-section equations for October–December 1970 are tabulated in Table 4. Composite elasticities, obtained as weighted averages (using message volumes as weights) of the elasticities across separate mileage bands, are also presented. The price elasticities are seen to increase (ignoring sign) and with length-of-haul; the income elasticities, in contrast, are seen to decrease. The weighted mean elasticities for price and income are -0.21 and 0.52, respectively.

Since the price elasticities being estimated refer to the impact on relative day/night volumes of changes in day/night price differentials, these results clearly suggest that long-haul calls are shifted more than short-haul calls. Given that long-haul calls are also longer in duration than short-haul calls, this result it probably to be expected since the charge for a long-haul call increases more than in proportion to the increase in distance. However, an explanation for the sharp decrease in the income elasticity after one hundred miles is not readily apparent.[22]

The results from the pooled cross-section/time-series equations are presented in Table 5. Two equations are estimated for each mileage band, the observations from 1968, 1970, and 1972 being used in one equation, and 1969, 1972, and 1973 being used in the other. The years are split in order to control for seasonality. Once again, price elasticities are seen to increase with length-of-haul, while income elasticities decrease. In this case, though,

[21] In the pooled equation, the population and distance variables are replaced with state dummy variables.

[22] Carl Pavarini has suggested that persons with high incomes may make proportionately more long-haul calls.

TABLE 5

Estimates of day/night price and income elasticities (Stuntebeck study, pooled sample)

Mileage Band	Price Elasticity	Income Elasticity
25–50 miles		
1968/70/72	-0.05	1.21
1969/71/73	-0.10	1.24
51–100 miles		
1968/70/72	-0.21	0.79
1969/71/73	-0.22	1.08
101–200 miles		
1968/70/72	-0.24	0.72
1969/71/73	-0.24	0.82
Weighted mean	-0.13	1.10

Source: Stuntebeck (1976, p. 32)

the price elasticities are uniformly smaller, and income elasticities uniformly larger, than the estimated pure cross-section elasticities in Table 4.

A lot of material has been covered in this section, and it will be useful to summarize what I consider to be the major findings. Although there is considerable variation in the estimated price and income elasticities from the state models in Table 1, there are also strong currents of uniformity. Intrastate toll demand is strongly influenced by the relative price of toll and income. The mean estimates of the long-run elasticities are 0.67 and 1.33 for price and income, respectively. The estimates of the price elasticities for intrastate toll are, in general, smaller than the estimates, presented in Table 4 for interstate (i.e., long-haul) toll, but since the average length-of-haul is longer for interstate calls than for intrastate calls, this is to be expected. On the other hand, the intrastate toll elasticities are, again, in general larger than the elasticities that have been estimated for local use. This, too, is to be expected. Thus, the pattern that has emerged is: The elasticity for the monthly service charge, which is smaller than the elasticity for the intrastate toll price, which is smaller than the elasticity for the interstate toll price. And in Section VI below, we shall see that the price elasticity for the interstate toll price is, in general, smaller than the elasticity for the price of international calls.

II. WATS AND PRIVATE LINE

We now turn to the demand for WATS and private-line services. WATS, which can be viewed as an extension of flat-rate service to long-distance calling, is of two types: inward WATS (now called 800 service) and outward WATS. With inward WATS, the called party pays for the service, while the outward WATS, the caller pays. With either type, calls are routed through special designated WATS-servicing central offices. With private line, however, telephones are connected via dedicated direct circuits, rather than through exchanges. In light of the discussion in Chapter 2, it is clear that the demand for inward WATS will be closely associated with the call externality imposed on callees. Willingness-to-pay in this case is identified with the amount that a subscriber is willing-to-pay in order to receive calls. The demand for outward WATS, in contrast, is related to more traditional benefit/cost calculations. A cost-minimizing subscriber will choose WATS over MTS and private line only if the anticipated volume of calls at the WATS rates is cheaper than paying MTS and private-line rates.[23]

The literature on the demand for WATS and private line is small. I have found only three studies that focus explicitly on these services, namely

1. Davis *et al.* (1973), who estimate demand equations for WATS (inward and outward combined) and private line, using quarterly time-series inter-state data for the United States.
2. Feldman (1976), who estimates equations for intrastate inward WATS and outward WATS separately, using cross-sectional state data for the United States.
3. Subissati (1973), who estimates equations for WATS (inward and outward combined) and business toll, using monthly time-series data for Bell Canada.

Of these three studies, the Feldman study is the most extensive, and will be reviewed in greatest detail. For both outward WATS and inward WATS, the Feldman study specifies equations for (1) the total number of WATS lines, (2) the number of lines with measured service, (3) the number of lines with full service,[24] (4) the total number of messages, and (5) the number of hours

---

[23] This is clearly a simplification, for many business customers subscribe to WATS and private line, in addition to having access to MTS. The relevant question, in this case, is how the optimal mix of MTS, WATS, and private line is determined. In the pre-1980 literature, theoretical analysis of this question was noteworthy for its absence. Post-1980, see Griffin and Egan (1985).

[24] Full-service lines refers to lines with unlimited use. With measured WATS, there is an initial allowance of ten or fifteen hours; subsequent hours are then charged for at tenths of hour intervals. Measured WATS is thus like measured local service with an initial allowance.

of use per line for lines with measured service. Double-logarithmic demand function are postulated with WATS price, DDD price, personal income, an exchange rate proxy, and regional dummy variables as independent variables. Intrastate cross-sectional data for forty-one states for November 1973 are used in estimation. The demand functions obtained, though, refer to intrastate WATS demand as opposed to interstate.

The price and income elasticities from the Feldman study are tabulated in Table 6. In addition to the own-price elasticities, cross elasticities with respect to the price of DDD and full or measured WATS (where relevant) are also presented.[25] While it might seem at first glance that estimated own-price elasticities are implausibly large, it must be kept in mind that businesses subscribe to WATS as a substitute for regular long-distance service. This is true for inward WATS, as well as outward WATS, since the alternative may be the acceptance of a large number of collect calls. Thus, the estimated price elasticities appearing in the table clearly present a picture of substitution. The large positive cross elasticity with respect to the price of DDD indicates that WATS and regular toll are strong substitutes. Not surprisingly, measured WATS and flat-rate WATS are also indicated to be substitutes, but the substitution is not as strong as for either measured WATS or flat-rate WATS with regular toll.[26] The weakest equations are the ones for hours per measured line. Price is absent from these equations, and income is of little importance. The absence of WATS price is surprising and may result from the use of an average price for the price variable, rather than the marginal price, which (as was discussed in Chapter 3) is theoretically more appropriate. Finally, most of the estimated income elasticities are seen to be in the neighborhood of 1.

Davis *et al.* (1973) estimate, as part of the AT&T FORECYT model, equations for deflated WATS revenue, deflated private-line revenue, and the number of private-line telephones. Logarithmic Koyck models are specified

---

[25] WATS price is defined as average revenue (per billing period) per line, and DDD price is measured as average revenue per DDD message.

[26] Cf. the cross-price elasticities for DDD and other WATS offerings in the equations for measured lines and full lines. The own price appears in the equations directly and as a deflator of the price of substitutes. In the equation for measured outward WATS, for example, the price variables are (all as logarithms): the price of measured WATS, the price of DDD divided by the price of measured WATS, and the price of flat-rate WATS divided by the price of measured WATS. The coefficient for the price of measured WATS then measures the own-price elasticity when the prices of measured WATS, flat-rate WATS and DDD all change in the same proportion. This elasticity is quite small (-0.30 in the case considered). Moreover, the t-ratio for this coefficient is always smaller than are the t-ratios for the price substitution terms. This is further evidence of the importance of substitution among the three forms of long-distance communication.

TABLE 6

Estimates of price and income elasticities of demand for WATS (Feldman study)

Dependent Variable	Own Price Elasticity	Cross-Price Elasticity			Income Elasticity
		DDD	WATS measured	WATS Full	
Inward WATS					
Total lines	-1.40	1.17			0.91
Measured lines	-2.34	1.52		0.64	0.75
Full lines	-2.83	0.78	1.82		1.01
Messages	-0.91	0.69			1.02
Hours/measured line					0.13
Outward WATS					
Total lines	-2.30	2.11			1.06
Measured lines	-3.25	2.07		0.88	0.78
Full lines	-3.37	1.90	1.08		1.09
Messages	-1.15	0.96			0.97
Hours/measured line					0.32

Source: Feldman (1976)

and estimated with quarterly data over the period 1961 through 1972.[27] In addition to the lagged dependent variable, independent variables are a WATS price index and sales of domestic airlines (since airlines are very heavy users of WATS) in the WATS equation, and a price index for private line and the number of private-line telephones in the equation for deflated private-line revenue.[28] The price and income elasticities estimated for WATS and private-line revenues are reproduced in Table 7.[29]

Subissati (1973) estimates equations for deflated WATS revenues (inward and outward combined) and deflated business toll revenue using monthly data

[27] The WATS revenue data are interstate WATS revenue. The private-line data, in contrast, refer to revenue from all Bell private-line telephones, local, intrastate, and interstate.

[28] The price indices for WATS and private-line revenues are deflated by the implicit deflator for GNP. Presumably, airline sales are also deflated, although the authors do not state this is the case.

[29] The coefficient for the lagged dependent variable in the equation for private-line telephones is so close to 1 that the calculation of a "long-run" elasticity is not a meaningful exercise. The short-run price elasticity is estimated to be -0.009.

TABLE 7

Estimates of price and income elasticities of demand for WATS and private line (Davis *et al.* study)

Service	Price Elasticity		Income Elasticity	
	Short-Run	Long-Run	Short-Run	Long-Run
WATS	-0.17	-0.84	0.18	1.04
Private line	-0.74	-1.03	–	–

Source: Davis *et al.* (1973, p. 38).

The elasticities in the equation for private-line revenues are conditional on the number of private line telephones.

for Bell Canada for the period 1967 through 1972. The settlement data used are from Bell Canada to the rest of Canada. Independent variables in the WATS equation are a WATS price index, the value of retail trade in Ontario and Quebec,[30] the two-quarter change in (deflated) business toll revenue, and a time trend. The WATS price index is deflated by a similar index for business toll, and retail trade for Ontario and Quebec is deflated by the national CPI. The time trend is intended to reflect the more rapid rate of growth in inward WATS as compared with outward WATS. Finally, the two-month change in business toll revenue is intended to capture the build-up in business toll calling that is required before the use of WATS becomes cost effective.

Independent variables in the business toll equation are a business toll price index, manufacturing shipments (for all of Canada), and the first difference in (deflated) WATS revenue. The business toll price index is deflated by the national CPI. Manufacturing shipments are included as a five-month moving average, beginning at $t - 5$ and going backward in time, using an "inverted" V lag structure. The first difference in WATS is intended to reflect the substitution between WATS and regular toll by business.

Because of the presence of WATS revenue in the toll equation, Subissati's model is simultaneous, and two-stage least squares is used in estimation. Subissati finds significant negative price effects in both equations, as well as significant income effects.[31] The coefficient for the two-month change

---

[30] Retail trade is introduced as a seven-month moving average, beginning in $t - 2$ and going backward in time, using an "inverted" V lag structure.

[31] The own-price elasticities estimated by Subissati are -0.33 and -0.25 for WATS and business toll, respectively, where the cross elasticity for WATS with respect to the price of business toll is estimated to be 0.33. The estimated income elasticities are greater than 1 in

in business toll revenue is also positive, in line with Subissati's *a priori* reasoning, but, surprisingly, the coefficient for the first difference in WATS revenue in the business toll equation is also positive. Subissati suggests, among other things, that this may be a reflection of a "free-calling" attitude developed by flat-rate billing. Also, since a WATS line serves only one call at a time, frequent queuing may occur, and many calls may be sent by MTS, rather than waiting their turn on the WATS line.

Despite the illuminating results obtained in the Feldman study as regards the substitution among regular WATS, measured WATS, and regular toll service, our knowledge of the demand for WATS and private-line service is, in general, still unsatisfactory. The biggest unknown is private line. The study of Davis *et al.* provides some evidence that the long-run price elasticity for real private-line revenues, holding the number of private-line telephones constant, is well within the range that has been estimated for the long-run price elasticity for regular toll. This is essentially all that the existing empirical evidence can tell us about private-line demand. The equation for private-line telephones in the Davis *et al.* study is unsatisfying, but it appears to be the state of the art. Neither do we know anything about the cross-price elasticities of demand between private-line and WATS and between private-line and MTS.

III. COIN STATIONS

Recent years have seen concerted efforts by telephone companies to increase the charge for local calls dialed from coin stations. However, as noted in Section I of Chapter 4, the literature on the demand for coin-station service is small and unsystematic. In my search through the literature, I found only one study that involves explicit econometric analysis of the demand for coin-station services, this being in Feldman (1976).[32] The focus in the Feldman study is on intrastate toll demand originating from coin stations, and models are estimated for (1) the number of operator-handled calls, (2) the number of person-to-person calls, (3) the average length-of-conversation for operator-handled calls, and (4) the average length-of-conversation for person-to-person calls. Intrastate Bell data for the fourth quarter of 1973 for the forty-eight contiguous states in the United States are used in estimation.

both equations.

[32] Brubacher and Hiscock (1978) provide an analysis of the impact of the increase in the price of a local call from 10 cents to 20 cents in 1974 and the subsequent return to 10 cents in 1977 in the parts of Ontario and Quebec served by Bell Canada. Box-Jenkins techniques are used in the analysis.

TABLE 8

Estimates of price and income elasticities of demand for pay-station toll calls (Feldman study)

Dependent Variable	Price Elasticity	Cross-Price Elasticity	Income Elasticity
Number of Calls			
Station	-0.88	0.04	–
Person-to-person	-2.86	2.04	–
Average Length of Conversation			
Station	-0.19	–	0.03
Person-to-person	-0.78	–	0.31

Source: Feldman (1976)

In the equations with the number of calls as the dependent variable, the independent variables are average revenue per call (as a measure of price), average length-of haul, population (Bell area), and regional dummy variables. The average revenue per operated-handled call is an additional predictor in the equation for person-to-person calls. Independent variables in the equations for average length-of-conversation are average revenue per minute, average length-of-haul, per-capita personal income, and the regional dummy variables. Double-logarithmic functions are specified throughout.

The price and income elasticities obtained in the study are tabulated in Table 8. The substantial price elasticity in the equation for person-to-person calls is something of an illusion, for it reflects a large cross elasticity with respect to the price of a station call. This cross elasticity is estimated to be 2.04. The "pure" price elasticity is thus -0.82, in keeping with the price elasticity in the equation for station-to-station calls, which includes only the own-price. In neither of the equations for average length-of-conversation is income significant statistically. Its t-ratio in the equation for person-to-person calls is 1.50 and only 0.20 in the equation for station calls. However, for income to be more important in the person-to-person equation clearly makes sense.

It is interesting to compare Feldman's results for toll calls made from coin stations with those for regular intrastate toll (cf. Table 3). In general, price elasticities for coin-station toll calls are somewhat larger than for toll calls from noncoin phones, while income elasticities are somewhat smaller. The most marked difference involves the coefficient for the exchange area proxy. In the noncoin toll equations, the coefficient is positive (and highly significant), whereas in the coin-station equations, it is negative (and also highly significant). It is not clear what this signifies.

IV. VERTICAL SERVICES[33]

Vertical services encompasses all equipment at the subscriber end, except for the main telephone. Included in vertical services, therefore, are residence and business extensions, PBX stations, PBS switchboards and switching equipment, Centrex, residence package plans, and other service and supplementary telephone equipment (hold features, intercom systems, special lights, bells, chimes, whistles, Mickey Mouse wagging his tail, etc.). The pre-1980 econometric literature on the demand for vertical services includes part or all of six studies, Feldman (1976), Huang (1975), Kearns (1978), New York Telephone (1976b), Reitman (1977), and Southern New England Telephone (1977d).

The Feldman study specifies equations for business and residence extensions separately, while Huang and Kearns both focus on residence extensions. The Feldman study uses state cross-sectional data in estimation, while Huang uses monthly time-series data for Minnesota. Reitman's primary focus, too, is on residence extensions, but an equation for the residential demand for total vertical services is also estimated. Reitman uses quarterly time-series for forty-five states for the period 1966–1974 in estimation. The NYT study estimates a model for total vertical services (business and residence combined) for New York State for the period 1965:2–1975:2. Finally, the SNET study estimates a model for total vertical services using quarterly data for the period 1970:2–1976:4.

Independent variables in the Feldman (double-logarithmic) equations are revenue per extension as a measure of the price of an extension, the price of local service, population, per-capita personal income, and regional dummy variables. The estimated elasticities with respect to the price of local service are -0.17 and -0.31 for residence and business, respectively. Kearns estimates a pooled time-series/cross-sectional model, using a data set consisting of observations on forty-seven geographical entities (states and cities) for thirty-seven quarters. The dependent variable in the analysis is deflated residence-extension revenue per capita, while the dependent variables are per-capita disposable income, the monthly basic service charge, the price of a residence

---

[33] With deregulation, the studies in this section are mostly of historical interest.

extension, and the service connection charge (all of the prices are deflated by CPI). The charge for additional message units (where applicable) was also included as a predictor, but its coefficient was insignificant, and the variable was dropped in the final model. A number of analysis-of-covariance models were used in the pooled analysis, and, in general, the results indicate that demand structures vary across states.

Huang estimates models for total residence extensions, inward movement of residence extension, and outward movement of residence extension. (The difference between inward and outward movement equals net change in extensions.) Independent variables are a price index for extensions and a measure (or measures) of the level of economic activity (usually residential construction). The number of residence main stations is also included in the model for total extensions. Static double-logarithmic equations are estimated using monthly time-series data. Autocorrelation is rampant in each case, and a correction for autocorrelation is applied. The strongest results are obtained for inward and outward movement.

The NYT study employs a logarithmic Koyck distributed-lag model, with a price index for terminal equipment, personal income, time, and a dummy variable to adjust for the effects of the fire in 1967 as predictors. The terminal-equipment price index and personal income are both deflated by the CPI for the New York metropolitan area. The dependent variable is defined as vertical-services revenue deflated by the price index for terminal equipment. Independent variables in Reitman's equations are a price index for residence extensions, per-capita personal income, and the number of residence main stations. The extension price index and personal income are both deflated by the national CPI. The equations are double-logarithmic, and are estimated using quarterly time-series data for each state separately and for all states combined. Reitman's results for all states combined are, in general, much stronger than for the states individually. In the combined equation, it is assumed that structures are homogenous across states, which, in light of the results obtained by Kearns, is probably not a valid assumption. Finally, the independent variables in the SNET study are real disposable income for Connecticut, a price variable, and the dependent variable lagged one period.

The price and income elasticities obtained in the six studies are tabulated in Table 9. The price elasticities are all less than 1 (in absolute value), suggesting that the demand for vertical services is inelastic with respect to changes in price. Kearns obtains an estimate of -0.33 for the price elasticity for residence extensions in his covariance model. Reitman obtains an estimate of -0.45. Kearns also finds a significant cross-price elasticity of -0.29 with respect to the monthly basic service charge. With exception of Feldman's equation

TABLE 9

Estimates of price and income elasticities of demand for vertical services

Study	Dependent Variable	Price Elasticity	Income Elasticity	Type of Data
Feldman (1976)	business extensions	-0.41	1.20	CS: states
Feldman (1976)	residence extensions	-0.16	0.52	CS: states
Huang (1975)	residence extensions	-0.008	0.002	TS: M, Minnesota
Huang (1975)	residence extensions (inward movement)	-0.26	0.44	TS: M, Minnesota
Huang (1975)	residence extensions (outward movement)	0.77	2.06	TS: M, Minnesota
Kearns (1978)	deflated residence-extension revenue per capita	-0.33	0.25	TS–CS: Q, 45 states
NYT (1976b)[a]	deflated terminal equipment revenue	(-0.16) -0.59	(0.22) 0.82	TS: Q, New York
Reitman (1977)	residence extensions	-0.45	0.52	TS–CS: Q, 45 states
Reitman (1977)	total residential vertical services	-0.99	0.29	
SNET (1977)[b]	deflated total vertical services	(-0.07) -0.15	(0.34) 0.79	TS: Q, Connecticut

[a] The NYT model is dynamic; short-run elasticities are in parentheses.
[b] The long-run in the SNET study refers to the elasticity calculated after the lapse of one year.
Symbols: TS: time-series; CS: cross-section; M: monthly; Q: quarterly.

for business extensions and Huang's equation for outward movement,[34] the estimated income elasticity for residence extensions is less then 1.

V. THE IMPACT OF SERVICE-CONNECTION AND OTHER NONCURRING CHARGES

The impact of service-connection and other nonrecurring charges on demand was of a great deal of interest in the 1970s because of pressure to unbundle local-service charges and, in particular, to bring installation charges into line with costs. The move toward cost-based installation charges became a serious matter on September 27, 1972, in Colorado when sharply high

---

[34] Huang's income elasticity for outward movement seems implausibly large.

service-connection charges were put into effect.[35] The charge for installing a telephone increased from a minimum of $7 to a minimum of $23 for a residence main station, while for a business, the minimum installation charge went from $7 to $15 for a phone on a private branch exchange (PBX) and to $60 for a non-PBX phone. The charge for disconnecting a residence phone, which previously was zero, was set at $12.

The Colorado case attracted considerable attention, and at least one formal study in an analysis by S.K. Black and P.V. Tryon, published in June 1976 by the Office of Telecommunications Policy of the U.S. Department of Commerce. Black and Tryon estimate econometric equations for both inward and outward movement of main stations and extensions for both business and residence customers, the purpose of the analysis being to estimate the impact of the September 1972 increase in service-connection charges.[36] Black and Tryon specify equations for inward and outward movement, with electric-meter installations, time, seasonal dummy variables, and a dummy variable for the change in the service-connection charge as independent variables. Electric-meter installations are included as a proxy for the economic and demographic factors that influence telephone movement. Monthly data for the period January 1969 through September 1973 are used in estimation.

Based on the coefficient for the dummy variable for the increase in the service-connection charge, Black and Tryon estimate that the increase in the service-connection charge resulted in a decrease in inward movement of 4,800 telephones per month and decrease in outward movement of 2,050 telephones per month. The net effect of the increased service-connection charge is thus estimated to have been 2,750 fewer new telephones per month. Of the decrease of 4,800 in inward movement, Black and Tryon estimate that 1,500 were potential residence main-station customers, 1,700 were potential residence extension customers, 400 were potential business main-station customers, and 1,200 were potential business extension customers.[37]

Unfortunately, Black and Tryon do not list the regression equations that generated these estimates, so that an evaluation of the statistical quality of the results is not possible.[38] Clearly, however, an increase in service-connection

[35] As stated in Decision No. 81320 (Docket 717, Colorado Public Utility Commission 1972, p. 16) "Failure to charge reasonably in line with the expense incurred is unjustly discriminatory to those that do not require the service, or at least require such service infrequently."

[36] Logically, the Black-Tryon study belongs in Section I of Appendix 1 with the analysis of access demand. I have included it in this section because of its explicit focus on service-connection charges.

[37] See Black and Tryon (1976, p. 7).

[38] Black and Tryon provide 95 percent confidence intervals for their forecasts. However, estimates of the other coefficients, standard errors, and so on could usefully have been provided as well.

charges of the magnitude of the one in Colorado should be expected to have an impact on inward and outward movement. Yet, at the same time, one should also expect the elasticities to be small.[39] And the price elasticities for main-station inward movement implicit in the Black-Tryon results clearly confirm this, being of the order of -0.02 for residential customers and -0.06 for business customers. These values agree closely with the estimates obtained by Perl (1978) and Waverman (1974).[40]

The only other econometric analysis of non-recurring charges that came to my attention in the first edition of this book is a study by the Southern New England Telephone Company (1977a). The dependent variable in the SNET analysis is deflated nonrecurring revenues in the area served by SNET in Connecticut. Independent variables are a deflated index of nonrecurring charges, disposable personal income, the change in Connecticut unemployment, the dependent variable lagged one period, and two dummy variables to correct for strikes in 1968:2 and 1971:3. A double logarithmic model is estimated with quarterly data for the period 1963:2 through 1976:4. The estimate of the price elasticity in the SNET model is -0.06 in the short run and -0.10 after a lapse of one year. Although they are larger, these values are, in general, in keeping with the values obtained by Black and Tryon, Perl, and Waverman. The one-year income elasticity is estimated to be 0.72. The t-ratios for the price and income coefficients are -2.72 and 2.53, respectively.

VI. INTERNATIONAL DEMAND

In previous sections, a number of studies of telephone demand in other countries have been reviewed, but the focus in each case was on domestic demand. Our attention in this section will be on international demand, where international is defined as communications to any point outside of the forty-eight contiguous U.S. states.

Let us begin with some general observations. Since an international telephone call is long-distance by definition, international demand should be expected to behave more or less the same as domestic toll demand. Depending on where one is calling, however, there are also some important differences.

---

[39] As was discussed in Section I of Appendix 1, we should expect "churning" caused by temporary changes in address (college students leaving for the summer, use of vacation homes, etc.) to be the most sensitive to increases in service-connection charges. Inward and outward movement associated with permanent changes of address will be less sensitive to changes in these charges because they are part of the larger costs of moving. Also, one should expect changes in service-connection charges to have a greater impact on extension phones than on main stations.

[40] See Section I of Appendix 1.

In the first place, domestic toll calling is routine with nearly everyone, but this is not necessarily the case with international calling; in fact, most people have never made an international call.[41] In the second place, even when adjusted for distance, an international call is about two to three times more expensive than a domestic toll call, and this may contribute to the mystique that makes an international call seem to be a very different product from a domestic toll call.[42] Also, with the exception of calls to Canada, an international call is typically a production compared with a domestic call. An operator is often required in the country originating the call, and, partly because of time differences, chances of reaching the party desired are usually substantially reduced. For example, the completion rate (in the mid-1970s) for domestic calls is about 70 percent, but usually around 50 percent for international calls. Moreover, for calls to some international points, equipment is limited, and it may be hours (or, in some extreme cases, days) before a call can be placed. Thus, the time required to initiate and complete an international call is an important addition to the out-of-pocket costs of the calls.[43]

Another substantive difference between international and domestic toll demand is the possible importance of telegraph and telex as competitive modes of communication. Much of the time, the purpose of an international call may be served equally well by a telegram or telex. This contrasts with domestic toll calls, where the time and out-of-pocket costs of a call are small in comparison with the costs of a telex or a telegram. Recognition of the competition provided by telegraph and telex has led, in some cases, to the specification of multi-equation models in which the international demands for telephone, telegraph, and telex are approached as a group.[44]

[41] This excludes calls between the United States and Canada. Also, the focus here in on calls made by U.S. residents. The statement may therefore not apply to residents of Western Europe.

[42] I have in mind the higher priority and the greater sense of urgency usually associated with an international call, particularly by people who do not frequently use this service. A similar mystique attaches, although less now than in the past, to a long-distance call vis-à-vis a local call. In the past, the phrase, "long-distance calling", was virtually certain to snap one to attention. With DDD, the stimulus has become more subtle; one listens for the long-distance "hum". For a discussion and analysis of a survey conducted in 1955 of motives and attitudes toward long-distance calls, see Adelson *et al.* (1956).

[43] However, it should be noted that, with the advent of modern cable technology (TAT III in 1963) and satellite communications in 1965, both the completion time and the real cost of an international call have been significantly reduced. Even the proportion of calls dialed by the customer has increased sharply in the last few years. In 1973, for example, only 35 percent of international (two-way) calls (not including Canada and Mexico) did not require an operator in either country. By 1976, this figure reached 60 percent. I am indebted to Robert Craver for these observations.

[44] See, in particular, Rea and Lage (1978), Lago (1970), and Yatrakis (1972).

Much of the research on international telephone demand has been undertaken at AT&T and Bell Canada,[45] so that, not surprisingly, most of the focus in the empirical literature is on the United States and Canada. In general, research at AT&T has focused on the development of models, on a country-by-country basis, for explaining the volume of voice communication between the United States and other countries. As of December 1977, AT&T had developed and were using some thirty-one different models for forecasting traffic between the forty-eight contiguous states and the rest of the world. Of these, twenty-five were annual models, three quarterly, and three monthly. Included in the "inventory" were models for twenty-eight countries, Alaska, Hawaii, Puerto Rico, and the Virgin Islands.

Besides the efforts of Craver and Khadem, other studies of international telephone demand include Communications Satellite Corporation (1969), Kumins (1967), Rea and Lage (1978), Lago (1970), Naleszkiewicz (1970), and Yatrakis (1972). As mentioned earlier, the studies of Rea and Lage, Lago, and Yatrakis focus on telegraph and telex, as well as on telephone. In each study, there is an attempt to estimate cross-elasticities of telephone demand with respect to the prices of telegraph and telex. Telegraph and telex as substitutes for voice communication are not considered in the models of Craver and Khadem. The studies of Rea and Lage, Lago, and Yatrakis also differ in the data that are used in estimation. In the studies of Craver and Khadem, the models are either of one country with another or of one country with the rest of the world, and time-series data are used in estimation. In the Rea-Lage, Lao, and Yatrakis studies, in contrast, the focus is not on specific country pairs, and either cross-section or pooled time-series/cross-section data are used in estimation.[46]

The price and income elasticities estimated by Craver, Khadem, Rea and Lage, Lago, and Yatrakis are tabulated in Tables 10 and 11. The estimated elasticities of Craver and Khadem are given in Table 10, while the estimates of Rea and Lage, Lago, and Yatrakis are given in Table 11. The results suggest price and income elasticities for international telephone demand that, on balance, are larger than the ones for domestic toll demand.[47] This is

[45]   See Craver (1975, 1976a, 1976b, 1976c, 1976d, 1977) and Khadem (1973b, 1976).

[46]   During the period under review, AT&T did not feel that competition between international calls and telegraph or telex was a significant factor. The use of international telegrams has been declining for several years, and was no longer of quantitative importance. Telex services require special terminal equipment and are thus used almost exclusively by business. Indeed, in AT&T's view, the business use of telex services is more a complement to voice communications, rather than a substitute, because of a customer's need to have a paper copy. Again, I am indebted to Robert Craver for these observations.

[47]   Rea and Lage use a pooled time-series/cross-sectional sample of observations for thirty-seven major routes. The data are annual for the years 1964–1973. Lago also uses a pooled time-

especially evident in Khadem's results for Canada. A second point to note is the impact of the prices of telegraph and telex. Both Lago and Yatrakis find a positive cross elasticity with respect to the price of telegraph, but Rea and Lage find this cross elasticity to be negative. Of the two positive estimates, the one obtained by Yatrakis is the only one with robustness, for the t-ratio for Lago's cross elasticity is only 1.7. On the other hand, the cross elasticity estimated by Rea and Lage is not only negative, but is also very large (-2.93) and highly significant statistically (its t-ratio is -7.52). In general, however, one should view this finding with skepticism.

Despite the attention that international telephone demand has received in recent years, much remains to be done. Existing results clearly indicate that price – as well as income – is an important factor, and, further, that the price of telex service should also be considered in order to better determine whether telephone and telex are substitutes or complements. More recent research has shown that trade volume, industrial structure, and ethnic overlaps are important variables. The results tabulated in Tables 10 and 11 suggest that international price and income elasticities – especially income elasticities – may be larger than their domestic counterparts. Given that an international call is clearly a luxury in most quarters, especially residence calls, this is not unreasonable. Nevertheless, one must be skeptical at this point of the size of the elasticities that have been obtained. The problem, as has been noted by Kumins (1967), is that most rate changes to date have been rate decreases associated with the introduction of new or expanded facilities. Consequently, it is not clear how much of the elasticity that is observed is the result of the releasing of a supply constraint, as opposed to a genuine demand response. While there has been some attempt to take circuit constraints into account (notably by Craver 1976d; Kumins 1967), the problem clearly requires more attention than is has been given.

VII. YELLOW-PAGES ADVERTISING

Up to this point in this review, we have considered the demand for access to the telephone system, the demand for the use of the telephone system, and the demand for certain types of telephone-related equipment. However, there is another service that telephone companies provide, but which is usually

series/cross-sectional sample consisting of annual observations on telephone traffic between the United States and twenty-three other countries for 1962–1964. Finally, Yatrakis uses a cross-sectional sample consisting of observations for sixty-six countries for 1967. The dependent variable for Yatrakis is the number of originating telephone calls from a country to all other countries to which it is linked via good-quality telephone facilities.

TABLE 10

Estimates of price and income elasticities for international telephone demand (Part I)

Study	Dependent Variable	Price Elasticity		Income Elasticity		Type of Data
		Short-Run	Long-Run	Short-Run	Long-Run	
Craver (1976c)	billed minutes U.S. to U.K.		(-0.38)		(0.09)	TS: A
Craver (1977)	messages, U.S. originating		(-0.51)		(2.37)	TS: A
Craver (1976d)	messages		(-0.46)		(2.67)	TS: A
Craver (1976d)	messages, U.K. to U.S.	-0.63	-1.02	–	–	TS: A
Craver (1976a)	messages, 2-way U.S. to Canada	-0.23	-0.62	0.44	1.18	TS: A
Craver (1976a)	messages, 2-way U.S. to Canada	-0.42	-0.52	1.28	1.60	TS: Q
Craver (1976a)	messages, U.S. to Canada		(-0.70)		(1.65)	TS: Q
Craver (1976a)	messages, Canada to U.S.		(-0.55)		(1.49)	TS: Q
Khadem (1976)	messages, Canada outward	-0.89	-3.65	2.19	9.03	TS: Q
Khadem (1973)	messages, Canada to U.S.	–	–	0.59	1.84	TS: Q
Khadem (1973)	deflated ARPM Canada to U.S.	-0.61	-1.67	–	–	TS: Q
Khadem (1973)	deflated revenues Canada to U.S.	-0.30	-1.12	0.94	3.2	TS: Q

Symbols: TS, time series; A, annual; Q, quarterly; ARPM, average revenue per message.

TABLE 11

Estimates of price and income elasticities for international telephone demand (Part II)

Study	Dependent Variable	Tele-phone	Tele-graph	Telex	Income	Type of Data
Rea & Lage (1978)	messages, U.S. outward	-0.73	-2.93	0.31	2.62	CS–TS: A, 37 point-to-point routes
Lago (1970)	messages, U.S. outward	-1.69	0.29	–	–	CS–TS: A, 23 countries
Yatrakis (1972)	messages, outward,	-0.82	1.31	-0.49	0.66	CS: 46 countries, 1967
Yatrakis (1972)	messages, outward	-2.31	2.73	-0.42	1.78	CS: 23 developed countries, 1967
Yatrakis (1972)	messages, outward	-0.96	–	–	–	CS: 23 developing countries, 1967

Symbols: TS: time-series; CS: cross-section; A: annual.

not considered in the same light as access and use, namely, yellow-pages advertising. Yellow-pages advertising is an important source of revenue for telephone companies. This section, accordingly, is devoted to a brief discussion of a study by Wang (1976) of the demand for yellow-pages advertising in the service areas of fourteen pre-divestiture Bell System operating telephone companies.

Since the topic is somewhat off the beaten path, I shall make the digression self-contained by considering a theoretical framework for analyzing the demand for Yellow-pages advertising. Accordingly, let us assume (following Wang) that the demand for yellow-pages advertising can be reduced to the demand for yellow-pages space and that the price charged for an advertisement is proportional to the space the advertisement requires. Space, however, is not perfectly divisible, but rather is offered for sale in blocks of different sizes, say, $s_1, s_2, \ldots, s_n$. Let p_i be the price of s_i, and assume that the p_i are ordered $s_1 < s_2 < \ldots < s_n$, so that $p_1 < p_2 < \ldots < p_n$.

Let us now assume that we have a population consisting of M firms and that each firm allocates a maximum amount that it is willing to spend for space in the yellow pages.[48] Let this amount for the jth firm be denoted by

---

[48] What determines this maximum amount is clearly an interesting and relevant question, but will not be considered here.

y_j. On the assumption that more space is preferred to less space, the firm will purchase the largest advertisement that it can afford. That is, the firm will purchase the maximum s_i for which $y_j > p_i$. Alternatively, s_i will be determined as the i for which

$$p_i \leq y_j < p_i + 1 \quad \text{for } i \leq n - 1$$

$$p_i < y_j \quad \text{for } i = n. \tag{4}$$

The number of advertisements of size s_i that will be purchased will then be given by the number of firms whose yellow-pages advertising budgets satisfy these inequalities.

More formally, let

$$\delta(p_i, y_j) = \begin{cases} 1 & \text{if } p_i \leq y_j p_{i+1} \text{ or } p_n < y_j \\ 0 & \text{otherwise,} \end{cases} \tag{5}$$

and let

$$N_i = \sum_{j \in M} \delta(p_i, y_j). \tag{6}$$

Further, let $F(y_j)$ denote the cumulative distribution function of yellow-pages advertising budgets over the M firms. Then,

$$N_i = F(p_{i+1}) - F(p_i) \tag{7}$$

defines the demand function for the ith size of yellow-pages advertisement.[49]

If we now assume that the distribution of yellow-pages advertising budgets is such that

$$F(p_{i+2}) - F(p_{i+1}) < F(p_{i+1}) - F(p_i) \tag{8}$$

for all i, then $N_i > N_{i+1}$, and N_i plotted against p_i will be a decreasing step function.[50] If the size of an advertisement were made to vary continuously, and if the number of firms is large, this step function would approach a smooth curve. This curve, which we shall denote by $N(p)$, can be viewed as the market demand function for yellow-pages advertising.

Let me now turn to the empirical results obtained by Wang. Wang assumes that the function $N(p)$ can be approximated by a double logarithmic function,

$$\ln N = \alpha + \beta \ln p + \alpha \ln T + u, \tag{9}$$

[49] The yellow-pages space of size s_i demanded will clearly be given by $N_i s_i$.
[50] A sufficient condition for this result is that the "yield" from a yellow-pages advertisement be a decreasing function of the ad's space.

where T and u denote the number of telephones and a random error term. The number of telephones is included as a surrogate for market size. Wang estimates the model in (9), using pooled time-series/cross-sectional data for fourteen pre-divestiture Bell System operating companies.

Wang's price elasticities vary from -0.72 to -1.49, and his elasticities with respect to the number of telephones range from 0.92 to 1.26. The medians of these estimates are -0.94 and 1.02. Wang's results will be illustrated with his equation for one OTC, namely:[51]

$$\ln N = \frac{-4.33}{(-17.81)} - \frac{0.72}{(-39.13)} \ln P + \frac{1.13}{(52.08)} \ln T. \tag{10}$$

Wang does not present any goodness-of-fit statistics, but the large values for the t-ratios suggest that the equation probably fits the data very well. This is the case in all of the equations estimated. The coefficient of 1.13 for the logarithm of the number of telephones is of particular interest, for it is significantly greater than 1, and is therefore consistent with the existence of a positive network externality.

VIII. NONECONOMETRIC APPROACHES TO FORECASTING TELEPHONE DEMAND

To this point, the focus has been on the econometric literature on telephone demand. By "econometric" I mean studies that focus on the quantification of the basic economic, sociological, and demographical determinants of telephone. In most of the studies reviewed, the emphasis has been on estimation of price and income elasticities of demand and the development of models for forecasting the impact on revenues of changes in telephone tariffs. When we consider forecasting per se, however, an econometric model is only one of several approaches that might be used. Time-series models have been used in a number of contexts, and, in this concluding section, we shall provide a brief summary of several of these.[52]

---

[51] T-ratios are in parentheses. This equation is estimated with pooled data from nineteen directories for the years 1970–1976. The sample contains 819 data points.

[52] Even more than in preceding sections, the discussion in this section is neither detailed nor exhaustive. The purpose here is merely to provide the readers with an introduction to the pre-1980 time-series literature on forecasting telecommunications demand.

1. Bhattacharya (1974)

Bhattacharya (1974) is concerned with forecasting the demand for a telephone in Australia. To this end, a Box-Jenkins ARIMA[53] model is applied to a demand series from which the effect of the connection charge plus annual rental have been removed. The model estimated thus takes the form of a regression model with one independent variable and an ARIMA error term. The dependent variable in the model is the twelve-month percentage change in the number of new telephones installed, while the independent variable is the twelve-month percentage change in the connection charge plus annual rental. Monthly data for the period July 1962 through June 1971 are used in estimation. The price elasticity estimated by Bhattacharya is -0.91 with a t-ratio of -8.27.

2. Dunn, Williams, and Spivey (1971)

Dunn, Williams, and Spivey (1971) focus on forecasting inward and outward movement of business and residence main stations in three Michigan cities, Battle Creek, Grand Rapids, and Flint. The data analyzed are monthly for the fifteen-year period 1954–1968. A number of forecasting models are examined, including a simple trend-seasonal-irregular time-series decomposition, adaptive exponential smoothing, and adaptive exponential smoothing with exogenous variables.[54] The authors emphasize the problems of obtaining meaningful exogenous variables for local areas, but note the gain in precision that is likely to be achieved if exogenous predictors can be found. In the case of Flint, a 15 percent reduction in the mean absolute forecast error was obtained through the use of the number of employees covered by unemployment compensation and the number of households as exogenous predictors.

3. Thompson and Tiao (1971)

Thompson and Tiao (1971) bring Box-Jenkins methodology to bear on forecasting monthly inward and outward movements in Wisconsin using data of the Wisconsin Telephone Company for the period January 1951 through October 1966. In contrast to Dunn, Williams, and Spivey, inward and outward movements are not decomposed to business and residence customers.

[53] AutoRegressive Integrated Moving Average. For a discussion of Box-Jenkins procedures, see Box and Jenkins (1976) or Granger and Newbold (1977).

[54] For discussion of adaptive forecasting models, see Nerlove and Wage (1964) and Theil and Wage (1964). Cf. also Chen and Winters (1966) and Crane and Crotty (1967).

Also, the series analyzed refer to the inward and outward movement of all telephones, rather than just main stations. As one might expect, Thompson and Tiao find strong seasonal effects in both inward and outward movement, as well as some effects between months. They test the assumption of constant seasonal effects over time, but find no evidence to refute it.[55]

4. Tomasek (1972)

Tomasek (1972) is concerned with developing a model to forecast inward movement of main stations in metropolitan Montreal. Tomasek notes that traditional predictors, such as the change in personal income and new residential construction expenditures, are difficult to find for an area as small as the one considered, and thus turns to an autoregressive time-series model. Ten years of monthly data (1961–1970) are used in estimation. Tomasek estimates a regression of inward movement on itself at one, three, five, twelve, thirteen, fifteen, and seventeen months in the past, and he also estimates a Box-Jenkins ARIMA model. On balance, however, the forecasts from the ARIMA model are not quite as good as the ones from the pure autoregressive model.

5. Wellenius (1970)

Wellenius (1970) focuses on the development of a model for forecasting the residential demand for telephones in Santiago, Chile. Wellenius postulates that residential telephone demand is determined solely by income, and defines demand as including the desire to have a telephone if income is sufficient to pay for it. This allows for suppressed demand arising from supply constraints on telephone availability. Income is assumed to be lognormally distributed, but with parameters that vary over time. Wellenius obtains an estimate from survey information of the "threshold" value of income for demanding a telephone. Forecasts of residential telephone demand at any other point in time can then be obtained by combining the threshold level of income, which is viewed as a parameter, with estimates of the appropriate parameters of the distribution of income.[56]

---

[55] Thompson and Tiao note that inward and outward movements are probably related – most disconnections lead to later reconnections – but the possibilities of this are not examined.

[56] Wellenius' model is very much along the lines of the one discussed in Section II of Chapter 2. The only really essential difference is an assumption that the threshold level of income for demanding access to the telephone system is independent of price and system size.

NETWORK EXTERNALITY AND THE DEMAND FOR RESIDENTIAL LONG-DISTANCE TELEPHONE SERVICE: A COMMENT*

Much of the debate in the first Interexchange Competition Hearing before the Canadian Radio-television and Telecommunications Commission in 1984 focused on the toll demand models submitted by Bell Canada in evidence and whether the estimated price elasticities of demand were implausibly small because of the coefficients for the market size variable being implausibly large. In 1985, Jon Breslaw (Breslaw 1985) wrote a searching critique of the Bell Canada models in which he purported to show that Bell's estimates of price and market size elasticities are degraded by multicollinearity. This appendix comments on Breslaw's analysis.

In the hearings before the CRTC (hereafter referred to as the IX hearings), CNCP advanced a value of -1.34 for the toll price elasticity, while Bell Canada argued that the elasticity is more of the order of -0.5. CNCP's figure was based upon models estimated by Breslaw (1980) and Fuss and Waverman (1981) using Bell Canada data and Bozman (1983) using data of B.C. Telephone. In testimony offered on behalf of Bell Canada (Taylor 1984), I noted that when the Bell and Breslaw-Fuss-Waverman models were estimated from the same data set, the size of the price elasticity depended upon the constraints that are imposed upon the coefficient of the variable representing "market size". A priori constraints were placed on this coefficient in the Breslaw and Fuss-Waverman models, but not in the Bell models. In rebuttal, CNCP argued that Bell's coefficients for market size implied an implausibly large network externality and suggested that the sensitivity of the toll price elasticity to constraints on the market-size coefficients is the result of harmful multicollinearity. In the paper under review, Breslaw develops these arguments in detail. He begins with a searching discussion of the conceptual basis of the network externality and the forms it might take. He advances a framework for measuring the externality which differs from that used by Bell Canada. Finally, using the collinearity diagnostic procedures developed by Belsley, Kuh, and Welsch (1980) and Belsley (1982), he reach-

---

* The original version of this comment was submitted by Bell Canada in evidence in the Price Elasticity Modelling Hearings before the CRTC in early 1989.

es the conclusion that the Bell Canada models are bedeviled with harmful multicollinearity.

I. A MODEL OF TOLL DEMAND

To facilitate the discussion, it will be useful to begin with a simplified version of the model which underlies Bell Canada's analyses. Suppose that we have two exchanges, A and B, that are not part of the same local calling area, so that calls between the exchanges are toll calls. Let the number of telephones in exchange A be T, and the number of telephones in exchange B be R. The total possible connections between the two exchanges will therefore be equal to $T \cdot R$. This is the measure of market size that is used in the Bell Canada models.[1] Let M denote the number of calls that are "sent paid" from A to B during some period of time (a quarter, say), and let θ denote the proportion of the potential connections $(T \cdot R)$ that M represents, so that

$$M = \theta T \cdot R. \tag{1}$$

Equation (1) might describe the relationship that would be observed in a completely stationary world – i.e., where income, price, and all the other factors that affect toll calling are constant. However, these other factors do not remain constant, and we can allow for them through the value of θ. In particular, let us suppose that income (Y) and price (P) of a toll call from A to B affect θ according to

$$\theta = aY^\beta P^\gamma, \tag{2}$$

where a, β, and γ are constants. The relationship in expression (1) accordingly becomes

$$M = aY^\beta P^\gamma (T \cdot R). \tag{3}$$

We come now to the question which is the focus in Breslaw's paper and of this comment: How does M vary with market size as measured by potential toll connections? In the Bell Canada models, it is assumed that an increase in

---

[1] There is a strong tendency in the literature to treat the telephone network as a closed system, in which case A and B coincide and TR would be equal to $T(T-1)$. For large T, this is essentially the same as T^2. This leads Breslaw to interpret Bell Canada's market-size variable as simply the square of the number of telephones. The error involved is empirically not serious in the case of aggregated data, but can lead to serious errors in interpretation, especially when the specification is usage per telephone.

the number of telephones in either A or B affects calling either more or less than proportionately, so that instead of equation (3) we have

$$M = aY^{\beta}P^{\gamma}(T \cdot R)^{\lambda} \tag{4}$$

where λ is a constant, presumably of the order of 1. If we take logarithms of both sides of this equation, we obtain

$$\ln M = \alpha + \beta \ln Y + \gamma \ln P + \lambda \ln(T \cdot R), \tag{5}$$

where $\alpha = \ln a$. With the addition of a random error term, equation (5) represents the model estimated by Bell Canada in the IX Hearings. The results for the four "Bell-Intra" models that were presented in my IX testimony are reproduced in Table 1. The Bell models appear on the fourth line of the table; the models on the first three lines should be ignored for the moment.

CNCP in the IX Hearings and Breslaw in his paper take issue with the Bell results because of what they interpret to be implausibly large network externalities. The basis for Breslaw's objection can be illustrated by rewriting equation (4) as

$$\frac{M}{T} = aY^{b}P^{c}R^{k}, \tag{6}$$

where, like a, b, and c, k is a constant. Breslaw's essential point is that, in a mature telephone system such as Canada's, usage per telephone should be largely independent of the number of telephones that can be reached, which is to say that k should be zero or close to zero. The results for the Bell Models in Table 1 strongly suggest otherwise, for the coefficients on potential toll connections $T \cdot R$ are much closer to one than to zero. What happens when prior constraints are imposed on k is evident in the first three models in Table 1. The models are identified with Breslaw (1980), Fuss and Waverman (1981), and Bozman (1983).

As all of the models are double-logarithmic, their comparison is facilitated by writing them with a common form for the dependent variable:

$$\ln M = \alpha + \beta \ln Y + \gamma \ln P + \lambda \ln(T \cdot R) \quad \text{[Bell Canada]} \tag{7}$$

$$\ln M = a_0 + a_1 \ln Y + a_2 \ln P + a_3 \ln \text{POP} \quad \text{[Breslaw]} \tag{8}$$

$$\ln M = b_0 + b_1 \ln Y + b_2 \ln P + (1 - b_1) \ln \text{POP} \quad \text{[Fuss \& Waverman]} \tag{9}$$

$$\ln M = c_0 + c_1 \ln Y + c_2 \ln P - -c_1 \ln \text{POP} + \ln T \quad \text{[Bozman].}^2 \tag{10}$$

----

[2] This represents the long-run equilibrium (or steady-state) form of Bozman's model.

TABLE 1

Comparison of price and market size elasticities from CNCP and Bell Canada toll demand models*.

Model	Short Haul (0–100 miles)				Long Haul (101+ miles)			
	Peak		Off Peak**		Peak		Off Peak**	
	Price	Market Size	Price	Market Size	Price	Market Size	Price	Market Size
Bredslaw	-0.317	4.220	-0.335	4.497	-0.634	2.892	-0.454	4.023
	(-3.57)	(56.32)	(-2.89)	(26.67)	(-5.77)	(9.48)	(-4.60)	(13.97)
			-0.054				-0.044	
			(-2.89)				(-2.49)	
Fuss/Waverman	-2.055	2.964+	-1.410	2.386+	-1.243	1.054+	-1.224	1.287+
	(-12.50)		(-5.87)		(-17.43)		(-10.10)	
Bozman	-1.595	1.240++	-1.147	0.888++	-0.927	-0.176++	-0.992	0.064++
	(-12.97)	(8.33)	(-6.06)	(4.94)	(-16.72)	(-2.28)	(-10.26)	(0.54)
		1.000	-0.221	1.000++		1.000	-0.108	1.000++
			(-8.79)				(-4.37)	
Bell Canada	-0.282	1.025	-0.265	1.158	-0.370	0.829	-0.354	1.043
	(-4.96)	(88.71)	(-3.40)	(40.35)	(-3.74)	(13.13)	(-3.99)	(16.57)
			-0.059				-0.036	
			(-4.82)				(-2.35)	

* All models estimated using quarterly data for Bell-Intra for 1974 Q1 – 1983 Q3. t-Ratios are in parentheses, when available.

** Two price variables are included in the off-peak models to take into account a change in the weekend discount structure which occurred in June 1977.

+ The coefficient for market size in the Fuss-Waverman model, from equation (12) in the text, is $(1 - b_1)$.

++ Market size in the Bozman model is represented by $\ln$ POP (whose coefficient is constrained to be the negative of the coefficient of $\ln Y$), and by $\ln T$ (whose coefficient is constrained to be 1).

Source: Taylor (1984, p. 28)

Population (POP) is the only variable not previously defined.

As is evident in Table 1, imposition of constraints on the coefficient for the market-size variable has severe consequences for the price elasticities, for they are much larger in the Fuss-Waverman and Bozman models. Since, apart from the different variables for market size, the models are estimated from a common data set (hereafter referred to as the "509" data set), the sensitivity of the price elasticities to constraints on the coefficient for market size must necessarily reflect sample intercorrelations between and among income, price, and market size. In my IX testimony, I took the position that the Bell Canada model is the correct model and that the Breslaw, Fuss-Waverman, and Bozman models are misspecifications. The differences in price elasticities can then be attributed (via the Theil theorem on the impact of an omitted variable) to the misspecifications. Breslaw, in contrast, adopts the view that, because the implied network externalities (on his interpretation of how to define the externality) are so large, the "tradeoff" must be a reflection of "harmful" multicollinearity. Breslaw attempts to establish that this is the case using the Belsley-Kuh-Welsch (BKW) and Belsley tests for harmful multicollinearity.

Breslaw's view is that the network externality, if it exists, will be manifested in greater usage per telephone in a larger system as opposed to a small system – i.e., usage per telephone will be a positive function of the number of telephones that can be reached.[3] Following de Fontenay and Lee (1983), Breslaw notes that the conventional formulation of the network externality does not distinguish between an increase in the penetration rate, with no expansion in the population (Type I externality), and an increase in the number of telephones, with no change in the penetration rate (Type II externality). Since Canada has effectively had universal service for years, Breslaw dismisses the Type I externality and focuses on the Type II externality. Properly in my view, Breslaw poses the Type II externality in terms of community of interest rather than simply the number of telephones. As he notes (Breslaw 1985, p. 5):

> Clearly, an individual living in a region composed of a population of 30 is going to make more calls when the population increases to 10,000. The reason is clear – the individual's community of interest will have increased, and thus the population growth will result in an increased demand for toll by each subscriber. The present empirical question is whether the

[3] As noted in Chapter 9, this is not a necessary implication of the network externality, because an externality can exist without it affecting usage per telephone. For what an increase in network size offers subscribers (and potential subscribers) is the *option* of reaching more telephones. This option can increase willingness-to-pay for access, but there is no necessity for this to be reflected in increased usage.

individual's community of interest expands when the population of a given region increases from say, 3 million to 6 million.

This is the right question. The task is to formulate it in a way that allows for unambiguous empirical testing. In pursuit of this, Breslaw specifies a Koyck double-logarithmic model as follows:

$$\ln(Q/H)_t = a + a_5 \ln P_t + a_6 \ln(Y/H)_t$$
$$+ a_7 \ln MS_t + a_8 \ln(Q/H)_{t-1} + \varepsilon_t, \qquad (11)$$

where:[4]

Q = price-deflated toll revenue per household, for off-peak calls of greater than 100 miles

P = four-quarter moving average of real toll price

Y = real personal disposable income per household in Ontario and Quebec

MS = market size, defined as the number of weighted potential toll connections

ε = random error term.

The results from estimating this model from quarterly Bell Canada data (1974:1 through 1983:3) for Ontario and Quebec are given in Table 2. Although the results are not directly comparable because of definitional differences with the results given in Table 1, the price elasticity is of the same order of magnitude as in the models labeled Breslaw and Bell Canada in that table. However, except for the seasonal effects, none of the coefficients is strong statistically, and Breslaw interprets this as an indication that multicollinearity is muddying the water. He is also concerned about the coefficient on market size, which he views as implausibly large.

The first question that needs to be asked is whether Breslaw's model is appropriate for the task at hand. In assessing this, it will be useful to rewrite Breslaw's model in the notation used earlier in this section. The steady-state form of the model will suffice:

$$\ln(Q/H) = a^* + a_5^* \ln P + a_6^* \ln(Y/H) + a_7^* \ln(T \cdot R) \qquad (12)$$

[4] $a = a_0 + a_1 QD1 + a_2 QD2 + a_3 QD3 + a_4$ RCENT, where QD_i, $i = 1, 2, 3$, denote seasonal dummy variables and RCENT denotes a shift variable for a change in the Toronto EAS in 1976.

TABLE 2

Unconstrained estimation; Breslaw model

| Method: | OLS | | | |
| Dependent Variable: | LnQ | | | |

| Variable | Short-Run | | Long-Run | |
	Coeff.	t-stat	Coeff.	t-stat
C	-16.6027	-3.24		
RCENT	0.0597	3.45		
QD1	-0.0600	-2.31		
QD2	-0.0990	-7.30		
QD3	-0.1842	-8.70		
LnP	-0.4667	-2.04	-0.5496	-2.36
LnY	0.4996	2.79	0.5884	2.94
LnMS	0.3982	2.72	0.4691	3.10
LnQL	0.1510	0.91		

SER = 0.01725   R-Squared = 0.9901

D.W. = 2.0270   Observations = 36

Durbin H = -0.8032

Source: Breslaw (1985, p. 8)

where H denotes the number of households and $MS = (T \cdot R)$ from earlier. For comparison, we rewrite the earlier model of this section:

$$\ln(Q/H) = \alpha + \beta \ln(Y/H) + \theta \ln P + \lambda \ln(T \cdot R) + (\beta - 1) \ln H. \quad (13)$$

Comparing equation (13) with equation (12), we see that the two models are equivalent for $\beta = 1$. However, from Table 2 we find that empirically this is not the case, for the long-run coefficient for income is seen to be about 0.6. The problem would seem to be in Breslaw's definition of market size. For, although the dependent variable and income are expressed per-household in Breslaw's model, market size continues to measured in terms of potential toll connections. This does not make sense. What matters to a household is not the number of potential toll connections but simply the number of telephones that can be reached. The number of potential toll connections is a relevant measure of market size from the point of view of the serving telephone company, but not for an individual household. If this point is accepted,the appropriate per-household specification would be

$$\ln(Q/H) = b_0 + b_1 \ln P + b_2 \ln(Y/H) + b_3 \ln R. \qquad (14)$$

Since during the period in question Ontario and Quebec essentially had universal service, T in equation (14) can reasonably be replaced by H, in which case (14) can be written:

$$\ln(Q/H) = \alpha + \beta \ln(Y/H) + \gamma \ln P + \lambda \ln R + (\beta + \lambda - 1) \ln H. \quad (15)$$

Comparison of this equation with equation (12) shows that equivalence of the two models now requires that $\beta + \lambda$ be equal to 1 – i.e., that the coefficients for income and market size sum to 1. In Table 2, we see that they in fact sum to 1.06, which is close enough to 1 to establish the point. This is an important result because it means that the differences between Breslaw and Bell Canada do not involve fundamentally different models. We can concentrate on finding the best way of allowing for the network externality and then assessing whether the estimation is compromised by harmful multicollinearity.

II. ISOLATION OF THE NETWORK EXTERNALITY

I now turn to an analysis of Breslaw's concerns regarding the size of the network externality and whether its empirical importance is exaggerated by harmful multicollinearity. A modified version of the model developed in the preceding section will be used, in which usage per telephone is related to real income per household, the real price of toll calling, and market size as measured by the number of telephones that can be reached:

$$\ln(Q/T)_t = \alpha + \beta \ln(Y/H)_t + \gamma \ln P_t + \varepsilon_t, \qquad (16)$$

where the variables are all as defined previously.

The results from estimating this model from the 509 data set for long-haul (greater than 100 miles) off-peak toll for Ontario and Quebec are given in column A in Table 3. The price and income elasticities are of the same magnitude as in the aggregate model [i.e., the model in equation (5), tabulated on the fourth line in Table 1], while market size continues to have a strong positive effect. The results with market size excluded from the model are tabulated in column F of the table. Once again, we see the effect that constraining the effect of market size has on the price elasticity, for it is seen to jump from -0.35 to -1.3.

In an effort to take a face value Breslaw's observation that the network externality should be expected to operate as a system goes from 30 to 10,000

TABLE 3A

Bell Canada DDD offpeak long haul; alternative measures of marketsize. (509 data, 1974 Q1 to 1983 Q3)

	Marketsize* A	Marketsize* B	Marketsize* C	Marketsize* D
Price.1	-0.3349	-0.3277	-0.3305	-0.3278
	(-3.7)	(-3.6)	(-3.6)	(-3.6)
Price.2	-0.0321	-0.0323	-0.0322	-0.0323
	(-2.0)	(-2.1)	(-2.1)	(-2.1)
Income	0.4442	0.4245	0.4330	0.4250
	(5.4)	(5.4)	(5.4)	(5.4)
Marketsize	1.4842	234.995	63.7905	240.945
	(8.5)	(8.7)	(8.7)	(8.7)
S.E.R.	0.0153	0.0150	0.0152	0.0151
D.W.	2.51	2.58	2.55	2.58
	Passes S/N Test	Passes S/N Test	Passes S/N Test	Passes S/N Test

* Dependent variable = PDR per residence NAS.
Income = Retail sales per household in Ont. and Que.
Marketsize A = Weighted residence toll connections/
   Residence NAS = No. of tels which can be reached.
Marketsize B = 1 - 1/(Marketsize A)**(1/4) (logged)
Marketsize C = 1 - 1/(Marketsize A)**(1/8) (logged)
Marketsize D = 1 - 1/(Marketsize A)**(1/4) (not logged).
Note: S/N test refers to the signal-to-noise test of Belsley (1982).

telephones, but is of questionable importance in a system going from 3 to 6 million, some models have been estimated in which the externality varies inversely with system size or even reaches an asymptote. The results for four such models are also tabulated in Table 3. The four models are as follows:

$$\ln(Q/T)_t = \alpha + \beta \ln(Y/H)_t + \gamma \ln P_t + \lambda \ln(1 - R^{-1/4}) + \varepsilon_t \qquad (17)$$

$$\ln(Q/T)_t = \alpha + \beta \ln(Y/H)_t + \gamma \ln P_t + \lambda \ln(1 - R^{-1/8}) + \varepsilon_t \qquad (18)$$

$$\ln(Q/T)_t = \alpha + \beta \ln(Y/H)_t + \gamma_t \ln P_t + \lambda \ln(1 - R^{-1/4}) + \varepsilon_t \qquad (19)$$

$$\ln(Q/T)_t = \alpha + \beta \ln(Y/H)_t + \gamma \ln P_t + \lambda Z_t + \varepsilon_t, \qquad (20)$$

TABLE 3B

Bell Canada DDD offpeak long haul; alternative measures of marketsize. (509 data, 1974 Q1 to 1983 Q3)

	Market-* size E	Market-* size F	Market-* size G	Market-* size H	Market-* size I
Price.1	-0.3312	-0.9537	-0.5999	-0.5894	-0.6515
(Static)	(-3.7)	(-9.4)	(-2.8)	(-6.7)	(-7.1)
Price.2	-0.0322	-0.1029	-0.0521	-0.0495	-0.0658
(Static)	(-2.0)	(-4.2)	(-2.8)	(-2.7)	(-3.5)
Income	0.4348	-0.1073	-0.2508	-0.2492	-2.526
(Static)	(5.4)	(-1.2)	(-3.8)	(-3.8)	(-3.5)
Marketsize	75.6684		1.3526	1.3661	1.2623
	(8.6)		(6.2)	(6.3)	(5.5)
S.E.R.	0.0152	0.0279	0.0187	0.0185	0.0200
D.W.	2.54	1.20	2.06	2.08	1.92
	Passes S/N Test	Income Fails Test	Passes S/N Test	Passes S/N Test	Passes S/N Test

* Dependent variable = PDR per residence NAS.

Income = Retail sales per household in Ont. and Que.

Marketsize E = 1 - 1/(Marketsize A)**(1/8) (not logged)

Marketsize F = 0 (no marketsize variable used)

Marketsize G
Marketsize H $\Big\}$ = Marketsize A if Marketsize A $\leq$ K, or K if Marketsize A $>$ K
Marketsize I

where K = Mean (Marketsize A) for Marketsize G

= Median (Marketsize A) for Marketsize H

= (Min(Marketsize A) + Max(Marketsize A))/2 for Marketsize I.

where R denotes the market-size variable and:

$$Z_t = \begin{cases} \ln R & R < R^* \\ \ln R^* & R \geq R^*. \end{cases} \qquad (21)$$

The conclusion which emerges from Table 3 is that, statistically, market size has a strong positive effect on calling per telephone that is largely independent of the number of telephones that can be reached. There is some evidence of an asymptote, but the data are probably too global to be able to identify the asymptote with precision. What is important in the present context is that the effect of market size is not confined to small systems, for the mean number of telephones that could be reached in Ontario and Quebec during the period of the sample was more than 2.5 million. A statistically strong system effect simply has to be accepted as a fact at this point, and the question becomes, what can account for this fact? Breslaw's view is that it is a bogus result, induced by harmful multicollinearity. Before assessing the multicollinearity argument, however, there is another possibility to consider, namely, that a call externality may be the cause.

The call externality, which arises from the fact that a completed call affects the welfare of the called party, has never received much attention in the literature because it has been thought that in a closed system its effect is internalized. As noted in the text, however, recent research suggests that the call externality can operate along another dimension, in that a call from A to B stimulates part (or all) of a call in return.[5] To illustrate the idea, consider the following two-equation, two-point, directional calling model:

$$\ln Q_{AB} = \alpha_0 + \alpha_1 \ln Y_A + \alpha_2 \ln P_{AB} + \alpha_3 \ln T_A + \alpha_4 \ln Q_{AB} \qquad (22)$$

$$\ln Q_{BA} = \beta_0 + \beta_1 \ln Y_B + \beta_2 \ln P_{BA} + \beta_3 \ln T_B + \beta_4 \ln Q_{AB}, \qquad (23)$$

where Q_{AB} denotes calls from A to B, Y_A income in A, P_{AB} the price of a call from A to B, T_A the number of telephones in A, etc. Note that any network externalities arising from the number of telephones that can be reached in B from A and in A from B are assumed away. Assumed to be present, however, is a reverse-traffic effect: the traffic from B to A and vice versa. Solving equation (23) and (24) for their reduced forms, we get:

$$\ln Q_{AB} = \frac{\alpha_0 + \alpha_4 \beta_0}{1 - \alpha_4 \beta_4} + \frac{\alpha_1}{1 - \alpha_4 \beta_4} \ln Y_A + \frac{\alpha_4 \beta_1}{1 - \alpha_4 \beta_4} \ln Y_B$$

$$+ \frac{\alpha_2}{1 - \alpha_4 \beta_4} \ln P_{AB} + \frac{\alpha_4 \beta_2}{1 - \alpha_4 \beta_4} \ln P_{BA}$$

$$+ \frac{\alpha_3}{1 - \alpha_4 \beta_4} \ln T_A + \frac{\alpha_4 \beta_3}{1 - \alpha_4 \beta_4} \ln T_B \qquad (24)$$

$$\ln Q_{BA} = \frac{\beta_0 + \beta_4 \alpha_0}{1 - \alpha_4 \beta_4} + \frac{\beta_1}{1 - \alpha_4 \beta_4} \ln Y_B + \frac{\beta_4 \alpha_1}{1 - \alpha_4 \beta_4} \ln Y_A$$

$$+ \frac{\beta_2}{1 - \alpha_4 \beta_4} \ln P_{BA} + \frac{\beta_4 \alpha_2}{1 - \alpha_4 \beta_4} \ln P_{AB}$$

[5] See Larson, Lehman, and Weisman (1990), Appelbe *et al.* (1988), and Acton and Vogelsang (1993).

$$+\frac{\beta_3}{1-\alpha_4\beta_4}\ln T_B + \frac{\beta_4\alpha_3}{1-\alpha_4\beta_4}\ln T_A. \tag{25}$$

If we assume that $\alpha_3/(1-\alpha_4\beta_4)$ and $\beta_3/(1-\alpha_4\beta_4)$ are approximately equal to 1, that income per household in A and B are approximately equal, and finally that $P_{AB} = P_{BA} = P$ (as is the case in Ontario and Quebec), then equations (24)–(25) can be written:

$$\ln(Q_{AB}/T_A) = A_0 + A_1 \ln(Y_A/H_A) + A_2 \ln P + A_3 \ln T_B \tag{26}$$

$$\ln(Q_{BA}/T_B) = B_0 + B_1 \ln(Y_B/H_B) + B_2 \ln P + B_3 \ln T_A. \tag{27}$$

These equations have the same form as the model in expression (16) in that calling per telephone depends upon income per household, the price of toll, and the number of telephones that can be reached. In this case, however, the network externality is zero by hypothesis. What this points up is the possibility (noted in Section V of Chapter 9) of being unable to distinguish empirically, with aggregate time-series data, between the network externality and the call externality. The two externalities simply may not be identified.

I now turn to Breslaw's conclusion that the strong market-size effect which is observed in the Bell Canada data is the result of harmful multicollinearity. In his analysis of multicollinearity, Breslaw uses the diagnostic tests which have been developed by Belsley, Kuh, and Welsch (1980) and Belsley (1982). The tests are based upon the singular value composition (SVD) of the matrix of observations on the independent variables of the model. To fix ideas, regarding SVD, it will be useful to revert for a moment to the standard linear model,

$$y = X\beta + u \tag{28}$$

where y, X, β, and u have their usual definitions. The SVD of the design matrix X utilizes two orthogonal matrices, U and V, such that

$$X = UDV' \tag{29}$$

where D is an $n x n$ diagonal matrix whose diagonal elements are the singular values of X. Pre-multiplying expression (29) by X'

$$X'X = VDU'UDV' = VD^2V', \tag{30}$$

it is seen that the squares of the singular values of X are the latent roots of $X'X$. Consider, now, the covariance matrix for the OLS estimator or β,

$$COV(\beta) = \sigma^2(X'X)^{-1}, \tag{31}$$

where σ^2 is the variance of u. From (30) we have (since V is an orthogonal matrix so that $V' = V^{-1}$)

$$COV(\beta) = \sigma^2 V D^{-2} V',$$ (32)

or for the ith element of β,

$$\text{var}(\beta_i) = \sigma^2 \sum_{j=1}^{n} \frac{v_{ij}^2}{\lambda_j^2},$$ (33)

where v_{ij} is the ijth element of V and λ_j is the jth singular value of X.

The decomposition in expression (33) is the point of departure for the SVD analysis of multicollinearity, for it provides a way of pinpointing troublesome collinear relationships among the independent variables. "Troublesome" in this context is inherently ambiguous, because short of a singular value of 0, which implies an exact linear relationship between two or more of the independent variables, there is no objective standard against which to define and measure troublesome. Belsley, Kuh, and Welsch approach this problem through the condition index of the matrix X defined over the n singular values of X as

$$\eta_j = \frac{\lambda_{\max}}{\lambda_j}, \quad j = 1, \ldots, n,$$ (34)

where $\lambda_{\max}$ denotes the largest of the singular values. Near linear dependencies among the columns of X are signaled by large condition numbers. Monte Carlo experiments undertaken by BKW suggest that condition numbers of 30 or more qualify as large.

In the variance decomposition given by formula (33), we see that each term in the decomposition is associated with a particular singular value. Since the singular values (or rather their squares) appear in the denominators, it is clear that small singular values can make large contributions to a variance. BKW formalize this as follows. From expression (33), define

$$\pi_{ij} = \frac{\theta_{ij}}{\theta_i}$$ (35)

where

$$\theta_{ij} = \frac{v_{ij}^2}{\lambda_i^2}$$ (36)

and $\theta_i = \sum_j \theta_{ij}$. θ_{ij} measures the proportion of the variance of the ith regression coefficient that is contributed by the jth singular value. Clearly, the smaller is a singular value, the larger will be its contribution to the variance. When the same singular value makes a large contribution to the variances of two or more regression coefficients, this is an indication that estimation of the coefficients is being adversely affected (or what BKW call degraded) by the near linear dependency associated with the singular value. Identifying such singular values and the coefficients affected is a key step for BKW in establishing the presence of harmful multicollinearity.

Once degradation is identified, the next step is to assess its severity. Breslaw pursues this through a test developed by Belsley (1982) of the signal-to-noise ratio. The test statistic used is the conventional t-ratio, i.e., the ratio of a regression coefficient to its estimated standard error. The hypothesis tested, however, is not with respect to the value of the regression coefficient, but whether the sample is informative with respect to the parameter in question. As Breslaw notes, the relevant question regarding the toll price elasticity is not whether its value is zero, but whether the sample is informative about its value, whatever it might be. The test that is conducted is whether the observed signal-to-noise ratio (defined as β_j / s_{β_j}) exceeds some reasonably chosen threshold level. The test can show that a sample is uninformative about a regression coefficient even though the t-ratio by conventional standards is highly significant.

If a coefficient fails the signal-to-noise test, the question then asked, following the Belsley-BKW script, is whether the failure is the result of multicollinearity or short data. ("Short data" in this context refers to inadequate variation in the independent variable failing the signal-to-noise test.) Failure of the signal-to-noise test combined with an ill-conditioned X matrix (as determined by the BKW collinearity diagnostics) is taken to define harmful multicollinearity.

Breslaw applies the Belsley-BKW procedure to the results for equation (11) that are presented in Table 2. The variance-decomposition matrix for the design matrix underlying the estimates is given in Table 4. The elements in the first column of this matrix represent the condition number as calculated from expression (34); the remaining elements are the variance proportions attributable to each of the singular values according to expressions (35) and (36). According to the BKW diagnostic criteria, the model has three potentially troublesome singular values, namely, the last three, for their condition numbers are well in excess of 30. The BKW rule-of-thumb (derived from Monte Carlo experiments) is that a near-linear dependency is degrading if 50% or more of two or more variances is associated with a large condition number.

In Table 4, we see that the largest condition number is 470.5, that 86% of the variance of the coefficient for the price variable is associated with this condition number, and that 46% of the variance of the coefficient for price

TABLE 4

Variance decomposition matrix for Breslaw model in Table 2

Condition Index	C	RCENT	QD1	QD2	QD3	LnP	LnY	LnQL	LnMS
1.0	.000001	.000716	.000303	.001120	.000473	.000004	.000006	.000007	.000009
2.6	.000000	.000003	.025318	.000053	.035033	.000000	.000001	.000000	.000000
2.6	.000000	.000000	.007365	.120414	.013297	.000000	.000000	.000000	.000000
5.3	.000000	.060929	.038511	.138125	.054621	.000009	.000002	.000016	.000037
6.0	.000019	.067176	.026671	.104654	.046405	.000158	.000099	.000000	.000011
20.8	.000016	.332823	.002588	.001780	.000629	.002542	.000351	.004285	.009205
93.8	.000396	.089977	.006122	.190239	.284762	.030688	.147643	.062159	.128198
206.9	.000001	.258066	.892646	.313704	.090347	.107116	.469493	.856189	.401215
470.5	.999568	.190310	.000477	.129911	.472632	.859483	.382406	.077345	.461325

Source: Breslaw (1985, p. 11)

is associated with it. The second largest condition number is associated with 86% of the variance of the coefficient for lagged dependent variable and 47% and 40%, respectively, of the variances of the coefficients for income and market size. The collinearities associated with these two condition numbers appear to be the troublesome ones.[6]

Breslaw's concern is whether the degradation manifested in the last two lines of Table 4 is harmful with respect to the estimate of the price elasticity. Attention is accordingly turned to the question of whether the variance of the estimate is large in relation to its expected value, that is, to whether the signal-to-noise ratio is unacceptably small. The Belsley test indicates that this is the case. From this, Breslaw concludes that the estimate of the price elasticity is harmed by collinear relationships among price, income, and market size and that Bell Canada is consequently not justified in concluding that toll demand is price inelastic.

Before turning to an assessment of Breslaw's conclusion, it will be instructive to apply his procedure to the model that I consider the proper specification for the question before us, namely, the model in equation (16). This models differs from Breslaw's [equation (11)] in that the dependent variable is price deflated revenues per telephone rather than per household and market size is measured by the number of telephones that can be reached rather than potential toll connections. Also, the lagged dependent variable is excluded since a dynamic specification does not seem warranted. The coefficients for this model, estimated from the 509 data set, are given in the first column of Table 3. The variance-decomposition for this equation is given in Table 5. This time, we see that there are only two large condition numbers (according to the BKW criteria) and that the near dependencies associated with the largest condition numbers are once again influential in the variance of the coefficients for the three economic variables, price, income, and market size. Application of the Belsley test to the signal-to-noise ratio for all three of these variables presents an interesting result: they all pass the test! Thus, with this specification, harmful multicollinearity appears not to exist.[7]

---

[6] For some reason, Breslaw concentrates on the aggregate proportion of a variance associated with the three largest condition numbers, rather than large proportions of different variances associated with the same condition number. BKW emphasize that for collinearity to be harmful, the variances of two or more regression coefficients must be adversely affected by the same near dependency.

[7] Breslaw defines the toll price in his model as a 4-quarter moving average. His results are sensitive to this, because when his model is re-estimated with price defined (as in the 509 data set) as the price for the current quarter, price *passes* the signal-to-noise test at the 0.75 level (but not at the 0.90 level). Breslaw's justification for defining price as a 4-quarter moving average is unconvincing.

TABLE 5

Variance-decomposition matrix for Equation (1) in Table 3

Condition Index	C	RCENT	QD1	QD2	QD	LnP1	LnP2	LnY	LnMS
1.0	1.38 E-08	9.52 E-04	2.96 E-04	0.0014	8.65 E-04	1.43 E-04	4.73 E-04	2.34 E-07	2.13 E-08
2.5	1.30 E-10	1.08 E-06	0.0250	1.99 E-05	0.0611	1.2 E-06	2.44 E-05	1.02 E-09	1.92 E-10
2.5	2.12 E-12	4.13 E-07	0.0073	0.1400	0.0236	4.80 E-07	8.39 E-05	1.07 E-10	3.89 E-12
4.2	7.22 E-08	0.0449	0.0094	0.0347	7.43 E-05	0.0134	1.27 E-06	1.03 E-07	
6.1	3.36 E-07	0.0134	0.0573	0.2582	0.1549	3.91 E-04	0.0024	6.43 E-06	5.04 E-07
15.8	3.51 E-07	.07468	6.43 E-04	7.1 E-04	0.0044	0.00451	0.2841	8.26 E-06	4.43 E-07
19.7	7.17 E-07	0.0675	1.88 E-04	0.0049	3.30 E-04	0.2323	.03598	1.50 E-05	9.35 E-07
536.6	0.0020	0.0313	0.2375	0.0307	0.0959	0.1531	0.0989	0.2791	0.0122
4287.6	0.9980	0.0952	0.6624	0.5163	0.6242	0.5689	0.5689	0.7208	0.9878

But back to Breslaw. Having concluded that multicollinearity is harming the estimation of the price elasticity (and by implication causing a significant market-size effect to appear where there should be none), Breslaw's next step is to employ a Theil-Goldberger mixed estimator,[8] whereby an estimate of the network externality from local-calling data is combined with the Bell-intra toll data. Breslaw's point of departure is the observation that if there is a network externality for the toll network, there should be one for the local network as well. And since local calling is free, price and income (except for the opportunity cost of time) will not be constraining factors, with the consequence that the externality should be easier to isolate with local data than with toll data.

Using annual data for Bell Canada, 1966–1983, for local non-business-day calling, Breslaw estimates the following model:

$$\ln \text{CON}_t = a_0 + a_1 \ln T_t + a_2 \ln \text{CON}_{t-1} + \varepsilon_t, \tag{37}$$

where:

CON = local conversations per household per average non-business day

T = number of residential main stations.

The results are tabulated in Table 6. The network externality (as measured by the coefficient for $\ln T$) is seen to be small, in the long run as well as the short run, and statistically insignificant.

Breslaw combines the long-run estimate of the network externality from this equation with the Bell-intra toll data using the Theil-Goldberger mixed estimation format. The results are given in Table 7. Comparing this table with Table 2, the changes are striking. The long-run market-size elasticity falls from 0.47 to 0.04, the long-run price elasticity jumps from -0.55 to -1.15 (with a t-ratio of 10), and the long-run income elasticity is more than halved.

The results from the mixed estimation have two problems. Breslaw's procedure is flawed conceptually and also is not clear that what Breslaw thinks was done is what was done in fact. Putting the conceptual problems aside for the moment, it is seen that the mixed estimation appears to combine a toll-based coefficient for market-size of 0.47 with a t-ratio of 3.10 with a local-based coefficient of 0.021 with a t-ratio of 0.47 to yield a mixed estimate of 0.045 with a t-ratio of 0.93. For the local estimate to "overwhelm" the toll estimate in this way, given their relative t-ratios, is implausible. One simply has to wonder whether the calculations are correct.

---

[8] See Theil and Goldberger (1961), also Theil (1971).

TABLE 6

Local conversations; Breslaw model

Variable	Short-Run		Long-Run	
	Coeff.	*t*-stat	Coeff.	*t*-stat
C	0.5890	(0.69)		
LnT	0.0229	(0.49)	0.0434	(0.47)
LnCONL	0.4727	(1.90)		

SER = 0.0208   R-Squared = 0.2028

D.W. = 1.8145   Observations = 18

Durbin H = n/a

Source: Breslaw (1985, p. 17)

TABLE 7

Mixed estimation; Breslaw model

Method: Iterative OLS

Dependent Variable: LnQ

Variable	Short-Run		Long-Run	
	Coeff.	*t*-stat	Coeff.	*t*-stat
C	-3.8426	(2.70)		
RCENT	0.0570	(3.01)		
QD1	-0.0987	(4.25)		
QD2	-0.1073	(7.44)		
QD3	-0.1587	(7.73)		
LnP	-0.7540	(3.45)	-1.1495	(10.20)
LnY	0.1765	(1.26)	0.2690	(1.23)
LnMS	0.0293	(0.91)	0.447	(0.93)
lNQL	0.3441	(2.12)		

SER = 0.0189   R-Squared = 0.9991

D.W. = 2.1057   Obwervations = 37

Durbin H = -1.9477

Source: Breslaw (1985, p. 17)

The conceptual problem is that in defining his mixed estimator, Breslaw is mixing apples and oranges. This can be seen with two simple "local" and "toll" models as follows:

local

$$\ln y_t = \alpha_0 + \alpha_1 \ln y_{t-1} + \alpha_2 \ln \mathrm{MSL}_t + u_t \tag{38}$$

toll

$$\ln z_t = \beta_0 + \beta_1 \ln z_{t-1} + \beta_2 \ln \mathrm{MST}_t + \beta_3 \ln x_t + v_t, \tag{39}$$

where MSL and MST denote market size in the local and toll markets and where x denotes income, price, etc. in the model. The parameter of interest is the long-run coefficient for market size, which is $\alpha_2/(1 - \alpha_1)$ and $+\beta_2/(1 - \beta_1)$ for local and toll, respectively. The presumption is that this coefficient has the same value in the two models. Denote this common value by γ. Question: How does one efficiently estimate γ using the information from the two models?

Assume for the moment that, not only does $\gamma_L = \gamma_T$ but that $\alpha_0 = \beta_0$, $\alpha_1 = \beta_1$, and $\alpha_2 = \beta_2$ as well. Also, let us rewrite (38) and (39) as:

$$y = W\alpha + u \tag{40}$$

$$z = X\beta + v. \tag{41}$$

Finally, assume that both u and v satisfy the OLS assumptions. In this case, the equations for the Theil-Goldberger mixed estimator will be

$$
\begin{aligned}
z &= X\beta + v \\
\hat{\beta} &= G\beta + \varepsilon
\end{aligned} \tag{42}
$$

or

$$w = H\beta + \eta \tag{43}$$

where:

$$\hat{\beta} = (W'W)^{-1}W'y$$

$$G = (1, 1, 1, 0)$$

$$w = \begin{pmatrix} z \\ \beta \end{pmatrix}$$

$$H = \begin{bmatrix} X \\ G \end{bmatrix}$$

$$\eta = \begin{pmatrix} v \\ \varepsilon \end{pmatrix}.$$

The Theil-Goldberger (i.e., GLS) estimator of β is then

$$\beta = (H'\Omega^{-1}H)^{-1}H'\Omega^{-1}w, \qquad (44)$$

where

$$\Omega = \begin{bmatrix} \sigma_v^2 I & 0 \\ 0 & \sigma_u^2(W'W)^{-1} \end{bmatrix}. \qquad (45)$$

An alternative to the foregoing is to assume that just the long-run coefficients in the two models are equal (i.e., $\gamma_L = \gamma_T$). In this case, the GLS formula in expression (44) is not appropriate; efficient least squares estimation would proceed by minimizing the sum of squared errors in (38) and (39) subject to the constraint that $\gamma_L = \gamma_T$, i.e., that[9]

$$\frac{\hat{\alpha}_2}{1 - \hat{\alpha}_1} = \frac{\hat{\beta}_2}{1 - \hat{\beta}_1}. \qquad (46)$$

Breslaw appears to confuse the two approaches. For what he has done is to take the estimate of the *long-run* coefficient for market size from the local model and use it as an estimate in the mixed-estimator formula of the *short-run* coefficient for market size in the toll model. This is the mixing of apples and oranges mentioned earlier, and undermines any conclusions that can be drawn from the mixed estimation.

III. CONCLUSIONS

Let me now respond to each of Breslaw's points:

1.   *The network externality is implausibly large in the Bell Canada model.*

In this case, implausibly large is in the eye of the beholder. Breslaw's point of departure is a strongly held maintained hypothesis that there should be no network externality in a system as large as Bell Canada's. So firmly is this hypothesis maintained that t-ratios of 8 or more are explained away as a consequence of harmful multicollinearity. I will respond to this conclusion below. Here the relevant comment is that, with aggregate time-series data, a pure network effect probably cannot be isolated, for it cannot be disentangled from a possible call externality. It has been shown that a model in the network externality is assumed not to exist but with a call externality that takes the form of calls giving rise to calls in return probably cannot be distinguished

---

[9] Should v and ε be correlated, a constrained Zellner-SUR format would be applicable.

empirically from a model in which a network externality is assumed but no call externality. In short, the two externalities probably cannot be separately identified. Consequently, the statistically robust market-size effect that is observed may reflect a strong call externality rather than a network externality.

2. *The large elasticity for market size and the small elasticity for toll price are consequences of harmful multicollinearity.*

Breslaw reaches this conclusion on the basis of the collinearity diagnostics developed by Belsley, Kuh, and Welsch and the signal-to-noise ratio test of Belsley. The conclusion is not warranted. For we have seen that in Breslaw's model with everything defined as Breslaw does except for the toll price, which is redefined as the current price rather than a smoothed 4-quarter moving average, all variables pass the signal-to-noise test (at least at the 0.75 level). The same is true when a per-telephone/per-household model is specified in which market size is measured by the number of telephones that can be reached rather than potential toll connections.

3. *Use of an extraneous estimate of the network externality from local-calling data in a Theil-Goldberger mixed estimation format causes the apparent network externality observed in the toll data in isolation to vanish.*

It was just shown that Breslaw errs in his application of the Theil-Goldberger estimator, so again the conclusion is not warranted.

So, where does this leave things? I do not mean in all this to diminish the contributions that Breslaw makes in his paper. He does much to sharpen and clarify discussion of the network externality and his use of the Belsley-Kuh-Welsch collinearity diagnostics is a seminal contribution to the applied telecommunications demand analysis. My own view at this point is that, for whatever reasons, market size is an important influence on toll calling in Ontario and Quebec, and I think that research should concentrate on attempting to explain why this is the case rather than on explaining it away. Whether it is a reflection of the network or the call externality probably cannot be answered with aggregate time-series data.

BIBLIOGRAPHY

Acton, J.P., Mitchell, B.M. and Mowill, R.S. (1976), "Residential Demand for Electricity in Los Angeles: An Econometric Study of Disaggregated Data," September, RAND R–1899–NSF, RAND Corporation, Santa Monica, CA.

Acton, J.P. and Vogelsang, I. (1992), "Telephone Demand Over the Atlantic: Evidence from Country-Pair Data," *Journal of Industrial Economics,* Vol. 40, No. 3, September 1992, pp. 305–323.

Adams, W.J. and Yellen, J.L. (1976), "Commodity Bundling and the Burden of Monopoly," *Quarterly Journal of Economics*, Vol. 90, No. 3, August 1976, pp. 475–498.

Adelson, J., Cannel, C., Heyns, R.W. and Lansing, J.B. (1956), "Motives, Attitudes, and Long-Distance Calls," April, Survey Research Center, Institute of Social Research, University of Michigan.

Aitchison, D. and Brown, J.A. (1957), *The Lognormal Distribution*, Cambridge University Press, Cambridge, England.

Albery, B.B. and Sievers, M.P. (1988), "The Averch-Johnson-Wellisz Model and the Telecommunications Industry," *Federal Communications Law Journal*, Vol. 40, No. 2, UCLA School of Law, April, 1988, pp. 157–192.

Alden, R.M. (1976), "Usage-Sensitive Pricing for Exchange Service," *New Dimensions in Public Utility Pricing*, ed. by H.M. Trebing, pp. 297–306, 7th Annual Conference, MSU Institute of Public Utilities, East Lansing, MI.

Alessio, F.J. *et al.* (1986), "Cost Support for Market Pricing: Challenges to Local Exchange Companies," in *Telecommunications in the Post-Divestiture Era*, ed. by A.L. Danielsen *et al.*, pp. 119–122, Lexington Books/DC Health, Lexington, MA.

Alleman, J.H. (1977), "The Pricing of Local Telephone Service," *OT Special Publications* 77–14, April, Office of Telecommunications, U.S. Dept. of Commerce, Washington, DC.

Alleman, J.H. and Beauvais, E.C. (1981), "Local Loops as Barriers to Entry?" in *Challenges for Public Utility Regulation in the 1980's*, ed. by H.M. Trebing, pp. 324–340, 12th Annual Conference, MSU Institute of Public Utilities, East Lansing, MI.

Alleman, J.H. and Jensik, L.W. (1978), "Self-Selecting Local Telephone Prices," in *Proceedings of the First NARUC Biennial Regulatory Information Conference*, Oct 18–20, 1978, National Association of Regulatory Utility Commissioners, Columbus, OH.

Alleman, J.H. and Schmidt, L.W. *et al.* (1984), "Telecommunications Pricing in a Fickle Regulatory Environment," in *Changing Patterns in Regulation, Markets, and Technology: The Effect on Public Utility Price*, ed. by P.C. Mann, pp. 20–32, 15th Annual Conference, MSU Institute of Public Utilities, East Lansing, MI.

Alston, H.L. (1982), "Preferences for Flat Rate and Measured Service Plans in New Mexico," *Report of Research & Statistics District in Finance Corporation Planning Dept.*, December, Mountain Bell, Denver, CO.

Amemiya, T. (1981), "Qualitative Response Models: A Survey," *Journal of Economic Literature*, Vol. 19, No. 4, December 1981, pp. 1483–1536.

Amemiya, T. (1985), *Advanced Econometrics*, Harvard University Press.

370

American Telephone and Telegraph Company (1976), "A Simulation of the Bell Revenue Loss and MCI Revenue Gain Based on Total Market Potential," Unpublished paper prepared for FCC Docket No. 20640.

American Telephone and Telegraph Company (1976a), Affidavit of P. Muench, Re: Execunet Service, FCC Docket 20614, August 18, 1976.

American Telephone and Telegraph Company (1976b), Price Index Project, Comptrollers Department, December 10, 1976.

American Telephone and Telegraph Company (1978), *1978 Annual FDC (Fully Distributed Cost) Report*, filed with the FCC.

American Telephone and Telegraph Company (1983), Emergency Petition, March 6 FCC Filing.

American Telephone and Telegraph Company (1984a), Emergency Petition, Response to FCC Data Reguest, March 6, 1984.

American Telephone and Telegraph Company (1984b), Reply to the FCC Public Notice of March 30, 1984, dated April 3, 1984.

Antonelli, C. (1990), "Information Technology and The Derived Demand for Telecommunications Services in The Manufacturing Industry," *Information Economics and Policy*, Vol. 4, pp. 45–55.

Appelbe, T.W., Snihur, N.A., Dineen, C., Farnes, D. and Giordano, R. (1988), "Point-to-Point Modeling: An Application to Canada-Canada and Canada-U.S. Long Distance Calling," *Information Economics and Policy*, Vol. 3, Issue 4, pp. 311–331.

Appelbe, T.W., Dineen, C.R., Solvason, D.L. and Hsiao, C. (1992), "Econometric Modelling of Canadian Long Distance Calling: A Comparison of Aggregate Time Series Versus Point-to-Point Panel Data Approaches," *Empirical Economics*, Vol. 17, pp. 125–140.

Arcate, J.A. and Doherty, A.N. (1984), "The Formulation and Measurement of Local Telephone Cost Output with Econometric Models," *Federal Communications Law Journal*, Vol. 37, Issue 3, pp. 521–541, July, UCLA School of Law/Federal Communications Bar Association.

Artle, R. and Averous, C. (1973), "The Telephone System as a Public Good: Static and Dynamic Aspects," *Bell Journal of Economics and Management Science*, Vol. 4, No. 1, Spring 1973, pp. 89–100.

AT&T-Long Lines (1978a), "Demand Analysis and Forecast of the Mexico-U.S. Telecommunications Market," January, AT&T-Long Lines Overseas Economic Research and Telmex-Rates and International Planning.

AT&T-Long Lines (1978b), "Demand Analysis and Forecast of the U.S.-Canada Telecommunications Market," January, AT&T-Long Lines Overseas Economic Research and TCTS-Network Development Forecasts.

AT&T-Long Lines (1977c), "Conclusive Evidence that Demand and Circuit Growth are Exponential," FCC Docket No. 18875, Section 7, pp. 1–58, August 31, 1977.

Auray, R.R. (1978), "Customer Response to Changes in Interstate MTS Rates," in *Assessing New Pricing Concepts in Public Utilities*, ed. by H.M. Trebing, pp. 47–81, 9th Annual Conference, MSU Institute of Public Utilities, East Lansing, MI.

Bailey, E.E. and Lindenberg, E.B. (1976), "Peak Load Pricing Principles: Past and Present," in *New Dimension in Public Utility Pricing*, ed. by H.M. Trebing, pp. 9–31, 7th. Annual Conference, MSU Institute for Public Utilities, East Lansing, MI.

Balestra, P. and Nerlove, M. (1966), "Pooling Cross-Section and Time-Series Data in the Estimation of a Dynamic Model: The Demand for Natural Gas," *Econometrica*, No. 3, July 1966, pp. 585–612.

Baughcum, A. *et al.* (1984), "Telecommunications Access and Public Policy," from Workshop on Local Access, 9/82, St. Louis, Ablex Publishing Corp., Norwood, NJ.

Baughman, M. and Joskow, P. (1975), "The Effects of Fuel Prices on Residential Appliance Choice in the U.S.," *Land Economics*, Vol. 51, February 1975, pp. 41–49.

Baumol, W.J. and Bradford, D.F. (1970), "Optimal Departures from Marginal Cost Pricing," *American Economic Review*, Vol. 60, No. 3, June 1970, pp. 265–283.

Beauvais, E.C. (1977), "The Demand for Residential Telephone Service Under Non-Metered Tariffs: Implications for Alternative Pricing Policies," Western Economic Association Meetings, June, Anaheim, CA.

Beilock, R. (1985), "Is Regulation Necessary for Value-of-Service Pricing?," *Rand Journal of Economics*, Vol. 16, No. 1, Spring 1985, pp. 93–102.

Bell Canada (1976), "Models of Message Toll Demand in Trans-Canada, Canada-U.S. and Canada-Overseas Settlements," Demand Analysis Group, December, Ottawa, Ontario.

Bell Canada (1984), "Econometric Models of Demand for Selected Intra-Bell Long-Distance and Local Services," Attachment 1 of Response to Interrogatory Bell (CNCP) 20 February 84–509 IC (Supplemental, July 1984), CRTC, Ottawa, Ontario.

Bell Canada (1986a), "Residence Network Access Service: Who Are the Non-Subscribers?," Responses to Interrogatory Bell (CRTC) 19 Feb 86–11 FP Attachment, Bell Canada, Hull, Quebec.

Bell Canada (1986b), "A Comparison of Subscribers and Non-Subscribers With Respect to Selected Household Characteristics," Corporate Economics, Bell Canada, Hull, Quebec, September 5, 1986.

Bell Canada (1989), "Intra-Bell Customer-Dialed Peak and Off-Peak Model Updates," Attachment 1, CRTC Telecom Public Notice 1988–45; Bell Canada and British Columbia Telephone Company-Review of Methodologies Used to Model Price Elasticities, March 3, 1989.

Bell Canada (1989), "Cross-Sectional Analysis of Residential Telephone Subcription in Canada – An Update Using 1987 Data," Attachment 4, CRTC Telecom Public Notice 1988–45; Bell Canada and British Columbia Telephone Company – Review of Methodologies Used to Model Price Elasticities, March 3, 1989.

Bell Communications Research, Inc. (1984), "The Impact of Access Charges on Bypass and Universal Telephone Service," Morristown, NJ, September 1984.

Bell Telephone Company of Pennsylvania (1976), Testimony and Exhibits of Hendrik S. Houthakker, Docket No. 367, November 1976 and Cross-examination, June 1977.

Bell Telephone Laboratories (1977), *Engineering and Operations in the Bell System*, Bell Telephone Laboratories, Murray Hill, NJ.

Belinfante, A. (1988), "The Analysis of Telephone Penetration: An Update," presented at the BELLCORE/Bell Canada Industry Forum on Telecommunications Demand Analysis, Key Biscayne, FL, January 26, 1988, Industry Analysis Division, Common Carrier Bureau, Federal Communications Commission, Washington, D.C.

Belsley, D.A. (1982), "Assuming the Presence of Harmful Collinearity and Other Forms of Weak Data Through a Test for Signal-to-Noise," *Journal of Econometrics*, Vol. 20, No. 2, November 1982, pp. 211–254.

Belsley, D.A., Kuh, E. and Welsch, R.E. (1980), *Regression Diagnostics: Identifying Influential Data and Sources of Collinearity*, John Wiley & Sons, New York.

Ben-Akiva, M. and Gershenfeld, S. (1989), "Analysis of Business Establishment Choice of Telephone System," Cambridge Systematics, Cambridge, MA, May 1989.

Ben-Akiva, M. and Lerman, S.R. (1985), *Discrete Choice Analysis*, MIT Press.

Benedetti, M. *et al.* (1974), "Planning Concepts in Providing Telecommunications Services," in *Gas/5 Manual*, Chapter XIII, September, International Telephone and Telegraph Consultative Committee.

Bergstrom, A.R. and Chambers, M.J. (1989), "Gaussian Estimation of a Continuous-Time Model of Demand for Consumer Durable Goods With Application to Demand in the United Kingdom, 1973–1984," Department of Economics, University of Essex, Essex, U.K.

Bernstein, J.I. (1980), "A Corporate Econometric Model of the British Columbia Telephone Company," *Forecasting Public Utilities*, ed. by O.D. Anderson, pp. 17–38, North-Holland Publishing Co.

Berryhill, E.B. (1984), "New Mexico Telephone Access Demand Model Based on Rate Group Data," Demand Analysis Group, Revenue Requirements, Mountain Bell, Denver, CO, August 31, 1984.

Berryhill, E.B. and Reinking, R.D. (1984), "Optional Local Measured Telephone Service-Economic Efficiency with Consumer Choice," *Public Utilities Fortnightly*, Vol. 177, No. 1., January 5, 1984, p. 30 ff.

Betteridge, W.W. (1973), "Description of Interstate Message Telecommunications Demand Model-Supplement," FCC Docket No. 19129, Phase II, November 1973.

Bewley, R. and Fiebig, D.G. (1988), "Estimation of Price Elasticities For An International Telephone Demand Model," *Journal of Industrial Economics*, Vol. 36, No. 4, June 1988, pp. 393–409.

Bhatia, M. (1989), "Econometric Models for Ten International Telephone Streams," presented at the Australasian Meeting of the Econometric Society, 12–15 July 1989, Armidale NSW, Australia, Overseas Telecommunications Commission, Sidney.

Bhattacharya, M.N. (1974), "Forecasting the Demand for Telephones in Australia," *Applied Statistics*, Vol. 23, No.1, pp. 1–10.

Bhattacharya, S.K. and Laughhunn, D.J. (1987), "Price Cap Regulations: Can We Learn from the British Telecom Experience?," *Public Utilities Fortnightly*, Vol. 120, Issue 8, October 15, 1987, pp. 22–29.

Black, S.K. and Tryon, P.V. (1976), "Increased Telephone Installation Rates: A Statistical Analysis of Colorado's 1972 Rate Change," June, OT Report 76–90, U.S. Department of Commerce. Edited version in *Business Communications Review*, November/December 1976.

Blattenberger, G.R. (1977), "Block Rate Pricing and the Residential Demand for Electricity," Ph.D. Dissertation, Department of Economics, University of Michigan.

Blomqvist, N. (1977), "On the Relation between Change and Initial Value," *Journal of the American Statistical Association*, Vol. 72, No. 4, December 1977, pp. 746–749.

Bodnar, J., Dilworth, P. and Iacono, S. (1988), "Cross-Sectional Analysis of Residential Telephone Subscription in Canada," *Information Economics and Policy*, Vol. 3, No.4, pp. 359–378.

Bodnar, J. and Lefebvre, S. (1992a), "Canadian Residential Telephone Penetration Rates in 1990," Bell Canada, Economics and Revenue Estimates, Hull, Quebec, April 9, 1992.

Bodnar, J. and Lefebvre, S. (1992b), "A Comparison of Canadian Households With and Without Residential Telephone Service in 1990," Bell Canada Economics and Revenue Estimates, Hull, Quebec, July 16, 1992.

Bohm, P. (1975), "Option Demand and Consumer's Surplus: Comment," *American Economic Review*, Vol. 65, No. 4, September 1975, pp. 733–736.

Bohmer, D.A. *et al.* (1979), "Operational Effects of Local Measured Service A Joint Industrial Paper," in *Perspectives on Local Measured Service*, ed. by J.A. Baude *et al.*, pp. 119–137, Telecommunication Industrial Workshop 3/13–3/14/1979, Telecommunication Industrial Organizing Committee, Kansas City, MO.

Boiteux, M. (1960), "Peak-Load Pricing," *Journal of Business*, Vol. 33, No. 2, April 1960, pp. 157–179.

Box, C.E.P. and Jenkins, G.M. (1976), *Time Series Analysis Forecasting and Control*, Revised Edition, Holden-Day, Inc., San Francisco, CA.

Bozman, S. (1983), "Intra B.C. Long Distance Telephone Demand Price Elasticities: An Empirical Investigation," M.A. Thesis, Department of Economics, University of Victoria, Victoria, B.C., August 1983.

Brander, J.A. and Spencer, B.J. (1983), "Local Telephone Pricing: Two-Part Tariffs and Price Discrimination," *Economic Analysis of Telecommunications: Theory and Applications*, ed. by L. Courville *et al.*, pp. 305–316, Elsevier Science Publishers/North Holland, New York.

Brandon, B.B., ed. (1981), *The Effect of the Demographics of Individual Households on Their Telephone Usage,* Ballinger Publishing Co., Cambridge, MA.

Brandon, B.B. and Brandon, P.S. (1981), "Introduction and Summary," *The Effect of the Demographics of Individual Households on Their Telephone Usage*, ed. by B.B. Brandon, Ballinger Publishing Co, Cambridge, MA.

Breslaw, J.A. (1985), "Network Externalities and the Demand for Residential Long Distance Telephone Service," Working paper No. 1985–13, Concordia University, Montreal, Quebec.

Breslaw, J.A. (1989), "Bell Canada and British Columbia Telephone Company: Review of Methodology Used to Model Price Elasticity," Evidence on behalf of the Government of Quebec before the Canadian Radio-Television and Telecommunications Commission, CRTC Telecom 1988–45, April 1989, Ottawa, Ontario.

Breslaw, J.A. and Smith, J.B. (1982), "Efficiency, Equity, and Regulation: An Optimal Pricing Model of Bell Canada," *Canadian Journal of Economics*, Vol. 14, No. 4, November 1982, pp. 634–648.

Bresnahan, J.F. (1989), "Empirical Studies of Industries With Market Power," in *Handbook of Industrial Organization*, Vol. 2, ed. by R. Schmalensee and R. Willig, North Holland Publishing Co.

Brock, G.W. (1981), *The Telecommunications Industry: The Dynamics of Market Structure*, Harvard University Press, Cambridge, MA.

Brock, G.W. (1984), "Bypass of the Local Exchange: A Qualitative Assessment," OPP Working paper No.12, Office of Plans and Policy, Federal Communications Commission, Washington, D.C., September 1984.

Brock, G.W. (1986), "Telephone Pricing to Promote Universal Service and Economic Freedom," OPP Working paper No. 18, Office of Plans and Policy, Federal Communications Commission, Washington, D.C., January 1986.

Brooks, J. (1976), *Telephone: The First Hundred Years*, Harper & Row, New York, NY.

Brubacher, S.R. and Hiscock, R.J. (1978), "An Application of Multivariate Box-Jenkins Techniques in Bell Canada," Joint ORSA/TIMS Conference New York, May 1978, Management Sciences Division, Bell Canada, Montreal.

Buckalew, A.C., Mount-Campbell, C.A. and Racster, J.L. (1979), "Synopsis of the Impact of Measured Telephone Rates on Telephone Usage by Government and Non-Profit Organizations," NRRI–79–47, National Regulatory Research Institute, Columbus, OH.

Burness, H.S. and Patrick, R.H. (1986), "Peak-Load Pricing with Continuous Interdependent Demand," NRRI–84–16, National Regulatory Research Institute, Columbus, OH.

Cain, P. and MacDonald, J.M. (1991), "Telephone Pricing Structures: The Effects on Universal Service," *Journal of Regulatory Economics*, Vol. 3, pp. 293–308.

Canadian Radio-television and Telecommunications Commission (1990), *Review of Methodologies for Modelling Price Elasticities*, Telecom Decision CRTC 90–25, November 27,

1990, Ottawa, Ontario.

Carne, E.B. (1983), "Potential Alternatives for Local Telephone Distribution Systems," in *Adjusting to Regulatory, Pricing and Marketing Realities*, ed. by H.M. Trebing, pp. 93–108, 14th. Annual Conference, MSU/Institute of Public Utilities, East Lansing, MI.

Carsberg, B. (1988), "The Control of British Telecom's Prices," in an *Office of Telecommunications Statement*, July 7, by Dr. Bryan Carsberg, Director-General of Tele London, OFTEL, Atlantic House, Holburn Viaduct, EC1N 2HQ.

Chaddha, R.L. and Chitgopekar, S.S. (1971), "Residence Telephone Demand," *Bell Journal of Economics and Management Science*, Vol. 2, No. 2, Autumn 1971, pp. 540–560.

Chalstrom, L.K. (1983), "Demand for Residential Telephone Service and the Measured Service Option," M.A. Thesis draft, University of Wyoming, Laramie, WY., December 1983.

Charles River Associates, Inc. (1982), "The Demand for Local Telephone Service Upon the Introduction of Optional Local Measured Service," CRA Report No. 61, prepared for Southern New England Telephone Co., Charles River Associates, 200 Clarendon St., Boston, MA, July 30, 1982.

Chen, G.K.C. and Winters, P.R. (1966), "Forecasting Peak Demand for an Electric Utility with a Hybrid Exponential Model," *Management Science*, Vol. 12, B531–B527, August 1966.

Chen, J.A. and Watters, J.S. (1988), "A Discrete-Choice Analysis of Customer-Specific Time-of-Day Usage Shares," Southwestern Bell Telephone Co., November 1988.

Chen, J.A. and Watters, J.S. (1989), "A Binary Discrete-Choice Model of Demand for IntraLATA 800 Service," Southwestern Bell Telephone Co., October 1989.

Chen, J.A. and Watters, J.S. (1992), "Estimating Telephone Usage Elasticities: A Shares Equation System Approach," *Applied Economics*, Vol. 24, December 1992, pp. 1219–1224.

Chessler, D. and Ferng, L.K. (1986), "On the Limited Use of Marginal Cost Pricing in Telephone Regulation," in *Issues of Regulating Imperfectly Competitive Telecommunications Markets*, ed. by J.L. Racster, pp. 43–94, NRRI–85–12, November 1986, National Regulatory Research Institute, Columbus, OH.

Chipman, J.S. (1982), "A Model of the Aggregate Residential Demand for Electricity Under Declining Block-Rate Pricing," in *Aggregate Residential Electricity Demand: Methods for Integrating Over Declining Block Rates*, prepared for the Electric Power Research Institute Palo Alto, CA, by National Economic Research Associates, EPRI EA–2767, Project 1361, December 1982.

Cohen, G. (1976), "Experimenting with the Effect of Tariff Changes on Traffic Patterns," November, 8th International Teletraffic Congress, Melbourne, Australia.

Cohen, G. (1977), "Measured Rates Versus Flat Rates: A Pricing Experiment," Fifth Annual Telecommunications Policy Research Conference, March 1977, Airlie, VA.

Cohen, G. and Garfinkel, L. (1982), "Predicting Local Telephone Usage Under Measured Service," *Public Utilities Fortnightly*, Vol. 115, August 5, 1982, pp. 39–43.

Cohen, G. and Huntoon, Z. (1973), "Measured Local Service Study: Experimental Tariff Design," *GTE Labs Technical Review*, November 1973.

Cole, L.P. and Beauvais, E.C. (1983), "The Economic Impact of Access Charges: Does Anyone's Ox Need to Be Gored?," in *Adjusting to Regulatory, Pricing and Marketing Realities*, ed. by H.M. Trebing, pp. 417–451, 14th Annual Conference, MSU Institute of Public Utilities, East Lansing, MI.

Colias, J. and Maddox, L. (1990), "Analysis of Demand for Kentucky Local Telephone Usage," Attachment to the Testimony of Lorraine Maddox, "An Investigation in to the Economic Feasibility of Providing Local Measured Service Telephone Rates in Kentucky," Administrative Case No. 285.

Coll, S. (1986), *The Deal of the Century*, Atheneum, New York.

Collins, S.M. and Infosino, W.J. (1978), "A Model to Estimate Cincinnati Local Residential Calling Rates from Demographic Variables," Unpublished Bell Laboratories Memorandum, January 1978.

Colorado Public Utility Commission (1972), Decision 81320, Docket 717.

Communications Satellite Corporation (1969), "Econometric Model of Demand for International Telecommunications," Comsat Satellite Corporation, Washington, D.C., April 1969.

Cooter, R.D. and Rubinfeld, D.L. (1989), "Economic Analysis of Legal Disputes and Their Resolution," *Journal of Economic Literature*, Vol. 27, No. 3, September 1989, pp. 1067–1097.

Copeland, B.L., Jr. and Severn, A. (1985), "Price Theory and Telecommunications Regulation: A Dissenting View," *Yale Journal on Regulation*, Vol. 3, No. 1, Fall 1985.

Cornell, N.W. and Pelcovits, M.D. (1983), "Access Charges, Cost and Subsidies: The Effect of Long Distance Competition on Local Rates," in *Telecommunications Regulation Today and Tomorrow*, ed. by E. Noam, pp. 307–350, Harcourt, Brace, Jovanovich, Orlando, FL.

Cosgrove, J.G. and Linhart, P.B. (1979), "Customer Choices Under Local Measured Telephone Service," *Public Utilities Fortnightly*, Vol. 111, August 30, 1979, pp. 27–31.

Courville, L., de Fontenay, A. and Dobell, A.R., eds. (1983), *Economic Analysis of Telecommunications: Theory and Applications*, North-Holland Publishing Co., Amsterdam.

Cox, A.J. and Ruud, P.A. (1988), "Modeling the Effects of Household Characteristics on Telephone Usage and Class of Service Choice," Department of Economics, University of California, Berkeley, CA.

Cozanet, E. and Gensollen, M. (1987), "Les Modèles de Prevision de la Demande Téléphonique en France," *Revue Economique*, Vol. 38, No. 2, March 1987, pp. 257–305.

C&P Telephone Company of Maryland (1977a), Rebuttal testimony of H. Kelejian, Docket No. 7025, March 29, 1977.

C&P Telephone Company of Maryland (1977b), Rebuttal testimony of A.P. Sprinkel, Docket No. 7025, March 29, 1977.

C&P Telephone Company of West Virginia (1977c), Testimony of Alan P. Sprinkel, Docket No. 8890, March 3, 1977.

Cracknell, D. (1986), "The Analysis of Revenue Growth in Telecommunications," paper prepared for the 6th International Conference on Forecasting and Analysis for Businesses Planning in the Information Age, Tokyo, November 30–December 3, 1986, British Telecom Economics Advisory Division, London, November 1986.

Cracknell, D. (1988), "The Analysis of Growth in Demand for Access: A Disaggregated Approach," paper prepared for Bell Canada-BELLCORE Demand Analysis Industry Forum, Key Biscayne, FL, January 25–27, 1988, British Telecom Economics Advisory Division, London, January 1988.

Cracknell, D. (1992), "Demand Modelling for Customer Options," paper presented to the 9th International Conference of the International Telecommunications Society, British Telecom Products and Services Management, London, April 1992. Crane, D.B. and Crothy, J.B. (1967), "A Two-State Forecasting Model: Exponential Smoothing and Multiple Regression," *Management Science*, Vol. 13, B510–B507, April 1967.

Cracknell, D. and White D. (1989), "The Use of Panel Data in Market Analysis: British Telecom's Experience," paper prepared for International Telecommunication Society Regional Conference, Leuven, Belgium, April 14–15, 1989, British Telecom Economics Advisory Division, London, April 1989.

Craver, R.F. (1975), "International Calling at Bargain Rates," *Telephony*, Vol. 189, December

15, pp. 34–35.

Craver, R.F. (1976a), "A Demand Analysis Study of Telecommunications Between Canada and the United States," Unpublished paper, January and April, AT&T Long-Lines Overseas Economic Research.

Craver, R.F. (1976b), "An Estimate of the Price Elasticity of Demand for International Telecommunications," *Telecommunications Journal*, Vol. 43, pp. 671–675.

Craver, R.F. (1976c), "A Look Into a Crystal Ball at the Future of International Calling," *Telephony*, Vol. 191, No. 5, August 2, pp. 35–37.

Craver, R.F. (1976d), "UK Forecast Analysis," Unpublished paper, September, AT&T Long-Lines Overseas Economic Research.

Craver, R.F. (1977), "The 'Utrility' of Econometrics – How to Forecast Demand," *Telephone Engineer and Management*, February 15, pp. 74–78.

Craver, R.F. and Neckowitz, H. (1980), "International Telecommunications: The Evolution of Demand Analysis," *Telecommunications Journal*, Vol. 47, pp. 217–223.

Craven, J. (1985), "Peak-Load Pricing and Short-Run Marginal Cost," *The Economic Journal*, Vol. 95, No. 3, September 1985, pp. 778–780.

Curien, N. and Gensollen, M. (1987), "A Functional Analysis of the Network: A Prerequisite for Deregulating the Telecomm Industry," *Annales des Télécommunications* (in English), Vol. 42, No. 11, November–December 1987, pp. 629–641.

Curien, N. and Gensollen, M. (1989), *Prévision de Demande de Télécommunications: Methodes et Modèles*, Eyrolles, Paris.

Curien, N. and Gensollen, M. (1992), *L'Economie des Télécommunications: Ouverture et Réglementation*, Economica, Paris.

Daggett, R.S. and Freedman, D.A. (1985), "Econometrics and the Law: A Case Study in the Proof of Antitrust Damages," in *Proceedings of the Berkeley Conference in Honor of Jerzy Neyman and Jack Kiefer*, Vol. 1, ed. by L.M. LeCam and R.A. Olshan, Wadsworth, Inc.

Dalton, M.M. and Mann, P.C. (1985), "Telephone Cost Allocation: Testing the Variability of Costs," *Land Economics*, Vol. 64, No. 3, August 1985, pp. 296–305.

Daly, G. and Mayor, T. (1980), "Estimating the Value of A Missing Market: The Economics of Directory Assistance," *Journal of Law and Economics*, Vol. 23, No. 1, April 1980, pp. 147–166.

Dansby, R.E. (1983), "Economic Analysis of A Measured Service Option," in *Economic Analysis of Telecommunications: Theory and Applications*, ed. by L. Courville *et al.*, Elsevier North-Holland, New York, NY.

Davidson, R. and MacKinnon, J.G. (1981), "Several Tests for Model Specifications in the Presence of Alternative Hypothesis," *Econometrica*, Vol. 49, No. 4, July 1981, pp. 781–794.

Davis, B.E., Caccappolo, G.J. and Chaudry, M.A. (1973), "An Econometric Planning Model for American Telephone and Telegraph Company," *Bell Journal of Economics and Management Science*, Vol. 4, No. 1, Spring 1973, pp. 29–56.

Deaton, A.S. and Muellbauer, J. (1980), "An Almost Ideal Demand System," *American Economic Review*, Vol. 70, No. 3, June 1980, pp. 312–326.

de Fontenay, A. and Lee, J.T. (1983), "B.C./Alberta Long Distance Calling," in *Economic Analysis of Telecommunications: Theory and Applications*, ed. by L. Courville *et al.*, pp. 199–227, Elsevier Science Publishers/North Holland, New York, NY.

de Fontenay, A., Shugard, H.M. and Sibley, D.S., eds. (1990), *Telecommunications Demand Modeling*, North-Holland Publishing Co., Amsterdam.

Denny, M., Fuss, M., Everson, C. and Waverman, L. (1981), "Estimating the Effects of Diffusion of Technological Innovations in Telecommunications: The Production Structure of Bell Canada," *Canadian Journal of Economics*, Vol. 14, No. 1, February 1981, pp. 24–43.

Deschamps, P.J. (1974), "The Demand for Telephone Calls in Belgium, 1961–1969," Birmingham International Conference in Telecommunications Economics, May 1974 Birmingham, England.

Deschamps, P.J. (1976), "Second-Best Pricing with Variable Product Quality: A Quantitative Decision Rule and an Existence Proof," Université Catholique de Louvain, Louvain, Belgium.

Deschamps, P.J. (1977), "Pricing for Congestion in Telephone Networks: A Numerical Example," Center for Operations Research and Econometrics, Université Catholique de Louvain, Louvain, Belgium.

Dobell, A.R., Taylor, L.D., Waverman, L., Liu, T.H. and Copeland, M.D.G. (1970), *Communications in Canada: A Statistical Summary*, study prepared for the Department of Communications, Ottawa, by the Institute for Policy Analysis, September 1970, University of Toronto.

Dobell, A.R., Taylor, L.D., Waverman, L., Liu, T.H. and Copeland, M.D.G. (1972), "Telephone Communications in Canada: Demand, Production, and Investment Decisions," *Bell Journal of Economics and Management Science*, Vol. 3, No.1, Spring 1973, pp. 175–219.

Doherty, A.N. (1978), "Econometric Estimation of Local Telephone Price Elasticities," in *Assessing New Pricing Concepts in Public Utilities*, ed. by H.M. Trebing, Ninth Annual Conference Proceedings, MSU Institute of Public Utilities, East Lansing, MI.

Doherty, A.N. and Oscar, G.M. (1977), "Will The Rates Produce The Revenues," *Public Utilities Fortnightly*, Vol. 99, May 12, 1977, pp. 15–23.

Domencich, T. and McFadden, D. (1975), *Urban Travel Demand: A Behavioral Analysis*, North Holland, Amsterdam.

Dubin, J.A. (1985), *Consumer Durable Choice and the Demand for Electricity*, North-Holland Publishing Co., Amsterdam.

Duncan, G.M. and Perry, D.M. (1992), "Demand Elasticities by Dynamic Analysis of Revenue and Usage Data: IntraLATA Toll in California," Department of Economics and Statistics, GTE Laboratories, Inc., Waltham, MA.

Dunn, D.M., Williams, W.H. and Spivey, W.A. (1971), "Analysis and Prediction of Telephone Demand in Local Geographical Areas," *Bell Journal of Economics and Management Science*, Vol. 2, No. 2, Autumn 1971, pp. 561–576.

Duvall, J.B. (1984), "Telephone Rates and Rate Structures: A Regulatory Perspective," in *Telecommunications Access and Public Policy*, ed. by A. Baughcum *et al.*, pp. 166–204, Workshop on Local Access, September 1982, St. Louis, Mo., Ablex Publishing Co., Norwood, NJ.

Egan, B.L. and Weisman, D.L. (1986), "The U.S. Telecommunications Industry in Transition: Bypass, Regulation and the Public Interest," *Telecommunications Policy*, June 1986, pp. 164–176.

Einhorn, M.A. (1987), "Pareto Improving Telephone Tariffs Under By-pass Alternatives," November, CTIS Conference Working Paper, Columbia University Graduate School of Business, New York, NY.

Einhorn, M.A. and Egan, B.L. (1987), "How to Set Long Distance Access Charges: A Multi-Tariff Approach," *Public Utilities Fortnightly*, Vol. 119, No. 10, May 14, 1987, pp. 19–23.

Eliasson, G., Folster, S., Lindberg, T., Pousette, T. and Taymaz, E. (1990), "The Knowledge Based Information Economy," The Industrial Institute for Economic and Social Research (Telecon), Almqvist & Wilsell International, Stockholm.

Engle, R.F. and Granger, C.W.J. (1987), "Co-Integration and Error-Correction: Representation,

Estimation and Testing," *Econometrica*, Vol. 55, No. 2, March 1987, pp. 251–276.

English, H.E., ed. (1973), *Telecommunications for Canada: An Interface for Business and Government*, Methuen, Toronto, Ontario.

Ergas, H. *et al.*, eds. (1984), "Changing Market Structures in Telecommunications: Proceedings of an OECD Conference," from OECD Conference, December 12–15, 1982, North-Holland, New York, NY.

Evans, D.A. (1953), "Experimental Evidence Concerning Contagious Distribution in Ecology," *Biometrika*, Vol. 40, pp. 186–211.

Evans, D.S. *et al.*, eds. (1983), "Breaking Up Bell: Essays on Industrial Organization and Regulation," North-Holland Elsevier, New York, NY.

Fask, A. and Robinson, P.B. (1977), "The Analysis of Telephone Demand by Dynamic Regression," Unpublished paper, AT&T, September 1977.

Faulhaber, G.R. (1987), *Telecommunications in Turmoil: Technology and Public Policy*, Ballinger Publishing Co., Cambridge, MA.

Federal Communications Commission (1985), Second Bypass Order, CC Docket 78–72, Phase I, January 18, 1985.

Feldman, J. (1976), "A Preliminary Cross Sectional Analysis of Services," Unpublished paper, AT&T, February 1976.

Feldstein, M.J. (1972a), "Distributional Equity and the Optimal Structure of Public Prices," *American Economic Review*, Vol. 62, No. 1, March 1972, pp. 32–36.

Feldstein, M.J. (1972b), "Equity and Efficiency in Public Sector Pricing: The Optimal Two-Part Tariff," *Quarterly Journal of Economics*, Vol. 86, No. 2, May 1972, pp. 175–187.

Fenton, C.G. and Schankerman, M.A. (1977), "The Demand for Basic Exchange Service: A Discrete Choice Model and Its Implications for Socially Preferred Subsidy Patterns," 5th Annual Telecommunications Policy Research Conference, March 30–April 2, 1977, Airlie, VA.

Finney, D.J. (1971), *Probit Analysis*, 3rd ed., Cambridge University Press, Cambridge, England.

Fisher, F.M. (1980), "Multiple Regression in Legal Proceedings," *Columbia Law Review*, Vol. 80, No. 4, May 1980, pp. 702–754.

Fisher, F.M. (1986), "Statisticians, Econometricians, and Adversarial Proceedings," *Journal of the American Statistical Association*, Vol. 81, No. 394, June 1986, pp. 277–286.

Forrest, H. *et al.*, eds. (1986), "Telecommunications 1986: Competition and Deregulation After the AT&T Divestiture," from Course Handbook Series No. 234, Practicing Law Institute, New York, NY.

Fowler, M.S., Halprin, A. and Schlichting, J.D. (1986), "'Back to the Future': A Model for Telecommunications," *Federal Communications Law Journal*, Vol. 38, No. 2, August 1986, pp. 145–200.

Fuss, M. and Waverman, L. (1981), "The Regulation of Telecommunications in Canada," Technical Report No. 7, Economic Council of Canada.

Gabel, D. and Kennet, M.D. (1993), "Pricing of Telecommunications Services," *Review of Industrial Organization*, Vol. 8, No. 1.

Gabor, A. (1955), "A Note on Block Tariffs," *Review of Economics Studies*, Vol. 23.

Gale, W.A. (1971), "Duration of Interstate Calls," March 1969, Unpublished Bell Laboratories Memorandum, Murray Hill, N.J., December 1971.

Gale, W.A. (1973), "Time of Day Distributions for Long Distance Calls," Unpublished Bell Laboratories Memorandum, Murray Hill, N.J., October 1973.

Gale, W.A. (1974), "Elasticity of Duration for Intrastate Calls," Unpublished Bell Laboratories

Memorandum, Murray Hill, N.J., October 1974.

Garfinkel, L. (1977a), "Practical Problems in Economic Theory and Rate Structure," in *Proceedings of 1977 Symposium on Problems of Regulated Industries*, February 1977.

Garfinkel, L. (1977b), "Planning for a Transition in Pricing Basic Exchange Service," Public Utilities Forecasting Conference, BOWNESS-ON-WINDERMERE, United Kingdom, March 24, 1977.

Garfinkel, L. (1979a), "Network Access Pricing – Practical Problems in Implementation," in *Issues in Public Utility Regulation*, ed. by T.M. Trebing, 10th Annual Conference, MSU Institute of Public Utilities, East Lansing, MI.

Garfinkel, L. (1979b), "Network Access Pricing," in *Issues in Public Utility Regulation*, ed. by H.M. Trebing, pp. 153–166, 10th Annual Conference MSU, Institute of Public Utilities, East Lansing, MI.

Garfinkel, L. and Linhart, P.B. (1979), "The Transition to Local Measured Service," *Public Utilities Fortnightly*, Vol. 111, August 16, 1979, pp. 17–21.

Garfinkel, L. and Linhart, P.B. (1980), "The Revenue Analysis of Local Measured Telephone Service," *Public Utilities Fortnightly*, Vol. 112, October 9, 1979, pp. 15–21.

Gatto, J.P., Kelejian, H.H. and Stephan, S.W. (1988), "Stochastic Generalizations of Demand Systems with an Application to Telecommunications," *Information Economics and Policy*, Vol. 3, No. 4, pp. 283–310.

Gatto, J.P., Langin-Hooper, J., Robinson, P.B. and Tryan, H. (1988), "Interstate Switched Access Demand," *Information Economics and Policy*, Vol. 3, No. 4, pp. 333–358.

Gilbert, R.J. (1983), "Technical Change in Regulated Industries," Department of Economics, University of California, Berkeley.

Globerman, S. (1988), "Elasticity of Demand for Long-Distance Telephone Service," Report prepared by Steven Globerman Associates, Ltd. for the Federal-Provincial-Territorial Task Force on Telecommunications, Ottawa, Ontario, February 29, 1988.

Goldberger, A.S. (1964), *Econometric Theory*, J. Wiley & Sons, New York, NY.

Goldfeld, S., Quandt, R. and Trotter, H. (1966), "Maximization by Quadratic Hill Climbing," *Econometrica*, Vol. 34, No. 3, July 1966, pp. 541–551.

Granger, C.W.J. and Newbold, P. (1977), *Forecasting Economic Time Series*, Academic Press, New York, NY.

Green, J.R. and Zarkadas, C.J. (1984), "Local Measured Service as an Option: The Experience of Southern New England Telephone Company," in *Changing Patterns in Regulation, Markets, and Technology: The Effect on Public Utility Pricing*, ed. by P.C. Mann *et al.*, pp. 268–282, 15th Annual Conference, MSU Institute of Public Utilities, East Lansing, MI.

Green, P.E., Carmone, F.J. and Wachpress, D.P. (1976), "On the Analysis of Qualitative Data in Marketing Research," Working paper, AT&T, May 1976.

Griffin, J.M. (1982), "The Welfare Implications of Externalities and Price Elasticities for Telecommunications Pricing," *Review of Economics & Statistics*, Vol. 64, No. 1, February 1982, pp. 59–66.

Griffin, J.M. and Egan, B.L. (1985), "Demand System Estimation in the Presence of Multi-Block Tariffs: A Telecommunications Example," *Review of Economics & Statistics*, Vol. 67, No. 3, August 1985, pp. 520–524.

Griffin, J.M. and Mayor, T.H. (1987), "The Welfare Gain from Efficient Pricing of Local Telephone Service," *Journal of Law and Economics*, Vol. 30, No. 2, October 1987, p. 465 ff.

Haavelmo, T. (1944), "The Probability Approach in Econometrics," *Econometrica*, Vol. 12, Supplemental, July 1944.

Hackl, P. and Westlund, A.H. (1992), "On Price Elasticities of International Telecommunications Demand," Department of Economic Statistics, Stockholm School of Economics, Stockholm, Sweden.

Harbus, F.I. (1975), "Comparison of Average Durations and Time of Day Distributions for WATS and Business MTS Calls," Unpublished Bell Laboratories Memorandum, Bell Laboratories, Murray Hill, N.J., August 1975.

Harbus, F.I. (1978), "Price Elasticity: A Basic Ingredient in Rate Planning," AT&T Demand Analysis Group, New York, NY, February 1978.

Hartley, N. and Culham, P. (1988), "Telecommunications Prices Under Monopoly and Competition," *Oxford Review of Economic Policy*, Vol. 4, No. 2, Summer 1988, pp. 1–19.

Hartman, M.G. (1976), "Customer Line Usage Studies," 8th International Teletraffic Congress, Melbourne, Australia, November 1976.

Harvey, H.E. (1983), "Pricing Telephone Service in the 1980s," in *Current Issues in Public-Utility Economics*, ed. by A.L. Danielsen *et al.*, pp. 265–277, Lexington Books/D.C. Heath, Lexington, MA.

Hasselwander, A.C. (1979), "The Impact of Intercity Rate Restructure on Local Telephone Rates," in *Issues in Public Utility Regulation*, ed. by H.M. Trebing, pp. 391–400, 10th Annual Conference, MSU Institute of Public Utilities, East Lansing, MI.

Hausman, J.A. (1981), "Exact Consumer's Surplus and Deadweight Loss," *American Economic Review*, Vol. 71, No. 4, September 1981, pp. 662–676.

Hausman, J.A. (1990), "Estimation of Dynamic Demand Models for New Telecommunications Products," presented at conference on Telecommunications Demand Analysis with Dynamic Regulation, Hilton Head, SC, April 22–25, 1990, sponsored by Bell Canada and BELLCORE, Department of Economics, M.I.T., Cambridge, MA.

Hausman, J.A. (1991), "Phase II IRD Testimony of Professor Jerry A. Hausman on Behalf of Pacific Bell Telephone Co.," before the Public Utility Commission of California, September 23, 1991.

Hausman, J.A., Kinnucan, M. and McFadden, M. (1979), "A Two-Level Electricity Demand Model," *Journal of Econometrics*, Vol. 10, No. 3, August 1979, pp. 263–289.

Hausman, J.A., Tardiff, T. and Baughcum, A. (1983), "The Demand for Optional Local Measured Service," in *Adjusting to Regulation, Pricing and Marketing Realities*, ed. by H.M. Trebing, pp. 536–556, 14th Annual Conference, MSU Institute of Public Utilities, East Lansing, MI.

Hausman, J.A. and Trimble, J. (1984), "Appliance Purchase and Usage Adaptation to a Permanent Time-of-Day Electricity Rate Schedule," *Journal of Econometrics*, Vol. 26, No. 1/2, Sept/Oct. 1984, pp. 115–140.

Hausman, J.A. and Wise, D.A. (1978), "A Conditional Probit Model for Qualitative Choice: Discrete Decisions Recognizing Interdependence and Heterogenous Preference," *Econometrica*, Vol. 46, No. 2, March 1978, pp. 403–426.

Hazelwood, A. (1951), "Optimal Pricing as Applied to Telephone Service," *Review of Economic Studies*, Vol. 18.

Hendry, D.F. and Mizon, G.M. (1987), "Procrustean Econometrics," Department of Economics, University of Southhampton, Southhampton, U.K.

Hill, D., Groves, R., Howrey, E.P., Lepkowski, J., Smith, M.A., Kline, C. and Kohler, D. (1978), "Evaluation of Federal Energy Administration Rate Design Experiments," report prepared for the Electric Power Research Institute, Palo Alto, CA., Institute for Social Research, University of Michigan, Ann Arbor, MI.

Hobson, M. and Spady, R. (1988), "The Demand for Local Telephone Service Under Optional

Local Measured Service," Bell Communications Research, Morristown, NJ.

Hoffberg, M and Shugard, M.H. (1981), "A Utility Theory Approach to Class-of-Service Choice and Usage Regression," Bell Laboratories Technical Memorandum, TM–59541–5, 81–59543–7, Murray Hill, NJ, October 1981.

Hood, W.C. and Koopmans, T.C. (1953), *Studies in Econometric Method*, Cowles Commission Monograph No. 14, John Wiley & Sons, New York.

Hopley, J.K. (1978), "The Response of Local Telephone Usage to Peak Pricing," in *Assessing New Pricing Concepts in Public Utilities*, ed. by H.M. Trebing, pp. 12–26, 9th Annual Conference, MSU Institute of Public Utilities, East Lansing, MI.

Hopley, J.K. (1984), "Lifeline Rates for Local Exchange Service: Integrating Lifeline Principles with Income Tariffs," in *Changing Patterns in Regulation, Markets, and Technology: The Effect on Public Utility Pricing*, ed. by P.C. Mann *et al.*, pp. 283–291, 15th Annual Conference, MSU Institute of Public Utilities, East Lansing, MI.

Houthakker, H.S. (1965), "New Evidence on Demand Elasticities," *Econometrica*, Vol. 33, No. 1, April 1965, pp. 277–288.

Houthakker, H.S. and Taylor, L.D. (1970), *Consumer Demand in the United States: Analyses and Projections*, 2nd ed., Harvard University Press, Cambridge, MA.

Huang, S. (1975), "Building a Demand Model for Residence Phone Extensions in Minnesota," Unpublished paper, Northwestern Bell Telephone Company.

Huber, P.W. (1987), "The Geodesic Network: 1987 Report on Competition in the Telephone Industry," U.S. Department of Justice/Antitrust Division, GPO, Washington, D.C., January 1987.

Hyman, L., ed. (1987), "The New Telecommunications Industry: Evolution and Organization," from publishers of *Public Utility Fortnightly*, Public Utilities Reports, Arlington, VA.

Iacono, S., Orr, F.D. and Taylor, L.D. (1990), "Telecommunications Demand Analysis in Canada: Issues and Implications," Presented at the Eighth International Conference of the International Telecommunications Society, Venice, Italy, March 18–20, 1990, Bell Canada, Hull, Quebec.

Illinois Bell Telephone Company (1976), Testimony of Arnold Zellner, Illinois Docket No. 76–0409, Co. Ex.11, July 2, 1976.

Infosino, W.J. (1976), "Estimating Flat Rate Residence Average Local Calling Rate from Demographic Variables," Unpublished Bell Laboratories Memorandum, Murray Hill, N.J., August 1976.

Infosino, W.J. (1980), "Relationships Between the Demand for Local Telephone Calls and Household Characteristics," *Bell System Technical Journal*, Vol. 59, July–August 1980, pp. 931–953.

Irish, W.F. (1974), "A Market Analysis of the Demand for Telephone Sets by Class of Service," North Carolina Utilities Commission, December 1974.

Jackson, C.L. and Rohlfs, J.H. (1985), "Access Charging and Bypass Adoption," study prepared for Bell Atlantic by Shoosan and Jackson, Inc., Washington, D.C.

Jensik, J.M. (1979), "Dynamics of Consumer Usage," in *Perspectives on Local Measure Service*, ed. by J.A. Baude *et al.*, pp. 141–159, Telecommunications Industry Workshop March 13–14, 1979, Telecom Industry Workshop Organizing Committee, Kansas City, MO.

Jensik, J.M. (1982), "Some Changes in Local Calling Habits Because of Conversion to Local Measured Service," in *Telecommunications Policy Handbook*, ed. by J.R. Schement, pp. 142–157, 7th & 8th Telecommunications Policy Research Conference, Praeger Special Studies/Praeger Scientific, New York, NY.

Jensik, J.M. and Stolleman, N. (1983), "Pick A Number: A Discussion of Usage Sensitive

Tariffs," in *Adjusting to Regulatory, Pricing and Marketing Realities*, ed. by H.M. Trebing, pp. 503–535, 14th Annual Conference, MSU Institute of Public Utilities, East Lansing, MI.

Johnson, L.L. (1988), "Telephone Assistance Programs for Low Income Households: A Preliminary Assessment," RAND/R–3606–NSF/MF, RAND Corporation, Santa Monica, CA., February 1988.

Johnson, N.L. and Kotz, S. (1970), *Distributions in Statistics: Continuous Univariate Distributions*, Houghton Mifflin, Boston, MA.

Johnson, N.L. and Kotz, S. (1972), *Distributions in Statistics: Continuous Multivariate Distributions*, John Wiley & Sons.

Johnston, J. (1962, 1984), *Econometric Methods*, 3rd ed., 1984, McGraw-Hill, New York.

Jones, A.P. (1981), "Telecommunications in Transition: Toward Deregulation and Competition," in *Challenges for Public Utility Regulation in the 1980s*, ed. by H.M. Trebing, pp. 12–17, 12th Annual Conference, MSU Institute of Public Utilities, East Lansing, MI.

Jones, D.N. (1987), "A Perspective on Social Contract and Telecommunications Regulation," NRRI Report 87–5, National Regulatory Research Institute, Columbus, OH., June 1987.

Judge, G.G., Griffins, W.E., Hill, R.C., Lutkepohl, H. and Lee, T.C. (1985), *The Theory and Practice of Econometrics*, 2nd ed., John Wiley & Sons, New York.

Kahn, A.E. (1966), "The Tyranny of Small Business Decisions: Market Failure, Imperfections, and the Limits of Economics," *Kyklos*, Vol. 19, January 1966, pp. 23–47.

Kahn, A.E. (1970a), *The Economics of Regulation: Volume 1: Economic Principles*, Wiley & Sons, Inc., New York, NY.

Kahn, A.E. (1970b), *The Economics of Regulation: Volume 2: Institutional Issues*, J. Wiley & Sons, New York, NY.

Kahn, A.E. (1983), "Some Thoughts on Telephone Pricing," *Implementing the AT&T Settlement: The New Telecommunications Era*, ed. by M. Forrest *et al.*, Workshop on Local Access, September 14–17, 1982, Practicing Law Institute, New York, NY.

Kahn, A.E. (1984), "The Road to More Intelligent Telephone Pricing," *Yale Journal on Regulation*, Vol. 1, No. 2.

Kahn, A.E. (1985), "Frontier Issues in Telecommunications Regulation," *1985 Mountain Bell Academic Seminar*, ed. by J.T. Dwyer, August 1985, Competition Analysis and Docket Management, Mountain Bell, Denver, CO.

Kahn, A.E. and Shew, W.B. (1987), "Current Issues in Telecommunications Regulations & Pricing," *Yale Journal on Regulation*, Vol. 4, Winter 1987, pp. 191–256.

Kahn, A.E. and Zielinski, C. (1976), "New Rate Structures in Communications," *Public Utilities Fortnightly*, Vol. 108, March 25, 1976, pp. 19–24.

Kaserman, D.L., and Mayo, J.W. (1988), "Long-Distance Telecommunications Policy – Rationality on Hold," *Public Utilities Fortnightly*, Vol. 123, No. 13, December 22, 1988, pp. 18–27.

Katz, M. and Willig, R. (1983), "The Case for Freeing AT&T," *Regulation*, pp. 43–49.

Katz, M. and Shapiro, C. (1985), "Network Externalities, Competition and Compatibility," *American Economic Review*, Vol. 75, No. 3, June 1975, pp. 424–440.

Kaufman, I. (1972), "Bell Canada Message Toll Market Response System," Bell Canada Management Science-Toll Studies, Ottawa, Ontario.

Kearns, T.J. (1978), "Modeling the Demand for Residence Extensions," Unpublished Bell Laboratories Memorandum, Murray Hill, N.J., February 1978.

Kelley, D. (1983), "Optional Calling Plans: Promotional or Predatory?," in *The Impact of Deregulation and Market Forces on Public Utilities: The Future Role of Regulation*, ed. by P.C. Mann *et al.*, pp. 279–286, 16th Annual Conference, MSU Institute of Public Utilities,

East Lansing, MI.

Khadem, R. (1973a), "An Economic Study of the Demand for Trans-Canada Long Distance Telephone Service," Bell Canada, Demand Analysis Group, Ottawa, Ontario, Canada.

Khadem, R. (1973b), "An Econometric Demand Model of Canada-U.S. Voice Telecommunications," Computer Communications and Network Services, Bell Canada, Ottawa, Ontario, Canada, December 1973.

Khadem, R. (1974), "An Econometric Model of the Demand for Overseas Voice Telecommunications," Computer Communications and Network Services, Bell Canada, Ottawa, Ontario, October 1974.

Khadem, R. (1976), "An Econometric Forecasting Model of the Demand for International Voice Telecommunication from Canada," *Teleglobe Canada*, Montreal, October 1976.

Kiss, F. and Lefebvre, B. (1987), "Econometric Models of Telecommunications Firms: A Survey," *Revue Economique*, Vol. 38, No. 2, March 1987, pp. 307–372.

Klein, R.W. and Willig, R.D. (1977), "Network Externalities and Optimal Telecommunications Pricing: A Preliminary Sketch," in *5th Annual Telecommunications Policy Research Conference Papers*, Vol. 2, Airlie, VA., pp. 475.

Kling, J.P. and Van der Ploeg, S.S. (1990), "Estimating Local Call Elasticities with a Model of Stochastic Class of Service and Usage Choice," in *Telecommunications Demand Modelling*, ed. by A. de Fontenay, H.M. Shugard and D.S. Sibley, North-Holland Publishing Co.

Konczal, E.F. (1973), "Model Building: Art and Science – Outline of Long Lines – DRI Seminar," Unpublished paper, AT&T Long-Lines, October 1973.

Koopmans, T.C. (1937), *Linear Regression Analysis of Economic Time Series*, Netherlands Economic Institute, Haarlem.

Koopmans, T.C. (1950), *Statistical Inference in Dynamic Economic Models*, Cowles Commission Monograph No. 10, John Wiley & Sons, New York.

Kowal, K.L. (1985), "Local Access Bypass," *Federal Communications Law Journal*, Vol. 37, No. 2, April 1985, pp. 325–376.

Kraepelien, H.Y. (1958), "The Influence of Telephone Rates on Local Traffic," L.M. Ericsson Technics, No. 2, L.M. Ericsson/Telefonaktiebolaget, Stockholm, Sweden.

Kraepelien, H.Y. (1977), "The Configuration Theory: The Influence of Multi-Part Tariffs on Local Telephone Traffic," 8th International Teletraffic Congress, Melbourne, Australia.

Kraepelien, H.Y. (1978), "Local Telephone Pricing: The Configuration Theory," paper prepared for the Office of Telecommunications, U.S. Department of Commerce, Boulder, CO., March 1978.

Kridel, D.J. (1987), *An Analysis of the Residential Demand for Access to the Telephone Network*, Ph.D. Dissertation, Department of Economics, University of Arizona, Tucson, AZ, January 1987.

Kridel, D.J. (1988), "A Consumer Surplus Approach to Predicting Extended Area Service (EAS) Development and Stimulation Rates," *Information Economics and Policy*, Vol. 3, No. 4, pp. 379–390.

Kridel, D.J., Lehman, D.E. and Weisman, D.L. (1991), "Option Value, Telecommunications Demand and Policy," Southwestern Bell Telephone Co., St. Louis, November 1991.

Kridel, D.J. and Taylor, L.D. (1993), "The Demand for Commodity Packages: The Case of Telephone Custom Calling Features," *Review of Economics and Statistics*, Vol. 75, No. 2, May 1993, pp. 362–367.

Kristian, B., Gaustad, O. and Kosberg, J. E. (1976), "Some Traffic Characteristics of Subscriber Categories and the Influence from Tariff Changes," International Tele-traffic Congress, Melbourne, Australia, November 1976.

Krutilla, J.V. (1967), "Conservation Reconsidered," *American Economic Review*, Vol. 57, No. 4, September 1967, pp. 777–786.

Kuh, E. (1963), *Capital Stock Growth: A Micro-Econometric Approach*, Amsterdam, North-Holland.

Kumins, L. (1967), "An Estimate of Price Elasticity of Demand for International Long-Distance Telephony," *Telecommunications Journal*, Vol. 34, No. 6, June 1967, pp. 214–215.

Kwok, P.K., Lee, P.C. and Pearce, J.C. (1975), "Econometric Models of the Demand for Bell Originated Message Toll," Bell Canada, CCNS Network Market Planning, Ottawa, Ontario, January 1975.

Laber, G. and Zamore, P.H. (1984), "Competition in Intrastate Telephone Service," *Public Utilities Fortnightly*, Vol. 116, July 5, 1984, pp. 27–30.

Lago, A.M. (1970), "Demand Forecasting Models of International Telecommunications and their Policy Implications," *Journal of Industrial Economics*, Vol. 19, November 1970, pp. 6–21.

Lang, H. and Lundgren, S. (1991), "Price Elasticities for Residential Demand for Telephone Calling Time: An Estimate With Swedish Data," *Economic Letters*, Vol. 35, pp. 85–88.

Larsen, W.A. and McCleary, S.J. (1970), "Exploratory Attempts to Model Point-to-Point Cross-Sectional Interstate Telephone Demand," Unpublished Bell Laboratories Memorandum, Murray Hill, N.J., July 1970.

Larson, A.C. (1988), "Specification Error Tests for Pooled Demand Models," presented at Bell Communications Research/Bell Canada Industry Forum on Telecommunications Demand Modeling, Key Biscayne, FL, January 25–27, 1988, Southwestern Bell Telephone Co., St. Louis.

Larson, A.C. and Lehman, D.E. (1986) "Asymmetric Pricing and Arbitrage," presented at the Sixth International Conference on Forecasting and Analysis for Business Planning in the Information Age, Southwestern Bell Telephone Co., St. Louis.

Larson, A.C., Lehman, D.E. and Weisman, D.L. (1990), "A General Theory of Point-to-Point Long Distance Demand," in *Telecommunications Demand Modelling*, ed. by A. de Fontenay, M.H. Shugard and D.S. Sibley, North-Holland Publishing Co, Amsterdam.

Larson, A.C., Makarewicz, T.J. and Monson, C. (1989), "The Effects of Subscriber Line Charges on Residential Telephone Bills," *Telecommunications Policy*, December 1989, pp. 337–354.

Leunbach, G. (1958), "Factors Influencing the Demand for Telephone Service," Paper presented at Second International Tele-traffic Congress, July 7–11, 1958, The Hague.

Levin, S.L. and Case, J.C. (1986), "Local Measured Service: The Present and Future," Paper presented at 14th Annual Telecommunications Policy Research, April 1986, Airlie, VA.

Lin, W., Hirst, E. and Cohn, S. (1976), "Fuel Choices in the Household Sector," Oak Ridge National Laboratory, ORNL/CON–3, October 1976.

Linhart, P.B. and Radner, R. (1984), "Deregulation of Long-Distance Telecommunications," *Policy Research in Telecommunications*, ed. by V. Mocso, 11th Annual Telecommunications Research Conference, Ablex Publishing Co., Norwood NJ.

Littlechild, S.C. (1970), "A Note on Telephone Rentals," *Applied Economics*, Vol. 2, No. 1.

Littlechild, S.C. (1970), "Peak-Load Pricing of Telephone Calls," *Bell Journal of Economics*, Vol. 1, No. 2, Autumn 1970, pp. 191–210.

Littlechild, S.C. (1975), "Two-Part Tariffs and Consumption Externalities," *Bell Journal of Economics*, Vol. 5, No. 2, Autumn 1975, pp. 661–670.

Littlechild, S.C. (1977), "The Role of Consumption Externalities in the Pricing of Telephone Service," *Pricing in Regulated Industries: Theory and Application*, ed. by J.T. Wenders, pp. 38–46, Economic Seminar, Carefree, Az., January 1977, Mountain States Telephone and Telegraph, Denver, CO.

Littlechild, S.C. (1979), "Elements of Telecommunications Economics," Published by Peter Peregrinus for the Institute of Electrical Engineers, New York, NY.

Littlechild, S.C. and Rousseau, J.J. (1975), "Pricing Policy of a U.S. Telephone Company," *Journal of Public Economics*, Vol. 4, No. 1, February 1975, pp. 35–56.

Lords, J. (1985), "Mountain Bell Telephone Access Demand Model Based on Wire Center Data," Demand Analysis Group, Unpublished Mountain Bell Study, Denver, CO.

Lowry, E.D. (1976), "The Demand for Telecommunications Services: A Survey," in *Competition and Regulation – Some Economic Concepts*, ed. by C.F. Phillipis, Washington and Lee University Press, Lexington, VA.

Maddala, G.S. (1971), "The Use of Variance Components Models in Pooling Cross-Section and Time-Series Data," *Econometrica*, Vol. 39, No. 2, March 1971, pp. 341–358.

Mahan, G.P. (1979), *The Demand for Residential Telephone Service*, Michigan State University Public Utilities Papers, East Lansing, MI.

Manski, C.F. (1991), "Regression," *Journal of Economic Literature*, Vol. 29, No. 1, March 1991, pp. 34–50.

Margeson, A.J. (1981), "Network Access Pricing," in *Challenges for Public Utility Regulation in the 1980s*, ed. by H.M. Trebing, pp. 149–164, 12th Annual Conference, MSU Institute of Public Utilities, East Lansing, MI.

Margeson, A.J. (1983), "Pricing Response to Increased Local Revenue Requirements," in *Diversification, Deregulation and Increased Uncertainty in the Public Utility Industry*, ed. by H.M. Trebing, pp. 496–512, 13th Annual Conference, MSU Institute of Public Utilities, East Lansing, MI.

Martin, C.P. (1982), "A Review of the Demand Analysis of Directory Assistance Charging," January, IL82–02–320, AT&T Demand Analysis Group, New York, NY.

Martins-Filho, C. and Mayo, J. (1993), "Demand and Pricing of Telecommunications Services: Evidence and Welfare Implications," *Rand Journal of Economics*, Vol. 24, No. 3, Autumn 1993, pp. 439–454.

McAfee, R.P., McMillan, J. and Whinston, M.D. (1989), "Multiproduct Monopoly, Commodity Bundling, and Correlation of Values," *Quarterly Journal of Economics*, Vol. 104, No. 2, May 1989, pp. 371–384.

McFadden, D.L. (1974), "Conditional Logit Analysis of Qualitative Choice Behavior," in *Frontiers of Econometrics*, ed. by P. Zarembka, Academic Press, New York, NY.

McFadden, D.L. (1976), "The Revealed Preference of a Government Bureaucracy: Empirical Evidence," *Bell Journal of Economics and Management Science*, Vol. 7, No. 1, Spring 1976, pp. 55–72.

McFadden, D.L. (1978), "Modelling the Choice of Residential Location," in *Spatial Interaction Theory and Planning Models*, ed. by A. Karquist *et al.*, North-Holland Publishing Co., Amsterdam.

McFadden, D.L. (1989), "A Method of Simulated Moments for Estimation of Discrete Response Models Without Numerical Integration," *Econometrica*, Vol. 57, No. 5, September 1989, pp. 995–1026.

Mead, J.E. (1985), "Analysis of Characteristics of Residential Telephone Calling and Propensities to Alter Calling Activity per Call," General Telephone Co. of California, Thousands Oaks, CA., November 15, 1985.

Meier, P. (1986), "Damned Liars and Expert Witnesses," *Journal of the American Statistical Association*, Vol. 81, No. 394, June 1986, pp. 269–276.

Meyer, C.W. (1966), "Marginal-Cost Pricing of Local Telephone Service," *Land Economics*, August 1966.

Meyer, L.S. and Kiesling, R. (1979), "Consumers' Viewpoints (on L.M.S.)," in *Perspectives on Local Measured Service*, ed. by J.A. Baude *et al.*, Telecomm Industry Workshop, March 13–14, 1979, Telecommunications Industrial Workshop Organizing Committee, Kansas City, MO.

Meyer, J.R. *et al.*, eds. (1980), "The Economics of Competition in the Telecommunications Industry," Oelgeschlager, Gunn and Hain, Cambridge, MA.

Michigan Bell Telephone Company (1976), Testimony, Exhibit, and Supporting Work Papers of Harold T. Shapiro, Docket No. U5125, September 7, 1976.

Michigan Bell Telephone Company (1976), Rebuttal Testimony and Exhibit of E. Phillip Howrey, Docket No. U5125, November 22, 1976.

Mirman, L.J. and Sibley, D.S. (1980), "Optimal Nonlinear Prices for Multiproduct Monopolies," *Bell Journal of Economics and Management Science*, Vol. 11, No. 2, Summer 1980, pp. 659–670.

Mitchell, B.M. (1976), "Optimal Pricing of Local Telephone Service," RAND R–1962–MF, RAND Corporation, Santa Monica, CA, November 1976.

Mitchell, B.M. (1978), "Telephone Call Pricing in Europe: Localizing the Pulse," in *Pricing in Regulated Industries: Theory and Application*, ed. by J.T. Wenders, Mountain Bell Academic Seminar, August 1978, Mountain Bell, Denver, CO.

Mitchell, B.M. (1978), "Optimal Pricing of Local Telephone Service," *American Economic Review*, Vol. 68, No. 4, September 1978, pp. 517–538.

Mitchell, B.M. (1979), "Pricing Policies in Selected European Telephone Systems," in *Proceedings of the 6th Annual Telecommunications Policy Research Conference*, ed. by H.S. Dordick, pp. 437–475, Conference on Telecommunications Policy Research, Arlie, VA, Lexington Books/D.C. Heath, Lexington, MA.

Mitchell, B.M. (1980a), "Alternative Measured Service Structures for Local Telephone Service," in *Issues in Public Utility Pricing and Regulation*, ed. by M.A. Crew, pp. 107–123, Lexington Books/D.C. Heath, Lexington, MA.

Mitchell, B.M. (1980b), "Economic Issues in Usage Sensitive Pricing," RAND Research Paper P–6530, RAND Corporation, Santa Monica, CA, September 1980.

Mitchell, B.M. (1983), "Local Telephone Costs and the Design of Rate Structures," in *Economic Analysis of Telecommunications: Theory and Application*, ed. by L. Courville *et al.*, pp. 293–304, Elsevier Science Publishing/North-Holland, New York, NY.

Mitchell, B.M. and Park, R.E. (1981a), "Repression Effects of Mandatory vs. Optional Local Measured Telephone Service," RAND Research Note N–1636–NSF, RAND Corporation, Santa Monica, CA, March 1981.

Mitchell, B.M. and Park, R.E. (1981b), "Repression Effects of Mandatory versus Optional Local Measured Telephone Service," in *Challenges for Public Utility Regulation in the 1980s*, ed. by H.M. Trebing, pp. 121–139, 12th Annual Conference, MSU Institute of Public Utilities, East Lansing, MI.

Moffitt, R. (1986), "The Econometrics of Piece-Wise-Linear Budget Constraints," *Journal of Business and Economic Statistics*, Vol. 4, July 1986, pp. 219–223.

Moffitt, R. (1990), "The Econometrics of Kinked Budget Constraints," *Journal of Economic Perspectives*, Vol. 4, No. 2, Spring 1990, pp. 119–140.

Moore, W.A. and Bowman, G.W. (1982) "The Demand for Local Telephone Use: Modeling the Effects of Price Change," in *Award Papers in Public Utility Economics and Regulation*, ed. by H.M. Trebing, pp. 270–291, MSU Public Utilities Papers, East Lansing, MI.

Mountain Bell (1977a), Testimony of E. Milker, Montana Docket No. 6496, October 9, 1977.
Mountain Bell (1977b), Testimony of J.L. Whiting, Idaho Docket No. U–1500–90, June 22, 1977.
Mount-Campbell, C.A., Neuhardt, J.B. and Lee, B. (1985), "A Methodology for Telephone Usage Studies Relating Usage to Demographic or Other Variables," NRRI–84–14, National Regulatory Research Institute, Columbus, OH, March 1985.
Murphy, M.M. (1985), "Volume Discount Pricing of Long Distance Telephone Service," in *The Impact of Deregulation and Market Forces on Public Utilities: The Future Role of Regulation*, ed. by P.C. Mann *et al.*, 16th Annual Conference, MSU Institute of Public Utilities, East Lansing, MI.
Musgrave, R.A. (1959), *The Theory of Public Finance*, McGraw Hill Publishing Co.
Myskja, A. and Walmann, O. (1973), "A Statistical Study of Telephone Traffic Data with Emphasis on Subscriber Behavior," 7th Annual International Tele-traffic Congress, Stockholm, Sweden.
Naleszkiewicz, W. (1970), "International Telecommunications – Testing a Forecasting Model of Demand," *Telecommunications Journal*, Vol. 37, September 1970, pp. 635–638.
Nall, D.W. and Ronayne, K. (1986), "Florida Toll Demand Elasticities: A Background Paper," Florida Public Service Commission, Tallahassee, FL, September 1986.
Nerlove, M. (1971), "Further Evidence on the Estimation of Dynamic Economic Relations from a Time Series of Cross Sections," *Econometrica*, Vol. 39, No. 2, March 1971, pp. 359–382.
Nerlove, M. and Press, S.J. (1973), "Univariate and Multivariate Log-Linear and Logistic Models," RAND Corporation, December 1973.
Nerlove, M. and Wage, S. (1964), "On the Optimality of Adaptive Forecasting," *Bell Journal of Economics and Management Science*, Vol. 10, January 1969, pp. 207–224.
New England Telephone and Telegraph Company (1978), Prepared Testimony of Hendrik S. Houthakker, Massachusetts Docket No. 18210 Phase II, May 15, 1978.
New Jersey Bell Telephone Company (1977), Testimony and exhibits of P.J. Dhrymes, Docket No. 7711–1136, November 1978.
New York Telephone Company (1976a), Testimony and exhibit of S.F. Cordo, Docket No. 27100, November 17,1976.
New York Telephone Company (1976b), Testimony and exhibit of A.N. Doherty, Docket No. 27100, November 17, 1976.
New York Telephone Company (1977a), Prepared testimony of T.R. Kershner, J.K. Kenney, and S. Schmidt, Docket No. 27100, July 20, 1977.
New York Telephone Company (1977b), Rebuttal testimony of A.N. Doherty, Docket No. 27100, March 29, 1977.
New York Telephone Company (1977c), Rebuttal testimony of S.F. Cordo, Docket No. 27100, March 29, 1977.
New York Telephone Company (1984), Testimony and Exhibits of A.N. Doherty, NYPSC Case No. 28961, November 1984.
Nieswadomy, M.L. and Brink, S. (1990), "Private Line Demand: A Point-to-Point Analysis," Department of Economics, University of North Texas, Denton, TX.
Nijdam, J. (1990), "Forecasting Telecommunications Services Using Box-Jenkins (ARIMA) Models," *Telecommunications Journal of Australia*, Vol. 40, No. 1, pp. 33–37.
Noll, R.G. (1983), "The Future of Telecommunications Regulation," in *Telecommunications Regulation Today and Tomorrow*, ed. by E.M. Noam, Law & Business, Inc./Harcourt Brace Jovanovich, New York, NY.

Noll, R.G. (1985), "Let Them Make Toll Calls: A State Regulator's Lament," *American Economic Association Papers and Proceedings*, Vol. 75, No. 2, May 1985, pp. 52–56.

Noll, R.G. (1986), "State Regulatory Responses to Competition and Divesture in the Telecommunications Industry," in *Antitrust and Regulation*, ed. by R.E. Grieson, pp. 165–200, D.C. Heath & Co., Lexington, MA.

Noll, R.G. (1987), "The Twisted Pair: Regulation and Competition in Telecommunications," *AEI Journal on Government and Society*, No. 3/4, American Enterprise Institute, Washington, D.C.

Norton, S.W. (1992), "Transaction Costs, Telecommunications, and the Microeconomics of Macroeconomic Growth," *Economic Development and Cultural Change*, Vol. 41, No. 1, October 1992, pp. 175–196.

Northwestern Bell Telephone Company (1978a), Testimony of L. Graff, Minnesota Docket No. GR–77–1509, May 8, 1978.

Northwestern Bell Telephone Company (1978b), Testimony of H.S. Houthakker, Minnesota Docket No. GR–77–1509, May 8, 1978.

Northwestern Bell Telephone Company (1978c), Testimony of J.W. Johnson, Minnesota Docket No. GR–77–1509, May 8, 1978.

Obuschowski, E.J. (1987), "Access Charges and Revenue Architecture," *AT&T Technical Journal*, Vol. 66, May–June 1987, pp. 73–81.

Ohio Bell Telephone Company (1976), Testimony and attachments to testimony of R.A. Billinghurst, Docket No. 7476–ITP–AIR, January 6, 1976.

Oi, W.Y. (1971), "A Disneyland Dilemma: Two-Part Tariffs for a Mickey Mouse Monopoly," *Quarterly Journal of Economics*, Vol. 85, No. 1, February 1971, pp. 77–96.

Opinion Research Corporation (1980), "The GTE Local Measured Service Experiment in Illinois: Attitude Research Among Residence and Business Customers 1975–1979," ORC Study No. 33604, Opinion Research Corporation, Princeton, NJ.

Ordover, J.A. and Panzar, J.C. (1980), "On the Nonexistence of Pareto-superior Outlay Schedules," *Bell Journal of Economics and Management Science*, Vol. 11, Issue 1, Spring 1980, pp. 351–354.

Ordover, J.A. and Willig, R.D. (1983), "Local Telephone Pricing in a Competitive Environment," in *Telecommunications Regulation Today and Tomorrow*, ed. by E.M. Noam, Law and Business, Inc./Harcourt Brace Jovanovich, New York, NY.

Ordover, J.A. and Willig, R.D. (1984), "Pricing of Interexchange Access: Some Thoughts on the 3rd Report and Order in FCC Docket 78–72," in *Policy Research in Telecommunications*, ed. by V. Mosco, 11th Annual Telecommunications Policy Research Conference, 1983, Ablex Publishing, Norwood, NJ.

Pacey, P.L. (1983), "Long Distance Demand: A Point-to-Point Model," *Southern Economic Journal*, Vol. 49, No. 4, April 1983, pp. 1094–1107.

Pacey, P.L. and Sinell, L. Jr. (1983), "Should Local Telephone Companies Advertise Measured Service?" Unpublished research for Mountain Bell, Denver, CO., May 1983.

Pacific Northwest Bell Telephone Company (1976), Testimony of L.K. Bumgarner, Docket No. U7540, Exhibits 66, 67, and 68, January 12, 1976.

Pagan, A.R. and Wickens, M.R. (1989), "A Survey of Recent Econometric Methods," *Economic Journal*, Vol. 99, No. 398, December 1989, pp. 962–1025.

Pakes, A. and Pollard, D. (1989), "Simulation and the Asymptotic of Optimization Estimators," *Econometrica*, Vol. 57, No. 5, September 1989, pp. 1027–1058.

Panzar, J.C. (1979), "The Pareto Domination of Usage-Insensitive Pricing," in *Proceedings of the Sixth Annual Telecommunications Policy Research Conference*, ed. by H.S.

Dordick, pp. 425–436, 6th Telecommunications Policy Research Conference, 1978, Lexington Books/D.C. Heath, Lexington, MA.

Park, R.E. and Mitchell, B.M. (1986), "Optimal Peak-Load Pricing for Local Telephone Calls," RAND R–3403–RC, RAND Corporation, Santa Monica, CA, June 1986.

Park, R.E. and Mitchell, B.M. (1987), "Optimal Peak-Load Pricing for Local Telephone Calls," RAND R–3404–1–RC, RAND Corporation, Santa Monica, CA, March 1987.

Park, R.E., Mitchell, B.M. and Wetzel, B.M. (1981), "Charging for Local Telephone Calls: How Household Characteristics Affect the Distribution of Calls in the GTE Illinois Experiment," RAND R–2535–NSF, RAND Corporation, Santa Monica, CA., March 1981.

Park, R.E., Mitchell, Wetzel, B.M. and Alleman, J. (1983), "Charging for Local Telephone Calls: How Household Characteristics Affect the Distribution of Calls in The GTE Illinois Experiment," *Journal of Econometrics*, Vol. 22, No. 3, August 1983, pp. 339–364.

Park, R.E., Wetzel, B.M. and Mitchell, B.M. (1983), "Price Elasticities for Local Telephone Calls," *Econometrica*, Vol. 51, No. 6, November 1983, pp. 1699–1730.

Parsons, E.M. and Stalon, C.G. (1979), "The Future of Local Measured Service-Regulator's Perspectives," in *Perspectives on Local Measured Service*, ed. by J.A. Baude *et al.*, pp. 177–187, Telecommunications Industry Workshop March 13–14, 1979, Telecommunications Industrial Workshop Organizing Committee, Kansas City, MO.

Pavarini, C. (1974), "Identifying Normal and Price-Stimulated Usage Variations of Groups of Customers, Part I, Distributional Comparisons – Case 49059–2," Unpublished Bell Memorandum, Bell Laboratories, Murray Hill, NJ, October 29, 1974.

Pavarini, C. (1975), "Identifying Normal and Price-Stimulated Variations of Groups of Customers – Part II: Individual Customer Comparisons," Unpublished Bell Memorandum, Bell Laboratories, Murray Hill, NJ, October 31, 1975.

Pavarini, C. (1976a), "Residence and Business Flat Rate Local Telephone Usage," Unpublished Bell Memorandum, Bell Laboratories, Murray Hill, NJ, July 7, 1976.

Pavarini, C. (1976b), "The Effect of Flat-to-Measured Rate Conversions on the Demand for Local Telephone Usage," Unpublished Bell Lab Memorandum, Bell Laboratories, Murray Hill, NJ, September 27, 1976.

Pavarini, C. (1979), "The Effect of Flat-to-Measured Rate Conversions on Local Telephone Usage," in *Pricing in Regulated Industries II*, ed. by J.T. Wenders, pp. 51–75, Mountain States T & T Co. Economic Seminar, Mountain States Regulatory Matters Division, Denver CO.

Pelcovits, M.D., Cornell, N.W. and Brenner, S.R. (1984), "Access Charge Theory and Implementation: A Slip Twixt Cup and Lip," in *Changing Patterns in Regulation, Markets, and Technology: The Effect on Public Utility Pricing*, ed. by P.C. Mann *et al.*, pp. 343–359, 15th Annual Conference, MSU Institute of Public Utilities, East Lansing, MI.

Perl, L.J. (1978), "Economic and Demographic Determinants of Residential Demand for Basic Telephone Service," National Economic Research Associates, Inc., March 28, 1978.

Perl, L.J. (1983), "Residential Demand for Telephone Service 1983," Prepared for Central Service Organization of the Bell Operating Companies, Inc. BOCs, National Economic Research Associates, Inc., White Plains, NY, December 1983.

Perl, L.J. (1984), "Revisions to NERA's Residential Demand for Telephone Service 1983," prepared for The Central Services Organization, Inc. of the Bell Operating Companies, National Economic Research Associates, White Plains, N.Y., April 24, 1984.

Perl, L.J. (1986), "The Consequences of Cost-Based Telephone Pricing," in *Telecommunications and Equity: Policy Research Issues, Proceeding of the Thirteenth Annual Telecommunications Policy Research Conference.* ed. by J. Miller, pp. 231–244.

Pousette, T. (1976), "The Demand for Telephones and Telephone Services in Sweden," presented at the European Meetings of the Econometric Society, Helsinki, Finland, August 1976.

Pratt, G. (1972), "Some Economics of a Public Utility," Working Paper No. 28, University of Warwick, Coventry, England, September 1972.

Pudney, S. (1989), *Modelling Individual Choice*, Basil Blackwell, Oxford, U.K.

Racster, J.L., Wong, M.D. and Guldmann, J.M. (1984), "The Bypass Issue: An Emerging Form of Competition in the Telephone Industry," NRRI Report 84–17, National Regulatory Research Institute, Columbus, OH, December 1984.

Ramsey, F.P. (1927), "A Contribution to the Theory of Taxation," *Economic Journal*, Vol. 37, March 1927, pp. 47–61.

Rash, I.M. (1971), "An Econometric Model of Demand for Residential Main Telephone Service," Bell Canada Working Paper, Ottawa, Ontario, September 1971.

Rash, I.M. (1972), "Residence Sector Demand for Message Toll Service," Bell Canada Working Paper, Ottawa, Ontario, April 1972.

Rea, J.D. and Lage, G.M. (1978), "Estimates of Demand Elasticities for International Telecommunications Services," *Journal of Industrial Economics*, Vol. 26, June 1978, pp. 363–381.

Reitman, C.F. (1977), "The Measurement and Analysis of Demand Elasticities of Residential Vertical Telephone Service," Unpublished Ph.D. Dissertation, New School for Social Research, May 1977.

Rohlfs, J. (1974), "A Theory of Interdependent Demand for a Communications Service," *Bell Journal of Economics and Management Science*, Vol. 5, No. 1, Spring 1974, pp. 16–37.

Rohlfs, J. (1978), "Economically Efficient Bell System Pricing," Unpublished Bell Laboratories Memorandum, attachment H, transmitted by R.L. McGuire of AT&T to Congressman Lionel VanDeerlin, October 31, 1978.

Rubinfeld, D.L. (1985), "Econometrics in the Courtroom," *Columbia Law Review*, Vol. 85, No. 5, June 1985, pp. 1048–1097.

Rubinfeld, D.L. and Steiner, P.O. (1983), "Quantitative Methods in Antitrust Litigation," *Law and Contemporary Problems*, Vol. 46, No. 4, Autumn 1983, pp. 69–141.

Samuel, P. (1985), "Telecommunications: After the Bell Break-up," in *Unnatural Monopolies*, ed. by R. Poole, pp. 177–203, Lexington Books/D.C. Heath, Lexington, MA.

Sands, B.N. and Trosset, M.W. (1990), "Nonnested Hypothesis Testing in Applied Economics," Discussion 90–14, Department of Economics, University of Arizona, Tucson, AZ.

Schankerman, M. and Stone, R. (1976), *A Project to Analyze Responses to Docket No. 20003, Final Report, Deliverable F*, prepared by T&E Inc., Cambridge, MA.

Schmidt, L.W. (1977), "Unbundling for Both Exchange and Extension Services," in *Proceedings of the 1977 Symposium on Problems of Regulated Industries*, Conference February 13–16, 1977, Kansas City, Mo., University of Missouri-Columbia/Extension Pub., Columbia, MO.

Schultz, W.R. and Triantis, J.E. (1982), "An International Telephone Demand Study Using Pooled Estimation Techniques," *Proceedings, American Statistical Association*, Business and Economic Section.

Scott, R.D. and Easton, D.C. (1986), "New Approaches to Estimating the Price Elasticity of Demand for Message Toll Service Within B.C.," B.C. Telephone Co., Vancouver, B.C., April 1986.

Selwyn, L.L. (1983), "Local Measured Telephone Service: The Known Costs and Dubious Benefits," in *Adjusting to Regulatory, Pricing and Market Realities*, ed. by H.M. Trebing, pp. 557–574, 14th Annual Conference, MSU Institute of Public Utilities, East Lansing, MI.

Sharkey, W.W. (1987), "Models of Competitive Telecommunications Markets," *Annales des Télécommunications*, Vol. 42, No. 11, November–December 1987, pp. 620–628.

Sheffield, V.K. and Murphy, J.W. (1985), "The Demand for Local Telephone Service in Iowa," Iowa State Commerce Commission, PRP–85–7, Des Moines, November 1985.

Shin, R.T. and Ying, J.S. (1992), "Unnatural Monopolies in Local Telephone," *Rand Journal of Economics*, Vol. 23, No. 2, Summer 1992, pp. 171–183.

Shugard, M.H. (1979), "Demand for Local Telephone Service: The Effects of Price and Demographics," Bell Laboratories Memorandum, MF–79–9541–42, Murray Hill, NJ, October 8, 1979.

Shugard, W. (1982), "Choice Dependent on Usage: Residence Class-of-Service Choice," Bell Laboratories Memorandum, TM:82–59543–14, Murray Hill, NJ, August 30, 1982.

Sichler, B.J. (1928), "A Theory of Telephone Rates," *Journal of Land and Public Utility Economics*, Vol. 4, pp. 180–184.

Sichter, J.W. (1985), "Bypass, Universal Service, and NTS Cost Recovery," in *The Impact of Deregulation and Market Forces on Public Utilities: The Future Role of Regulation*, ed. by P.C. Mann *et al*, pp. 103–127, 16th Annual Conference, MSU Institute of Public Utilities, East Lansing, MI.

Simon, S.A. and Whelan, M. (1985), "After Divestiture: What the AT&T Settlement Means for Business and Residential Telephone Service," Knowledge Industry Publ., Inc, White Plains, NY.

Sjoholm, K.R. (1991), "The Telephone Use in Sweden and Its Sensitivity to Prices," Working Paper No. 292, The Industrial Institute for Economic and Social Research, Stockholm, February.

Smith, S.A. and Benjamin, R.I. (1984), "Telecommunications Demand in Automated Offices," in *Policy Research in Telecommunications*, ed. by V. Mosco, 11th Annual Telecommunications Policy Research Conference, 1983, Ablex, Norwood, NJ.

Smith, V.L. (1982), "Microeconomic Systems as an Experimental Science," *American Economic Review*, Vol. 72, No. 5, December 1982, pp. 923–955.

Snow, M.S. and Jussawalla, M. (1986), *Telecommunication Economics and International Regulatory Policy: An Annotated Bibliography*, Bibliographies & Indexes in Economics and Economic History #4, Greenwood Press, New York, NY.

Sonenklar, H. and Taschdjian, M.G. (1986), "The Economics of Residential AT&T-OCC Choice," GTE Sprint Communications Corp.

Southern Bell Telephone and Telegraph Company (1976), Testimony of R.E. Brinner, Florida Docket No. 76–0842–TP, November 29, 1976.

Southern Bell Telephone and Telegraph Company (1977), Testimony of R.E. Brinner, North Carolina Docket No. P100–Sub 45, December 6, 1977.

Southern New England Telephone Company (1977a), Curtailment testimony of J. Jeske, Connecticut Docket No. 770526, June 27, 1977.

Southern New England Telephone Company (1977b), Basic Residence Revenue Curtailment Study, Connecticut Docket No. 770526, June 1977.

Southern New England Telephone Company (1977c), Study on Usage Sensitive Pricing, presented to the Public Utilities Control Authority, February 1, 1977.

Southern New England Telephone Company (1982a), Testimony, Exhibits and Workpapers of B.P. Sullivan, DPUC Docket No. 82–04–16.

Southern New England Telephone Company (1982b), "Exchange Coin Demand Study," by Anthony Jones, Business Research Division, May 1981.

Southern New England Telephone Company (1982c), "Coin User Demographics Study,"

Business Research Division, June 1982.

Southern New England Telephone Company (1982d), "SLUS II Class of Service Usage Analysis," Business Research Division, August 1982.

Southern New England Telephone Company (1982e), "Analysis of SLUS II Usage Data With Regard to Distance," Business Research Division, August 1982.

Southern New England Telephone Company (1982f), "Demographic Analysis of SLUS II Residence Subscribers' Usage," Business Research Division, August 1982.

Southwestern Bell Telephone Company (1978a), Testimony of B. Egan, Kansas Docket No. 110–941–U, July 7, 1978.

Southwestern Bell Telephone Company (1978b), Testimony of J.M. Griffin, Kansas Docket No. 110–941–U, July 7, 1978.

Southwestern Bell Telephone Company (1982), Cross-Examination of B.L. Egan, Texas Docket 4545, November 1982, pp. 7132–7155.

Spann, R.M. (1977), "Pricing Within Urban Telephone Networks: Welfare, Allocation and Distribution Effect of Alternative Pricing Policy," in *Expanding Economic Concepts of Regulation in Health, Postal, and Telecommunications Services*, ed. by C.F. Phillips, Jr., Washington and Lee University, Lexington, VA.

Spanos, A. (1989), "On Rereading Haavelmo: A Retrospective View of Econometric Modeling," *Journal of Econometric Theory*, Vol. 5, No. 3, December 1989, pp. 405–429.

Spence, A.M. (1980), "Multi-Product Quantity-Dependent Prices and Profitability Constraints," *Review of Economic Studies*, Vol. 47, No. 5, October 1980, pp. 821–842.

Squire, L. (1973), "Some Aspects of Optimal Pricing for Telecommunications," *Bell Journal of Economics and Management Science*, Vol. 4, No. 2, Autumn 1973, pp. 515–525.

Stannard, R. (1978), "The Impact of Imposing Directory Assistance Charges," in *Assessing the Impact of New Pricing Concepts in Public Utilities*, ed. by H.M. Trebing, MSU Institute of Public Utilities, East Lansing, MI.

Statistics Canada (1986), *1985 Household Income (1984)*, 1986 ed., December 1986, Ottawa, Ontario.

Stern, C. (1965), "Price Elasticity of Local Telephone Service Demand," *Public Utilities Fortnightly*, Vol. 90, February 4, 1965, pp. 24–34.

Stone, R., Schankerman, M. and Fenton, C. (1976), *Selective Competition in the Telephone Industry: An Independent Appraisal Based on Responses to FCC Docket 20003*, T&E, Inc., Cambridge, MA.

Stuntebeck, S.V. (1976), "The Relation of Day/Night Price Differentials and Message Volume Distributions for Intrastate Toll Calls – Case 49059–1," Unpublished Bell Laboratories Memorandum, Murray Hill, NJ, October 25, 1976.

Subissati, E. (1973), "An Econometric Model for WATS and Business Toll Services," Computer Communications and Network Services Bell Canada, Ottawa, Ontario, August 1973.

Swamy, P.A.V.B. (1971), *Statistical Inference in Random Coefficient Regression Models*, Springer-Verlag, New York, NY.

System Applications Inc. (1977), "The Market Outlook for Telecommunications Equipment and Services," Final Report (TF77–15), San Rafael, CA, February 18, 1977.

Tardiff, T.J. (1991), "Modeling the Demand for New Products and Services," presented at the NTDS Forum, Santa Fe, NM, September 27, 1991, National Economic Research Associates, Cambridge, MA.

Taschdjian, M.G. (1986), "Residential Selection of Interexchange Carriers," presented at the Fourteenth Annual Telecommunications Policy Research Conference, Airlie, VA., April 28, 1986, GTE Sprint Communications Corp.

Taylor, L.D. (1975), "The Demand for Electricity: A Survey," *Bell Journal of Economics and Management Science*, Vol. 6, No. 1, Spring 1975, pp. 74–110.

Taylor, L.D. (1979), "Modeling the Class of Service Choice," Department of Economics, University of Arizona, Tucson, AZ, October 1979.

Taylor, L.D. (1980), "The Demand for Telecommunications: A Nontechnical Exposition," in *Issues in Public Utility Pricing and Regulation*, ed. by M.A. Crew, pp. 93–106, Lexington Books/D.C. Heath, Lexington, MA.

Taylor, L.D. (1983), "Problems and Issues in Modeling Telecommunications Demand," in *Economic Analysis of Telecommunications: Theory and Applications*, ed. by L. Courville *et al.*, pp. 181–198, Elsevier Science Publication/North Holland, New York.

Taylor, L.D. (1984), "Evidence of Lester D. Taylor on Behalf of Bell Canada Concerning The Price Elasticity of Demand for Message Toll Service in Canada," Canadian Radio-television and Telecommunications Commission, November 1984.

Taylor, L.D. and Blattenberger, G.R. (1986), "Energy Demand by U.S. Households: Pre-and Post O.P.E.C.," Department of Economics, University of Arizona, Tucson, AZ, January 1986.

Taylor, L.D., Blattenberger, G.R. and Verleger, P.K. (1977), "The Residential Demand for Energy," Electric Power Research Institute, EPRI EA–235, Palo Alto, CA, January 1977.

Taylor, L.D. and Houthakker, H.S. (1991), "Co-Integration and Habit Formation: A Reformation of the Dynamics of the Houthakker-Taylor Model," revision of paper presented at the 6th World Congress of the Econometric Society, Barcelona, Spain, August 1990, Department of Economics, University of Arizona, Tucson, AZ, December 1991.

Taylor, L.D. and Kridel, D.J. (1990), "Residential Demand for Access to the Telephone Network," in *Telecommunications Demand Modelling*, ed. by A. de Fontenay, M.H. Shugard and D.S. Sibley, North-Holland Publishing Co, Amsterdam.

Taylor, L.D., Waverman, L. and Wall, G.W. (1990), "Equity Considerations and Ramsey Pricing in Telecommunications," Centre for International Studies, Trinity College, University of Toronto, Toronto, Ontario, M55 1A1.

Taylor, W.E. and Taylor L.D. (1993), "Post-Divestiture Long-Distance Competition in the United States," *American Economic Review Papers and Procedures*, Vol. 83, No. 2, May 1993, pp. 185–190.

Temin, P. (1987), *The Fall of the Bell System*, Cambridge University Press, Cambridge, MA.

Theil, H. (1959), *Economic Forecasts and Policy, Second Revised Edition*, North-Holland Publishing Co., Amsterdam.

Theil, H. (1971), *Principles of Econometrics*, John Wiley & Sons, New York.

Theil, H. and Goldberger, A.S. (1961), "On Pure and Mixed Statistical Estimation in Economics," *International Economic Review*, Vol. 2, No. 1, pp. 65–78.

Theil, H. and Wage, S. (1964), "Some Observations on Adaptive Forecasting," *Bell Journal of Economics and Management Science*, Vol. 10, January 1964.

Thompson, H.E. and Tiao, G.C. (1971), "Analysis of Telephone Data: A Case Study of Forecasting Seasonal Time Series," *Bell Journal of Economics and Management Science*, Vol. 2, No. 2, Autumn 1971, pp. 515–541.

Tomasek, O. (1972), "Statistical Forecasting of Telephone Time Series," *Telecommunications Journal*, Vol. 39, December 1972, pp. 725–731.

Train, K.E. (1986), *Qualitative Choice Analysis*, MIT Press.

Train, K.E. (1991), "Self-Selecting Tariffs Under Pure Preferences Among Tariffs," Department of Economics, University of California, Berkeley, CA, March 1991.

Train, K.E., Ben-Akiva, M. and Atherton, T. (1989), "Consumption Patterns and Self-Selecting

Tariffs," *Review of Economics & Statistics*, Vol. 71, No. 1, February 1989, pp. 62–73.

Train, K.E., McFadden, D.L. and Ben-Akiva, M. (1987), "The Demand for Local Telephone Service: A Fully Discrete Model of Residential Calling Patterns and Service Charges," *The Rand Journal of Economics*, Vol. 18, No. 1, Spring 1987, pp. 109–123.

Trimble, D.B. (1992), Revised Direct Testimony of Dennis B. Trimble for GTE Florida Incorporated, before the Florida Public Utility Commission, Docket No. 920188–TL.

U.S. G.A.O. (1986a), "Telephone Communications: Bell Operating Company Entry Into New Lines of Business," GAO/RCED–86–138, U.S. General Accounting Office/GPO, Washington, D.C, April 1986.

U.S. G.A.O. (1986b), "Telephone Communications: The FCC's Monitoring of Residential Telephone Service," GAO/RCED–86–146, U.S. General Accounting Office/GPO, Washington, D.C, June 1986.

U.S. G.A.O. (1986c), "Telephone Communications: Bypass of the Local Telephone Companies," GAO/RCED–86–66, GPO, Washington, D.C, August 1986.

U.S. G.A.O. (1987a), "Telephone Communications: Issues Affecting Rural Telephone Service," GAO/RCED–87–74, U.S. General Accounting Office/GPO, Washington, D.C, March 1987.

U.S. G.A.O. (1987b), "Telephone Communications: Cost and Funding Information on Lifeline Telephone Service," GAO/RCED–87–189, U.S. General Accounting Office/GPO, Washington, D.C, September 1987.

U.S. G.A.O. (1987c), "Telephone Communications: Controlling Cross-Subsidy Between Regulated and Competitive Service," GAO/RCED–88–34, U.S. General Accounting Office/GPO, Washington, D.C, October 1987.

U.S. House of Representatives (1981), "Telecommunications in Transition: The Status of Competition in the Telecommunications Industry," in *Subcommittee on Telecommunications, Consumer Protection, Finance of Committee on Energy and Commerce*, Committee Print 97–V (97th Congress, 1st Session), U.S. Government Printing Office, Washington, D.C, November 3, 1981.

U.S. Telephone Association (1984), Bypass Study, filed October 5, 1984 in response to FCC Public Notice of March 20.

Vaartbou, E. (1981), "The Demand for Long Distance Calls: Review of the Literature and Derivation of a Model," B.C. Tel(BCG) 1981–12–15–1001 Attachment 2, B.C. Telephone Co., Vancouver, B.C., December 15, 1981.

Vickrey, W. (1981), "Local Telephone Costs and The Design of Rate Structures," Department of Economics, Columbia University, March 1981.

Vilmin, E. and Curien, N. (1985), "Influence of Time-of-Day Pricing on Telephone Traffic Profile (in French)," *Annales des Télécommunications*, Vol. 40, Nos. 9–10, September–October 1985, pp. 451–465.

Von Rabenau, B. and Stahl, K. (1974), "Dynamic Aspects of Public Goods: A Further Analysis of the Telephone System," *Bell Journal of Economics and Management Science*, Vol. 5, No. 2, Autumn 1974, pp. 651–669.

Wade, S.H. (1980), *The Implications of Decreasing-Block Pricing for Individual Demand Functions: An Empirical Investigation*, Ph.D. dissertation, Department of Economics, University of Arizona, Tucson, AZ, April 1980.

Wallace, T.D. and Hussian, A. (1969), "The Use of Error Components Models in Combining Cross-Section with Time-Series Data," *Econometrica*, Vol. 55, No. 1, January 1969, pp. 55–60.

Wang, R.C. (1976), "Demand for Yellow Pages Advertising Space," Unpublished paper,

Mountain Bell, Denver, CO, October 1976.

Watters, J.S. and Grandstaff, P.J. (1988), "An Econometric Model of Interstate Access," presented at BELLCORE/Bell Canada Telecommunications Demand Analysis Industry Forum, Key Biscayne, FL, January 25–27, 1988, Southwestern Bell Telephone Co, St. Louis, MO.

Watters, J.S. and Roberson, M.L. (1991), "An Econometric Model for Dedicated Telecommunications Services: A Systems Approach," Southwestern Bell Telephone Co., St. Louis.

Watters, J.S. and Roberson, M.L. (1992), "An Econometric Model of the Demand for IntraLATA MTS Pricing Plans," Southwestern Bell Telephone Co., St. Louis.

Waverman, L. (1974), "Demand for Telephone Services in Great Britain, Canada and Sweden," International Conference on Telecommunications Economy, University of Acton, Management Centre, May 29, 1974.

Weisbrod, B.A. (1964), "Collective-Consumption of Individual Consumption Goods," *Quarterly Journal of Economics*, Vol. 78, No. 3, August 1964, pp. 471–477.

Weisman, D.L. (1988), "Default Capacity Tariffs: Smoothing the Transitional Regulatory Asymmetrics in the Telecommunications Market," *Yale Journal on Regulation*, Winter 1988, pp. 149–178.

Weisman, D.L. and Kridel, D.J. (1990), "Forecasting Competitive Entry: The Case of Bypass Adoption in Telecommunications," *International Journal of Forecasting*, Vol. 6, pp. 65–74.

Wellenius, B. (1969), "The Effect of Income and Social Class on Residential Telephone Demand," *Telecommunications Journal*, Vol. 36.

Wellenius, B. (1970), "A Method for Forecasting the Demand for Urban Residential Telephone Connections," *Telecommunications Journal*, Vol. 37, June 1970, pp. 262–267.

Weller, D. (1985), "Toll Pricing Without Premium Access," in *The Impact of Deregulation and Market Forces on Public Utilities: The Future Role of Regulation*, ed. by P.C. Mann *et al.*, 16th Annual Conference, MSU Institute of Public Utilities, East Lansing, MI.

Wenders, J.T. (1979), "Economic Efficiency of Local Measured Service," in *Perspectives on Local Measured Service*, ed. by J.A. Baude *et al.*, pp. 59–69, Telecommunication Industry Workshop March 13–14, 1979, Telecommunication Industry Workshop Organizing Committee, Kansas City, MO.

Wenders, J.T. (1986), "Rejoinder: Throttling Competition," *Telecommunications Policy*, June 1986, pp. 177–180.

Wenders, J.T. (1987), *Telecommunications Economics*, Ballinger Publishing Co., Cambridge, MA.

Wert, G.M. (1976), "The Effects of Day/Night Price Ratios on Residence Weekday Interstate MTS Traffic," Unpublished Bell Laboratories Memorandum, Murray Hill NJ, June 1976.

White, D. and Sandbach, J. (1985), "Reconciliation of Short- and Medium-Term Models of Business Telephone Connections," British Telecom Economic Advisory Division, London, October 1985.

Wilkinson, G.F. (1983), "The Estimation of Usage Repression Under LMS: Empirical Evidence from the GTE Experiment," in *Economic Analysis of Telecommunications: Theory and Application*, ed. by L. Courville *et al.*, pp. 253–262, Elsevier North-Holland, New York, NY.

Williamson, O.E. (1966), "Peak-Load Pricing and Optimal Capacity Under Indivisibility Constraints," *American Economic Review*, Vol. 56, No. 4, September 1966, pp. 810–827.

Williamson, O.E. (1974), "Peak Load Pricing: Some Further Remarks," *Bell Journal of Economics and Management Science*, Vol. 5, No. 1, Spring 1974, pp. 223–228.

Williamson, R.B. and Chen, J.S. (1991a), "Operator Services Directory Assistance Study – Business Econometric Demand Analysis," Demand Analysis District, Southwestern Bell

Telephone Co., November 1991.

Williamson, R.B. and Chen, J.S. (1991b), "Operator Services Directory Assistance Study – Residential Econometric Demand Analysis," Demand Analysis District, Southwestern Bell Telephone Co., December 1991.

Willig, R.D. (1976), "Consumer Surplus Without Apology," *American Economic Review*, Vol. 66, No. 4, September 1976, pp. 587–597.

Willig, R.D. (1978), "Pareto-Superior Nonlinear Outlay Schedules," *Bell Journal of Economics*, Vol. 9, No. 1, Spring 1978, pp. 59–69.

Willig, R.D. (1979a), "Customer Equity and Local Measured Service," in *Perspectives on Local Measured Service*, ed. by J.A. Baude *et al.*, pp. 71–78, Telecommunication Industry Workshop March 13–14, 1979, Telecommunication Industry Workshop Organizing Committee, Kansas City, MO.

Willig, R.D. (1979b), "The Theory of Network Access Pricing," in *Issues in Public Utility Regulation*, ed. by H.M. Trebing, pp. 109–152, 10th Annual Conference, MSU Institute of Public Utilities, East Lansing, MI.

Wisconsin Bell Telephone Company (1976), Prepared testimony of J. Tang, Docket No. 2U8030, Exhibit 94, July 20, 1976.

Wong, T.F. (1980), "How to Estimate Usage Changes Due to Flat-to-Measured Service Conversion," Research Memorandum 80–9541–17, Bell Laboratories, Murray Hill, NJ, December 18, 1980.

Yatrakis, P.G. (1972), "Determinants of the Demand for International Telecommunications," *Telecommunication Journal*, Vol. 39, pp. 732–746.

Ying, J.S. (1992), "The Price of Breaking Up: Local Telephone Rates After the Divestiture," Department of Economics, University of Delaware, July 1992.

Zoglo, D.P. (1984), "Long Term Repression of Local Calling By Customers Who Switched to Measured Service," Mountain Bell Memorandum, Denver, CO, November 6, 1984.

Zona, J.D. and Jacob, R. (1990), "The Total Bill Concept: Defining and Testing Alternative Views," presented at BELLCORE/Bell Canada Industry Forum, Telecommunications Demand Analysis with Dynamic Regulation, Hilton Head, SC, April 22–25, National Economic Research Associates, Cambridge, MA.

INDEX